Varieties of Capitalism in History, Transition and Emergence

Economics tends to teach that developed countries have good institutions while developing countries do not, and that this is the factor that constrains the latter's growth. However, the picture is far messier than this explanation suggests.

Building on the varieties of capitalism framework, this book brings together the tools of institutional economics with historical analyses of institutional evolution of different kinds of property rights and legal systems, protected by different kinds of state, giving rise to distinct corporate governance structures. It constructs institutional development histories across leading liberal capitalisms in Britain and the United States, compared with continental capitalisms in France and Germany, and contemporary transitional capitalisms in China and Tanzania. This volume is innovative in combining both historical and economic insights, and in combining developed country with developing country institutional emergence, dispelling the prevailing sense of complacency about the inevitability of the path of institutional development for the developed areas of the world and the paths that developing countries are likely to follow.

This volume will be of great importance to those who study international economics, development economics and international business.

Martha Prevezer is Senior Lecturer at the School of Business and Management, Queen Mary University of London, UK. She has worked in various policy arenas, at the Bank of England, the National Economic Development Office (NEDO) and London Business School.

Routledge Studies in the Modern World Economy

For a full list of titles in this series, please visit www.routledge.com/series/SE0432

158. The Financialization of Housing
A political economy approach
Manuel B. Aalbers

159. Fiscal Policy in Dynamic Economies
Kim Heng Tan

160. The Political Economy of China's Great Transformation
Xingyuan Feng, Christer Ljungwall and Sujian Guo

161. The Russian Economy and Foreign Direct Investment
Edited by Kari Liuhto, Sergei Sutyrin and Jean-Marc F. Blanchard

162. Information Efficiency and Anomalies in Asian Equity Markets
Theories and evidence
Edited by Qaiser Munir and Sook Ching Kok

163. Agricultural Growth, Productivity and Regional Change in India
Challenges of globalisation, liberalisation and food insecurity
Surendra Singh and Prem Chhetri

164. The Political Economy of Special Economic Zones
Concentrating Economic Development
Lotta Moberg

165. Varieties of Capitalism in History, Transition and Emergence
New Perspectives on Institutional Development
Martha Prevezer

166. Human Evolution, Economic Progress and Evolutionary Failure
Bhanoji Rao

Varieties of Capitalism in History, Transition and Emergence

New Perspectives on Institutional Development

Martha Prevezer

LONDON AND NEW YORK

First published 2017 by Routledge

2 Park Square, Milton Park, Abingdon, Oxfordshire OX14 4RN
52 Vanderbilt Avenue, New York, NY 10017

Routledge is an imprint of the Taylor & Francis Group, an informa business

First issued in paperback 2019

British Library Cataloguing in Publication Data
A catalogue record for this book is available from the British Library

Library of Congress Cataloging in Publication Data
Names: Prevezer, Martha, author.
Title: Varieties of capitalism in history, transition and emergence : new perspectives on institutional development / Martha Prevezer.
Description: 1 Edition. | New York : Routledge, 2017. | Includes index.
Identifiers: LCCN 2016047667 | ISBN 9780415735407 (hardback) | ISBN 9781315819228 (ebook)
Subjects: LCSH: Capitalism. | Institutional economics. | Corporate governance.
Classification: LCC HB501 .P69247 2017 | DDC 330.12/2--dc23
LC record available at https://lccn.loc.gov/2016047667

ISBN: 978-0-415-73540-7 (hbk)
ISBN: 978-0-367-86910-6 (pbk)

Typeset in Times New Roman
by Taylor & Francis Books

For Sam, Hannah and Sol

Contents

	Preface	viii
	Acknowledgements	x
	List of abbreviations	xi
1	Introduction	1
PART I		**15**
2	Primary institutions: Property rights, legal systems and the state – theories and concepts	17
3	Meso-institutions	51
PART II		**75**
4	How did Britain's 'good institutions' evolve, and how good were they?	77
5	Continental variety of capitalism: France and Germany compared with Britain	118
6	The United States compared with Britain	151
PART III		**185**
7	Institutions debate for development: Theories, concepts and institutional development in Tanzania	187
8	China in its institutional transition to capitalism	223
9	Conclusions	256
	Index	274

Preface

This book arose out of my teaching about the role of institutions in economic development. The significance of institutions in shaping capitalisms has been well established in the literature. The idea that property rights and legal systems underpin the workings of capitalism has become a truism. Also well established and frequently discussed is the idea that there are very different varieties of capitalism – different coalitions between, and weights given to, the various interest groups and parties involved in capitalisms in different countries – owners, managers, employees or workers, and the state.

But this appears to me to be only the start of the enquiry. Property rights are a catch-all concept. There are numerous types of property rights when thought of as valuable assets and skills: in addition to various different types of land rights, there are rights over different types of assets such as stocks and shares in companies, government securities, and assets that are not traded on markets, that are built up within firms and people as intangible, tacit knowledge. Different capitalisms protect some types of assets more than others. Different countries have opted for different kinds of property rights in land too, with the alternatives of customary land rights competing with individual private land rights and land ownership vested in the state. And the role of the state, who the elites are, whether the elites are in or out of the state, whose property rights get supported, and whose property rights get renounced are all also a part of the entangled picture.

The main avenue of enquiry for this book is to answer the historical question about the pathways, trajectories, and evolutions into the particular diverse patterns that we see today across both developed and developing country capitalisms. The literature seemed to leave unanswered questions about how those evolutions occurred, the ways in which institutions of property rights and legal systems interacted and occurred *sequentially* to lead capitalisms down diverse paths. In other words, the histories of different capitalisms told in terms of the evolution of institutions remained to be explained.

Property rights have had different meanings in different places at different times; the law, the use of law, and legal systems have evolved differently between countries. The extent and ways in which property rights were protected by the law has varied over time. The book's aim is to explore those different paths and sequences. This involves disentangling these issues historically and outlining when particular types of property rights became established, through which type of legal system and by which type of state – and doing this across both leading examples of the variety of developed capitalisms – the liberal British and American ones and the coordinated continental European ones – across an example of a developing country sub-Saharan post-colonial capitalism in Tanzania; and across the leading transitioning country into capitalism, China.

This is an ambitious task, and one to which I have undoubtedly failed to do justice. Nevertheless, an outline, however contentious, is there. What this book primarily aims to do is to indicate or, in its better moments, show how the historical path matters, of course, in shaping these institutions. It is written for students and others with an interest in these issues, regardless of whether or not they possess a familiarity with the literature and academic field of economics.

This book is interdisciplinary in the sense that it imposes some of the theory-building coming out of historical sociology, institutional economics and anthropology onto this historical material with the aim of discerning patterns across this field. At this point, I must mention the influence of Mary Douglas' *How Institutions Think* (1986), if not in very concrete ways, still in providing a kind of superstructure in suggesting the ways in which these evolutions occur and the way people's choices are shaped by the institutions they find themselves living in. The passages on and references to her work are there to point to a different way than either rational choice theory or deterministic theory of thinking about the interactions between individuals and societal structures.

The book's structure is as follows. The theoretical approaches that I use throughout the book are laid out in Chapters 2 and 3, the former relating to institutions of property rights, legal systems, and the nature of the state, and the latter relating to the institutions associated with the varieties of capitalism literature. These two chapters, along with Chapter 1, form Part I. Part II contains Chapters 4, 5 and 6, which contain historical case studies of Britain, continental Europe, and the United States, respectively. Part III switches to the modern era to look at case studies of developing and transition countries in Chapters 7 and 8, with a correspondingly different emphasis in the theories used, which are set out in introductory pages of Chapter 7. In all the case study chapters, however, the purpose is the same: to trace the evolution and interaction between property rights and legal system, and between the nature of the state, its elites and state capacity; and to determine how these features shaped corporate governance, organizational forms and structures. Chapter 9 concludes the book by returning to theory-building in suggesting patterns between which types of property rights became protected, whose property rights they were, and the kinds of legal systems and states that supported these patterns.

Acknowledgements

This work was aided by a sabbatical year by Queen Mary University of London, School of Business and Management in 2013–2014. I am very grateful to Brigitte Granville and Frances Bowen for supporting the project at the outset. Many thanks to David Alberman, Eva Alberman, Liam Campling, Dread Scott, Briony Fane, Camilla Loewe, Marion Coutts, Jaume Martorell Cruz, Anna Fairbank, Hanna Heffner, Nicky Mayhew, Jenny Polak, Enid Prevezer, Simon Srebrny, Brendon Swedlow and Andrew Wilson for their interest, encouragement and helpful comments. I thank Stella Warren for her careful editing and Laura Johnson at Routledge for her encouragement and patience. Perri 6 and Frances Bowen gave detailed and insightful comments on a first draft, and I am extremely grateful for their engagement and help.

Abbreviations

CCI	Coercion-Constraining Institution
CCM	*Chama Cha Mapinduzi*
CCP	Chinese Communist Party
CDD	Cooperative Development Department
CEI	Contract-Enforcement Institution
CEO	Chief Executive Officer
CME	Coordinated Market Economy
CRMP	Cooperative Reform and Modernization Program
CSRC	China Securities Regulatory Commission
DCO	District Cooperative Officer
FAO	Food and Agriculture Organization of the United Nations
FDI	Foreign Direct Investment
GDP	Gross Domestic Product
GmbH	Gesellschaft mit beschränkter Haftung
GNP	Gross National Product
HRS	Household Responsibility System
ICA	International Co-operative Alliance
IMF	International Monetary Fund
IPO	Initial Public Offering
JP	Justice of the Peace
KCNU	Kilimanjaro Native Cooperative Union
KNPA	Kilimanjaro Native Planters Association
LAO	Limited Access Order
LME	Liberal Market Economy
LPC	Local People's Congress
LSE	London Stock Exchange
MRS	Management Responsibility System
NPC	National People's Congress
NYSE	New York Stock Exchange
OAO	Open Access Order
PRs	Property Rights
RSTGA	Rungwe Smallholder Tea Growers Association
SACCO	Savings and Credit Cooperative Society

SARL	Société à *Responsabilité Limitée*
SEZ	Special Enterprise Zone
SOE	State-Owned Enterprise
SPC	Supreme People's Court
SPO	Small Producer Organization
SSA	Sub-Saharan Africa
TCB	Tanzania Coffee Board
TFC	Tanzanian Federation of Cooperatives
TOI	Timing of Industrialization
TTA	Tanzanian Tea Authority
TVE	Township and Village Enterprise
WATCO	Wakulima Tea Company
WTO	World Trade Organization

1 Introduction

In June 2016, England (population 55 million) lost to Iceland (population 330,000) in the Euro 2016 Football Championship and failed to make it into the quarter-finals of the tournament. I live down the road from the Arsenal Football Club in London, which is an internationally competitive club in England's Premier League, attracting players, sponsors and resources from around the world. Why is there such a gap between the fortunes of England's club football and its national team? Why do resources, energy, and ethos coalesce around the enterprises that are premier football clubs in England but cannot do so when it comes to fielding a national team? The answer lies in the history of England's institutional development of its particular form of capitalism.[1]

My starting point is to build on the varieties of capitalism literature of Hall and Soskice (2001), which divided developed capitalisms into liberal market economies (LMEs), such as those of Britain and the United States, and coordinated market economies (CMEs), exemplified in the first instance by continental European countries such as Germany and France. These varieties of capitalism have different characteristics in terms of what I call their 'meso-institutions' – their labour market institutions of employment protection and mobility of labour, and the types of skills and training these cultivate – and their capital market institutions, such as the degree to which firms use equity markets to finance their activities and the extent to which they are publicly-listed and issue shares that are freely tradable on those markets. LMEs have been characterized as having less employment protection, greater mobility of labour and changing of jobs, and an emphasis on the general and portable skills that people carry with them between different firms. Firms in LMEs use equity markets to raise finance and are publicly-listed on stock markets. There is more shareholding by individuals and institutions, an example of the latter being pension funds that are external to the firms whose shares they hold. There is a more active takeover market, meaning that companies and assets are bought and sold through the market for corporate control. In this process, acquired companies typically have to change strategic direction, destroying skills and assets that had been built up under the previous regime. These assets and skills are not well protected under liberal institutions. Paramount in these economies is using markets to maintain the tradability of assets.

The coordinated market economy has greater employment protection, more coordinated wage bargaining, longer job tenure and greater training in skills relating to specific firms. Firms use close relationships with their banks rather than using public equity markets and public listing of companies. Shareholding structures are more concentrated, with leading owners having blockholdings of shares. Owners keep control of their companies, and there are numerous obstacles in the way of hostile takeovers. These obstacles take the form of concentrated ownership itself, which cannot be bought out; of proxy votes by banks; and of different classes of shares, which enable capital to be raised without lessening owners' control over their firms. They result in the protection of strategic assets – the skills and assets built up inside companies – rather than an emphasis on the tradable nature of assets and the protection of that tradability.

Making this distinction between the kinds of property rights that are protected is new to the literature. I am building on this in two ways. First, I believe there to be a substantial truth in the distinction between these different ways of running capitalism, and I want to understand how they got to that point, that is, to bring out the histories of their institutions. Second, I would like to forge the connection between the meso-institutions of the varieties of capitalism and the primary institutions that underpin capitalist economies. Neither of these elements has been explored before. When property rights have been discussed, it has been assumed that they are all of one nature or one type. Here, I bring out the differences and tensions that exist between different kinds of property rights: tradable versus strategic, individual versus customary, and privately ordered versus publicly backed by the state.

How I do this is through outlining institutional histories across different countries that have been classed as running their capitalisms in different ways. This book is largely about joining up the dots, bringing together different literatures so as to focus, historically and conceptually, on the linkages between the protection of different kinds of property rights in the different varieties of capitalism and the historical routes and underpinnings that offer an explanation as to how and why they became so different. Of necessity, the joining together is sketchy and schematic – it highlights different building blocks – the different natures of property rights, the contrasts between legal systems and differing conceptions of the rule of law, and the variety of and changing constructions of state apparatuses and structures. These I label primary institutions, the institutions that are deemed to underpin capitalism and enable contract enforcement to occur.

I want to emphasize that we cannot understand the way capitalism works in any country – how its meso-institutions are constructed and operate – without a grasp of how a given country's primary institutions were constructed and how they evolved. I give a more nuanced view of how each country evolved institutionally and how it arrived at its very different variety of capitalism, but I also bring out the deep-rooted nature of institutional evolution: the centuries-old build-up and incremental change that entrenches ways of doing and seeing things. This in turn brings out the crucial interaction and dynamic between informal structures in a country and the evolution of formal institutions. I am not able to explore this at all adequately, but nevertheless I do want to emphasize the importance of, for example, the individualistic ordering in Britain as it took root from the post-Black-Death 15th century and compare it with the more hierarchical bureaucratic structures that took shape in France and some parts of what would become Germany. And when I come to look at how property rights 'take' in developing contexts, I also want to emphasize the importance of the more collectivist group-orderings in Tanzania, of villages and cooperatives, which also have deep roots.

These different informal structures mean that the same size of state by some measure of state expenditure in GDP have given rise to very different degrees of regulation or state intervention or public presence in the economy. States comprising the institutions of government, of administration, and of the judiciary have taken different shapes across countries and have different relationships, types of legal capacity, degrees of centralization or decentralization, and extent of independence of their judiciaries from the state executive. For example in France, state administrations have played a more direct and interventionist role in settling disputes between parties, such as disputes over property rights, whilst in liberal economies state administrations have kept out of such disputes, which have been dealt with through the courts.

I want to suggest the importance of private orderings of maritime property rights, which were significant in the building up of commercial roots in Britain through the chartering of companies, through privateering and letters of marque, and through the symbiotic relationship between the growth of the fiscal capacity of the British state and its naval capacity. This story intersects with the history of landed property rights, which themselves were bound up with the 17th-century shift of power from Crown to Parliament; the strengthening of common law and a decentralized legal system somewhat removed from direct state executive control; and the creation of constraints on executive power through a constitutionally limited government. This contrasts with the continental European states' administrative systems, which have historically featured more centralized civil codification, stronger state influence over the judicial system, more limited fiscal capacity and yet greater interventionist powers – a set-up which has been variously known as *dirigisme* or *étatisme*. Critical to this contrast is the intertwining of financial market development with liberal states' ability to issue public debt: the priority and ability of Britain and the United States to service public debt from taxation and not default and to honour and protect property rights linked to those markets, a policy which in turn enabled naval expansion, victory in war, commercial extension, and, in the case of the United States, territorial expansion across North America. It raises the questions of why the continental European states did not go down the route of developing fiscal capacity through equivalent financial markets, and whether their *étatisme* led to more privately-held companies, as has been argued.

Why these countries? I take as my sample countries the two supposedly liberal economies – Britain and the United States – the two leading continental European economies that were originally central to the conception of the coordinated market economy – France and Germany – and two contrasting emergent capitalisms, Tanzania and China. In each coupling, there are similarities and large contrasts to highlight. The United States carried certain institutional orderings over from Britain – common law, the importance of chartered companies and the corporation, and a certain individualism. But it was also constructed institutionally very differently with regard to its separation of powers, its decentralized federal executive, and the role of race and slavery within its domestic economy. France and Germany of course also have different institutional histories. France is known for its highly centralized state apparatus, its prolonged absolutist government, and the importance of its state administrative structures. Germany, on the other hand, was an amalgam of differing states and orderings between the Hanseatic north, the Bavarian Catholic south, the commercial Rhineland states in the west, and the Junker estates in the east. Somehow these were gathered together into one country in the late 19th century. But there are certain institutional similarities, which include the importance of state administration and bureaucracy; centralized legal codifications; and the role of the state in providing education, infrastructure, and skills for industrialization. Tanzania and China in 2016 are widely differing. But in 1980 their per capita GDPs were $601 and $1,061 (in 1990 international Geary-Khamis (GK) dollars), respectively, as Table 1 shows. They were both poor agricultural and socialist nations with legacies of *dirigiste* authoritarian leaders. Between then and 2010, China's per capita GDP grew tenfold whilst Tanzania's increased by 30 per cent. I unpick their institutional histories – their property rights, legal systems, and the nature of their states. I connect these with their meso-institutions of enterprise development: the corporate governance of listed firms in China and the governance of cooperatives and their place in commercial supply chains in Tanzania. This reveals the urban-rural divides that exist in both countries and suggests the institutional underpinnings of Chinese growth and of Tanzanian relative stagnation.

Institutions matter for enterprise development and investment, for their development leads to economic growth and increased wealth. This much has been established by decades of research evaluating the relative importance of institutions, geographical characteristics and trade in stimulating development (North and Thomas 1973; Rodrik, Subramanian and Trebbi 2004; Acemoglu, Johnson and Robinson 2001; and Robinson 2012). The institutionalist camp argues that institutions trump geography and trade as a meta-explanation for development, *contra* others such as Diamond (1997) or Findlay and O'Rourke (2007), who argue for the supreme importance of geographical characteristics or world trade. The institutionalist argument, crudely paraphrased, goes

Table 1.1

	Variety of capitalism	*OAO or LAO*	*1700*		*1800*		*1850*		*1900*		*1980*		*2000*		*2010*	
			Per capita GDP	*Population (millions)*	*Per capita GDP*	*Population (millions)*	*Per capita GDP*	*Population (millions)*	*Per capita GDP*	*Population (millions)*	*Per capita GDP*	*Population (millions)*	*Per capita GDP*	*Population (millions)*	*GDP per capita*	*Population (millions)**
Britain	LME	OAO from 1850	1513	8.565	2,097	10.75	2,330	27.181	4,492	41.155	12,932	56.314	21,0456	59.522	23,777	62.8
United States	LME	OAO from 1850	n.a.	1.0	1,296	6.0	1,849	23.58	4,091	76.391	18,577	228.0	28,702	282.0	30,491	309.3
France	CME	OAO from 1870	n.a.	21.47	1,135 (in 1820)	29.0	1,597	36.35	2,876	40.598	17,647	55.11	20,392	61.137	21,478	65.0
Germany	CME	OAO from 1871, with break 1933–1945	939	15.0	986	18.0	1,428	33.746	2,985	54.388	14,114	78.297	18,944	82.188	20,661	81.8
Tanzania	EMC	Basic LAO	n.a	n.a.	n.a.	3.0	n.a.	5.468	424 (in 1950)	4.995	601	18.665	547	33.712	804	45.0
China	EMC	Mature LAO	n.a.	138.0	n.a.	330.0	600	412.0	545	400.0	1,061	982.0	3,421	1,260.0	8032	1337.7

Sources and units. Per capita GDP in 1990 international Geary-Khamis (GK) dollars. Maddison Project through Clio-Infra Project, Max Roser, https://ourworldindata.org. Database and paper Jutta Bolt and Jan Luiten van Zanden (2013) 'The First Update of the Maddison Project – Re-Estimating Growth before 1820'. Population: Clio-Infra Data from https://ourworldindata.org/world-population-growth/long-run-historical-perspective-country-trends-in-the-last-500-years. *Population data for 2010 from the World Bank.

something like this: if good institutions are not present, economic development does not occur; economic development is correlated with the presence of good institutions. And by good institutions, proponents of this position mean clarity of property rights, good contract enforcement, a functioning legal system independent of interference from the state executive, and an effective state in terms of its having a monopoly over violence (with no competing armies or factions able to challenge it) and sufficient administrative capacity to provide public goods. This set in train the search for a blueprint of 'good institutions' with the aim of importing or constructing them such that growth will follow.

But this is much too simplistic. To be fair, this characterization underplays the puzzlement in the literature over how one does attain good quality institutions (Rodrik 2004), which I go into further in the following chapter. But there has been an assumption that clarity of property rights is a relatively straightforward concept, which can be understood and adopted. My argument is that in order to understand how institutions matter, we need a better grasp of the differences between types of property rights, legal systems and states across the different varieties of capitalism. And to do that, we need a better grasp of their histories – of how those institutions of different property rights evolved.

My contribution is twofold: the first thread I entwine is, for each country in my sample – Britain, France and Germany; the United States; and then Tanzania and China – to tie together the historical evolution of their property rights and legal systems alongside the nature of their states. To do this, I need to decompose the idea of property rights. Property rights need protecting, but what type of property rights – which types of assets – need protecting? Whose property rights are protected in each country? And when did this become institutionalized? Linked to property rights are the different natures of legal systems. Legal systems are structured differently across countries and have different functions. In liberal countries, for example, legal systems are more decentralized, more reliant on common law; lawyers are prominent and are numerous and widely used to settle disputes and to challenge existing laws. In other countries, however, administrative structures counterbalance judicial systems, which themselves are more centralized and less accessible. When did these differences crystallize, and how do they link to the nature of the state?

The nature of the state is a large and complex concept. The links that I develop are between state fiscal capacity – the power of the state to raise money through taxation and public debt – and the state's effective capacity to expand – through wars in terms of territory, commerce and wealth. The liberal states' capacity to issue public debt was built on their credibility in borrowing and not defaulting. In turn, this arose from the greater protection and priority those states gave to tradable assets in the form of government securities. This was a particular type of coevolution – liberal states honoured promises to finance public debt, which was done out of taxation. This created a low-risk form of asset and contributed to expanding the financial market in those assets. This supported the development of financial institutions, particularly localized financial markets in equities as well as government securities, which were much more pronounced in the LMEs from an early stage. Linked to those markets was the pre-eminence in organizational form of companies and corporations that used those financial markets.

This goes together with ideas about the state – the ideological stance about what states should do, in the economic sphere particularly – and the drawing of different boundaries between private and public spheres. The second thread that I entwine, then, is what is meant by 'constraints on the state'; a state executive with power reined in in particular ways. I argue that in relation to tradable property rights in particular, the liberal states have been more constrained, and I outline where those constraints came from. I then contrast this with less-constrained state power over property rights in continental Europe and unconstrained states in Tanzania and China. This involves linking the protection of different types of property rights with what North, Wallis and Weingast (2009) call the 'dominant elites', their relationship to their states in each country, and the ideologies or stance of those states – how protectionist or mercantilist and how liberal they were and how they evolved to sanction the protection of one type of property rights over another.

These elements of the nature of the state are all inter-related: the dominant elites are typically in charge of courts and judicial-making structures, and they are usually influential in the legislative assemblies; the dominant elites feature in the administrative structures and bureaucracies. But some states – England – allowed much greater autonomy and power to the large landowning elites, gentry and notables in their roles as justices of the peace, in local courts, and in running other local municipal services, schools and hospitals, whereas other states – France – were more centralized from the 17th century and superseded judicial structures by administrative structures that were run by the administrative bureaucracy and largely bypassed the more regional nobility and the seigniorial courts. Prussia and then Germany also did a lot more through the bureaucracy, administrative structures and the centralized state than did Britain or the United States.

These contrasts – between states and the types of elites and their power – link back into the differential protection of types of property rights between states. In particular, the primacy of individualized and tradable property rights was embedded in the maritime economy in England (Paine 2013) and built into individualism in the countryside from the 15th century (Macfarlane 1978); they became entrenched and built on after the civil war in England in the 17th century and carried from England to the United States. The priority given to these tradable property rights was combined with Lockean possessive individualism as the cornerstone of individual rights in those countries, independent of the state, acting as a constraint on the state executive and coming prior to any great extension of the franchise.

One difference between England and the United States has been the role that race has played in their development. I bring out the colonial heritage of the United States – which was a patchwork of settlements founded by chartered companies and other groups – and the institutional elements that were brought over from England. I emphasize the post-1787 settlement of separated powers between states, the federal government and the Supreme Court, focusing on democracy and decentralized states' sovereignty – which were designed to constrain executive power – in addition to the expansionary tendencies of the Republic alongside racial division between northern and southern states, the strength of attachment to slavery-based capitalism in the southern states, and the exclusion of African Americans from citizenship. The decentralized role of the corporation and the Supreme Court in being pro-capitalist and constraining executive power also contributed to boosting the power of employers vis-à-vis employees. This combined with racial division and meant that labour movements were weaker and more violently put down by employer armies and that class interests were not politicized into a representative party as they were in Britain. Alongside this and in common with Britain were the growth of financial markets, the role of the corporation, and the partial democratization of shareholding through its dispersal in the early twentieth century. The rights of smaller shareholders needed protecting and led to the upholding of shareholder primacy that characterizes the LMEs.

This contrasts with both France and Germany. In the continental European states, property rights were to a greater extent in the gift of the state, despite the existence of old noble family lineages. From the 17th century (according to Tocqueville (1856)), and more so after the French Revolution (Rosenthal 1992), property rights were at the mercy of a more centralized administration and greater state intervention in terms of moving judicial litigious disputes over property into the realm of administrative decision-making, creating a different balance between individual property rights and state power. In addition, whereas in England property rights were more independent of the state executive before any real democracy took shape, in France the Revolution brought notions of *égalité* and *fraternité* alongside the *liberté* that itself was never as anchored on property rights as it was in England. The contrast is between England's freedom of property and intellect from the reaches of the state and its suspicions of those reaches, and France's equal rights for all before the law and its looking to the state to enforce those rights. It was not just that the English reacted to the French Revolution by recoiling from the uprising of the masses; they held substantially different ideas and were ruled by substantially different elite groups. The chasm had opened up in the 18th century and is bound up in very different histories of such institutions as the Financial Revolution in England from the end of the 17th century, which saw the growth of stock jobbing, joint stock companies and local stock exchanges; the transformation of the government's fiscal capacity and the extension of the national debt through new financial instruments, including the Bank of England; and the growth of the tax-raising power of the English state that in turn fuelled a huge extension of the navy's powers, which transformed British commercial and colonial adventures abroad.

This is a very distinct historical turning point, attributable substantially to the different lay-out of the fundamental institutions of property rights and the state between the two countries. The state in France in the 18th century, with its nobility largely exempt from taxation, which, as Tocqueville (1856) argues, was its payoff for its loss of real political power, was much less able to raise taxes, relying as it did more heavily on taxing the poor. This led to a series of military and naval defeats during the heavily war-driven long 18th century (from 1689 to 1815). It may also be linked to it being in England that the Industrial Revolution took off in the second half of the century, with France thereafter becoming a second-order power. Braudel (1983), contrasting financial developments in the two countries, argues that by the end of the 18th century France lagged well behind Britain in terms of the financial institutions – banking and stock markets – that played a part in financing new industries and enterprises.

I tell a complementary story about comparative organizational forms, about the importance of joint stock companies and then limited liability corporations in the liberal economies and more closely held private companies and partnerships in continental Europe. I discuss the presence of these different forms as a response to the absence of state regulation and pervasiveness and the tendency for self-regulation, especially of the financial sectors in the liberal economies, and as a counteraction to more pervasive state regulation on the Continent. This may be linked, I argue, to the protection of assets tradable on financial markets in the liberal economies, where mercantile-financial elites held more power. Whereas the assets protected in continental Europe were and continue to be more strategic, less tradable, assets built up in those more closely held companies owned by the industrial-state-bureaucratic elites in those countries. This protection of tradable assets in liberal economies is linked with an openness and competitiveness and less protection for many sectors in those economies, which in turn means that the English national football team is less nurtured and protected than the internationalized football club teams that live in the United Kingdom.

The final part of the comparison of institutional structures within the developed countries in my sample is to look at the evolutions of their corporate governance structures: When did dispersed shareholding come to characterize company ownership in the United States and United Kingdom? How is that linked to the evolution of different corporate organizational forms? Why did concentrated shareholding structures characterize our continental European countries (and continue to do so)? And why might that be linked to the financing institutions that were available to them and also to the greater strength of other stakeholder voices, especially employee voices, present therein? I do this by tracing the links between the Codetermination Act and works councils in the newly unified Germany in the late 19th century under Bismarck both to present-day corporate governance structures such as two-tier boards and labour force participation, but also to the powers of the state to intervene and take responsibility for regulating the welfare of the labour force in the interests of national policy. In a different fashion in France, the state has seen its role as intervening more directly in regulating labour conditions and setting centralized standards across industry, which is a tradition with deep roots in the nature of the French state.

This is one theme that I develop – how the different lay-outs and balances between different types of property rights and natures of the state influenced the future shapes and lay-outs of the capitalisms that we find in the late 20th and early 21st centuries.

The other main theme of the book – and it is not a secondary theme but is more heavily emphasized in contrasting the developed countries' histories with the developing countries' institutional evolutions – is to pick up the institutionalist theme of 'institutions matter' for economic development. Here, the contrast that is made in this debate is between the so-called 'good institutions' of the already developed economies – of clarity of property rights, good contract enforcement, strong state capacity but with constraints on the state – with the poor institutions of developing countries that appear to lack these (Acemoglu et al. 2001; and Robinson 2012). I have two contrasting countries in my developing country sample: China and Tanzania. They each bring out different aspects of the comparison with the developed country case studies. In each case, I approach them in a parallel way to those of the earlier case studies, bringing out the history of property rights and the nature of the state, but in more recent periods and in both cases focusing on their capitalist periods and structures rather than their pre-capitalist or socialist structures. This means picking up China's history from the post-Mao period in the late 1970s and picking up Tanzania's history from independence in 1961, although with a greater emphasis on the post-liberalization period from the 1990s. In both cases, property rights and the nature of the state are highly intertwined.

The emphasis in the Tanzanian story for primary institutions is on contrasting the different types of property rights – customary, statist and private – and, as with other African states (Boone 2014), on establishing that the power of the particular elites in the state goes hand-in-hand with the influence of customary or statist property rights. In Tanzania, statist property rights have predominated. Political power means power over land allocation. The plight of smallholder farmers in Tanzania is tied up with the loss of customary property rights and the assertion of statist rights. Property rights are not established independently of the state, and there is little scope for a market in land or land rights to develop.

North et al. (2013) outline the trade-off for what they call basic limited access orders (LAOs) (which characterize developing countries) between states centralizing their capacity to quell violence and division between ethnic groups and nurturing groups that are more independent of the state – through opposition parties, independent media, private sector enterprises – that constrain the state. Tanzania, through its post-colonial history, has created a highly centralized, relatively unconstrained state that maintains stability but stunts rural development. This follows from decades of taxation of agricultural surpluses in efforts to build urban industry, with the centralized state's long favouring of urban industrial development (Bates 1982, 2014) in *dirigiste* fashion leading to a narrowly based and concentrated industrial structure and a long exploitation of the agricultural smallholder in terms of price-fixing and taxation (through various structures such as marketing boards, auctions, and the centralized buying of exporting crops such as coffee, tea and sisal). This, in combination with the loss of customary land rights, has created an urban-rural divide.

In terms of meso-institutions in Tanzania, I look at the governance of cooperatives in coffee and tea and at how state influence penetrates into decision-making on the selection of representatives for primary societies and secondary unions. I emphasize how cooperatives are caught between these state influences and the pressures from the market through direct buying from individual farmers, which threatens the collective cohesiveness and financial viability of the cooperative, with groups breaking away. I also touch on centrifugal pressures on the cooperative arising from inequality between farmers. Smallholder farmers in cooperatives have been squeezed between weakness in individual land rights and their inability to use property as collateral on the one hand, and their strong collective identities and investments through cooperatives on the other (yet with cooperatives being subservient to state policies that have shifted surpluses from the rural agricultural sector to the urban industrial sector). A different squeezing of the smallholder farmer is illustrated in the tea industry: the tea association buys shares in and integrates down the value chain into tea processing, but individual farmers are still in a weak bargaining position vis-à-vis managers in those companies down the value chain when it comes to the terms of trade achieved for their green leaf tea.

An urban-rural divide is true also for China. The Chinese story is also based on how to interpret property rights and how those rights are tied up with (regional and central) state power and relationships with the state. In this case, property rights have to be seen not in an absolute Western sense of being upheld by the rule of law and being independent of the state, but as being 'good enough' property rights, providing security of the proprietor (not being arrested and put in jail for owning property and not having property taken away by the state) rather than absolute security of property itself (Huang 2008; Coase and Wang 2014). This was sufficient during the 1980s to get going a wave of rural enterprises and town and village enterprises, which were essentially privately owned but disguised as 'red hat' enterprises to fit with the socialist market ideology. There was a hiatus after the Tiananmen crackdown in 1989, which gradually thawed after 1992 – although some would argue that the 1980s was a more enterprise-driven decade, and especially a more rural-enterprise-driven decade, than the 1990s (Huang 2008) – and which ended in the early 2000s. I also emphasize the intricate nature of the state administrative structures and how control over state officials' careers at the centre, alongside incentive structures that pushed for decentralized economic growth (at various levels of decentralization), created a pact between non-state enterprises and entrepreneurs that ran them with the local officials, who were responsible not only for securing property rights but for various infrastructural investments that would support such enterprises. In terms of meso-institutions, I also bring in the peculiarity of Chinese corporate governance structures, which feature strong state holding of listed companies (not only of the state-owned companies) and strong state influence on top management careers (even for listed companies), and which are highly skewed in supporting shareholder/manager rights rather than labour rights and conditions despite being formally modelled on the German two-tier board system. There is, therefore, a different kind of principal-principal issue at play: while small shareholders can be exploited at the expense of larger shareholders in Western-concentrated shareholding structures, in China small shareholders can be exploited by the state, which is always the principal that has superior influence.

These more detailed and nuanced development stories about the different types of property rights and the nature of the state and their contrasting effects on economic development – highly successful in creating a type of capitalism in China and thwarting development to a large extent in Tanzania, but with distinct winners and losers in each case – cast a different light on the way in which institutions matter and how they matter for economic development.

And finally, in laying out the stories of some of the key developed countries in terms of their institutional development – of different types of property rights and natures of the state – in parallel with the institutional development of developing countries, one can also pick out certain common themes around the sequencing of events: did property rights get settled before and independent of democratic state power? And if not, how did that state power shape those property rights? One can also pick out a common theme around the private-public boundary: how much economic growth and development was done through private enterprises and privately organized institutions (financing institutions, private corporations) rather than through state-sponsored initiatives or state-regulating organizing structures? Here, the parallels cut across the developed-developing divide: I think you can pick out greater similarities between German or French paths of development and Chinese ones than between English and US paths and continental European paths. This can be seen in terms of who provides infrastructure and education – with different private-public boundaries in the LME than both the CME and developing country scenarios. Key to this difference is a sequencing issue: which came first, property rights and common law based on private property rights, or the type of state that comes to dominate development?

There are links to present-day policy debates that arise from this study. In arguing for the greater rootedness of institutional systems, it highlights the difficulties inherent in implanting harmonization of legal systems, of regulation, and of ways in which regulation is thought about between Britain and continental Europe. If fundamentally different kinds of assets are protected in the different systems, this means that the fault-lines are constructed orthogonally and cannot be mapped onto each other. If LMEs, such as Britain and the

United States, are constructed deliberately *not* to protect untradable skills and assets but to foster the development of tradable assets and to encourage openness and level playing fields in that tradability across national boundaries, then the vulnerable constituents in this kind of capitalism are indigenous groups, the less internationalized, the unprotected lacking tradable assets and portable skills; and those without capital assets be they houses, land or shares. The recent Brexit vote and the current support for Donald Trump (among some Americans) are in part protest votes by these unprotected indigenous 'outsiders', who are left out – particularly when the playing field is level and open. Harmonization between Britain and the European Union (EU) has had more profound obstacles than had previously been recognized in the form in which the primary institutional set-ups are very different, with different types of assets being protected.

The rest of the book is structured as follows: Chapters 2 and 3 outline the various theoretical frameworks and ideas used throughout the book, the former covering the primary institutions and the latter covering the meso-institutions of varieties of capitalism, as well as the literature and debates which prompted this enquiry to begin with. Chapters 4, 5 and 6 are the historical case studies, Chapter 4 of Britain, Chapter 5 of France and Germany, and Chapter 6 of the United States, forming Part II. Part III consists of Chapters 7, 8 and 9. Chapter 7 introduces two further theoretical ideas that inform the developing country cases with the study of Tanzania in Chapter 7 and of China in Chapter 8.Chapter 9 concludes the book by making conceptual linkages that contribute to theory-building in this literature. All case studies are structured around the evolution of primary institutions of different types of property rights, legal systems, and natures of the state, and the development of the meso-institutions of organizational forms and corporate governance.

Note

1 I develop a fuller answer to this particular question in Chapter 3.

References

Acemoglu, D., Johnson, S. and Robinson, J. (2001) 'The Colonial Origins of Comparative Development: An Empirical Investigation', *American Economic Review* 91(5): 1369–1401.

Acemoglu, D. and Robinson, J. (2012) *Why Nations Fail: The Origins of Power, Prosperity and Poverty.* London: Profile Books.

Bates, R.H. (1982) *Markets and States in Tropical Africa: The Political Basis of Agricultural Policy.* Berkeley: University of California Press.

Bates, R.H. (2014) 'The New Institutionalism', in I. Sened and S. Galiani (eds), *Institutions, Economic Growth and Property Rights: The Legacy of Douglass North*, 50–65. Cambridge: Cambridge University Press.

Boone, C. (2014) *Property and Political Order in Africa: Land Rights and the Structure of Politics.* Cambridge: Cambridge University Press.

Braudel, F. (1983) *Civilization and Capitalism, 15th – 18th Century, Vol. 2: The Wheels of Commerce.* London: Collins.

Coase, R. and Wang, N. (2013) *How China Became Capitalist.* New York: Palgrave Macmillan.

de Tocqueville, A. (1966 [1856]) *The Ancien Regime and the French Revolution.* London: Collins/Fontana.

Diamond, J. (1997) *Guns, Germs and Steel: The Fates of Human Societies.* New York: W.W. Norton.

Findlay, R. and O'Rourke, K. (2007) *Power and Plenty: Trade, War and the World Economy in the Second Millennium.* Princeton: Princeton University Press.

Hall, P. and Soskice, D. (2001) *Varieties of Capitalism: The Institutional Foundations of Comparative Advantage.* Oxford: Oxford University Press.

Huang, Y. (2008) *Capitalism with Chinese Characteristics: Entrepreneurship and the State.* Cambridge: Cambridge University Press.

Macfarlane, A. (1978) *The Origins of English Individualism.* Oxford: Basil Blackwell.

North, D. (1989) *Institutions and Economic Growth: An Historical Introduction.* London: Elsevier.

North, D. (1990) *Institutions, Institutional Change and Economic Performance.* Cambridge: Cambridge University Press.

North, D. (1991) 'Institutions', *Journal of Economic Perspectives* 5(1): 97–112.

North, D. and Thomas, R. (1973) *The Rise of the Western World: A New Economic History.* Cambridge: Cambridge University Press.

North, D., Wallis, J.J., Webb, S. and Weingast, B. (2013) *In the Shadow of Violence: Politics, Economics and the Problems of Development.* Cambridge: Cambridge University Press.

North, D., Wallis, J.J. and Weingast, B. (2009) *Violence and Social Orders: A Conceptual Framework for Interpreting Recorded Human History.* Cambridge: Cambridge University Press.

Paine, L. (2013) *The Sea and Civilization: A Maritime History of the World.* New York: Alfred A. Knopf.

Rodrik, D. (2004) Getting Institutions Right, Working Paper. Cambridge, MA: Harvard University.

Rodrik, D., Subramanian, A. and Trebbi, F. (2004) 'Institutions Rule: The Primacy of Institutions over Geography and Integration in Economic Development', *Journal of Economic Growth* 9(2): 131–165.

Rosenthal, J.-L. (1992) *The Fruits of Revolution: Property Rights, Litigation and French Agriculture, 1700–1860.* Cambridge: Cambridge University Press.

Part I

2 Primary institutions

Property rights, legal systems and the state – theories and concepts

Establishing that institutions rule

This chapter starts by taking stock of the institutional debate and setting out the tools it has used. As set out in Chapter 1, there are two broad aspects to this debate. One is that 'good institutions' are the key to the development of markets and capitalism. The other is that advanced capitalisms have developed distinct variants in terms of corporate governance structures and institutions that underpin corporations or companies, as set out in the varieties of capitalism literature (e.g., Hall and Soskice 2001). The first aspect relates primarily to the gap between developed and developing nations in the range, type and quality of primary institutions of property rights, contract enforcement, state capacity and constraints on the state. The second aspect concerns the different varieties of capitalism within the developed world. A central argument of this book is that differences in corporate governance across countries stem from how primary institutions in those countries evolved; in other words, these two aspects are connected.

Institutions within a country matter. Migration has been towards countries where there is no war against outsiders or between groups within its borders; where the rule of law applies to all, including to relatively more powerful elites; where disputes are settled through due process of law (again broadly speaking); where property rights apply and are upheld by law; where corruption, although present in areas, is not rife and is not the predominant form of transacting with those in office; and where, broadly speaking, political processes allow people a voice and apply, again roughly speaking, to all citizens in the country.

How has this insight been translated into proveable research in the academic debate to establish that institutions matter? Following North's ground-breaking work (1990, 1991, see below), there has been an enormous research effort to identify the main causes of the huge disparity in income levels between rich and poor countries. Three main groups of determinants have been identified in one body of work as the geography and resources of countries; countries' trading stance – how prominent trade is and how open countries are to trade; and the quality of countries' institutions – whether or not they have secure property rights, good contract enforcement, a robust legal system and a judiciary that is independent of the government (Rodrik, Subramanian and Trebbi 2004; Acemoglu, Johnson and Robinson 2002, 2001). The methods this work uses are econometric: regressing equations with income levels *per capita* on the left-hand side of the equation determined by variables on geography, trade and institutions. A panel of data across countries, from rich to poor countries, with between 79 and 137 countries in the various panels are constructed. The variables relate to fairly recent periods: trade data stretching from the 1950s to 1990; and geographical and institutional data relating to the 1990s for the most part.

I take three examples. First, *Institutions Rule: The Primacy of Institutions over Geography and Integration in Economic Development* by Rodrik, Subramanian and Trebbi (2004) estimates the contributions of geography, trade and institutions to economic growth. It contrasts the three explanations found in the literature: how rich a country is determined by geography through natural resources, climate and disease *versus* how open a country is to trade determines *versus* the quality of a country's institutions. The three authors find that the quality of institutions trumps the other two explanations in determining the income growth of a given country.

A second example is Acemoglu, Johnson and Robinson's article *The Colonial Origins of Comparative Development: An Empirical Investigation* (2001), which also argues that good institutions are the fundamental cause of economic growth. The authors do this by looking for institutional variation between countries and find it by contrasting countries colonized by Europeans: those countries where disease rates were high and where the colonists could not settle became 'extractive states', a prime example of this being the Belgian colonization of the Congo. These states did not protect private property, and there were no checks and balances on the state against government expropriation. The main purpose was to transfer the resources of the colony to the colonizer. The authors then contrast extractive states with 'neo-Europes', such as the United States, Australia and Canada, where, it is argued, the settlers replicated European institutions with a strong emphasis on private property and checks on government power. The particular colonization strategy was determined by how feasible it was to settle in the colony. The type of institutions persisted after independence and still affect the quality of those institutions to the present day.

One issue that these researchers have tackled is that of the complexity of causation within the econometrics, namely, that the regression analysis is so constructed that the right-hand-side variables determine or cause the left-hand-side income level, per capita gross domestic product (GDP). There is great inter-relation between the different right-hand-side variables: geographical place and resources are bound up with trade variables, which in turn are bound up with the quality of the institutions in the country. Also, there is endogeneity between independent and dependent variables, with income levels (dependent variable) feeding back into and affecting institutional quality and trade policy. Establishing cleanly the influence of institutions on income levels is difficult.

The way these papers and others have tackled this issue is to construct instrumental variables, particularly for institutional variables, that are correlated with the original institutional variables but that are not in themselves connected to, or affected by, income levels. The main instrumental variable for institutions has been mortality rates amongst settlers taken from Curtin's (1989) *Death by Migration* on the mortality of European troops from 1817 to 1848 and Curtin's (1998) *Disease and Empire* on the mortality of soldiers in the second half of the 19th century. The idea behind this is that settler mortality provides 'an exogenous source of variation' that is not influenced by income levels but that is related to institutional quality. The argument these papers make, then, is that colonizations can be divided into two categories: 1) those countries where mortality rates were high, where settlers could not become established, and where 'good institutions' were not built – instead 'extractive institutions' that plundered and extracted wealth from those countries were constructed (Acemoglu and Robinson 2012); and those countries where mortality rates were low, the neo-Anglo colonial countries, where settlers became established and constructed inclusive institutions that went on to become fertile ground for capitalism to thrive. For example, from Acemoglu, Johnson and Robinson's *Reversal of Fortune* we see that 'historical and econometric evidence suggests that European colonialism caused "an institutional reversal": European colonialism led to the development of institutions of private property in previously poor areas while introducing extractive institutions or maintaining extractive institutions in previously prosperous places' (2002: 3). In *The Colonial Origins,* the same authors argue that 'Europeans adopted very different colonization strategies with different associated institutions. In one extreme, as in the case of the US, Australia and New Zealand, they went and settled in the colonies and set up institutions that enforced the rule of law and encouraged investment. In the other extreme, as in the Congo or the Gold Coast, they set up extractive states with the intention of transferring resources rapidly to the metropole… The colonization strategy was in part determined by the feasibility of European settlement' (2001: 1395). And the rest, as they say, is history.

But that is the main issue that I have with this material. I agree with the focusing of the debate on institutions and their development and quality. But the picture that one takes away is deterministic and benign: where settlers managed to survive, they created good, benign institutions in accordance with democratic principles that were inclusive in the sense that they allowed most people to participate in the spread of commercial capitalism and thence industrial capitalism. These institutions were secure property rights, good contract enforcement, rule of law, and limited government. But this picture has led to an unduly simplistic template of what constitutes 'good institutions', and ahistorical policy advice to create institutions in this vein that ignores the much more complex trajectory that each country has taken. To be fair, Rodrik (2000) also argues against the template mentality that makes identifying what good institutions are straightforward. On the contrary, Rodrik says that there is no unique mapping between markets and the non-market institutions underpinning them and that the variation in 'institutional set-ups' is larger than usually supposed. As Rodrik says, the American style of capitalism is different from the Japanese style, that both differ from European capitalism, and that within Europe there are large differences between capitalisms (Rodrik 2000).

Acemoglu and Robinson (2012) also stress the specifics of historical contingency and that unforeseen events shift the balance of power, which then cumulates in an undeterministic way. In *Why Nations Fail,* Acemoglu and Robinson (2012) seek to explain the 'huge differences in incomes and standards of living that separate the rich countries of the world...from the poor' (Acemoglu and Robinson 2012: 1). In the argument they put forward about the Arab Spring of 2011 in Egypt, they say that the Egyptians were held back by an ineffective and corrupt state dominated by a narrow elite, and that the economic impediments they faced were in fact due to the way political power was exercised. They contrast this with England in 1688, when, they argue, the Glorious Revolution transformed political rights and in doing so expanded economic opportunities, with this expansion eventually leading into the Industrial Revolution (Acemoglu and Robinson, 2012: 4). But even this contrast sweeps away the difficulties in the process of achieving limited government; what constituted limited government in terms of who the dominant elites or elite coalitions in the country were; and why these elites should seemingly cede power for the sake of achieving limited government. The rational choice model that is used infers that exchanging elite privileges for more impersonal political rights was perceived as beneficial by those elites and was therefore the path that was chosen.

The problem with this approach is that it obscures the more complex and messy political, ideological, pragmatic and economic rationales that contributed to these historical processes. As Abba Lerner said, 'Economics has gained the title Queen of the Social Sciences by choosing solved political problems as its domain' (Lerner 1972: 259).

De Castella and Westcott (2013) of BBC News list 20 reasons why the infrastructure project HS2, the second stage of the High Speed 2 rail link between London and the north of England is going to take two decades to finish. The building of HS1, the Channel Tunnel Rail Link, took 16 years after Secretary of State for the Environment Michael Heseltine announced it to the Conservative Party Conference in 1991. HS1 was only 68 miles long; HS2 will be 330 miles long. Amongst the reasons for the delay are the need for consultation, and the buying of the land and people's houses: 'It can be a big business blocking the route or Bob in his allotment. Everyone needs to be talked to and negotiated with' (de Castella and Westcott 2013). The list cites the difficulties of building tunnels, the archaeological investigation, the regeneration involved, the Parliamentary approval that is necessary, concerns for the environment and protected species, and then the franchising and timetabling with the train operating companies, health and safety, contingency, and the laying of the rails. It includes the phrase 'The UK isn't

China'. The 1,318km Beijing-Shanghai high-speed route went from design to completion in 39 months. This is not possible in a democracy like the UK. One can contrast this too with the building of the TGV, the French High Speed Rail Network, which started up in 1981. The Déclaration d'Utilité Publique was granted by the French government in 1976 to build the LN1 route from Paris to Lyon. In that year, the prototype electric TGV was completed, having been developed by Alstom and SNCF. The first stage of the line was opened in 1981; the second stage, which included a further 116km of high-speed line, was opened in 1983. In the course of the 1980s up to 1996, further lines were constructed. In 2000, the billionth passenger was carried on the TGV (Bunn 2015).

The point I wish to make is that this story represents a fundamentally different stance both towards individual property rights in Britain, France and China, and by the state towards the building and financing of major infrastructure. These differences in type and strength of property rights and their intertwining with the nature of the state cannot be captured simply in the idea of 'the clarity of property rights'. We need, rather, to better understand the complex historical evolution of these structures – which property rights, whose property rights, what kind of state, and what kind of legal system enforces these rights – in order to understand the different institutional settlements, which is a precursor to looking at any policy prescriptions or negotiations.

Institutions are social constructs. They are humanly devised (North 1990), but not by rational design. They appear to humans as 'there', the way things are done, the way we behave (Douglas 1986). Mary Douglas' work (1986) and interpretations of her work (6 and Richards 2016) provide me with a lens through which to interpret the concepts developed in the institutional economics and historical institutionalism literature. So first I set out Mary Douglas' ideas about 'how institutions think' and how she rejects the rational choice path that the institutional economics debate has taken. Then, in interpreting the various concepts that the institutions debate employs – of property rights, contract-enforcement institutions (CEIs), private and public enforcement, effective states and state capacity, constraints on the state, and different types of state power – I ask such questions as: Why did common law property rights and limited government under a constitutional monarchy make sense in late-17th-century England? and with what did they fit?

Property rights, aligned with legal systems, are also not a straightforward concept. Not only are there different types of property rights (Boone 2014), but property rights have different functions (of protection, of coordination, of signalling) in the context of differently structured legal systems (Milhaupt and Pistor 2008). In this chapter, I set out the concepts which are used throughout the book, namely, property rights and legal systems, CEIs, constraints on the state, state legal and fiscal capacity, and the role and position of dominant elites in the state, and I connect them with the Douglas' (1986) and Milhaupt and Pistor's (2008) perspectives.

The book is structured using country case studies that span institutional evolution both within advanced capitalism and across transitional (China) and emerging market (Tanzania) capitalisms. In each chapter, I connect the institutions of property rights and legal systems with both the kind of state and the state capacity in that country; with the organizational forms of enterprises, the place of the corporation (its legal status), and alternative enterprise forms to the corporation in that country; and with the connection between these organizational forms and the institutions of stock markets and state regulation of markets and banks, which, in turn, have influenced the ownership structures of enterprises.

My argument, which unifies the book, is that different kinds of capital became protected through the different routes taken and different relationships between legal systems and nature of the states. Liberal states grew into protecting tradable property, whereas more coordinated states grew into protecting firms' strategic assets; and in my transition/emerging examples, state and foreign assets have been more protected at the expense of private assets and rural farmers' assets.

This book, through its case studies, builds on the prior work done on institutions, attempting to inject greater nuance and historical specificity into understanding how the particular institutions of property rights and the kind of state and the dominant elites in that state came to be there. The borders between inclusive and extractive institutions are more grey and porous than the original picture paints. Institutions are not created inclusive or extractive: particular groups have power, often through the state, which allows them to create rules that secure property rights in their favour. It matters which groups are the dominant elites and whether they are in coalition with, or in opposition to, other groups. Theoretically, I favour thinking about institutional evolution through the lenses of Douglas (1986) and Mann (1993; 2012), theorizing about social power and how that power is naturalized and absorbed into the minds and choices of people in different societies (Douglas 1986; 6 and Richards 2016).

The theoretical chapters of this book (this one and the next) flesh out the key concepts using building blocks identified in the literature. This chapter deals with the fundamental or primary institutions that underpin markets and capitalist development. These primary institutions are property rights; legal systems; contract enforcement; state capacity, which refers to legal capacity and the rule of law, courts, and the judicial system; and fiscal capacity, which refers to the ability to tax and spend on public goods. This chapter will also deal with the structure of the state that creates and enforces these institutions, whether centralized or fragmented and whether possessing collective and/or distributive power; and it will look at the political nature of the state, how liberal states like Britain and the US became liberal and when and why this occurred, contrasting them with the continental European, Chinese and Tanzanian states with their greater centralization or nation-building impetus, broader public spheres of activity and less liberal stances towards regulation and the private sector. This chapter then goes on to outline how that relates to the different variants of state, according to the North, Wallis and Weingast (2009) framework of limited access orders (LAOs) and open access orders (OAOs). It also explores how to interpret the idea of constraints on state power that limit the powers of the state; what the variety of institutions or organizations that constrain state power look like; whether constraints occurred through the need for taxation (and the forms that consent to taxation took); whether constraints took the form of non-state organizations in civil society that acted as a counterweight to state power; and whether constraints took the form of individual property rights that were independent of state power.

I use the ideas that Milhaupt and Pistor (2008) set out in their book *Law and Capitalism: What Corporate Crises Reveal about Legal Systems and Economic Development around the World.* I use their framework, which distinguishes between the degree to which legal systems are decentralized/centralized, and which links this to their protective versus coordinative functions and to the degree of contestability of law within the legal system. Milhaupt and Pistor emphasize how legal systems and capitalist institutions have coevolved and how law 'rolls with' the market. They use corporate crises across different countries to show how crises expose differences in the protection of different groups and the different capacities of countries to use law to settle conflicting claims. This is useful for my purposes in showing how the legal system is not, and has never been, a fixed institution but how it was intricately related to the power structures in each society and how its evolution has been bound up with – influencing and being influenced by – the social structures in each society, particularly those of the dominant elites, who shaped and used the legal system as capitalist structures evolved.

The story in brief

The thesis of this book is that property rights and different kinds of state coevolve and lead to the protecting of different types of property rights.

I connect the joining together of individual property rights backed by common law with a highly decentralized and protective legal system in the liberal economies. This in turn is connected to the interests of the dominant elites in those liberal states. Legal status and prominence was given in these liberal states to the corporation on the one hand and to the growth of self-regulated, localized capital markets on the other. The prominence of capital markets and the absence of state regulation, combined with the larger role for the 'private attorney general' (Milhaupt and Pistor 2008) in a decentralized legal system, led to the dual features of more dispersed shareholding in the early decades of the 20th century alongside greater protection for those minority shareholders (from the 1930s), the one leading to the other. The primacy given to (relatively mass or democratic) shareholding in turn has led to an emphasis on the protection of these tradable property rights over and above the protection of specific strategic assets (another form of property rights) built up within firms.

This contrasts with a very different institutional route for continental economies. More centralized state administrations (France) or nation-building bureaucracies (Germany) combined with more centralized civil code legal systems, giving less power to independent judges and more power to state administrators in decision-making on property rights and placing a greater emphasis on the coordinating function of property rights than on their protective function. In turn, the corporation with its legal status did not develop; instead, alternative company forms, such as partnerships with limited liabilities, developed and enabled the private blockholding of companies to be retained to a much greater extent than they otherwise would have. There was little demand for the growth of capital markets, this demand being inhibited in part by stronger state regulation; instead, companies were more reliant on closer relations with their banks and networks for financing. Part of this institutional route saw a corresponding emphasis on coordinating different groups within the firm and across the economy – employees and employers – to protect their interests, something which was fostered by state regulation where interest groups were not sufficiently cohesive. This in turn inhibited demand for capital markets – both due to the more intrusive role of state regulation and due to larger owners' unwillingness to cede control through dilution of shareholding and public listing of companies. The kind of property rights that have been protected in this system are those of strategic assets – investments in skills, capabilities, and routines that have been those built up within firms – with obstacles to their disruption and tradability. These investments have been protected against takeover by institutions reflecting the vested interests of these groups – cross-shareholdings, banks' holdings of proxy votes, codetermination, and works councils giving employees a voice in decision-making – with an overall an emphasis on wider stakeholder concerns above pure shareholder primacy.

I extend the same framework to the development chapters on China and Tanzania. In both cases, customary and rural land rights have been quashed by stronger state rights. In China in the 1980s, there was a 10-year spell of stronger liberalization, which allowed rural enterprise to flourish; this was reversed after Tiananmen, and state-controlled urban development has had stronger rights ever since. In Tanzania, strong state capacity and state-vested property rights have been asserted at the expense of rural customary land rights. In terms of coalitions in corporate governance, strong state alliances with managers have diminished the rights of workers and employees and the independence of cooperatives with a variety of capitalism that favours state-controlled, if not state-owned, assets over the rights of shareholders, employees and other stakeholders.

There are a lot of building blocks to establish. This book is about institutions and what constitutes 'good institutions' from the point of view of economic performance. Economic performance can be thought of first as the extension

Table 2.1 Putting together the theoretical framework for this story

	PRIMARY INSTITUTIONS				*TOWARDS MESO-INSTITUTIONS*
	Types of property rights	***Type of state***	***Legal system – characteristics and functions***	***Type of property rights protected***	***Production system in industrialization***
LMEs	Individual private property rights (PR) – large holdings, enclosures, strong PRs creating incentives for improvements.	Liberal state – no direct representation of interest groups in state but dominated by larger landholders, merchants, financial interests.	Decentralized, contestable by individuals through lawyers, courts (Milhaupt and Pistor 2008), protective function of law for minority shareholders.	Through prominence of markets and protection of smallholder rights, tradable assets protected – shares, land tradable – alienable rights high.	Industrialization based on unskilled landless labour, no employer groups, no incentives to invest in skills, managerial autonomy, representation through ownership in shares.
	Importance of property rights in other assets – rights over maritime contracting, commercial assets.	CCIs through decentralized legal system plus its protective function. Individual and class action lawsuits.		Contract enforcement through courts by individuals, corporations – contracts enforced over values of tradable assets.	

Table 2.1 (continued)

	PRIMARY INSTITUTIONS				*TOWARDS MESO-INSTITUTIONS*
	Types of property rights	***Type of state***	***Legal system – characteristics and functions***	***Type of property rights protected***	***Production system in industrialization***
CMEs	Private PRs in land less strong. More dispersed and developed later than England. Stronger state eminent domain property rights – smallholdings and tenure widespread – state administration coordinating between smallholders for dispute resolution.	Non-liberal regulating state – representative of economic interests of groups in state (Iversen and Soskice 2009). State administrations and bureaucracies centralized (Mann 1993). More encompassing state regulation, more extensive infrastructure publicly financed – fewer tradable assets, undeveloped equity markets, less openly held companies. Weaker CCIs – less independence of elites from state, more biased towards insiders.	Civil code, centralized, groups already represented in state, function of law to coordinate groups in order to regulate. CCIs – what form? Contestability of law low, CCIs weaker, less power of judges, lawyers, class actions.	Protection of strategic assets high – obstacles to tradability and transfer of ownership/control. CEIs – upholding of longer-term strategic contracts, relating to skills acquisition in firms.	Skills development – co-specific assets – stronger groups of guilds with skills and unions – consensual industrial relations. Incorporation of labour into governance – stakeholders more aggregated/organized, more consensual, more cooperation.

	PRIMARY INSTITUTIONS				*TOWARDS MESO-INSTITUTIONS*
	Types of property rights	***Type of state***	***Legal system – characteristics and functions***	***Type of property rights protected***	***Production system in industrialization***
EMERGENT MARKET ECONOMIES	Property Rights system in land contested: China – state-vested rights. Tanzania – state vested wins over customary. Customary property rights in land – unwritten, traditional, communal, hierarchical, decentralized *vs* state-vested rights *vs* individual private property rights – colonial legacy of private rights.	Developing Limited Access Order (North et al.2009) – dominance of elites, large privileged bureaucracies, lack of impersonality of law, of organizations. Strong state capacity over control of violence, at expense of CCIs, checks and balances (independent parties, media, judges).	Often legal transplant of civil code. What is the demand for legal enforcement? By which group? State dominates/chooses enforcement – legal rules but weak implementation.	Whose/which property rights protected? China, Tanzania – not rural farmers – urban developers and foreign investment favoured since 1990s.	Corporate governance – capital-labour relations. Labour rights weak, unskilled industrial, smallholder agricultural. Political/state holdings of companies mean state-managerial coalition – no labour voice.

of markets and commercialism and second as industrialization and technological development. These two types of performance are not the same thing, however, and institutions that encourage the spread of commercial markets are not the same as those that have underpinned industrial and technological change. This book is not concerned with measuring or assessing performance, but rather with unpacking the notion of 'good institutions'. It is concerned with the relationship between different aspects of good institutions and how they influenced or created a particular type of capitalism.

Definitions and conceptualizations of institutions

What do I mean by institutions? I am concerned here with capitalist institutions as a premise, not with socialist or planning institutions. The role of markets is therefore prominent, as the spread of capitalism is intimately connected to the spread and extension of markets (Greif 2006, 2005). I expand on Greif's work below. I start with the very famous quote from Adam Smith's *Wealth of Nations*: 'Commerce and manufactures can seldom flourish long in any state which does not enjoy a regular administration of justice, in which people do not feel themselves secure in the possession of their property, in which the faith of contract is not supported by law, and in which the authority of the state is not supposed to be regularly employed in enforcing the payment of debts from all those who are able to pay. Commerce and manufactures in short can seldom flourish in any state in which there is not a certain degree of confidence in the justice of government' (Smith 1776: 472). This highlights the main types of primary institutions that I am concerned with in this book: security of private property rights, contract enforcement backed by law, state authority to back up this framework, and the justice (and fairness) of government. Implicit is the issue of violence – that the government or state needs sufficient capacity to control incipient violence possessed through the power of rival groups and that there need to be institutions or organizations or practices that create sufficient constraints on that government to control its power and capacity for predation.

However, as the following discussion shows, there are many variants of institutions that fulfil these roles, and these are historically and culturally determined and specific to particular countries, nations, or regions within nations. Contract enforcement institutions (CEIs) are not uniform across different types of contracts: decentralized legal systems based on common law, where individuals or groups can bring actions through lawyers to localized courts, will tend to protect tradable, codified assets that can stand up to scrutiny by outsiders to a greater extent than more centralized, legal code systems where the number of lawyers might be restricted and where it is not encouraged for individuals to contest decisions using the legal system. Instead, different types of contracts are more respected and enforced. As Milhaupt and Pistor (2008) argue, the demand for law and legal enforcement plays a huge role above and beyond the formal law on the books that protects property rights. As they put it, how the law coevolves with the market varies significantly between countries.

North defines institutions as 'the rules of the game in a society or more formally…the humanly devised constraints that shape human interaction' (North 1990: 3). These include formal rules, written laws, formal social conventions and informal norms and shared beliefs in a society plus the means of enforcement. This definition sees institutions as the constraints on the behaviour of individuals. North's 1990 work, *Institutions, Institutional Change and Economic Performance,* was pivotal in setting the scene for integrating institutions into economic change. He writes: 'We cannot see, feel, touch or even measure institutions; they are constructs of the human mind' (North 1990: 107).

But as North asserts, they are the fundamental determinant of long-run economic performance. North builds his theory of institutions and institutional change on the back of individual rational choice theory as a function of information-processing by individuals and the costs of transacting.

North et al. (2009) argue that the operation of institutions shapes the formation of beliefs, so that there is a virtuous circle of functional institutions creating belief in those institutions and their functioning, which then in turn reinforces those beliefs. They distinguish between institutions and organizations, the latter being groups of individuals pursuing goals through coordinated behaviour. They also distinguish between adherent organizations that are self-enforcing, not requiring outside parties to enforce agreements, and contractual organizations, which use third parties to enforce contracts and agreements amongst members.

Superstructure: How do institutions arise? Social construction versus rational choice

I want to set the discussion in the context of Mary Douglas' *How Institutions Think* (1986). Douglas is concerned with the issue of how institutions get off the ground. She argues that posing the problem as a rational choice one, that individuals seek out, create and choose those institutions to solve problems of violence or of contract enforcement as they appear to them, is not an accurate way of depicting how individuals think within their institutional orders, both formal and informal. She argues instead that the choices that individuals make are set within the context of their social order: 'It is more in the spirit of Durkheim to…think of the individual mind furnished as society writ small. The entrenching of an idea is a social process…the whole process of entrenching a theory is as much social as it is cognitive…The individual's most elementary cognitive process depends on social institutions' (Douglas 1986: 45). She sees institutions as conventions, as arising when individuals see a need for coordination; but to turn the convention into a legitimate social institution requires a cognitive convention that is legitimated by society. She argues against an instrumental view of the legitimation of institutions for rational purposes or convenience, but instead says the answer to 'Why do you do it like this?' lies in terms of the way the planets are fixed or how humans naturally behave. She objects to institutional economics' rationalization of institutions because it doesn't explain how institutions get started and acquire legitimacy and stability. Douglas argues that this stabilizing comes from 'the naturalization of social classifications' (1986: 45) through analogies which explain to the individual that the institutions bear some sort of relation to the natural world or supernatural world. She describes this legitimizing process as a back-and-forth from a set of social relations to nature and between sets of social relations. Conventions may arise, for instance, over the division of labour in order that society doesn't have to renegotiate every time there is work to be done. Efficiency pressures and power structures will exert some argument over what that division of labour should be, and this acquires legitimacy through analogy with being natural, which then creates a political hierarchy. Shared analogies are devices used to legitimate fragile institutions (Shapin and Barnes 1976). Individuals need institutions to create their own identities, or, as Douglas puts it, to make institutions do the thinking for them instead of their having to start from scratch every time a choice has to be made. So the very categories and classifications that people use to think about things and confer authority are themselves constructed conventions or institutions, that is, socially accepted artefacts. For institutions to become socially accepted, they need to fit with what is already in place. Douglas uses a discussion of scientific discovery to illustrate that, only when society is 'ready' – that is, when there are supporting conventions and institutions in place – do discoveries get recognition and legitimacy. She gives several examples of this phenomenon – Condorcet's formulation of the discovery of the paradox of social welfare in 1785 was not taken up until 1948 by Arrow, when the context was right for thinking about the problems of majority voting. A further argument Douglas makes is that 'institutions do the classifying', or what Hacking calls 'making up people by labelling them' (Hacking 1985). The taxonomies we use to fit people into classes or income ranges are social constructs of a particular period and country. This classification is not static but goes round 'from people making institutions to institutions making classifications to classifications entailing actions, to actions calling for names, and to people… responding to the naming, positively and negatively' (Douglas 1986: 102). This classification process is fluid; individuals have some autonomy, they react to their identities and create new ones, and new institutions evolve. A further argument that Douglas makes that I want to use is that institutions are responsible for the major decisions, the life and death decisions, of individuals and not the minor ones. Individuals confer authority for making major decisions to institutions and work around the margins, making their individual decisions within the context of these larger life and death decisions. The tests of coherence and non-arbitrariness are not individual subjective preferences, but are socially created by the institutions. Individuals still do judge between different systems of institutions. Douglas is arguing not that there is moral relativism, but that individuals' choices and decision-making are socially shaped.

North comes close to this when he writes: 'Ideas and ideologies matter, and institutions play a major role in determining just how much they matter. Ideas and ideologies shape the subjective mental constructs that individuals use to interpret the world around them and make choices' (North 1990: 111). But North and his followers do not escape from the basic imperative behind rational choice ideas that if only actors had complete information then the costs of transacting could be lowered: 'There is nothing the matter with the rational actor paradigm that could not be cured by a healthy awareness of the complexity of human motivation and the problems that arise from information processing. Social scientists would then understand not only why institutions exist, but also how they influence outcomes' (North 1990: 111). But in the light of decades of behavioural research (e.g., Kahneman 2011) and following Douglas, we cannot reduce the response to incentives in terms of economically determined rational choices.

I subscribe to Douglas' view rather than to institutional economics' presumption of economic rationality in the choice of institutions. I agree that incentives are shaped by institutions and that individuals respond to those incentives, but I contend that these incentives and institutions themselves are not shaped according to rational choice and that they are not driven entirely or even principally by economic considerations. Rather, political, ideological and social forces and customs play their roles, and we cannot attribute particular importance to any one of these forces in an ahistorical manner: we have to read the history and bend our theorizing to assert that at times political forces have trumped economic or that social forces, such as racial histories in the United States, have trumped economic forces. This view follows Michael Mann's (1993, 2012) theorizing about sources of social power as coming from economic, political, ideological (including religious), or social and military origins, which posits that at different times in different countries one source of power has predominated over others. This theorizing eschews the primacy of economic power that institutional economics puts forward and argues against the dual balancing of political and economic power that North et al. (2009) argue for. In some cases, at particular points in time, military power comes to the fore – for example during Britain's revolutionary wars against France in the 1790s, which led to changes in tax-raising and in the nature of the state. Or in China in the 1980s, economic liberalization and enterprise creation was not accompanied by any corresponding increase in political liberalization and democracy. The case studies in this book illustrate the interaction between different sources of power in the evolution of key institutions.

The other issue that needs to be highlighted is the relationship between formal and informal institutions. I pay most attention here to the development of formal institutions – legal systems, types of property rights, and the natures of the state. But informal institutions matter hugely. Formal institutions rest and depend on informal ones. But they also create tensions with them because negative feedback against formal institutions is expressed through alternative informal orderings (6 2016). Through the Douglas (1982) lens, informal institutions are influential in cultivating thought-styles. The arguments made in the case studies to follow do not have much to say explicitly about informal institutions, which go beyond the scope of this book. But I do not want to underplay their significance, and I allude to some of the informal orderings as I go through the case studies. For example, individualism and individualistic and private property rights that developed in England during and after the 16th century depended on greater economic power for tenants after the Black Death as much as they did on the protection of property through formal institutional means. Macfarlane's (1978) English individualism and demise of 'peasanthood' in England was a product of the interaction between the state of mind or way of thinking about the household economy and the means open to it to survive and accumulate, as well as the formal institutions that protected private property. The development of institutions protecting maritime or naval property rights, which form an important part of the British story of protecting tradable property rights, arose out of the growth of maritime cities in England from the 17th century onward and their dependence on seaborne trade and interaction with the British naval state's procurement and supply chain in the 18th century (Knight 2013). Similar examples of informal orderings leading to and legitimizing formal institutional development can be found in France and Germany, and they will be discussed in Chapter 5.

In order to understand the different informal orderings that I discuss, I outline a version of Mary Douglas' schema of four types of social environments, which she refers to as 'grid and group'. The group dimension measures how much or how tightly individuals consider themselves part of a group with distinct boundaries: 'The group itself is defined in terms of the claims it makes over its constituent members, the boundary it draws around them, the rights it confers on them to use its name and other protections and the levies and constraints it applies' (Douglas 1982: 191). She contrasted individualist (weak) groups with strong groups such as hierarchies or clans. The grid dimension measures how regulated the social environment is: '[It] suggests the cross-hatch of rules to which individuals are subject in the course of their interaction…At the strong end there are visible rules about space and time related to social roles; at the other end, the formal classifications fade, and finally vanish' (Douglas 1982: 192). The strong end of the grid means individuals are highly regulated and do not freely transact with one another. For example, the male does not compete with the female, and sons do not define their relations with their fathers. Signs of discrimination occur, for example, through clothing and food. The weak end of the grid means individuals transact more freely and transact across boundaries. Douglas herself made a connection between the lowering of grid (weaker social regulation) and the development of markets: 'The fall-out from any system which pitches individuals against each other, contract by contract, man by man, is that in the end the only reckoning of achievement depends on size of support…it tempts individuals to get benefits of scale…When competing to get the largest following, market principles apply (Douglas 1982: 196). I am unable to do justice here to the fineness of the grid-group distinctions and combinations (6 and Richards 2016). However, I refer to these distinctions – of group and grid – in the case studies when considering the transition to a market-based capitalism in England in the 16th century and the breakdown of feudal structures; when thinking about the contrasts between Britain and continental Europe in the 18th century in terms of the nature of relationships between individuals and their states; and when thinking about how to characterize the mercantilist state, the liberal state and non-liberal state, and the growth of the more regulatory state and its compatibility with liberalism.

As far as how the primary institutions of capitalism (e.g. markets) developed, it is worth briefly discussing just what is meant in the literature by the term 'capitalism' and what I intend by it here. Braudel (1983: 237) discusses the etymology of the word. He argues that the word 'capital' did not begin to have the meaning now associated with it until around 1770. He attributes it to Turgot. *Capitale*, based on the Latin *caput* meaning head, emerged in the 12th century to mean 'funds' or 'stocks of merchandise': a sum of money. Italy was at the forefront of this idea, and it is found in Villani, Boccaccio and Velluti. Marco Datini, 'The Merchant of Prato', wrote in 1399 of taking out insurance on the capital and on the profit to be made. The word gradually came to mean the monetary capital of a firm or a merchant. Other words were also used such as *fonds* and *richesses*. Turgot in 1757 talks of advances circulating in enterprises, with 'advances' meaning investments. A letter from Van Robais, a manufacturer in Abbeville in 1722, speaks of *plus de la moitié du capital* in damages. Gradually, the word 'capital' triumphs over its synonyms – as an instrument of production and as a store of wealth, but also as the notion of productive money. Quesnay made a distinction in 1764 between idle capital and active capital – *capitaux oisifs* and *capitaux agissant*. There are then a few steps to make to turn it into Marx's means of production.

The word 'capitalist' dates from the mid-17th century, according to Braudel, but at that time it meant men of wealth – millionaires, *nouveaux riches,* those with fortunes. During the 18th century, it came to mean owners of pecuniary fortunes, that is, owners of public bonds, stock and shares, and liquid money for investing. In 1788, describing the foundation by the Dutch of the colony of Surinam in Guiana, Malouet distinguished between entrepreneurs, who designed plantations and drainage schemes, and the capitalists to whom they applied for money. In the run-up to the French Revolution, the term was one of abuse, along with 'tax-farmers,' 'financiers' and 'speculators'. This is not an idea about investment and entrepreneurship *per se*, but of the pursuit of money or wealth for its own sake. But Braudel's (1983) thesis, and one which I follow, is that capitalism predates industrial production.

British historians date the Industrial Revolution to around 1750. Capitalism as a word only comes into use in the mid-19th century. Louis Blanc writes of it in 1850 (161–162), calling it the 'appropriation of capital by some to the exclusion of others' (in Braudel 1983: 237). And Proudhon (1851) talks of land as the 'fortress of capitalism'. He defines it as an economic and social regime in which capital, the source of income, does not generally belong to those who make it work through their labour. Sombart (1902) talks of 'the modern capitalism'. Marx never used the term. It is a political term. The subsequent furore over the term was to try to tie it to the era of industrial production. Gerschenkron says: 'Capitalism, that is the modern industrial system' (1970: 4).

Braudel (1983) goes through the idea that modern growth came from savings. But who saved? If the elite were five per cent of the population owning 25 per cent of national income, it is they who were the savers. The rate of capital reproduction in pre-1750 Europe was very modest. Braudel's argument is that the kind of capital that existed pre-1750 depreciated very rapidly – it only lasted two to three years before needing replacement. Equipment was made of wood, and there were many fires. Land was fragile, and fertility was reduced. Bridges and buildings needed constant repairing. Kuznets' (1965) view is that there was little that could be classified as durable capital. The idea of fixed capital is a product of the industrial age, when materials such as iron and steel lasted longer.

About the lack of fixed capital before 18th-century industrialization, Kuznets says: 'At the danger of exaggeration, one may ask whether there was any fixed durable capital formation, except for the "monuments" in pre-modern times, whether there was any significant accumulation of capital goods with a long physical life that did not require current maintenance (or replacement) amounting to a high proportion of the original full value...the whole concept of fixed capital may be a unique product of the modern economic epoch and of modern technology' (1965: 48).

So the combination of a small elite and the technical structure of production meant that capitalism was in the commercial sector, circulating in the trading sector and not in the production sector. The paradox was that, in underdeveloped countries, capital, which could be amassed by the protected and elite sectors, had few outlets for investment. Looking at pre-industrial, *ancien régime*, economies can show us which sectors were unprofitable. For example, the French bourgeoisie stopped advancing money to peasants after 1550 and lent it to nobles or to the king. And cities of Castile stopped investing in the agriculture of the countryside after the mid-16th century. Yet Venetian merchants were investing in the country, and landlords of Bohemia were farming carp instead of rye. So capitalism was a hunt for profits and profitable opportunities; if they did not exist, then those investments did not take place. Following Braudel, I construe capitalism as a motor for seeking profitable opportunities. Braudel's argument is that capitalism resided in commerce and trade in the 15th to 18th centuries – because that is where the profitable opportunities were and not in production – before the advent of technological advances that would make investing in fixed and durable capital a profitable endeavour. Feudal structures – the yoke on the peasant of church, state and lord – meant that any attempts at innovation or progress would be opposed and thwarted. Even attempts to grow potatoes or sugar cane in Sardinia in 1816 failed when the workmen who had been brought in were assassinated (Braudel 1983).

Market development and contract enforcement institutions

Markets rest on institutions. For markets to develop, transactions must be secure. Greif (2006, 2005) discusses the joint planks of contract-enforcement institutions (CEIs) and coercion-constraining institutions (CCIs), which I use throughout the book. He makes the distinction between private-order institutions, which enforce contracts within private groups, and public-order institutions, which are supported by the state. The dictum is that for markets to grow, a combination of contracts being enforced and property rights being secured from predation, either by other agents or by the ruler, is required. So the starting point is not the control of violence *per se*, although that is involved in thinking about CCIs. As Weingast says, 'a government strong enough to protect property rights and enforce contracts is also strong enough to confiscate the wealth of its citizens' (1995: 1). For trade and contracting to occur, there must be the assurance that the state will not abuse property rights; in short, there must be constraints on the state. These constraints can take the form of limited state capacity; the state has too little administrative or military power to tax or expropriate citizens' wealth. If the CCIs are based on this, then property rights are secure from the state, but this limited state capacity is incompatible with the development of public-order CEIs. The development of public-order CEIs implies that property rights are less secure.

Most exchange is sequential, with a gap between making the contract and delivering on it. There is risk and uncertainty involved, but the contract would not be undertaken in the first place had there not been some sort of enforcement mechanism in place. The CEIs need to ensure that parties to the exchange fulfil any promises made when the contract is undertaken, some kind of credible commitment to the exchange, so that promises are not reneged on (Greif 2006). There need to be credible threats so that the contract will be honoured, so that there is no incentive to shirk or abuse it. Greif distinguishes between organic and designed CEIs, with organic CEIs emerging spontaneously out of individual interests, roughly corresponding to North's (1990) informal institutions. Designed CEIs are the product of conscious intention, roughly corresponding to North's formal institutions.

Markets rest on different combinations of CEIs and CCIs, with different combinations of private and public law. Private-order CEIs do not rely on the coercive power of the state but rather on family loyalty, reputation, and beliefs. Public-order CEIs rely more on the power of the state (although they also relay on such private mechanisms as networks, reputation, beliefs and trust). Markets can work and expand even in the absence of public-order CEIs and without limited government and the rule of law.

Greif argues that different combinations and types of CEIs and CCIs will depend on whether they are private or public and whether the society is collectivist (e.g., clan-like), where there will be greater reliance on private institutions, or individualist (e.g., nuclear-family-based), which leads more readily to the development of public-order law. An example of a private-order CEI is the community responsibility system which operated to secure trade in medieval Europe. The group undertook to punish those other members of the trading group who cheated on contracts. This allowed longer distance trade to develop, which was backed by sanctions within the group. Private-order institutions are smaller, faster and can deal with complex information that is not verifiable. Greif (2005) argues that private-order CEIs are more likely to develop in collectivist, clan-like societies where reputation effects carry weight and where policing within groups can be done through trust and reputation. However, individualistic systems need not be based on the nuclear family; the Roman republic was individualistic with competitive patrons and clients, with a family system that was multi-generational and extended. Its public and private CEIs depended on each other (Badian 1972; 6 2016). The clan is not the only kind of collective group. In the Tanzania case study (Chapter 7), I consider the tensions that exist between cooperative societies, which is one type of collective group, in their relationship to the development of markets and in their relationship with the state.

Public-order CEIs work through the enforcement of the state and through the rule of law, the judicial system and the courts, which enforce impersonal justice on all traders. Greif's (2006) main argument is that various combinations of CEIs and CCIs support markets and that other combinations do not. If you have CCIs where property rights are secured only because the state's administrative capacity is limited (as in China in 1500), that is not compatible with public-order contract enforcement, which itself requires a high degree of administrative capacity on the part of the state.

The CEIs determine the extent of the market, an idea which builds on Adam Smith's specialization determining the extent of the market, but applied to institutions (Greif 2006). What this means is that markets can develop to the extent that CEIs – either private or public – are in operation. In terms of the mix of public and private, at one extreme there are public-order institutions, like impartial courts, that can support impersonal exchange between strangers when conduct can be verified. An internal community-based CEI cannot support impersonal exchange with non-members. Private-and public-order CEIs generally complement each other, and exchange often relies on several types of CEIs. Public-order CEIs supported by the power of the state can support private-order CEIs. Often, there are hybrid types with both elements: laws and regulations combine with reputation. Markets expand as more CEIs are used. When public-order CEIs are created, such as a legal system that enforces contracts, an infrastructure is required that can capture individuals and penalize them for not honouring contracts. This power can protect or abuse rights.

Constraining the state

Weingast (1995:1) says that CCIs need to be designed to solve the problem that 'a government strong enough to protect property rights and enforce contracts is also strong enough to confiscate the wealth of its citizens'. Greif adds that for trade and contracting to occur, there must be assurance that the state will not abuse property rights; there must be constraints on the state. What kinds of institutions constitute CCIs? States can be constrained simply by not having sufficient administrative capacity or geographical reach to be able to exert power, collect taxes, and enforce contracts. Or states can be constrained by the strength of forces and organizations outside the state, in civil society, that act as a countervailing power. If civil society organizations do not exist and all social activity is controlled by the state, the state is not constrained and property rights and contracting are less secure. Corporatist states bring organizations within the ambit of the state, restricting the independence of civil society and its force as a countervailing constraining power.

In the absence of CCIs in the form of a countervailing power, public-order CEIs can reduce the security of property rights and undermine the market. So the Greif (2006) framework is a balance between the power of the CEI and the CCI. If there is countervailing power by economic agents such that they can flee or self-govern, then the CEI is less likely to be abusive. The more CCIs can protect rights, the more public-order CEIs expand markets. But the effectiveness of public-order CEIs also depends on their relation to private-order CEIs: if most people belong to private-order CEIs, then public-order CEIs will fail, as no one will use them. One can think of mafias or private vigilante groups as an example here. Greif argues that collectivist societies (based on kinship, religion, tribe or network) are more likely to use private-order CEIs (and will see a lower demand for public-order institutions), whereas individualist societies, based on individual and family, are more likely to develop public-order CEIs. This balance will also hinge on the extent of intra-group exchange as opposed to inter-group exchange: the greater the extent of trading between different groups, the greater the need and demand for public-order CEIs. Greif makes two main arguments: that the combination of private- and public-order CEIs will influence whether the market expands or contracts; and that CCIs based on weak state administrative capacity (inability to enforce contracts) are incompatible with effective public-order CEIs (Greif 2006). The more effective CCIs are in protecting security, the more effective public-order CEIs will be in expanding the market. The relations between private-order and public-order CEIs matter in that, if the former are effective, there will be less demand for the latter.

This links to the nature of the state, which I come to below. Organizations of all sorts represent types of private-order CEIs: they are social capital, associations that build trust, reputation, and knowledge between people with different cross-sectional groupings. They occur spontaneously and are often organic as opposed to designed. The density of this framework of social organizations underpins the formal construction of public-order CEIs.

Property rights

One problem in discussing property rights is the confusion in defining them. In debates about the roots of capitalism, property rights are central. An early and key type of capitalist property rights was in land, which is why there is such attention on how 'owning the earth' evolved (Linklater 2014). But not all property rights in land are capitalist, and one of the crucial distinctions is between non-capitalist, traditional property rights and individual written-down, legally enforceable property rights that were critical to capitalist development. And not all property rights are or were in land; the development of trade and markets depended on security of tenure over goods and, as discussed above, constraining others, including the state, from stealing from an individual. The development of securities and securities markets in shares of companies – joint stock companies – from the 16th century in England is an example of property in traded goods and ventures. Extremely important too in the case of England was the development of maritime property rights, which accompanied the growth of the maritime business and trading companies such as the Royal African Company, the East India Company, and Lloyd's of London from the 17th century.

In discussing property rights in the following chapters, I will be distinguishing between different types of property rights in land and analysing their relationship to capitalist development. I will also be tracing the evolution in importance of property rights from those in land and those at sea towards those in goods, in shares of corporations, and in the securitization of assets of various sorts (applying to both assets on land and at sea). The idea of CCIs applies to the security of property rights in general, but there are different degrees and types of security that have evolved in different countries at different times between land, maritime and financial assets and between different kinds of corporate assets.

Linklater (2014) in *Owning the Earth* and de Soto (1989, 2000) in *The Other Path* and *The Mystery of Capital* stress the influence of private property rights in land in shaping capitalism through altering incentives towards commercializing assets and creating profit-making opportunities, which transform landowning into capitalist tenure from a pre-capitalist, often collective or communal tenure over land. De Soto (2000) argues how the West turned property assets into capital through bringing extra-legal ownership into a unified legal system in each country. His argument is that property assets, when made into capital through becoming legal, are then assembled into more valuable combinations; used as collateral and security; enable connections between people; and promote markets through underpinning impersonal transactions between people who do not know each other.

Boone (2014) sets out three types of property rights to highlight these distinctions in talking about various types of land tenure in different African states. But these distinctions can equally be applied to historic forms of landholding in Western Europe and the United States. The oldest type of landholding was, and in places still is, traditional or customary property rights, where landownership depends on traditional usage over the generations and often involves communal ownership of 'common lands', where rights to those lands are not written down and are not individualized but depend instead on allocation by a group leader (i.e. chieftain, headman, feudal lord, or seignior).

Another type of property rights is individualized property rights, where land ownership is sanctioned by a legal framework – in England by common law from the 16th century for instance – where rights become written down and encoded in law, and where these rights can be challenged or fought over through the common law courts. The third type of property rights, which needs to be distinguished from the second, is what Boone (2014) calls 'statist property rights', where ultimate landownership is held by the state and where property rights are allocated by the state. With this third type of property rights, there is a much less independent relationship between those rights and the state: those in power in the state are able to reallocate property rights to their supporters or to their chosen projects, as property rights and state power are intimately connected.

Individual property rights encoded in law are to a much greater extent independent of state power, although state power of eminent domain exists in liberal states, namely, the right of states to compulsorily purchase private property and the right of property owners to be compensated for this. And in some jurisdictions, a court is involved.

By and large private property rights are not changed or threatened by a change in the political party in power, although even here one has to be careful. For example, Clause 4 of the British Labour Party's Manifesto from the 1950s to the 1990s pledged to alter the property rights of particular industries. Note here the British power to nationalize the means of production in industries, to change ownership of strategic assets, whereas the nationalization of land or tradable assets has been much rarer and not done without compensation (e.g., to coal owners in 1946 when the British coal industry was nationalized). Making assets tradable on the other hand, through privatizing them via selling shares, has been commonly done in Britain since the 1980s. Changing their ownership between individuals and corporations through trading of shares is the norm in Britain.

I develop a distinction between property rights in tradable assets (shares, bonds, securities, land), which depend on markets in those assets being developed and on there being a legal system that values the protection of the tradability of assets, and property rights in strategic assets, which are not tradable and which are bound up within entities such as firms through skills and routines and tacit knowledge and competences. The argument I make is that some countries' legal systems tend to protect those strategic property rights to a greater extent than the legal systems of other countries.

Property rights and legal systems

Milhaupt and Pistor's (2008) book *Law and Capitalism: What Corporate Crises Reveal about Legal Systems and Economic Development around the World* develops several arguments on the different relationships between legal systems and how they relate to market development around the world. First, the authors characterize legal systems according to how decentralized they are, how open to being used by individuals or groups through class actions in an economy. They contrast this with more centralized systems that are not as accessible by individuals, but rely more on statutory law-making from the centre. This coincides with the distinction between the common law and civil code systems, but the differences, they argue, do not stem from the legal family origins *per se* but from how the legal system is used and by whom. In particular, they stress the importance of demand for legal procedures, arguing that in a more decentralized system, populated by powerful groups of attorneys and barristers, the 'private attorney general' is stronger and the system is more contestable, inviting dispute resolution to be resolved using the courts and legal system. In more centralized civil code systems, the legal profession is not as prominent; access to the courts is not as easy; and there is greater emphasis on settling disputes through state-administered routes or through consensual bargaining and coordination. In line with this distinction, Milhaupt and Pistor (2008) emphasize the different functions that property rights serve: more decentralized legal systems based on common law, case law brought to courts by individuals, give more weight to the protective function of law to protect the property rights of smallholders or minority shareholders. Centralized legal systems based on civil codes, however, give greater weight to the coordinating and signalling functions of property rights; they are designed to give different groups a seat at the bargaining table rather than to protect weaker investors against their stronger counterparts. The power of the private attorney general is weaker in more centralized systems, as is the power of individuals to bring cases to court. Disputes in a more centralized system tend to be resolved through state administrative power rather than through the legal system itself.

I argue that this lines up with the different types of property rights: more decentralized legal systems place greater weight on individual private property rights and greater weight on the protective function of those property rights; more centralized legal systems tend to emphasize the coordinating function of property rights and give greater weight to state eminent domain and statist rights. This is a spectrum: it is not that individual protective property rights do not exist in a more centralized civil-code-based system; rather, it is that the constituencies that enable individual cases to come to court – lawyers, attorneys, class actions – exist to enable individuals to fight their corner. As

Milhaupt and Pistor argue, it is a question of how competing interests are resolved, that is, through formal mechanisms such as litigation in the courts in a system that protects individual rights, or through some kind of state-administered mediation or bargaining in a system that brings out the coordinating function of property rights (2008: 181).

This difference affects constraints on the state: decentralized legal systems place greater emphasis on public-order contract enforcement (through the courts, backed by law), and the legal system itself, in its independence from the state, works as a formal constraint on state power. More centralized legal systems, however, with more powerful state administrative civil codes and more extensive regulation, I would argue, place greater emphasis on private-order contract enforcement: there is a shying away from the court system to settle disputes and a greater reliance on statutory regulation and private networks for dispute resolution.[1] Formal constraints on the centralized civil code state are weaker in the public domain. This perhaps explains why private interests in these states protect themselves to a greater extent through private holdings.

State capacity, CCIs and property rights

States differ both over time and between countries in their structures (e.g. centralized, fragmented, dispersed, uncoordinated), and these structures affect both their legal and fiscal capacity and their coercive power and security of property rights. States with dispersed but uncoordinated capacity have better security of property rights (from the individual owners' perspective, and when security is from the state), but the power resides with those with force. Property rights are most secure when power is dispersed but the state is coordinated, depending on the balance between those with power and the ruler, as coordinating agent, protecting those without power. The more cohesive and powerful the ruling group, the less secure the property rights of those without power. So Greif (2006) describes a knife-edge between the security of property rights of those without power being protected when there is sufficient state capacity to create public-order CEIs to enforce the law impersonally; but this degree of state power threatens property rights unless constrained by the balance of power between ruler and elite groups.

Dincecco (2009) frames the issue from a slightly different perspective, namely, that of the fiscal capacity of the state, which is the ability of the state to raise tax revenues. He contrasts what he calls 'Old Regime' states with centralized power with those with fragmented power; and contrasts those with absolute government with those with limited government (i.e., a government constrained by a parliamentary democracy of sorts). He constructs per capita revenues for 11 countries over the period 1750–1913, which include the most important countries in Europe. He identifies the times when fiscal centralization occurs and when limited government occurs in each country. I use his datasets and results when discussing Britain and France and Prussia/Germany in Chapter 4 and Chapter 5, respectively. The results to emphasize here are as follows. Centralized states and those with limited government had higher per capita public revenues and were able to both set taxes and enforce tax collection from their populations. Centralized and limited states raised 12.56g of gold in per capita revenue compared with fragmented and limited states, which raised 12.15g. Both of these categories yielded significantly higher results than centralized and absolutist states (7.68g) and much higher results than fragmented and absolutist states (2.40g). (France is classed as having limited government only after 1870, England after 1688, and Prussia after 1848. Fiscal centralization is classed as having occurred in England in 1066, in France in 1790, and in Prussia in 1806.) Dincecco's (2009) main conclusion is that limited government or constraining the power of government also raises its ability to raise taxes, arguing that there is more security that taxes will be spent on public goods and not on the ruler's projects (e.g., wars). The relationship between state formation and waging war is a complex and much-debated one (Tilly 1992), and whether war itself should be considered a public good, rather than a ruler's project benefiting only the ruler, is also an issue. I discuss this relationship in the case study chapters.

Schumpeter (1918) was one of the first to identify the fiscal history of a people as playing a significant part in the rise of the nation. Besley and Persson (2009) are also interested in the origins of fiscal capacity, defined as the ability to raise taxes for either redistribution towards the ruling group or for public goods, and its relationship to legal capacity, seen as security of property rights from private expropriation. Empirically, looking at the situation in the early 21st century, they find a clear positive relationship between private credit to GDP, as a proxy for legal capacity, and share of income taxes in GDP, as a proxy for fiscal capacity. Rich countries have more of both kinds of state capacity, whereas poor countries have less of both. Dincecco (2009) emphasizes the role that ability to impose a uniform tax system across its territories played in the rise of the effective state in Europe from 1650 to 1913.

Hoffman (2015) argues that there has been undue emphasis on constraining the power of the state and insufficient attention on the processes of the state acquiring positive capacity for public and collective goods. As he says, 'we still know too little about what public goods states furnish or what determines the laws, regulations and policies that states adopt. Worse yet, we do not really understand how states arise in the first place and how they gain the ability to tax' (Hoffman 2015: 303). I think that Hoffman slightly overstates his case, although his general point is grist to the mill of this book. There is a lot known and written about the origins and purposes of states and how taxes were raised. But the answers need to enter into the debate and connect with the mainstream institutional theories of the state.

Different kinds of state and state power

Mann (1993, 2012) discusses concepts of social power. His model of power in society is one of 'organizational materialism', a blending of ideas and practices in four spheres: economic, political, military and ideological (which includes the forces of religion, Darwinism, racism, socialism, nationalism and liberalism). His theory of power is about the relationship between these four sources of power, with some aspects being more prominent than others in particular periods. As states grew and diversified, he argues, there were two control mechanisms – representation and bureaucracy. Representative conflicts were over which classes and groups were represented and where – how centralized, national or local state power was. The struggles were between a centralized nation and local-regional power which took place everywhere and which were intertwined. He argues that states become less coherent as they grow, with disjunctions between domestic and foreign policies: classes are obsessed with domestic politics, whereas political and military elites have power over foreign policy.

Mann (1993) makes three sorts of distinctions in terms of state power. The first is between the extensive and intensive power that states have: extensive power is when states have power over large numbers of people over large territories, and intensive power is when there is a high level of commitment from participants. The second is between authoritative power and diffused power: authoritative power means a willed power of command and obedience by subordinates, especially in military and political power, whereas diffused power is not directly commanded but spreads in unconscious or spontaneous ways, constraining people to act in a particular way. Market exchange in capitalism, for example, involves a constraint on people but is impersonal and is perceived as natural. And the third is between ideas of collective and distributive power: distributive power is of actor A over actor B; for B to get more distributive power, A must lose some. Collective power is joint power of actors A and B cooperating to exploit nature or another actor, C. During the period that this book considers, from the 17th century to the present, the collective powers of Europe and the West grew dramatically. Commercial capitalism and then industrial capitalism gave much greater power over nature; military power was enhanced, and the modern state emerged and created a new collective, the nation. The changes in distributive power are less clear cut: the rise in collective power of states gave elites less political power over subjects with the rise of democracy over monarchies (Mann 1993).

Different kinds of state

North et al. (2009) make the issue of managing violence their central organizing principle for classifying states. They argue that the natural state – as distinct from Hobbes' state of nature – is controlled by a dominant elite or coalition with special privileges. The elites are members of this dominant coalition. The dominant coalition agrees to suppress the violence (the means of or power for which it possesses), to cooperate with each other in exchange for receiving rents or privileges from society, and to respect each other's privileges. These elites stretch across societies in the religious, economic, and political domains, and they have personal relations between them – it matters who you are and whom you know – and there is limited access for individuals outside the elites to form organizations.

North et al. (2009) and North, Wallis, Webb and Weingast (2013) argue that elites must agree, must have a tacit pact, not to fight each other. They do this because it is in their best interest not to fight, as they reap rents from peace. As long as the rents from peace are high enough – the land, labour and resources they control are sufficiently more productive in peacetime than in times of violence – then the mutual pact in favour of peace is credible by all parties of the dominant elite. Each elite group has a privileged position in relation to a particular part of society. They are all bound to mutually enforce their privileges, one of which is the formation of organizations which the state will support. An example of this might be the East India Company or the Bank of England, which were granted monopolies by the English state in return for providing services to the state, with the elites running these entities gaining rents from them.

The logic of the natural state is that elites have privileges which give them rents in exchange for the control of violence. There is a double balance, according to North et al. (2009), between the distribution and organization of the potential for violence and political power on the one hand and economic power on the other. There need to be compatible incentives between these two sources of power, that is, the political and the economic.

In terms of the nature of the state, North et al. (2009) depart from Weber's famous maxim that the state is the organization with a monopoly on the legitimate use of violence (Weber 1947: 156), where the state is a monolithic ruler. North et al. (2009) decompose this claim to argue that the state is a collection of organizations. They emphasize that a central issue is how to organize things between the dominant elites, such that they can agree to hold a monopoly over violence: this is a matter for negotiation and a matter of balancing relationships between powerful people or groups in society.

The natural state has a dominant elite or collection of people or groups – a coalition in their terms – who possess the means of violence in the society and who have to be bought off by means of being paid rents, such that it is worthwhile that they cooperate. The agreement between them is that they respect each other's rights, including property rights and privileges. So it is the economic rents from the privileges that secure political cooperation. The members of the coalition may specialize in different activities, whether military, religious, political or economic; the idea is that they have to perceive that it is in their better interests not to fight each other but to receive rents in return for peace. Rents differ between each sphere of the society, and members of the dominant elite need to be in a position to mobilize and collect those rents. These elites in each specialist aspect of society have incentives to support each other and maintain the coalition. The state needs to enforce and support what the elites are doing. It is unclear from North et al. (2009) how far the elites recognize what they are doing and consciously maintain their power bases and whether this jostling between them is done unconsciously and out of a desire for self-preservation. They do stress, however, the dynamic and unstable nature of these coalitions, which are subject to continuous shocks, adjustments and redistributions of power. Their argument is that when negotiations or redistributions fail, then you get outbreaks of violence or civil wars or coups (e.g., Biafra against Nigeria, Bangladesh against Pakistan, the Yugoslavian break-up, Chile in 1973, Spain in 1936).

They distinguish between limited access orders (LAOs) and open access orders (OAOs). I discuss LAOs in greater detail in Part III. OAOs are characterized by impersonal relations between citizens and the freedom of those citizens to create organizations across society, with the result that OAOs have large numbers of such organizations, or what Greif (2006) calls 'corporations'. My main focus is on the characteristics of the different types of natural states and the conditions for their transition to OAOs, which, when it has happened at all, had occurred in the 19th century (North et al. 2009). Natural states limit access to organizations, whereas OAOs do not.

OAOs control violence with consolidated, powerful, monopolistic military and police organizations, which are themselves under the control of the political system. The political system limits the illegitimate use of violence, and it is broadly supported by economic and social interests.

The idea of openness is that economic and political endeavours should be open or accessible to a broad swathe of the population. All citizens should have the right to form organizations and do so without needing the consent of the state. All actors can compete for political control, and this keeps in check the power that political force has over those agents that control violence, the military and the police.

The importance of impersonality is stressed for the OAO: people can form organizations not based on who they are or on whom they know, but on the basis of having equal rights to do so and in practice doing so. North et al. (2009) also introduce the notion of the perpetually-lived organization that has a life beyond – or not commensurate with – any particular person or people, which is attached to the organization itself. This is not to say that the organization itself is immortal, but that its duration or life-span is independent of any person: they have an impersonal identity. The OAO can support a large number of perpetually-lived organizations. North et al. (2009) stress the nature of competition in an OAO between organizations that is Schumpeterian (and capitalistic) in being part of the process of creative destruction: new organizations will spring up and enter and erode the profitability and rents of older organizations and be able to replace them. There will be no obstacle to their entry and competition. This idea of an OAO places much greater emphasis on the economic and political spheres of activity outside the control of the state; there is continuous change in an OAO with new interests arising and forming organizations to reflect them. North et al. (2009) further argue that rent-seeking is constrained in OAOs by competition from new entrants; open access in economics and politics are complementary and supportive of each other.

OAOs have larger states but more decentralized ones; they spend more on infrastructure and public services than LAOs (North et al. 2009: 10). High-income countries sustain larger governments, but especially at the local and regional levels; they also provide more public goods, better infrastructure, and better education and health programmes, and they do so impersonally to all citizens.

There is considerable attention paid to the conditions of transition from the natural state to the OAO: why should elites make this transition from their position of privilege to one where they face competition from everyone? North et al. (2009) argue that the transition occurs in two stages: the first stage is a transition from personalized privileges to impersonal rights, which elites find it in their interest to move to, while the second stage requires fulfilling a set of what they call 'doorstep conditions' that allow elites to support extending access to non-elites. These conditions entail applying the rule of law to elites; having perpetually-lived organizations in public and private domains; and there being consolidated control over the military. These conditions create impersonal relations between elites. North et al. (2009) and Greif (2006) place great importance on the creation of impersonal relationships within the state as a sign of movement towards OAOs. Impersonal relationships are defined as being those not involving personal knowledge and those in which everyone is treated the same. Applying for a driving licence is an example: you need to fulfil certain criteria, and it does not matter who you are as an individual or whom you know.

North et al. (2009) argue that these transitions occurred for Britain and the United States between 1800 and 1850, having had doorstep conditions in the late 18th century, and for France by 1880. The transitions themselves occur quite quickly, although the build-up can take centuries. Almost all states were natural states before 1800, and a few transitioned to open access states during the 19th century (North et al. 2009: 257).

Another consideration is the identity of the leader. Is the king or ruling party above or below/within the law? Typically in LAOs the king is above the law – *l'etat c'est moi*. In OAOs, the king is within the law. Is the leadership of any organization a personalized office, depending on the personality of the leader, or is it impersonal? If the privilege of using the organization lies with the identity of the individual leader, then the society is based on personal relationships (North et al. 2009: 35). Societies develop ways of creating legal entities out of organizations, independent of their personalities.

This goes back to the relationship between the person's individual and social persona. It is not that property rights are not enforced in LAOs, but that they are enforced through networks of protection or patronage. The heads of networks are powerful and provide protection for their clients' property and persons. The heads of networks are part of the dominant elite or coalition. Any social mobility that occurs happens through the workings of the dominant elite's patronage and networks.

North et al. (2009) address the issue of the size of the dominant coalition. They argue that the size of elite coalition is limited in natural states because rents are dissipated between too many of them as the coalition grows (39).

I look at who the dominant coalition are, or were, in the England of the 17th and 18th centuries prior to the transition; in France and Germany in the 18th and 19th centuries; the United States in the 19th century; and Tanzania and China in the late 20th century. The case studies explore the coalitions between different interest groups (between merchants and financial capital in England against industrial capital; between industrial groups and bureaucracies in continental Europe; and between dominant parties in government and state bureaucracies and urban and foreign elites against rural agricultural groups in Tanzania and China).

Organizations as CCIs

Organizations are seen as tools to create human contact and relationships, to coordinate actions and to dominate others (North et al. 2009: 7). Their existence and the ability to form organizations are seen as very important in the transition from LAO to OAO. Fukuyama (1995) stresses the importance of social capital, people working together for common purposes in groups and organizations. Capitalism and democracy are closely linked, according to Fukuyama, because capitalism requires social capital in society to allow businesses, corporations and networks to be self-organizing. In his view, spontaneous sociability is key both to building businesses and to political organization (Fukuyama 1995: 356–357).

The importance of organizations *per se*, of all types, is an indicator of an OAO. The process of forming and running organizations is an important aspect, underpinning civil society. (There is an enormous literature on the character of civil society — for example Putnam (1993, 2000) and then back to Hegel (1820) and Tocqueville (1835) – but this goes beyond the scope of this book.)

North et al. (2009: 8) report a key and very interesting table looking at the number of organizations within countries by income group.[2] Countries with over $20,000 in per capita income had 64 organizations per million inhabitants compared with 2.8 organizations per million inhabitants for countries in the $300 to $2000 per income range. The number increases steadily as incomes rise. This table covers only a fraction of organizations in OAO societies. Looking at the historical statistics of the United States, they compare data on numbers of organizations in 1776/1800 with numbers at the end of the 20th century (1997): there were 200 formal business incorporations at the end of the 18th century compared with 23 million for-profit organizations in 1997. The ability of individuals to form organizations of different sorts – business, social, for-profit and non-profit – is a key variable, not just because it is testimony to open access but because the process of making organizations is key to creating social capital, which itself underpins democratic decision-making habits and abilities. Their existence also forms an essential part of the CCIs in the state.

These building blocks are used unevenly throughout the case studies. I make some connections between these different building blocks: the LAO/OAO distinction, the balance between CEIs and CCIs, the public versus private CEI, and the degree of centralized versus localized government. But I also want to throw some spanners into the works of smoothly associating numbers of organizations, density of civil society, and democracy with economic growth. The case studies highlight the different capacities to form firms that are independent of the state, influenced by the type of property rights that are established; the relationship between those property rights and the legal system; and the relationship between both of those to the kind of state. All are tied together and feed into the degree to which civil society develops.

In each case study chapter, there are three broad themes: the nature and evolution of property rights and their connection with the legal system; the nature of the state according to various dimensions of state capacity, the state structure, which groups constitute the dominant coalition, and how this fits with the North et al. (2009) framework; and the types of organizational forms and corporate governance structures, the theories of which I explore in the following chapter.

Notes

1 It has been pointed out that this is not always the case. The Byzantine Empire had a highly centralized legal system, but was dependent on public judicial dispute settlement (likewise Venice at the height of its power) (6 2016).
2 See their Table 1.3.

References

6, P. (2016) Private correspondence.

6, P. and Richards, P. (2016) *Mary Douglas: Explaining Human Thought and Conflict*. New York: Berghahn.

Acemoglu, D., Johnson, S. and Robinson, J. (2001) 'The Colonial Origins of Comparative Development: An Empirical Investigation', *American Economic Review* 91(5): 1369–1401.

Acemoglu, D., Johnson, S. and Robinson, J. (2002) 'Reversal of Fortune: Geography and Institutions in the Making of the Modern World Income Distribution', *Quarterly Journal of Economics* 117(4): 1231–1294.

Acemoglu, D. and Robinson, J. (2012) *Why Nations Fail: The Origins of Power, Prosperity and Poverty*. London: Profile Books.

Badian, E. (1972) *Publicans and Sinners: Private Enterprise in the Service of the Roman Republic*. Ithaca, NY: Cornell University Press.

Besley, T. and Persson, T. (2009) 'The Origins of State Capacity: Property Rights, Taxation and Politics', *American Economic Review* 99(4): 1218–1244.

Blanc, L. (1850) *Organisation du travail*. Paris: Bureau du nouveau monde.

Boone, C. (2014) *Property and Political Order in Africa: Land Rights and the Structure of Politics*. Cambridge: Cambridge University Press.

Braudel, F. (1983) *Civilization and Capitalism, 15th – 18th Century, Vol. 2: The Wheels of Commerce*. London: Collins.

Bunn, M. (2015) 'The History of the French High Speed Rail Network and TGV'. Available at: http://electric-rly-society.org.uk/the-history-of-the-french-high-speed-rail-network-and-tgv/.

Curtin, P. (1989) *Death by Migration: Europe's Encounter with the Tropical World in the 19th Century*. New York: Cambridge University Press.

Curtin, P. (1998) *Disease and Empire: The Health of European Troops in the Conquest of Africa*. New York: Cambridge University Press.

de Castella, T. and Westcott, K. (2013) 'HS2: 20 Reasons Why it Can Take 20 Years to Build a Railway', *BBC News*. Available at: http://www.bbc.com/news/magazine-21231044.

de Soto, H. (1989) *The Other Path: The Economic Answer to Terrorism*. New York: Harper and Row.

de Soto, H. (2000) *The Mystery of Capital: Why Capitalism Triumphs in the West and Fails Everywhere Else*. New York: Basic Books.

de Tocqueville, A. (1969 [1835]) *Democracy in America*. New York: Anchor Books.

Dincecco, M. (2009) 'Fiscal Centralization, Limited Government, and Public Revenues in Europe 1650–1913', *Journal of Economic History* 69(1): 48–103.

Douglas, M. (1982) *In the Active Voice*. London: Routledge and Kegan Paul.

Douglas, M. (1986) *How Institutions Think*. Syracuse, NY: Syracuse University Press.

Fukuyama, F. (1995) *Trust: The Social Virtues and the Creation of Prosperity*. London: Penguin Books.

Gerschenkron, A. (1970) *Europe in the Russian Mirror: Four Lectures in Economic History*. Cambridge: Cambridge University Press.

Greif, A. (2005) 'Commitment, Coercion, and Markets: The Nature and Dynamics of Institutions Supporting Exchange', in C. Menard and M.M. Shirley (eds), *The Handbook for New Institutional Economics*, 727–786. Norwell, MA: Kluwer Academic Publishers.

Greif, A. (2006) *Institutions and the Path to the Modern Economy: Lessons from Medieval Trade*. Cambridge: Cambridge University Press.

Hacking, I. (1985) 'Making Up People', in T.C. Heller, M. Sosna and D.E. Wellbery (eds), *Reconstructing Individualism: Autonomy, Individuality, and the Self in Western Thought*, 161–171. Stanford: Stanford University Press.

Hall, P. and Soskice, D. (2001) *Varieties of Capitalism: The Institutional Foundations of Comparative Advantage*. Oxford: Oxford University Press.

Hegel, G.W.F. (1952 [1820]) *Philosophy of Right*. Oxford: Clarendon Press.

Hoffman, P.T. (2015) 'What Do States Do? Politics and Economic History', *Journal of Economic History* 75(2): 303–332.

Iversen, T. and Soskice, D. (2009) 'Distribution and Redistribution: The Shadow of the Nineteenth Century', *World Politics* 61(3): 438–486.

Kahneman, D. (2011) *Thinking Fast and Slow*. London: Penguin Books.

Knight, R. (2013) *Britain against Napoleon: The Organization of Victory, 1793–1815*. London: Allen Lane.

Kuznets, S. (1965) *Economic Growth and Structure: Selected Essays*. New York: Macmillan.

Lerner, A. (1972) 'The Economics and Politics of Consumer Sovereignty', *American Economic Review* 62(1/2): 258–266.

Linklater, A. (2014) *Owning the Earth: The Transforming History of Land Ownership.* New York: Bloomsbury.

Macfarlane, A. (1978) *The Origins of English Individualism.* Oxford: Basil Blackwell.

Malouet, P.V. (1788) *Mémoire sur l'esclavage des nègres dans les possessions françaises.* Paris.

Mann, M. (1993) *The Sources of Social Power, Vol. 2: The Rise of Classes and Nation-States, 1760–1914*. Cambridge: Cambridge University Press.

Mann, M. (2012). *The Sources of Social Power, Vol. 3: Global Empires and Revolution, 1890–1945*. Cambridge: Cambridge University Press.

Milhaupt, C.J. and Pistor, K. (2008) *Law and Capitalism: What Corporate Crises Reveal about Legal Systems and Economic Development around the World.* Chicago: University of Chicago Press.

North, D. (1990) *Institutions, Institutional Change and Economic Performance.* Cambridge: Cambridge University Press.

North, D. (1991) 'Institutions', *Journal of Economic Perspectives* 5(1): 97–112.

North, D., Wallis, J.J., Webb, S. and Weingast, B. (2013) *In the Shadow of Violence: Politics, Economics and the Problems of Development*. Cambridge: Cambridge University Press.

North, D., Wallis, J.J. and Weingast, B. (2009) *Violence and Social Orders: A Conceptual Framework for Interpreting Recorded Human History.* Cambridge: Cambridge University Press.

Proudhon, P.J. (1851) *General Idea of the Revolution in the Nineteenth Century.* Fair Use Repository. Available at: http://fair-use.org/p-j-proudhon/general-idea-of-the-revolution/.

Putnam, R. (1993) *Making Democracy Work: Civic Traditions in Modern Italy.* Princeton: Princeton University Press.

Putnam, R. (2000) *Bowling Alone: The Collapse and Revival of American Community.* New York: Simon and Schuster.

Quesnay, M. (1764) *Traite de la suppuration*. Paris: Gallica.

Rodrik, D. (2000) Institutions for High-Quality Growth: What They Are and How to Acquire Them, Working Paper No. 7540. Cambridge: National Bureau of Economic Research.

Rodrik, D., Subramanian, A. and Trebbi, F. (2004) 'Institutions Rule: The Primacy of Institutions over Geography and Integration in Economic Development', *Journal of Economic Growth* 9(2): 131–165.

Schumpeter, J. (1991 [1918]) 'The Crisis of the Tax State', in R. Swedberg (ed.), *The Economics and Sociology of Capitalism*, 99–140. Princeton: Princeton University Press.

Shapin, S. and Barnes, B. (1976) 'Head and Hand: Rhetorical Resources in British Pedagogical Writing 1770–1850', *Oxford Review of Education* 2(3): 231–254.

Smith, A. (1970 [1776]) *The Wealth of Nations.* London: Penguin Pelican.

Sombart, W. (1902) *Der modern Kapitalismus.* Munich: Duncker und Humblot.

Tilly, C. (1992) *Coercion, Capital and European States.* Cambridge: Blackwell.

Weber, M. (1947) *The Theory of Social and Economic Organization*. New York: The Free Press.

Weingast, B. (1995) 'The Economic Role of Political Institutions: Market-Preserving Federalism and Economic Development', *Journal of Law, Economics and Organization* 11(1): 1–31.

3 Meso-institutions

Introduction

This chapter traces the links from the evolution of primary institutions set out in the previous chapter (of property rights, of contract-enforcement institutions (CEIs), of coercion-constraining institutions (CCIs), and of state legal and fiscal capacity) to comparative corporate governance institutions that I term 'meso-institutions'. At above a certain (undefined) level of economic development, once basic contract enforcement is viable, there arises the demand for public or larger-scale firms.[1] Connections need to be made between political and economic theories of the formation of primary institutions and legal theory on both the legal forms that business enterprise takes and how legal form relates to the forms of ownership – be it public or private ownership or be it publicly traded share ownership or privately held concentrated ownership.

This chapter develops the argument that there is a connection between a country's primary institutions, as outlined in Chapter 2, and the varieties of capitalism framework that was developed by Hall and Soskice (2001) and that has been extended since (Hall and Gingerich 2009; Hancké, Rhodes and Thatcher 2007; Thelen 2014). I argue that this connection rests on the development and protection of different types of property rights between the two main types of variety of capitalism: property rights in tradable assets in liberal market economies (LMEs) and property rights in non-tradable, strategic assets in coordinated market economies (CMEs). I extend this to developing and transition countries, which have developed a variety of capitalism that has protected state assets and foreign assets more than non-state indigenous private assets, and urban industrial assets over rural agricultural assets.

To arrive at this connection, there are three main planks of the argument developed in this chapter. The first plank is about different organizational forms: the corporation as independent legal person backed by the common law system in the LMEs; the various forms of limited partnerships and unincorporated private companies that combine some form of limited liability with non-public non-listing in both France and Germany; and the various forms of state control over assets and organizations in both Tanzania and China.

The second plank is linked to these organizational forms. It is the differential development of instruments for corporate finance: equity markets with their surrounding institutions of analysts, financial institutions (pension funds, insurance companies), their places of trading and dealing, contrasted with the use of banks – the Universal Bank, *Hausbank*, main bank within a holding group – with close relations between this financing institution and the company. For China, I look at the extension in the use of equity market, but retention of state control over the trading of shares and listed companies. For Tanzania, I link the lack of collateral in landed property with the absence of bank finance for indigenous rural enterprises.

The third plank focuses on coalitions between different groupings: shareholders, managers, employees, and the state. This builds on Aguilera and Jackson (2003, 2010), who look at the issue of who aligns with whom and why. These coalitions determine whether there exist strong shareholder rights aligned with managers, and weak employee rights and no voice for labour on the one hand, as opposed to weaker formal shareholder rights, with a stronger coalition between managers and employees giving employees a stronger voice, on the other hand. The third, developmental, coalition is between the state and managers, typically limiting the influence of both other shareholders and employees. For Tanzania, I look at the tension and coalition between the cooperatives, a significant organizational form for rural agricultural enterprises, and the state, in their governance structures that mediate between state and market.

Where does the state sit in this? I argue that the liberal state is kept out of business, partly through the ideology of *laissez-faire* and the separation of state from business, and partly from its association with majoritarian politics and not social democracy, an association that is largely linked to the disposition of power within a relatively decentralized and contestable legal system, with the judiciaries tending to back corporations and standing more independently as a constraint on the state.[2] This contrasts with the continental state, which is more entangled with business, which variously upholds worker rights and codetermination through the legal system, which is less constrained in terms of its regulatory power, and which pits itself against the more concentrated shareholders and supports the manager-employee coalition in terms of the provision of training and infrastructure. This, in turn, differs from the development/transition position of the state, where the state is centre-stage, not very constrained at all, entangled through its elites with businesses that control the legal system and with the formation of law and judiciary, and suppresses the independence of organizations outside the state.

In order to make these links, I need to place the role of corporate governance, broadly interpreted (Aguilera and Jackson 2003, 2010) to include not just the evolution of the governance of companies in terms of their corporate forms and the issue of ownership structure and investor protection (Franks, Mayer and Rossi 2009; Franks, Mayer and Wagner 2006; Fohlin 2005; Murphy 2005), but also the context of corporate governance's relationship to the primary institutions of property rights, rule of law and contract enforcement.

Varieties of capitalism: What is meant by this?

Hall and Soskice (2001) set out the parameters of a division within developed capitalisms between LMEs, whose institutions of labour markets and corporate governance operate with a strong influence of market mechanisms, and CMEs, which coordinate strategically through groups in their economies, groups such as employer federations, trade unions and business associations. They pointed to distinctions between methods of collective bargaining, for example where in CMEs this was organized for large chunks of the economy at the sectoral or industry level through the high-level bargaining of relatively few trade unions and employer associations. The Anglo-American LME variety is characterized as having liberal labour markets, high labour mobility, weaker trade unions, relatively low emphasis on training by the firm, relatively low levels of employee protection, high scores for ability to hire and fire, and high inequality between managers' salaries and employees' salaries since the 1980s (Hall and Gingerich 2009). There has been low and falling trade unions density and bargaining coverage during the 1980s and 1990s in the LMEs than in CMEs; the LMEs also had lower employment protection, benefits entitlement and social spending as a proportion of GDP. In terms of labour market flexibility, there have been longer hours worked, more part-time employment, higher income inequality, shorter job tenures and higher CEO compensation in LMEs than in CMEs during the 1980s and 1990s (Hall and Gingerich 2009; Aguilera and Jackson 2003). Stock market capitalization is much higher and debt/equity ratios much lower in LMEs than in CMEs.

Ownership data reflect this division. US and UK companies are more predominantly owned by outsiders external to the company (individuals, other financial institutions such as pension funds or foreign holdings), rather than insiders (family, holding companies connected to the company, or insider banks). Figures on ownership are from Tricker (2009) and relate to early-21st-century ownership patterns. US companies have much higher proportions of individual ownership (51 per cent) compared with France (23 per cent) or Germany (17 per cent) or even the UK (19 per cent). Both US and UK companies have high ownership by institutional investors (US 41 per cent, UK 58 per cent) compared with France or Germany (12 per cent and 15 per cent, respectively). This is counterbalanced by lower ownership by banks and government (3 per cent and 5 per cent for the US and UK, respectively), compared with France and Germany (14 per cent and 17 per cent, respectively), or of holding companies (0 per cent in the United States and 2 per cent in the United Kingdom), compared with France and Germany (14 per cent and 39 per cent, respectively).

On the financial side, there is greater weight in the LME (than in the CME) on equity markets for financing companies and less weight on debt or loan

Table 3.1 Different capital structures: Balance of listed company ownership

Country	*Individuals*	*Institutional investors*	*Banks and government*	*Holding companies*	*Foreign investors*
Canada	20%	34%	4%	11%	31%
France	23%	12%	14%	14%	37%
Germany	17%	15%	17%	39%	12%
Japan	20%	21%	23%	28%	8%
US	51%	41%	3%	0%	5%
UK	19%	58%	5%	2%	16%

Source: Tricker 2009: 182

financing. Associated with equity markets, there is greater dispersal of shareholding (Aguilera and Jackson 2003; Franks et al. 2009) and lower incidence of concentrated dominant shareholding. Alongside the dispersal of shareholding, there is greater protection of minority shareholding rights. In terms of shareholder versus stakeholder rights within the firm, US and UK firms are pictured as putting shareholder rights above those of other stakeholders, and accompanying this there is greater inequality in the LME in terms of control or decision-making, with CEOs having greater autonomy and a higher multiple of pay than the average in the firm (than in the CME). There are no dual boards, nor are there voices for labour or banks on company boards.

A further distinction between the LME and the CME has been in the nature of the state and its relation with business. The essence of the idea of the LME state is that it is kept out of organizing business interests, that it does not directly intervene or mobilize business interests, and that various parts of the economy – especially in infrastructure and education, and to some degree health – are seen as legitimate areas for private business and as therefore being outside the ambit of the public sector.[3] Whereas the CME state has been characterized as mediating and coordinating the framework for negotiation of collective bargaining and standard-setting. Hancké et al. (2007) consider the LME state as being at 'arm's length', since it keeps out of organizing business interests. This contrasts with the interventionist French *étatisme* state and the German mediating state (Martorell Cruz 2016; Granville, Martorell Cruz and Prevezer 2015). There has been substantial work looking at more recent trends in liberalization, in dualization of labour markets, in social solidarity, and in countries' differing responses to the challenges posed by increased competition from internationalization (Thelen 2014; Iversen and Soskice 2015; Rueda, Wibbels and Altamirano 2015).

Coalitions of managers, shareholders, employees, stakeholders and the state

I make two departures in the premises of this chapter: understanding the configuration of the varieties of capitalism and their different comparative corporate governance ownership modes and complementary institutions requires integrating politics into the model and understanding the coalitions of interest groupings, capital, labour, managers and the state (Roe 2003; Aguilera and Jackson 2003, 2010); and requires integrating the historical evolution of the institutions. There is path dependence in the origins and persistence of particular institutions at particular times (Bebchuk and Roe 1999); a striking feature is how persistent the distinction between the LME and CME is over time alongside institutional change and adaptation (Jackson and Deeg 2012).

I set out the integration of politics and coalitions into the model of the shaping of corporate governance in this chapter and go on to connect these ideas in the following chapters to the particular histories of institutional evolution: of Britain in Chapter 4, of continental Europe – France and Germany – in Chapter 5, and of the United States in Chapter 6.

The other element that I integrate into this conceptual chapter is a discussion of organizational forms. An important distinction between the LME and the CME revolves around the different uses and positions of the corporation as a legal form both in contrast to unincorporated forms and also in contrast to the other organizational options available for business enterprises to adopt (Deakin 2011; Lamoreaux and Rosenthal 2004).

The final element is to link up these corporate governance forms with the primary institutions of property rights and contract enforcement, state legal and fiscal capacity and the political nature of the state. What do I mean by property rights of capital, and different types of capital, as well as of labour, and how do those concepts figure in the coalitions between shareholders, managers and employees? And how do I relate contract enforcement institutions in the private and public spheres, as discussed in the previous chapter, with the nature of contract enforcement in insider corporate governance relationships as compared with outsider corporate governance relationships?

Comparative corporate governance as coalitions

So how do I get from the formation of primary institutions of CEIs and CCIs, discussed in the previous chapter, to the varieties of capitalism both amongst developed countries and between developed and emerging markets? This chapter sets out the varieties of capitalism framework in terms of comparative corporate governance systems. It defines corporate governance broadly as the relationships between parties with a stake in the firm and how their influence on corporate decision-making is shaped by their institutions (Aguilera and Jackson 2010).

It builds on Aguilera and Jackson's (2010, 2003), Gourevitch and Shinn's (2005) and Roe's (2003) modelling of the coalition groupings between the three main stakeholding groups: owners, managers and employees. First, I set about explaining why the different types of coalitions between these groups give rise to different varieties of capitalism in terms of the organization of corporate governance and then, to set up the enquiry for the following chapters of this book, I link these varieties of capitalism to the evolution of the primary institutions of CEIs and CCIs.

The absence of theory on the politics of corporate governance has quite recently been highlighted (Roe 2003; Gourevitch and Shinn 2005; Aguilera and Jackson 2003, 2010). This literature highlights the different – sometimes opposing and sometimes allied – interests between labour, capital and management. The political coalitions between different groups determines how to divide the surpluses between shareholders, managers and employees, but these political coalitions themselves are formed by the interaction of political preferences and institutional incentives, for instance in the form of degree of coordination across the political economy (Gourevitch and Shinn 2005).

I draw heavily here on the work of Aguilera and Jackson (2003, 2010). Comparative corporate governance is seen as having two dichotomous models – the Anglo-American and the continental European. The former is characterized as financed through equity and as having dispersed ownership, active takeover markets and flexible labour markets, called a liberal market economy (LME) in Hall and Soskice's (2001) varieties of capitalism framework; the latter is characterized as financed through debt and as having large blockholder owners, inactive markets for corporate control and inflexible labour markets, called a coordinated market economy (CME) in the Hall and Soskice (2001) parlance.

I follow Aguilera and Jackson (2003, 2010) in putting forward the three main stakeholder groups: capital, labour and management. Then I add to it by trying to conceptualize the role of the state in the different systems, to understand the difference between a more interventionist social democratic state and a more liberal *laissez-faire* state and what has pushed each country towards one or the other or both at different times.

Aguilera and Jackson show how shareholders, employees and managers react to institutions, but also that institutions are formed by what these groups do. This is in line with Douglas's (1986) ideas (outlined in the previous chapter), which also relate to this area.

Aguilera and Jackson (2003) argue that a country's property rights, its financial system and its inter-firm networks (in the form of overlapping ties between firms such as directors on boards, or networks of suppliers) shape the role of capital. The country's representation rights, union organization and skill formation shape the role of labour; and management ideology and career patterns shape the role of management.

Conceptualizing corporate governance involves the representation of an interplay of actors and institutions. How is this theorized in the economics and law literature? Comparative corporate governance has been driven by two strands of theory: agency theory and institutional theory. Aguilera and Jackson (2003) argue that agency theory is under-socialized: it treats the interests of owners and managers and employees as determined exogenously in their separate spheres, whereas institutional theory, they argue, is over-socialized and overemphasizes the role of the country and national model in determining actors' motives. For example, individualism means different things in different countries and across different sectors within the same country. Why? Because nations are institutionally diverse internally so that allocating a nation to one elementary form does not capture the diversity within the country. Exploring this fully is beyond the scope of this book. But I do discuss in the case study chapters the nature of individualism and liberalism in the context of those particular nations and periods being considered. For example, state-business relations in 19th-century Britain differed across tariff and trade policy from relations with rail and telegraph companies.

Agency theory starts from the premise of a separation of owners from managers and the need for an alignment of their interests. It assumes that shareholders maximize their returns and that managers may have different interests when it comes to expanding the firm or shirking in terms of effort. So shareholders have to find ways of monitoring management while having less information than managers about the constraints facing the firm and while struggling with free-rider problems of minority shareholders wishing to benefit from the efforts of larger shareholders without doing any work, leading to preferences to exit rather than to monitor managers (Eisenhardt 1989). Aguilera and Jackson (2003) stress that comparative corporate governance is usually then seen in terms of minimizing agency problems and costs, with different institutions such as the market for corporate control (the existence of takeovers) and legal regulation monitoring managers in the Anglo-American system, whereas blockholders, exercising direct control, perform that function in the continental European system.

But, as they argue, these explanations do not account for the different identities of the actors and the institutions in each system: banks, institutional investors and families have different interests themselves, especially as they too are governed by their own institutional constraints or incentives. Aguilera and Jackson point to interdependencies between the different groups, whereas agency theorists assume that employment relations are determined by labour markets, despite the interconnections between employee voice and corporate boards in many countries. For example, markets for corporate control (takeovers) affect not only managers but also employees who may find their interests threatened by an active takeover market (Aguilera and Jackson 2003).

They also point to the 'thinness' in institutional analysis behind agency theory, stating also that governance needs to be understood in the context of a wider range of institutional domains (Aguilera and Jackson 2003: 450). So, in their articles, Aguilera and Jackson (2003, 2010) set out to conceptualize corporate governance in terms of its embeddedness in different social (and institutional/historical) contexts.

The Hall and Soskice framework (2001) argues that there are institutional complementarities within countries: institutions around labour markets and financial markets go together to create comparative institutional advantage. Aguilera and Jackson (2003) argue that the role of institutions at the national level in these models is over-stylized and causes the firm-level actions to recede. Instead, we need a model that both contains firm-level actions, shaped by their institutions, and shows how institutions themselves are shaped by firm-level and other interactions. The roles of each stakeholder related to the firm are shaped by their institutional domains and therefore generate different conflicts and coalitional groupings (Aguilera and Jackson 2003): 'Most scholars interested in cross-nationally comparative corporate governance now agree that "institutions matter" for corporate governance, but how they matter remains a hotly contested question' (Aguilera and Jackson 2010: 490).

Interaction of institutions and stakeholders related to the firm

Drawing on Aguilera and Jackson (2003) I set out three distinctions in types of capital: between financial capital and strategic capital; between liquidity and commitment; and between debt and equity. What does this mean? Financial capital is primarily interested in the financial return on investments which is sometimes equated with portfolio investment as opposed to direct investment: investors are trying to maximize the value of their shares (O'Sullivan, 2000). Strategic capital is motivated by non-financial goals such as control rights. Shareholders might be other firms or banks and they want to have strategic influence over the firms they hold shares in. These interests include regulating competition, underwriting relational contracts, gaining access to markets, having influence over technological dependence and protecting managerial autonomy from outsider shareholders (Aguilera and Jackson, 2003). The liquidity versus commitment dimension relates to shareholders' desire to be able to trade shares quickly or exit from the firm, and this is traded off against the commitment to and direct control or voice in the firm (Hirschman, 1970; Becht and Roel, 1999; Aguilera and Jackson, 2003). Shareholders favouring liquidity are not seeking to have a direct voice in monitoring management; those preferring commitment (often larger, more concentrated block holders) will monitor management through voice and direct influence. A similar contrast is made between equity and debt capital, with debt capital having few control rights and receiving a fixed income, whereas equity confers some control (voting) rights usually and carries the residual risk in the case of insolvency.

These distinctions, then, translate into different types of property rights and different degrees of protection of those rights: between financial capital's property rights protecting liquid tradable returns to outside investors, strategic capital's property rights protecting non-tradable assets built up within the firm, and state capital's property rights protecting state assets over those of non-state actors and perhaps transferring resources from non-state sectors to the state.

In the context of corporate governance institutions, capital's property rights may be protected in some countries via the legal system through corporate law, bankruptcy law and contract law, which are the mechanisms or rights by which shareholders exert control. However, an important question is how far corporate law, bankruptcy law and contract law confer control in a particular national context. For example, veto rights, voting caps and mandatory information disclosure are rules that, in some countries, give particular power to certain groups of shareholders, such as small shareholders. Aguilera and Jackson (2003) argue that in countries where property rights favour large shareholders, capital will tend to pursue strategic interests rather than financial interests and will tend to exercise control through commitment rather than liquidity. Conversely, in countries where property rights protect minority shareholders, capital will tend to pursue financial interests and tend to exercise control through liquidity or exit.

Financial systems are usually divided into bank-based or equity (stock market)-based. In the first, banks are the key financial institutions for firm finances, and this goes with a closer relationship between firms and their leading banks. Part of this relationship entails closer monitoring of management and involvement in decision-making by those banks, with the lead bank having seats on boards and exercising proxy voting rights. In market-based systems, firms issue public equity, which expands securities markets. Capital markets are active, and shareholders pursue financial interests; they can exit from companies through selling, and there is an active takeover market for companies, which has a function of monitoring managers through keeping their interests aligned with those of shareholders.

For labour, there are three main areas of institutional influence: representation rights, union organization, and skill formation. As Aguilera and Jackson (2003) say, the role of labour is largely neglected in the corporate governance literature. This is in part due to the weak role of employee participation in the United States relative to Germany and Japan, where labour participation in decision-making has played a larger role in their competitive success. In the distinction between employees' internal or external control in corporate governance (Bamber and Lansbury 1998 in Aguilera and Jackson 2003), the Anglo-American system conforms to employees having an external influence; decision-making is seen as the prerogative of management and objections to it are made through external action such as strikes. Employee representation is through unions and kept separate from management.

The continental/Japanese alternative is an internal influence, where employees are either formally represented and have a role in decision-making, through codetermination in Germany for instance, or through more democratic decision-making on the shop-floor in Japan, which fosters cooperation and consensus (Streeck 2002). Complementary to this, there is the distinction made between the kinds of skills that labour build up through the workplace. The external, Anglo-American model, stressing labour mobility between firms also emphasizes generic skill-building outside the firm, which is portable between firms and non-proprietary. Employees favour exit rather than voice; they have shorter average tenures with any one firm; they want to be able to carry around their skills. Firms do not train employees in firm-specific skills and routines as much, fearing that employees will be poached or leave the firm. The insider, continental/Japanese system favours skill-building that is specific to the firm, given that core employees are likely to be kept within the same firm for a great length of time. If skills are firm-specific, that ties employees to the firm and makes their leaving, or exit, less likely. This complements the emphasis on greater voice and participation by employees.

The sets of institutions that determine participation and skill formation are the representation rights of workers at the firm level, how unions are organized and the institutions surrounding skills. Labour rights of representation have been a question of rights being fought for, such as the right to organize into a trade union. Employee representation rights have varied enormously across countries from rights to consultation, or codetermination, to rights to collective bargaining over wages and conditions. In the United States, for example, labour's representation rights are weak, with managers having autonomy to pursue strategic decisions without consulting employees. Germany, on the other hand, through codetermination, embodies strong employee representation rights statutorily on the boards of companies. Alternatively, employee ownership can establish representation rights through property rights, employees owning shares.

Union organization can vary by being by class, occupation, or enterprise (Streeck 1997). Again the distinction is whether unions influence governance through internal participation or external control. Craft unions, industrial unions, or class-based unions tend towards external control, as in the United States or United Kingdom. Employees go across different enterprises, so internal participation is complex and interests of employees threaten those of shareholders or management. Enterprise-based unions within a particular firm are more consensual and aim for internal participation, as in Japan. On skill formation, again there is the distinction between the United States and the United Kingdom, where skills come from outside the firm, and Germany and Japan, where internal training is emphasized and skills are formed within the firm (Dore 2000; Aguilera and Jackson 2003).

In considering management, Aguilera and Jackson (2003) make the distinction between ideologies and careers, between autonomous and committed managers, determining how independent managers are from the firm. They include the issue of the managers' functional background: whether they are financially trained or technically specialized. The distinction again is made between the autonomous and financially trained managers in the US and UK systems versus the committed and technically specialized managers of Germany and Japan. Their ideologies mimic this distinction: the legitimacy of managerial goals depends on their world views, educational backgrounds and models of control. A US manager is trained in general management; the shareholder value model is uppermost in teaching and is likely to have a financial orientation in terms of training. German management ideology is less prone towards shareholder value as the driving force. German managers are more likely to have PhDs in engineering or chemistry, are ideologically more likely to be corporatist, have a stakeholder view of the firm, and be less inclined towards individualism in leadership. The structure of managerial labour markets also reflect this, being more closed in the Germany/Japan model with emphasis on internal promotion based on seniority and with less inequality between managers and employees in terms of remuneration. In the US/UK model, the managerial labour market is more open, with shorter tenures for top management, greater inequality in remuneration, higher risk of termination, and more performance-related pay.

I integrate Roe's (2003) work into this picture and argue that politics shapes corporate governance. The forces for labour protection, for giving employees a voice on the board, or for favouring the stability of insider employees in the labour force are what Roe refers to as social democracy favouring more redistribution to incumbent employees (Roe 2003). Roe's argument is that if you have social democracy, then managerial agency costs are too high for there to be diffuse shareholding. Why? Because managers will tend to protect employees and are not persuaded to put shareholders' interests to the fore for there to be primacy of shareholders' rights. If this is the case, then shareholders cannot be assured, even in the presence of good corporate law protecting minority shareholders, that managers will take on projects that shareholders would wish. The assumption is that managers will be more risk-averse and that they will shy away from restructuring when technologies and product markets change, as this will require sacking employees, downsizing and upsetting existing vested interests. Good corporate law will not protect minority shareholders' interests, as what law does is protect against violations of the law, such as tunnelling private benefits to majority shareholders, not the quality of business decisions, which is beyond the scope of the regulator, law or state. Roe's (2003) argument is that the forces of social democracy are far-reaching in shaping decision-making over business orientation and business decisions that managers will choose to make, even when corporate law is of good quality.

A political approach to corporate governance takes the interests of shareholders, managers and employees in the public firm as being inherently different – not necessarily opposed, but pulling in different directions when it comes to making decisions about expansion, contraction, restructuring, new technologies, and new markets. And to make it more complex, there will not necessarily be cohesion in interests between all employees or between all types of managers: there are likely to be different interests between insider and outsider employees and between different sectors of industry (exporting sectors from domestic, technological sectors from non-technological).

Without expanding on each element, but as a way of indicating the kinds of issues involved in these different varieties of corporate governance, I list here the kinds of differences that are observable between countries in their corporate governance: ownership concentration versus diffusion; managerial compensation and the role of incentive schemes; labour influence in the firm through codetermination, lifetime employment, or works councils; degrees of employment protection embodied in law; different degrees of income inequality within the firm; social democracy, favouring employees over shareholders and associated with more protected or rigid labour markets; different degrees of domestic stock market capitalization/GDP, which tends to be inversely related to social democracy (Rajan and Zingales 2001); different degrees of pro-shareholder norms, such as favouring shareholder-value norms through transparent accounting, incentive compensation, or hostile takeovers; political scientists' ranking governments as being 'left' or 'right', with left-leaning social democratic governments tending not to have diffuse shareholding; and different degrees of product market competition, with higher levels of product market competition associated with less social democracy. This list is here to suggest the scope that is involved in making connections with *some* of the features of corporate governance that are outlined in the various case study chapters in this book, not that I do in fact pick up on all these features in each chapter. These differences have been developed and thought about in relation to post-war developed economies. Their purpose here is to begin to tie some of these ideas into the historical and developing country outlines that I present in the case study chapters.

The corporation and its legal status alongside alternative organizational forms

Linked to the discussion above of shareholder primacy versus stakeholder considerations are the organizational legal forms which business enterprises adopt and the way in which they have been used politically.

The theory of the firm in economics and law – the ideas of shareholder primacy as the driving motivation behind companies and of shareholders as principals – does *not* have its roots in company law. As Deakin (2011) argues, company law regimes are complex phenomena, coevolving with the emergence of firms and markets. There is a great variety of solutions to coordination problems and the evolution of the corporate form. Deakin distinguishes the economic idea of the firm from the legal concept of the corporation. The enterprise has organizational capacity: it can realize surpluses, absorb and control risk and, through the function of management, can meet its contractual obligations to the owners of assets. The corporation is a legal mechanism which has legal personality and legal capacity that underpins its organizational capacity. This allows it to undertake activities on a larger scale and for a longer time; it has permanence, which creates organizational continuity. Its legal personality protects against legal claims by creditors from principal investors – banks, commercial contractors, and workers. There is a separation of the firm's legal identity from its members that protects its asset base, which allows workers, suppliers and investors to make a credible commitment to it over a period of time (Deakin 2011).

Other features of the corporation that are useful from the point of view of business enterprise are delegated management under the board, limited liability for shareholders, and transferable shares (Deakin 2011: 354). As Deakin says, this allows for a division between investors and managers with a specialized management function, and it enables the diversification of share ownership. The corporation has organizational and contractual capacity.

Not all corporations are business enterprises with profit-making as a motive. For example, charities, churches and universities can be non-profit corporations. And not all business enterprises are corporations, particularly historically and looking across countries. The corporation has been particularly prominent in the common law countries, the United States and the United Kingdom, particularly in its capacity as a legal person in case law. The judiciary in the Supreme Court backing the corporation has shaped the political climate for business enterprise in favour of shareholders' and managers' interests and against employees' interests. In France and Germany other organizational alternatives, unincorporated forms with some of the functions that corporations perform in the United States and the United Kingdom of some sort of limited liability and transferability of shares, combined with civil code legal systems and greater state administrative powers, have meant that the corporation, especially in the form of the publicly-listed incorporated enterprise, has not occupied the same prime position as in the LMEs (see Chapters 4, 5 and 6). Under civil codes, directors' duties are seen in terms of pursuing 'the company interest, or maintaining the enterprise as a going concern'. Under common law systems, the idea of shareholder value is more prominent, although even under common law the board has discretion over how to interpret and balance the interests of the different groups (Deakin 2011: 361). Organizational form, therefore, needs to be integrated as an element of the story, along with the legal system and different types of state, that has led to divergent modes of capitalism.

Ownership of the corporation

What Deakin (2011) is at pains to argue, talking particularly about the United Kingdom, is that there is nothing legally in the constitution of the corporation that makes it put shareholders first as owners of the corporation. They are not owners of the corporation, which as a legal person cannot be owned, nor are they owners of the firm's assets. The firm's assets are vested in the corporation. Shareholders own shares; they have rights of voice and voting rights over members of the board and in relation to distributions out of the property in which they have a share. But they do not have rights to property in the firm itself nor in its assets, nor do any property claims give them a legal right to manage the assets of the firm (Deakin 2011: 356). What national company law does is give discretion to firm boards over their size and the timing of distributions to shareholders. As Deakin says, 19th-century British law was clear on locking shareholders into long-term, indeterminate relationships, whereby they could not demand their capital back, in the interests of investment and growth of the firm. The description of shareholders as principals, or of shareholder primacy as a leading objective, is not a product of company law.

The argument here in this book is that these different objectives – shareholder primacy in the LME and stronger stakeholder rights in the CMEs – need to be seen as political outcomes of the power of particular groups in their respective societies and as represented in the kind of states in those countries. Economic theorizing that argues for the primacy of shareholders in the interest of efficiency of markets contains a political stance that privileges this group of stakeholders, and such theorizing has tended to originate in the liberal market economies.

Making connections to primary institutions

Here I trace the links between primary institutions of CEI and CCI outlined in Chapter 2 onto the comparative corporate governance / varieties of capitalism framework. I argue for the need to incorporate additional elements to the frameworks of Aguilera and Jackson (2003, 2010): first, to take a historical view of how these institutions evolved, of corporate ownership and corporate forms, of financial markets and their role in financing companies, of investor protection, of labour representation and the choice between exit and voice, and of management ideologies and career structures. And second, I include the role of the state and the links between state formation (legal and fiscal capacity), degree of coordination between capital, labour and management within a national economy that a country variety ends up with, and whether the state evolves towards a *laissez-faire* view of itself or towards greater involvement and social democracy. So I want to forge the linkages between the different coalitions, between capital-labour-management, in different countries and the role the state has played in supporting particular interest groupings and bolstering property rights in a particular direction, supporting certain coalitions at the expense of others.

Linking to property rights

Roe (2003) makes the argument that, in social democracy states, where stakeholders have a voice in corporate governance and the labour voice is stronger, this lines up employee interests with manager interests against shareholder interests. He argues that this leads to ownership concentration or stronger blockholder control to counteract the management-employee coalition.

I also build on Rueda's (2005) distinction between insiders and outsiders in the labour market. The distinction between insider and outsider employees builds upon work on the difference between primary and secondary labour markets: insiders with secure full-time jobs and outsiders with precarious and often part-time jobs. Factors affecting insiderness include the nature of employment protection legislation and ease of hiring and firing. The distinction maps somewhat onto full-time and part-time employment. There are two aspects to employed outsiderness: precariousness of employment – fixed-term and part-time jobs have low wages, low protection and low rights; and the involuntary nature of that employment – most outsiders would rather be insiders. The interests of the two groups differ: insiders care about job security more than about the unemployment of outsiders. Outsiders care about unemployment and precariousness more than about the employment protection of insiders (Rueda 2005). Rueda makes the link between this insider-outsider division and the politics of social democracy in the post-1970s period in the developed world.

His argument is that insiders and outsiders have fundamentally different interests. For instance, employment protection works in favour of insider workers (those currently in jobs or in longer-term jobs) and works against outsider workers (those who are unemployed or in temporary or zero-hour type contracts). When I factor that into the corporate governance alliances between owners, managers and employees, I can formulate an argument distinguishing between more social democratic regimes and more liberal regimes. There operates in countries with stronger coordination and with more government involvement, which tends to go with more concentrated ownership, also an alliance between managers and insider-employees that pushes for and is the result of stronger employment protection legislation. Paradoxically, the less social democratic and more conservative regimes, which have more diffuse corporate ownership patterns and less employment protection, are possibly more favourable to outsider employees vis-à-vis insider employees, in that the liberal labour market flexibility that they engender more readily levels the playing field between insider and outsider employees.

How do I make the link both to different corporate governance regimes and to different types of state that go with those different regimes and finally to the underlying institutions and how they evolved? Rather than tying it to the party political argument, I want to formulate a more general connection between the nature of the state and which groups it supports, which relates to who its dominant elite is, who constitutes the state, and whose interests it supports to sustain itself. This can't be done without a historical explanation of the transition to open access order.

The political nature of the state

Does the state support insiders or outsiders and why? If the state supports insiders (in social democratic, CME regimes), why does that tend to coalesce with concentrated ownership, how does that alliance evolve, and why? Why did the UK/US states become more *laissez-faire* liberal states and the continental European states become social democratic?

The arrival at the Weberian state, the gaining of infrastructural power and a certain security of property rights – security from external invasion and internal order, and having a monopoly of violence – does not prescribe the kind of state that will be achieved.

The discussion of security of property rights as a prerequisite for private investment takes place as though all states with 'good institutions' have achieved a certain threshold of security of those rights, that states either have security or not. I need a more nuanced and graded view of this issue, especially to understand how different forms of state tie in with differing degrees of security of property rights, differing ways in which states might intervene, expropriate wealth, and protect some areas of property rights and not others. This applies particularly when considering the varieties of capitalism debate.

Property rights are not equally secure across the spectrum of types of property rights: rights over land, rights over inventions, rights against state expropriation, rights against private expropriation, and labour property rights over labour investments in human skills as opposed to capital property rights over capital investments. There are different degrees of protection over different types of capital such as financial liquid capital or industrial strategic capital, tradable or untradable capital. It is these differences in security of different types of property rights that I build on here.

Connecting property rights (of what types of investment) to different types of state in varieties of capitalism

Property rights of investors can be divided into various forms of capital – land, ideas, machines, portfolio investments in shares of companies, and investments by labour into skills. Investments in skills can be generic skills or specific to firms that labour works in. The different varieties of capitalism vary in how much they protect these labour skills, and different forms of capital can be seen as forms of property rights investments. The LME protects capital and in particular tradable property rights more securely – through minority share protection, free trading, and exit from companies through liquid markets. The LME does not protect employees' property rights. Nor does it protect strategic capital – skills built up in companies. Its emphasis on freedom of markets (which forms part of the protection of capital's tradable property), comes at the expense of employment protection rights and of strategic capital's protection rights.

In order to be able to protect (insider) employment rights, there need to be restrictions on changes in ownership and, therefore, a tendency towards concentrated blockholder shareholding and restrictions on hostile takeovers. This accompanies a coalition between management and insider employees against owners of companies.

In order to protect tradable capital property rights, there cannot be restrictions on restructuring and laying off employees. These capital property rights depend on the trading of shares, the disciplinary force of the managerial labour market through the market for corporate control. Trying to protect insider employees in this market system in the United Kingdom led to direct confrontation between managers and workers in the 1970s and the dismantling of many of the props that defended employees' rights, such as trade union power and rights in bargaining. This confrontation was not compatible with the Schumpeterian drive of technological development that depended on labour productivity being kept high, which, in a form of capitalism that did not give incentives to protecting labour's property in skills through long-term employment, came down to a straight fight between capital and labour over control of the workplace and ownership of capital. In the CME on the other hand, property rights over tradable capital are weaker and labour's property rights over skills and strategic capital's property rights are stronger. There tends to be a coalition of managers and insider employees against owners. Roe (2003) argues that this requires capital owners to have countervailing power through blockholding and concentration. Roe (2003) and Gourevitch and Shinn (2005) argue that these tend to be social democratic states with greater support for interventionist policies where ownership of capital is concentrated.

What is the link between the evolution of primary institutions – of CEIs and CCIs – and the protection of these different types of property rights? I go back to Greif's (2005) look at the interaction between CCIs and CEIs developed in Chapter 2 to tease out the linkages between the kind of contract enforcement and property rights institutions that develop in relation to the development of institutions constraining the state. I make the following arguments: there is a link between the development of individual property rights, backed by common law and independent of the state, and stronger constraints on the state itself; and these constraints on the state enhance the development of markets and the financing of enterprises through markets. These markets form part of the CCIs. The balance between CEIs and CCIs becomes more heavily weighted in favour of publicly-ordered but non-state market-based CEIs, which in turn act as CCIs. In regimes with stronger state eminent domains, CCIs are weaker because property rights are not as independent of the state and are not as based on markets. As Martorell Cruz (2016) puts it, LME state elites are more tightly constrained compared with CME state elites with greater discretional power.

The case study chapters ask the following questions: How did these different states come into being and when? What is the relationship between shareholders and the state in the LME, and how did it get there? What are the connections between having a liberal state and having more diffuse shareholders leading to a shareholder-manager alliance and very little labour voice? It matters who the governing elite were when the institutionalization of property rights happened. In the case of the United Kingdom, the elite included merchants and commercial people as well as landed gentry and some industrialists. It came in the mid-19th century at a time when the ideology was one of *laissez-faire* and retraction of state boundaries.[4] This contrasts with the more protectionist and mercantilist, 18th-century British state. I will develop these historical stories in the following chapters.

The other issue that the case study chapters address is how big the state is; in other words, how much gets done within private-order institutions and how much in public-order institutions? For example, the private sector can include canal building, railway companies, hospitals, schools or charitable organizations described in Mokyr (2012) for 18th-century Britain, where one sees the involvement of the private elite in constructing public infrastructures that on the continent were done through public financing and ownership.[5]

Three illustrations: Football clubs, orchestras and universities

I outline here three mini case studies of organizations across different parts of the economy – football teams, orchestras and universities – to illustrate this distinction in governance structures and aims between the LME and the CME. It contrasts football teams at the club and national level for England and Germany (Chelsea and Arsenal to England compared with Bayern Munich and Borussia Dortmund to Germany). For orchestras, it contrasts the London Symphony Orchestra with the Berlin Philharmonic, and for universities it contrasts Russell Group universities in the United Kingdom with leading German universities.

The idea behind these brief case studies is to illustrate the way in which conditions of international competitiveness, openness, and absence of what one may (in an old-fashioned way) call 'protection' in an LME differ from the greater coordination, greater restriction of access, and national protection in a CME and create corresponding differences in behaviour and results within those organizations. These are differences in degree rather than absolute differences, but will more clearly come across through outlining the details of particular examples.

One aspect of the 'LME-ness' of Britain is its openness. Why is it that the English national football team fares poorly, but the English clubs are world class? The openness of British football to foreign players and owners is in line with its being an LME: there are no restrictions on ownership of the clubs, and the clubs attract players from all around the world. There are similarly few restrictions on footballers' and managers' pay, and these tend to be higher and 'more competitive' than in other countries. For example, take one top Premier Club, Chelsea, and compare the number of British-born players in the top 26 listed in the squad in August 2013 (6) against the number of non-British players (22 from 13 different countries). Likewise for Arsenal or Manchester United. Ownership is typically non-British: Chelsea, owned by Roman Abramovich since 2003, through a takeover and then delisting, Arsenal by American Stan Kroenke (66.6 per cent) and Russian Alisher Usmanov (29.1 per cent), who took the club out of public trading.

Yet England as a national team struggles to qualify for the World Cup, failed to do so in 1994, and just managed it for 2014 (and disgraced itself in Euro 2016). There appears to be a shortage of world-class players to draw from in England, and apparently for the under-21 team in particular. England is a good place for world-class football to thrive, but not for nurturing English-born or naturalized players.

One can compare that scenario with the German (CME) picture. Germany's top clubs are Bayern Munich and Borussia Dortmund. Of their 26 squad members listed in 2013, 14 are German. The club is privately owned, with 82 per cent of shares owned by the club. Foreign ownership (in German football) is restricted to 15 per cent of shares. Commensurately, Germany has more resources directed at growing footballers at home. It is less open to trading in players and less open to foreign ownership. Germany has no difficulty in qualifying for the World Cup, or in winning it on occasion.

Let us now consider a comparison between the leading UK and German orchestras: the London Symphony Orchestra (LSO) versus the Berlin Philharmonic. The LSO is one of at least 5 competing orchestras in London. It is a fully open, international, self-run and self-managed orchestra, where the musicians are technically self-employed as members of the orchestra. The composition is highly diverse, attracting people from all over the world. It receives some public funding. London is a competitive venue for freelance work such as in films and advertising, and the orchestra schedule is very full based on being available for three-tier days, seven days a week, comprising touring, education work, sessions and domestic rehearsals and concerts.

The Berlin Philharmonic has pride of place as the leading orchestra in Berlin and is not in competition with other orchestras. It is largely state-funded and is an autonomous trust which employs its musicians, who are salaried, with civil-servant-like conditions comprising teaching, concerts, and pension rights. It is more insulated from competition and has more rehearsal time and a less frenetic schedule. Both orchestras are world-class, but the LSO is built in an environment of international and domestic competitiveness and less public protection, whereas the Berlin Philharmonic is built on more protectionist principles. The Berlin Philharmonic's touring work is not a major source of its income, as it is for the LSO. The LSO earns more from concert work abroad than in the United Kingdom; it exports its services heavily.

A similar scenario could be painted for the university sectors comparing Russell Group universities with top German universities: for the leading universities in the United Kingdom, they are highly international both in their global recruitment of staff and in the composition of their student bodies. The sector is seen as an area of UK exports, with growing numbers of international (non-EU) students from many countries. This 'globalizing' trend has been becoming more marked in the last 15 years, with the gradual withdrawal of state funding for domestic students. One can chart the introduction of fees for domestic students in the late 1990s and their raising from £1,000 to £3,000 and in 2012 to £9,000 with the full removal of the state subsidy. In terms of university earning capacity from domestic students, this narrows the differential between domestic and international students' fees and removes the former special status, not entirely but substantially, of UK domestic students being educated in domestic UK universities. As of 2012, UK students have had to compete for places against non-EU students, with very little preferential treatment given to them. In (most) institutions, there still remain some quotas for domestic students, but government policy has shifted in favour of expanding the number of places for higher-end-of-the spectrum qualifications and restricting access to those with below ABB grades at A level. The impact is to make access to those places more competitive across the spectrum of domestic and international students, on a meritocratic basis, with little protection given to home-grown students. In terms of international competitiveness, LME universities outperform CME ones: in the Times Higher Education World University Rankings for 2015–2016, 24 out of the top 25 universities are from the United States and the United Kingdom. German universities remain within the public sector; there are no student fees, and fees are much lower for foreign students; staffing is less international and less open to global competition; there is less competitive pressure to increase student numbers, to be ranked in research through league tables and research evaluation exercises, and to outperform their fellow national institutions.

The point to make about the LME-CME contrast is that there are advantages and disadvantages to both systems, winners and losers. The openness and competitiveness of the LME governance system makes its organizations more international, more world-class and competitive, and more successful at attracting good people. The downside of an LME is if one is considering England plc: that the losers are the indigenous people without international skills. Resources are not devoted to nurturing and training those indigenous peoples in a comparable way to the CME. German football teams, or orchestras, or universities may be more protected and less international, but they are simultaneously better endowed and protected against the competitive conditions that can detract from being first-class – more training time, more practising time, more research time, and less-crowded competitive freelance schedules. And German youth are more protected in terms of training and preparation – for their football teams, orchestras and universities. This has resonance with the 2016 divisions in political climate, where anti-immigration feeling in LMEs (and associated with Brexit for example) may be linked to greater competitiveness and less protection for indigenous people compared with CMEs, where the threat of international competition is not perceived to be as great.

The following chapters trace the histories of both the primary institutions outlined in Chapter 2 and the meso-institutions outlined in this chapter, and explore the links between them. How did institutional differences emerge out of the different ways in which the respective political economies developed historically? I examine this in Chapter 4 for Britain, Chapter 5 for France and Germany, and Chapter 6 for the United States. I then move on to relating these institutional questions to my developing and transition countries, Tanzania and China, especially revolving around property rights and the roles of the state, with implications for corporate governance.

Notes

1 There also exist large-scale firms in states where private sector enforcement is weak, such as imperial China and Russia (both in the Tsarist and Soviet periods). Where

contract enforcement is weak or poor for the private sector, private firms can exist on quite a large scale, but they need state or baronial patronage (e.g., the Fugger bank in early modern Italy grew on the back of patronage by princes from Italy, Spain and Germany (6 2016). My point, though, is that if public sector contract enforcement is viable and secure, then larger-scale firms are more likely to grow independently of the state or its patronage.

2 This is a generalization that depends on what is meant by 'liberal' and the period being referred to. The monopolized chartered companies such as the East India Company and Royal African Company were chartered by the Crown and operated from the 17th century through to the mid-19th century, implying state involvement in business. On the other hand, contract enforcement was 'liberal' in Britain well before the era of free trade and the repeal of the Navigation Acts in 1849. For a fuller discussion of what I mean by 'liberal' in the context of the particular histories of Britain and the United States, see Chapter 4 and Chapter 6.

3 This is a characterisation that is made particularly for the post-1980s period, in the Varieties of Capitalism literature. The case studies in the book examine the extent to which this was accurate historically. There is considerable evidence of British state involvement in business in particular sectors, especially in certain infrastructure and defence sectors and particularly related to waging war. State-business relations need to be carefully nuanced, and what is meant by liberal needs to be elaborated on, which I do in the case study chapters.

4 Even though the period of *laissez-faire* ideology was relatively brief, in the mid-19th century in Britain, and was modified from the post-1873 Depression period, free trade ideology nevertheless coincided with the period of extension of the franchise, and certain facets of this ideology have persisted, albeit not across all sectors of industry, as some areas (e.g., defence industries) had always been subject to close relations with the state. My argument, which I develop further in Chapter 4 for Britain, is that less state involvement and less regulation in certain industrial sectors may be linked to the institutionalization of both diffusion of shareholding and diminution of labour voice and participation in the early 20th century.

5 Again, this is a generalization that requires nuancing, as the picture of state involvement in infrastructure financing and ownership shifted over the course of the 19th century. I maintain, however, that there is a distinction between UK/US relationships with infrastructure financing and ownership, and continental European state relationships with these sectors.

References

6, P. (2016) Private correspondence.

Aguilera, R. and Jackson, G. (2003) 'The Cross-National Diversity of Corporate Governance: Dimensions and Determinants', *Academy of Management Review* 28(3): 447–465.

Aguilera, R. and Jackson, G. (2010) 'Comparative and International Corporate Governance', *Academy of Management Annals* 4(1): 485–556.

Bamber, G.J. and Lansbury, R.D. (1998) *International and Comparative Employment Relations.* Thousand Oaks, CA: Sage.

Bebchuk, L. and Roe, M. (1999) 'A Theory of Path Dependence in Corporate Ownership and Governance', *Stanford Law Review* 52: 127–170.

Becht, M. and Röell, A. (1999) 'Blockholding in Europe: An International Comparison', *European Economic Review* 43(4–6): 1049–1056.

Deakin, S. (2011) 'Legal Evolution: Integrating Economic and Systemic Approaches', *Review of Law and Economics* 7(3): 659–683.

Dore, R. (2000) *Stock Market Capitalism: Welfare Capitalism.* Oxford: Oxford University Press.

Douglas, M. (1986) *How Institutions Think.* Syracuse, NY: Syracuse University Press.

Eisenhardt, K. (1989) 'Agency Theory: An Assessment and Review', *Academy of Management Review* 14(1): 57–74.

Fohlin, C. (2005) 'The History of Corporate Ownership and Control in Germany', in *A History of Corporate Governance around the World: Family Business Groups to Professional Managers,* 223–282. Cambridge: National Bureau of Economic Research.

Franks, J., Mayer, C. and Rossi, S. (2009) 'Ownership: Evolution and Regulation', *Review of Financial Studies* 22(10): 4009–4056.

Franks, J., Mayer, C. and Wagner, H. (2006) 'The Origins of the German Corporation – Finance, Ownership and Control', *Review of Finance* 10(4): 537–585.

Gourevitch, P. and Shinn, J. (2005) *Political Power and Corporate Control: The New Global Politics of Corporate Governance.* Princeton: Princeton University Press.

Granville, B., Martorell Cruz, J. and Prevezer, M. (2015) Elites, Thickets and Institutions: French Resistance versus German Adaptation to Economic Change, 1945–2015, Working Paper No. 63. Queen Mary University of London: Centre for Globalisation Research.

Greif, A. (2005) 'Commitment, Coercion, and Markets: The Nature and Dynamics of Institutions Supporting Exchange', in C. Menard and M.M. Shirley (eds), *The Handbook for New Institutional Economics,* 727–786. Norwell, MA: Kluwer Academic Publishers.

Hall, P. and Gingerich, D. (2009) 'Varieties of Capitalism and Institutional Complementarities in the Political Economy: An Empirical Analysis', *British Journal of Political Science* 39(3): 449–482.

Hall, P. and Soskice, D. (2001) *Varieties of Capitalism: The Institutional Foundations of Comparative Advantage.* Oxford: Oxford University Press.

Hancké, B., Rhodes, M. and Thatcher, M. (2007) *Beyond Varieties of Capitalism: Conflict, Contradictions and Complementarities in the European Economy.* Oxford: Oxford University Press.

Hirschman, A. (1970) *Exit, Voice, and Loyalty.* Cambridge, MA: Harvard University Press.

Iversen, T. and Soskice, D. (2015) 'Democratic Limits to Redistribution: Inclusionary versus Exclusionary Coalitions in the Knowledge Economy', *World Politics* 67(2): 185–225.

Jackson, G. and Deeg, R. (2012) 'The Long-Term Trajectories of Institutional Change in European Capitalism', *Journal of European Public Policy* 19(8): 1109–1125.

Lamoreaux, N. and Rosenthal, J.L. (2004) Legal Regime and Business's Organizational Choice: A Comparison of France and the United States, Working Paper No. 10288. Cambridge: National Bureau of Economic Research.

Martorell Cruz, J. (2016) *One Money, Multiple Institutions: Capitalist Diversity under the Euro-Zone.* Unpublished PhD Thesis, Queen Mary University of London.

Mokyr, J. (2012) *The Enlightened Economy: An Economic History of Britain, 1700–1850.* New Haven: Yale University Press.

Murphy, A. (2005) 'Corporate Ownership in France: The Importance of History', in R. Morck (ed.), *A History of Corporate Governance around the World,* 185–222. Cambridge: National Bureau of Economic Research.

O'Sullivan, M. (2000) *Contests for Corporate Control: Corporate Governance and Economic Performance in the United States and Germany.* New York: Oxford University Press.

Rajan, R.G. and Zingales, L. (2001) 'The Influence of the Financial Revolution on the Nature of Firms', *American Economic Review* 91(2): 206–211.

Roe, M. (2003) *Political Determinants of Corporate Governance.* Oxford: Oxford University Press.

Rueda, D. (2005) 'Insider-Outsider Politics in Industrialized Democracies: The Challenge to Social Democratic Parties', *American Political Science Review* 99(1): 61–74.

Rueda, D., Wibbels, E. and Altamirano, M. (2015) *The Origins of Dualism in The Politics of Advanced Capitalism.* Cambridge: Cambridge University Press.

Streeck, W. (1997) 'German Capitalism: Does It Exist? Can It Survive?' in C. Crouch and W. Streeck (eds), *Political Economy of Modern Capitalism: Mapping Convergence and Diversity*, 33–55. London: Sage.

Streeck, W. (2002) 'Introduction: Explorations into the Origins of Nonliberal Capitalisms in Germany and Japan', in W. Streeck and K. Yamamura (eds), *The Origins of Nonliberal Capitalism: Germany and Japan Compared*, 1–28. Ithaca, NY: Cornell University Press.

Thelen, K. (2014) *Varieties of Liberalization and the New Politics of Social Solidarity.* Cambridge: Cambridge University Press.

Tricker, B. (2009) *Corporate Governance: Principles, Policies and Practices.* Oxford: Oxford University Press.

Part II

4 How did Britain's 'good institutions' evolve, and how good were they?

Introduction

Britain is the reference point and benchmark for the literature and policy-making on 'good institutions'. This is partly because it was the first country to have its agricultural and then industrial revolutions in the 18th century, the starting point of the Great Divergence between those countries whose growth rates accelerated in the 19th century and Asian countries – whose per capita GDP had been on a level with Western Europe's in 1700 but who were left behind at that point (Piketty 2014: 73; Pomeranz 2000; Landes 1998).

Britain's institutions are then looked at in the 21st century institutional economics literature, as a template for successful commercialization and industrialization. But it is unclear what it is that should be copied, because it is unclear, abstracting from the historical contingencies, which lessons should be drawn from the British experience in terms of its institutional evolution (Rodrik 2000). The shopping list of institutions which Britain is thought to have acquired consist of secure and clear property rights, limited government with constraints on the state, clear contract enforcement, strong legal and fiscal capacity creating an independent legal system and rule of law that apply to all its citizens impersonally, and fiscal capacity to create public goods.[1]

But it is not clear how, whose, and what type of property rights – in land, traded assets or industrial assets – were established and clarified and whose property rights were weakened in this process. 'Independent legal system and judiciary' does not spell out how a legal system, set up by and administered by the state, becomes independent of that state; how the rule of law is made impersonal and applicable to those in government as impartially as to everyone else; and indeed how, when, and the extent to which that happened in Britain.

This issue connects with state legal and fiscal capacity, which has to be seen in terms of both power to enforce law and to raise taxes. The state needs to be strong enough to provide functions such as defence and to have a monopoly of violence in doing so (Tilly 1992); to have enough administrative capacity to collect taxes and enough legal capacity to provide contract enforcement that is backed up by the state's legal machinery; and to provide public or collective goods that cannot be provided in the private realm. States differ, however, in how they acquire the ability to tax, what they tax, and what they spend revenues on. As outlined in Chapter 2, states with strong effective legal and fiscal capacity can overstep the mark and encroach on the property rights of their citizens. There has been a lot of emphasis in the literature on the necessity for institutions that constrain the state and limit the powers of government; indeed Hoffman (2015) argues that the literature places too much emphasis on constraining the state and too little on how states acquired their legal and fiscal capacities and what they used them for. In addition, states differ in whether 'public' goods such as infrastructure and education were provided by the public sector or by the private or semi-private sector.

This chapter first outlines the histories of how individual private property rights and the common-law legal system coevolved in Britain, especially after the Civil War (1642–1651) and the Glorious Revolution (1688), with the triumph of common law courts and statutory law over prerogative courts and the establishment of parliamentary sovereignty – a parliament composed of large landowners and merchants – limiting the power of both the Crown and the executive government. These private property rights were protected from the state, forming one of the main constraints on state power. They were protected by the common law and by law passed in Parliament, and by a largely independent and decentralized judiciary formed of notables. This constituted the decentralized and contestable legal system (Milhaupt and Pistor 2008), with property and contractual disputes being settled in courts rather than by state administration.[2]

Another theme here is the process of how Britain developed its exceptional fiscal capacity in the 18th century. It is true that limited government and fiscal capacity developed alongside each other. But I argue that it is not true that the raising of taxes and consent to them implied that revenues would be spent on public goods such as domestic infrastructure. The 18th-century British state waged war a lot. This required parliamentary cooperation to raise taxes, which were spent on extending the navy, on war and on expanding the Empire and trading routes, all of which in turn increased revenues.[3]

I trace a line from the creation of the liberal state in the late 18th century to the 1820s, which was a coalition of interests between the landed and commercial gentry and middle classes, with a priority given to private property and freedom of expression and intellect over political rights. British economic liberal institutions were built despite political institutions, such as the mass franchise, lagging behind. This was especially the case for the populations of Scotland and Ireland, whose political capacity was highly restricted. This in itself brings out a distinction between England – whose institutional evolution has set the template for and has dominated the rest of the United Kingdom – and Scotland and Ireland, whose institutional evolutions were in fact quite distinct and different from that of England. I return to this in Chapter 9 when I relate it to the implications of the Brexit vote in 2016.

I discuss the distinctive nature of this liberal state, some aspects of which form a continuity with the 1820s state through to the post-1980s state, although certain aspects are very different. 6 (2015) argues that the post-1980s British state regulation in a number of spheres has been more prescriptive, mandatory and intrusive particularly compared with immediate post-war Britain and that it is wrong to characterize the post-1980s British state as having a liberal resurgence. How does one square this with the varieties of capitalism characterization of the post-1980s British state as liberal and arm's length? Is there any resemblance or continuity between the liberalness of the 1820s–1870s state and that of the post-1980s period, as suggested by Mandler (1989)? To explore this fully is beyond the scope of this book, but I wish to sketch out an argument for future work.

Rather than seeing this liberal state as 'small' in terms of government expenditure as a proportion of GDP – which it is not, in comparison with its continental counterparts and in historical terms – the continuity rests in the nature of state-business relationships; the type of regulation through setting a legal framework; the use of courts in interpreting that legal framework; and the role of local officials for monitoring and inspection. This contrasts with a continental tradition of more centralized and direct state bureaucratic and administrative oversight of and links with industrial enterprise (which I explore in Chapter 5).

I use the ideas about English individualism (Macfarlane 1978) and the social fabric of England in the 18th century (Porter 1982) combined with Douglas' (1982) schema outlined in Chapter 2 of grid (degree of social regulation) and group (extent of social integration) to suggest that the particular type of individualism that grew up in commerce and various types of enterprise in Britain from relatively early on – the post-Black-Death 15th century, well before the agricultural and industrial revolutions, but the process continued into the 18th and 19th centuries – was accompanied by a large degree of self-regulation that relied on Acts of Parliament setting the framework for regulation, backed up by courts adjudicated by local notables, rather than on centralized bureaucratic regulation (Moran 2003; Bartle and Vass 2005). This was combined with guidance and standard-setting in the form of 19th-century inspectors of certain sectors of industry, finance, health and education. This has to be set against very close state-business relations in areas of government procurement, such as the defence industries, a closeness that goes back centuries, with examples of British state involvement in the supply chain in provisioning the navy fighting the Napoleonic Wars (Knight 2013). It is in the form of some areas of state-business relations, the institutions underlying those relations, that there is both the distinction from continental European structures and the continuity over time between the embryonic version of these relations in the 19th century and their version in the post-1980s liberal state.

This liberal state, despite periods of challenge and expansion – such as during the Age of Reform in the 1830s and during the 30-year period after the Second World War – has re-emerged since the 1980s with a different composition of groups with aligned interests, but around similar economic interests of private tradable property protection, as opposed to political interests of worker solidarity and civic equality. Critical to this process has been a further blurring of the distinctions between private and public interests, allowing private interests to expand further in Britain (and the United States) than in continental Europe. Constraints on the state through independence of the rule of law – common law and the judiciary and judicial appointments – from the central government were consolidated in England after the Glorious Revolution, from the late 17th and 18th centuries.[4] The triumph of common law after the Civil War meant that the legal system was decentralized and contestable, to use the parlance of Milhaupt and Pistor (2008). Old Corruption remained – Hanoverian privileges and appointments – but was diminished by the Age of Reform, at least in central government by the end of the 19th century. By and large commentators, such as North, Wallis and Weingast (2009), argue that private property was independent of the state by around 1832.[5]

The post-Glorious-Revolution period saw the growth of decentralized, self-regulated financial institutions of local stock and bond markets in the 18th century. Alongside this was the use of the corporation as a business form, of joint stock companies, of the issuing of shares and securities, and of the precocious development of local stock exchanges, which were unregulated by the state executive but were overseen by the courts. These created a capitalism around publicly-listed companies that were relatively free from state regulation. Major infrastructure – canals and railways – was built by private enterprise (although authorized by public courts in issues of access to land) and financed by local stock exchanges. Local government rather than central government was key in the provision of other public goods, such as water or schools, and much spending on public goods was done through the voluntary and quasi-private sphere – of charities and voluntary organizations – although local government spending did also increase. This chapter argues that the crystallization of these institutions in the first half of the 19th century around landed-mercantile-financial interests, but not around manufacturing interests, protected the property rights of tradable assets of shares and bonds at the expense of property rights in strategic non-tradable assets built up in industrial firms and their labour forces.

All the case studies in this book are structured in a parallel way: they pick up on the frameworks developed in Chapters 2 and 3 on primary institutions and on the meso-institutions of the varieties of capitalism. The next section in this chapter is on primary institutions of property rights and the legal system; then I look at primary institutions of the state, its fiscal capacity, and who the dominant elites were; and the last section is on meso-institutions of corporate governance and organizational forms related to business.

Primary institutions: Property rights and the legal system

The story of this section is that property rights in Britain evolved towards private property rights backed by the rule of law, which became independent of the state executive, although the rule of law was enforced through the judiciary.[6] This took centuries of incremental change. Property rights were not only in land, but, importantly for a maritime trading kingdom, concerned property at hazard in trade and such issues as contract enforcement, insurance, bills of exchange over goods, and assets traded through seafaring business. There were laws over property rights in goods traded at sea and in the units of financing for maritime trade since medieval times, but particularly since the maritime expansions of the 16th century. By Tudor times, these property rights in valuing goods at hazard in trade and in financial instruments for them were quite advanced, if we think of Antonio in Shakespeare's *The Merchant of Venice*. Such rights were particularly developed in Venice or Genoa and in the northern Hanseatic League, when England was still relatively speaking a trading backwater (Paine 2013: 328–345).

In thinking about the balance between different kinds of property rights prior to the 17th century – maritime trade and in land and commerce – the focus in the institutional economics literature has been on those based on landed property. To some extent, I redress that balance here and want to highlight the significance and development of property rights in maritime trade, in forestry, and in artisanal commerce in the post-Black-Death, post-feudal era from the late 14th century in England (Paine 2013; Braudel 1983). But I also argue that the reason the focus has been on rights to landed property from the 16th century and particularly on the settlement that was the Glorious Revolution at the end of the 17th century, is that this period represents a major crystallization of English and then British institutions around the shift in power from Crown to Parliament. This elevated the status of Parliament as a law-making body, the importance of local courts in implementing the law, and the importance of landed wealth in the formation of that aristocracy of the 18th century. This institutional settlement was significant in the rise to power of Britain through that century. British power in the 18th century was less based on agrarian wealth than that of its continental rivals; but the power base within Britain was reflected in ownership of land.

Property rights are complex. When the institutional economics literature talks about rights to property (de Soto 1989), in the first instance it means property as land, especially in an agrarian society. But property was also in British trading companies, joint stock companies, which grew in importance from the 17th century, and property rights also referred to security of rights over those commercial and financial assets. Piketty (2014: 114), in assessing the stocks of wealth of England and France in 1700, argues that a large part in England was held in non-land form as financial assets (usually government bonds). In 1674, a former landowner wrote: 'I choose rather to keep my estate in money than in land for I can make twice as much of it that way, considering what taxes are upon land and what advantages there are of making money upon the public funds' (HMC Fifth Report Appendix I 375 in Hill 1961: 236). This became more so in the 18th century. Dean Swift wrote in *The Examiner*: 'The wealth of the nation that used to be reckoned by the value of land is now computed by the rise and fall of stocks' (Hill 1961: 236). Hill argues that moneyed and landed interests were not opposed, but that the former became the senior partner. Property rights in goods at hazard in trade, which had been developed from the 15th century, themselves became more tradable. What developed from the late 17th century was the alienability, the tradability, of these assets through the development of capital markets in those property rights.

North and Weingast's (1989) thesis is that the development of English land law was central to developing the legal system and rule of law. It was also central to shaping the nature of the state, as the dominant elite used the control of land to structure their relationships. North and Weingast (1989: 803) 'interprets the institutional changes on the basis of the goals of the winners', which were to secure their property rights and protect their wealth from an overweening government. Central to this process is evolution towards making property rights – in land in particular – independent of the state executive; by the 18th century, the British state had no rights of interference in private property relations. This was not the case before the Civil War.[7]

Private individualist property rights

Britain developed economically on the basis of private property.[8] Land was central to feudal relationships, and feudalism crumbled earlier in Britain, in the 13th and 14th centuries, after the Black Death, than elsewhere (North et al. 2009: 78; Braudel 1983: 281). Legal concepts over landownership in England crystallized in the 12th and 13th centuries. Macfarlane (1978: 103) argues that land became owned by individuals rather than the family group from the 13th century. The influence of this development on enterprise is stressed by Bracton, writing in the 13th century, who argues that 'a citizen could scarcely be found who would undertake a great enterprise in his lifetime if, at his death, he was compelled against his will to leave his estate to ignorant and extravagant children and undeserving wives' (Macfarlane 1978: 103). The creation of a market for land, through its alienability, progressed through the 13th century. Macfarlane stresses that land was sold outside the family: 'There was no legal link between family and land under Common Law' (Macfarlane 1978: 104). North et al. (2009) stress the breakdown of feudal structures as manifest in the establishment of fee tail and fee simple: De Donis in 1285 regulated fee tail, creating alienability of land with conditions; and Quia Emptores in 1290 governed alienation without conditions, leading eventually to tenure of free and common socage, meaning the alienation of land without any obligation of feudal services. This was transferred to the colonies and became known as fee simple in the United States (North et al. 2009: 82; see Chapter 6). Rather than focusing on a transition from feudal society to capitalist structure, Macfarlane (1978: 34) argues that the transition should be seen as one from a peasant society, which was over in England by the late 14th century, towards an individualist capitalist one, with production by farmers being not for their own use but for the market. The more 'informal' institutional features that Macfarlane highlights in this transition are individual ownership of land with landholdings being sold outside the family, as opposed to the family stewardship of landholdings more commonly practiced in peasant structures; the greater geographical mobility within families, with sons settling away from their father; and the greater use of the market in commercializing the earnings from agricultural activity and rents (Macfarlane 1978: 94–100). Individual ownership of land combined with primogeniture meant that land was inherited and passed on, but there was also greater mixing up of social ranks, with second and other sons going into other occupations, and mixing through marriages. This contrasts with the French custom of both keeping land within the family and of partible inheritance, dividing it into smaller holdings amongst children (see Chapter 5). This was furthered by the shortage of labour in England after the Black Death in the 14th century, which shifted power away from landlords and towards tenants, forcing landlords to offer more generous terms for tenancy, including options to buy after a period of tenancy (6 2016).

Linklater (2014) highlights the importance of individual landownership in Henry VIII's reign, with the shift from communal obligations around the manor. He attributes the shift from arable strip farming in feudal manorial arrangements towards seeking profit from pasture, wool and enclosure to the incentives of rising wool prices from 1450 to the 1530s alongside a rising population. The dual incentives of enclosure and individual ownership led to more intensive farming; pasture with its increased manure on fields, less labour and higher prices for wool meant a wave of enclosures of the land of those who lacked written tenancy agreements. For example, in a day in 1567 Sir Thomas Gray of Chillingham in northern England cleared off his manor 340 people, villeins, cottagers and labourers whose rights were by tradition, or customary, rather than by written agreement. Villages and townships were emptied. It proved more difficult to shift tenants who did have written leases, but landlords could double rents and dues (Linklater 2014).

The 16th century was therefore the time when these customary rights to the land were challenged in England. The Crown and Church in 16th-century England often defended customary rights against those of the nobles who were evicting their tenants. The new Church of England had a prayer pleading with landlords not to raise rents; Sir Thomas More in *Utopia* condemns the powerful magnates who 'enclose all in pasture, throw down houses, plucke downe townes' (More 1516; Linklater 2014: 17). There were 9 statutes, royal proclamations and government commissions trying to prevent enclosures, which turned land to pasture, depopulated the countryside, and created homelessness, all of which threatened security. The royal courts fined and imprisoned those who broke the law against enclosures in the period 1517–1537. This land revolution, as Linklater terms it, affected only 5 per cent of the country, but was a shocking change in attitude of promoting individual interests with no thought to the consequences on the community. The shifting power towards Parliament against the King is evidenced by the House of Commons rejecting the royal bill against enclosure in 1547.

The battle over the monasteries represents another episode where aristocrats increased their power and rights over land. The monasteries were rich and Henry VIII needed funds for wars, so the Crown confiscated the land and sold it off. As Linklater says, within two generations England's most productive land had been bought and sold twice over and the people who got it were not ancient nobles but those with cash – merchants, farmers, and officials – which included Oliver Cromwell, who bought 20 properties in the southeast of England. Profits were made from the rising value of land (Linklater 2014).

Braudel (1983: 281) describes the change from feudal relations to capitalist farming relations as follows: feudal relations and traditional life was swept away, with feudal dues replaced by taxes to the state; large landowners leased rural property to tenant farmers, who took over responsibility for it themselves; tenant farmers employed landless labourers who constituted a rural proletariat; and there was a vertical division of labour whereby the landowner leased land and took the rent, the tenant farmer was the entrepreneur, and the wage labourer 'brought up the rear' (Braudel 1983: 282). This Braudel termed the English model, which was taken up in various other parts of Europe, but not as early as in England and not as completely in other countries.

Civil War effects on landownership

Hill (1961) argues that property rights swung in favour of landlords and enclosure before 1688 as a result of the Civil War. Land had become capitalist with all the accoutrements of capitalism: profit and loss, bookkeeping, and the virtues of thrift and accumulation that stemmed from mid-17th-century puritanism. There was an extension of cultivable land over commons, marshes and royal forests, which was drawn by the incentive of private ownership.

The Civil War had profound effects on landownership. Royalist lands were confiscated much like Church lands during the Dissolution of the Monasteries. Parliament became the guardian of private property from the 1650s (Hill 1961). Landowners acquired greater rights to settle inheritance, although copyholders remained insecure and could be evicted for enclosure and consolidation. This was a victory for large landowners over small landowners. The Civil War had seen popular protests against enclosure of common lands, but the Restoration defeated the radicals; new areas were brought under cultivation by rich men. In the 1660s, Parliament passed an Act for the drainage of the Fens.

The first Bill for Enclosure dates to 1621, but in 1633 there was still a powerful anti-enclosure lobby, with depopulators being prosecuted for enclosures. Enclosures were at the same time a violation of smallholder and customary property rights, and an enforcement of large landowners' private property rights. Enclosures aided agricultural improvement (Hill 1961) – they resulted in larger farms, greater clarity, and enforceability of property rights for those who won them.

Landowners – freeholders or copyholders – had certain inalienable rights over common land if they paid rents; neighbours could graze animals after the harvest was in; and when legal rights were extinguished, compensation was paid. But for traditional rights over common lands, no compensation was paid when they were lost through enclosure. The losers were smallholders with informal rights over other lands, who were supplementing their incomes and fuel from common lands. The winners were those with larger plots. Enclosures changed the geography of the land, creating larger plots. In 1700, the average farm size in open-field land was 65 acres; in 1800, it was 150 acres in southern England and 100 acres in the north.[9] Farms were enclosed, and then run by professional stewards on market principles. By the early 19th century, the peasant proprietor had disappeared from England;[10] land was owned by landlords and leased to tenant farmers who employed day labourers, with farmers supplying capital and know-how. Jane Austen has the Martin family in *Emma* portrayed as sturdy tenant farmers. According to Mokyr (2012: 172–176), by 1790 75 per cent of British soil was cultivated by this kind of tenant.

In Britain, primogeniture, inheritance by the oldest male child, played an important part in fostering larger-scale and more capitalistic estates. Primogeniture kept the estate together, increasing the economic burden on the head of the family to run the estate in commercial fashion, and forced the rest to earn their livings. This kept the larger holdings together and gave incentives for improving them in money-earning ways (Landes 1998: 67). Landowners leased land to tenants, enclosed land, concentrated holdings, and found tenants who would introduce crop rotation and new agricultural techniques. Improving landlords formed part of the agricultural revolution. Landes (1998), through Arthur Young's observations, also argues that the concern of British gentlemen to acquire a fortune pushed them towards social mixing between nobles and gentry; below the level of gentry, there was no barrier between land and trade (Landes 1998: 70).

Inheritance created a lot of stability and continuity: Tawney (1941: 2) estimates that of the 62 leading landowners in the 1642 Parliament, one half of their descendants owned over 3,000 acres in 1874. It is clear that by the end of the 17th century the land was capitalist, was run according to profit and loss with bookkeeping, and that the freeholders to the land had secure rights although copyholders did not. Lands confiscated during the Civil War were restituted, and North et al. (2009) gauge that by the end of the 17th century landownership was outside political control and manipulation by the state, which they argue is a characteristic of a mature natural state.

Legal system: Triumph of common law and statutory law over prerogative law

Property rights of landowners were increasingly protected through the rising power of Parliament as a result of Parliament's victory in the Civil War over absolute monarchy, which culminated in the Glorious Revolution, or what Winston Churchill called the Bloodless Revolution, when the English aristocracy, Anglican and Catholic, banded together to invite William of Orange to replace the absolutist-leaning and Catholic James II (T. Harris 2006; Pincus 2009; Churchill 1956). Pincus argues that in James II's reign there was an attempt to create a centralized, bureaucratic state based on monarchical authority, along the lines of Louis XIV's state, and that it was this that was toppled by the Whig aristocrats inspired by the Dutch model of modernity (Pincus 2009; Pincus 2010).

John Locke's *Two Treatises of Government,* written in the 1670s (after the Civil War but before the Glorious Revolution) underscores the English connection between individual property rights and liberal government to which there is active consent of the people. For Locke, the formation of political society rests on individual property. Locke emphasizes that 'every Man has a Property in his own Person...that whatsoever he removes out of the state that Nature hath provided and left it in, he hath mixed his Labour with...and thereby makes it his Property' (II para 27 in Laslett 1960). In retrospect, this view captured something (although at the time Locke was in exile and was read only by a few radical Whigs). Property extended from man's labour to the land. It established that rather than everything being commonly owned, the relationships between men in society were based on their contacts with the world of property (Laslett 1960: 115). Civil society and government were set up in order to preserve and regulate this property. By property, Locke meant man's life and liberty as well as material things; abstract rights of the individual were bound up with this broad idea of property.

The establishment of common-law-based property rights independent of the state executive is also bound up with the nature of the rule of law in England. The rule of law operating impersonally across the whole society including over elites and over government requires that all government officials and all citizens be bound by law. It binds officials and also constrains the state by imposing legal limits on law-making power (Tamanaha 2007). Villaverde (2015) argues that the rule of law in England needs to be interpreted in its 'thick' version (Tamanaha 2004), going back to *Magna Carta*, embodying commitments to individual liberties, especially property rights. He traces the formation of 'rule of law' through Bracton in the 13th century, with the King subject directly to the law 'for there is no rex where will rules rather than lex' (Bracton 2: 33), through to Sir Edward Coke in the 17th century, who upheld the common law as embodying 'common right and reason' even in the face of statutory Acts of Parliament. Villaverde argues that it was the English Constitution of Coke that upheld limited government of checks and balances on the King by the lords and commons. He traces this through to A.V. Dicey's 1885 treatise *Introduction to the Study of the Law of the Constitution*: 'For Dicey the law in rule of law was the common law and its protection of individual freedoms' (Chapter IV: 145–146 in Villaverde 2015: 6). The Glorious Revolution unleashed parliamentary sovereignty, as argued by Blackstone, which was defended by the winners of 1688 and was opposed by both Tory monarchists and radicals like John Wilkes (Villaverde 2015: 14). There was a shift of power towards Parliament and a strengthening of common law in the course of the Civil War and Glorious Revolution that reinforced each other and reflected the interests of the propertied elites in protecting their assets.

Decentralized, contestable legal system and constraints on the state

The Lex Mundi project on 'Courts' of Djankov, La Porta, Lopez-de-Silanes and Shleifer (2002, 2003) emphasizes the difference in legal systems between common law systems of the United States and the United Kingdom and the civil code systems of continental Europe. In tracing through how Britain gained this conceptualization, institutional economists have focused on the transitions in England and then Britain of the Glorious Revolution. But what were those transitions? How accurate is it to describe this transition as a triumph for common law?

The thesis of North et al. (2009) and Acemoglu and Robinson (2012) is that after the Civil War property rights of the dominant elite were established. All freehold tenures of land in fee simple or common socage gave owners impersonal rights beyond the reach of the state. Their argument is that elite privileges were turned into rights, as it was in the propertied classes' interests – as rural capitalists required alienable rights in land – to have property rights made independent of the state, severing their status as privileges and placing them under the rule of law.

The balance between different types of law was shifted in the course of the 17th century. Pre-Civil-War, royal and church prerogative courts, such as the Star Chamber and the High Commission, were dominant, with notables in charge of local courts. This ran in parallel with the courts of common law, administered by local Justices of the Peace, also composed of local notables. There were three common law courts, Common Pleas, King's Bench and Exchequer, which were institutionalized in the formation of English common law between the 12th and 14th centuries (R. Harris 2000: 25). The Civil War was, in part, a fight over the relative status of the common law courts against the prerogative courts controlled by the Crown, but also about the status of statutory law made by Parliament. The Civil War and then Glorious Revolution shifted power, including law-making power, towards Parliament. Private Acts of Parliament were chiefly responsible for enacting enclosures, as well as for incorporating the Bank of England, as they had been responsible for chartering the great monopoly companies earlier.

Before the Civil War, one of Charles I's offences had been to disregard both common law courts and the authority of Parliament over fiscal matters in bringing cases to the Star Chamber (Hill 1961). Prior to the Civil War, the King had control of the judicial bench. He could dispense with Parliament if there was no war and hence no need to raise taxes to finance war. He had the Privy Council and Star Chamber to enforce his will. The pre-Civil-War courts of High Commission and church courts ran as a parallel system, and were financed by tithes and fines. During the Civil War, the courts of Star Chamber and High Commission were abolished and not restored, along with other prerogative and church courts. The ecclesiastical courts lost power, and the bishops never controlled government again.

Through the Civil War, common law and statute law triumphed over prerogative and church courts. The common law courts – of the King's Bench and of Common Pleas – were overwhelmingly in favour of private property rights and larger landowners. The local Justices of the Peace, largely coming from the local gentry, came to play an important role in the enforcement of order and business contracts. The revolt against Charles I was not fought to defend common law (Adamson 2007); rather, as Porter (1982: 69) puts it, 'the purposeful solidarity of property interests in rejecting James II heralded greater cohesion to come'. It resulted in diminishing royal court control, which freed business from government regulation, abolished government privileges of granting industrial monopolies, and loosened state regulation of wage rates.

Post-1660, with the Restoration and then the Glorious Revolution, the common law courts increased their power. The King's Bench and Parliament took over supervision of legal processes of the Privy Council. This saw the primacy of the common law of Coke and the Parliamentarians, adapting medieval law to commercial society. There was a common lawyer as Lord Chancellor. In 1668, it was ruled in the House of Commons that it was illegal for judges to menace juries. Justices of the Peace came out of local notables; judges were under the control of Parliament but not of the King. This was a big step towards constraining the monarchy. Macaulay (1848: 200) argues that the transfer of supreme control of the executive administration from Crown to House of Commons was done noiselessly but rapidly and stealthily. Just how noiselessly this revolution was accomplished is challenged by more recent historians (Pincus 2009; T. Harris 2006), who stress the violence involved, especially in Scotland and Ireland (the Battle of the Boyne), in transferring authority to Parliament. There is a distinction between the evolution of English institutional forms and their imposition on Scotland and Ireland, whose tensions resound to the present day.

Implementation of law became more decentralized and contestable (in Milhaupt and Pistor's (2008) framework), although the increasing 'Parliamentarization' of the 18th century has been characterized by Tilly (1997) as centralized contention. Nevertheless, private Bills of Parliament (for instance, of enclosure) were initiated from all over Britain. Tilly (1997) highlights the tensions between decentralizing and centralizing pulls in the 18th century, between localized assemblies of notables in English politics and the growing power of centralized Parliament in politics from the 1780s, as well as in law-making during the 18th century.

So how does this link to the 'legal origins' debate about the differences between common law, more reliant on judge-made case law, and civil law systems, more grounded on civil codes and statute law, in being shaped by different political power and in turn affecting the kinds of investment that economies undertook (Glaeser and Shleifer 2002; La Porta, Lopez-de-Silanes and Shleifer 2008; Hayek 1960). The economics literature has focused on the cross-country comparative adaptability and flexibility of legal systems, comparing case law/common law against civil codes/statute law, especially in the area of company law (Anderlini, Felli and Riboni 2008), whereas the historical literature in assessing the evolution of differential powers of types of law within any country, such as Britain, has pointed to the mix of statute and common law and has highlighted which types of law were strengthened in particular periods.

The point I would make is that, in parallel with the tradition of individual property rights, England, Britain and then the United Kingdom have been characterized as having a longstanding common-law-based legal system, going back at least to the 13th century, and that common law was bound up with interpreting property rights. This was bolstered by increasing use of statute law affecting property rights in the post-1688 period. Overall, I conclude that the legal systems of the United Kingdom (and the United States) have been structured differently, in a more localized, decentralized, contestable fashion than those on the Continent, and that this has formed one of the pillars that supported the protection of private property rights and that constrained the government from encroaching on those rights. Kagan (2001) has labelled this *Adversarial Legalism* for the United States, with law as a bulwark against government. It applies also to the United Kingdom. The prominence of lawyers, the use of the courts, and accessibility of the legal system has continued to the present. If one compares numbers of lawyers per thousand citizens in the early 21st century, the United Kingdom (1.49) is behind the United States (3.11), but well ahead of Germany (0.53) and France (0.41) (Cross 2003).

Distinguishing between landed elites and non-landed wealth

Land was an important source of wealth and status. But the English economy and society had grown up since the 15th century on the backs of the great seafaring cities of Bristol and London, with their property rights associated with trade, shipping and victualling, as well as with other forms of enterprise. There were property rights associated with forestry, which was vital for wood for shipbuilding; and the artisan community not based on land but involved in smithing, tavern-running, and wheelwright workshops had property rights in their traded goods. Journeymen in artisan businesses made the transition from apprentices without property into property-owning enterprises; the textile industry was not only about sheep-farming but had artisan operations in workshops, in traded raw materials and in semi-finished goods. In these kinds of enterprises, property-owning was not about inheritance but about tradability. The key argument being made throughout this book is that the 'liberal' economies were based on and protected tradable property rights, and that they emphasized their tradability to a much greater extent than the continental or developing economies in my other case studies.

Why then the focus on landownership? To be in the elite you had to be a large landowner, and this was a highly concentrated structure. Porter (1982: 78) describes the establishment in 18th-century England of the 'more or less autonomous magnates as satraps of local communities, scarcely checked by

Crown, Church or intendants of the kind who emerged in France'. These magnates dominated parliamentary legislation, sponsoring local private bills – for enclosure, canals and regulating trade. The Great House, Parliament, was the power-house of dominion (Porter 1982: 78). Moreover, this autonomy of the magnates had been strengthened by the Glorious Revolution, having been restored to levels that they had not enjoyed since the 15th century prior to Henry VII, whose dynasty had been consolidated by curbing the power of the local nobility (Penn 2011; Porter 1982).

The problem of concentration of ownership is complicated by concepts of seisin – title that could be held by multiple people – and the difference between proprietary and possessory rights, between those who owned and those who worked the land. North et al.'s (2009) estimate for the end of the 15th century is that between 50 and 200 nobles owned 20 per cent of the land; between 200 and 2,000 powerful gentry controlled a substantial proportion of land but were not in Parliament; and 5,000 and 8,000 lesser gentry had above average landholdings. They estimate the nobility and gentry to have been 0.5 to 1 per cent of the population, that the nobles, gentry and lesser gentry owned 45 per cent of the land, the King owned 5 per cent, and the Church owned 20 per cent. The other 99 per cent of the population did not own much at all, but were spread over the land (North et al. 2009: 93). By 1688, based on Gregory King's estimates of social categories, ownership was somewhat more diffuse and not just in land, with 1.2% of society classified as landowners, 24% farmers and freeholders, 3% professionals, 4% merchants and shopkeepers, 4% artisans, 27% labourers, 30% cottagers and paupers, and 7% in armed forces (Porter 1982: 63). Porter says that these figures underestimate the numbers of merchants, shopkeepers and craftsmen.

Porter (1982) makes the argument that English society in the post-Glorious-Revolution century was a gently graded one, with very fine differences in status all along the gradations in the social ladder. Yes, there were huge differences between rich and poor at either end of the social spectrum. But there were myriad grades in between, who had a stake in society: 'England had more prosperous folk than any other nation: self-employed masters and men of movable property, men of money' (Porter 1982: 85). These included master craftsmen, manufacturers, tailors, jewellers, carriage-builders, and then men servicing the 'quality market': lawyers, bailiffs, clergy, surveyors, stewards and mortgage-brokers.

The post-1688 settlement tilted the balance in favour of parliamentary settlement of property rights: there was an explosion of Parliamentary Acts relating to enclosure and a major clarification of property rights. Acts were used for constructing roads and canals, for draining wetlands and embanking, as well as for other infrastructure-related activities such as building workhouses, paving streets, and constructing marketplaces. Post-1690 Parliamentary Acts took off in number compared with the Stuart reigns. The number of Acts from 1600 to 1815 was as follows: on roads 2,692; on canals 255; on ports 248; for river navigation 188; for urban improvements 553; for drainage 123;

and for churches 198. Acts authorizing property sales leapt up after 1689 compared with the early 17th century. Parliament was a forum for modernizing property rights in a way that was 'voluntary, effective, peaceful and permanent' (Bogart and Richardson 2011). On Enclosure Acts, over 4/5 of individuals possessing rights in villages drafted petitions, which formed the basis for Bills of Enclosure. Parliament appointed a commission to implement the terms of the Acts; Bogart and Richardson (2011) argue that this extended the range of contract and made investment in infrastructure easier and that Parliament reacted flexibly to economic opportunities.

Mokyr (2012) contrasts formal property rights with customary rights; he argues that the 18th-century British state came down in favour of formal property rights against historical custom, against the customary rights of the poor and in favour of written rights, of the rich. Adam Smith, writing in 1776, says: 'Civil government so far as it is constituted for the security of property is in reality constituted as a defence of the rich against the poor'. Tocqueville noted the same in the 1830s: those whose property rights were denied were colonials, smallholders, cottagers, beggars, vagrants and women. Parliament acquired greater powers in the 18th century and reallocated property away from privileges, but also away from common rights. Britain was characterized by a greater spread and evenness of commercialization and industrialization.

Protection of tradable assets

Land was central to 18th- and 19th-century wealth and dominion. Most millionaires were landowners. They became colliery owners, and as urban land values rose landowners bought into urban transport. Canals and railways raised values for adjacent land. Landowners' investments went into commerce, through private banks and law, through the City into government stocks and trade. But English industrial and commercial capitalism was not based on land, nor was it a spillover from agrarian landownership. The English and Scottish cities had thriving trading capitalism and forms of property rights with sophisticated financial instruments operating before the 18th century. There were stock and commercial property bubbles and busts in the 1690s in London, the products of long commercial and maritime development (Dillon 2006).

Investments in infrastructure and stock exchanges, financial instruments and joint stock companies grew together. Investments were made through banks, discount houses and bill brokers; land was mortgaged and savings went into insurance companies that lent to landowners for their investments and consumption. Commercialization was good for property owners. Shareholding grew and was given to younger sons, elderly women in marriage and unmarried daughters, widows and aunts, who could own property from the mid-19th century. New provincial stock exchanges to finance infrastructure, such as railways, grew together. In 1865, 157 MPs and 49 peers were directors of railway companies. Investors were gentry, professionals, businessmen, merchants from commercial areas, and propertied middle class with savings to buy shares. This was the development of rentier capital, with wealth moving from land and commerce into industry (Landes 1998). The wealthy had got rich since the 16th century in commerce, finance and transport as merchants, bankers, shipowners, merchant bankers, stock and insurance brokers, as well as manufacturers. Fortunes were made in trade and the colonies, and were invested in land, titles and government stocks. Marriage was into land and industry; aristocrats and landowners were on the boards of city and manufacturing enterprises. Finance replaced land as the business interest (Cain and Hopkins 1986, 1987; Landes 1998; Mandler 1989; Mann 1993). Property rights of tradable assets were the concern of these moneyed layers of society.

Primary institutions: Nature of the state

State fiscal capacity and limited government

Mark Blyth says of the state: 'can't live with it, can't live without it, don't want to pay for it' (Blyth 2013: 98). In a sense, this was not true for the 18th-century British state. Its fiscal capacity grew stealthily via indirect taxation based on increasing commercialization and spreading of markets and increasing public debt, which also stimulated the growth of markets in government securities, which in turn enabled the extending of the empire and the increase of trade, further enhancing its fiscal capacity.

Besley and Persson (2009) demonstrate the complementarity in the 21st century between legal and fiscal capacity, charting the positive relationship between legal capacity – strength and clarity of property rights and their enforcement through the courts – and fiscal capacity – the ability of the state to raise taxes and the depth of its administration that enables it to do so. They chart both the positive correlation between these two aspects of state capacity and the positive relationship with per capita income: richer countries have higher legal and fiscal capacities, whereas poorer countries remain stuck in the southwest corner of the graph, lacking both types of state capacity. But what was the process of building this, and how does it connect with the building of constraints on the state?

The story for Britain was of strengthening property rights and growing legal and fiscal capacity of the state alongside growing constraints on the state. One argument is that limiting government also enabled the British state to raise more revenue through increasing fiscal capacity. Dincecco (2009) argues that centralized states with limited government brought with them increased state capacity through a greater ability to tax than both fragmented states with absolutist powers and centralized states with absolutist powers. Absolutist regimes in France and Spain in the 18th century raised lower levels of taxes per head than the parliamentary ones in England and the Netherlands (Dincecco 2009: 52).

How did centralization, tax-raising and constraining state powers happen in England? The English state had never been terribly centralized and absolutist. Greif (2006) looks at the balance of military power between Crown and barons in the 13th century; centralized monarchical power was relatively precarious. Out of that conflict, the cities got charters of self-governance with 500 autonomous towns (boroughs) being created that collected taxes, administered justice and formed military units, all of which constrained the Crown. There was the transformation of the Great Council into Parliament with representation of the towns. In 1265, in response to Henry III dissolving the Great Council and raising taxes, there was a revolt by Simon de Montfort. Edward I's Model Parliament of 1295 included representatives of the commercial urban sector. In 1297, Edward I confirmed in *Magna Carta* that tax-raising required the assent of Parliament. The expansion of English law and the legal system in the 13th century extended markets. And while the Crown respected the rights of those in England with countervailing power, it did not respect those outside the realm (for example, Italian traders) (Greif 2006).

By the 15th century, public order CEIs took the form of common law courts, with increasing administrative power and independence of jurisdiction. The case of negotiable credit instruments in 1436 is a case in point: it was a tussle between the Mayor of London and the King, where the Mayor's court had customary rights in cases involving merchants. The King tried to transfer jurisdiction to the King's Bench; the Mayor refused to consent, and the King withdrew. Negotiated credit instruments became legal, expanding the CEIs of credit and bonds.

Henry VII reversed much of this development. His was a brutally centralizing and extractive state which sought to quash the independence of the barons, thereby ending much of the decentralization of fiscal oversight which had been achieved under the later Plantagenets (Penn 2011). It was regained only partially in Elizabeth I's time. Only with the decay and defeat of the Stuart aspiration towards absolutism was the trend of the early 15th century restored (6 2016).

A further aspect of state power that became more constrained from the 16th to the 17th centuries was in the demise of the Crown granting monopolies and charters to municipalities and craft guilds (North et al. 2009: 71). Guilds were monopolies, exclusive institutions with high barriers to entry and a set of privileges. In the mid-16th century, the chartering of joint stock companies granted by the Crown was important in overseas trade and colonization. Such companies as the Russia Company, Virginia Company, East India Company, Massachusetts Bay Company and Hudson Bay Company were granted charters by the Crown. Commercial and trading interests were an intrinsic and important part of the English economy from the 16th century.

Dincecco's (2009) argument is that fragmented states did not have the administrative capacity to collect taxes and that absolutist states did not have the consensus of the people to pay taxes. He argues that unconstrained absolutist monarchs spent on wars, and limited government was a way to curb that and create credible commitment to redirect spending towards public services. Constraining government created a pact between government and people, with the people consenting to paying more in taxes, which would be spent on public goods.

However, Dincecco's argument doesn't take account of the role of war in making the state (Tilly 1992), the 'war machine' (Harling and Mandler 1993: 47), the 'fiscal-military state' (Brewer 1989: 18) that was the 18th-century British state that paid for its wars through the tax system. The 18th century was a period of almost continuous war and military expenditure for Britain. Harling and Mandler (1993) calculate that wartime public spending, in real terms, rose from £94.7m in 1701–1713 to £118.7m in mid-century during 1756–1763, to the highs of £671.95m during the French Wars of 1793–1815. The proportion of government spending that went to defence, and the debt that serviced that defence spending, rose from around 90 per cent to 94 per cent, meaning that spending on civil government services fell from the meagre 10 per cent at the beginning of the century to 6 per cent (although of a larger absolute total) at the end of the century. This was not a state that was constrained from spending on wars and towards spending on public goods. O'Brien (2011) makes the further argument that Britain's fiscal exceptionalism of the 18th century was grounded in building its capital-intensive naval capacity in order to police the oceans and defend its trading interests and growing empire. This military and naval capacity rested on an already well-developed set of commercial maritime capabilities, which were in turn dependent on property rights secured for those capabilities. In other words, its ability to tax and its capacity for war went together during the 18th century. As Queralt (2016) argues, in line with Tilly (1992), the effect of war on state-building depended on how warfare was financed between taxes and loans.

The dominant classes feared aristocratic revolts, like the Monmouth Rebellion (1685) and attacks from the Pretenders. They were determined to defend the Protestant constitution from the threat abroad of absolutism (Pincus 2009). O'Brien (2006) argues that Britain attained the first Weberian state, since it was able to defend itself against external takeover; it was politically stable (in England although not in Ireland); and it commanded sovereignty with a level of revenue, administrative capacity and efficiency that enabled it to deliver a certain level of order in terms of legal and judicial systems and other institutions. External security and internal order were indispensable for the expansion of the commercial economy.[11] Mathias and O'Brien (1976) illustrate the building of fiscal capacity, looking at the growth in share of taxation in GDP, which rose in Britain from around 16 per cent in 1715 to 20 per cent in 1759 to 36 per cent in 1803–1812.

O'Brien (1988) examines which taxes were increased and who paid them. The tax burden on land rose during the 1690s and in the early 19th century under the threat of French invasions, but stabilized and declined between 1710 and the 1780s until William Pitt's introduction of income tax in the early 19th century. The burden of taxation on the aristocracy fell during the 18th century, but during the late 17th and early 19th century wars, landowners paid the state to defend their property. The bulk of increased taxation was increased excise and stamps paid on luxury domestic consumption, which hit city and town merchants as well as landowners. There were many partial exemptions for the rapidly growing sectors of industry (cottons, woollens, metallurgy, pottery, canals, banking), although these sectors also paid additional taxes. Excise taxes were increased for domestic industries and services such as legal instruments, licences, paper, vinegar, patent medicines plus decencies such as beer, candles, coal, soap, and leather; and they fell more on those who could afford it, being levied on the more expensive types of those items. In terms of explanations of policy, O'Brien (1988) stresses that the governments were constrained more by structure than by events: income taxes were not feasible; customs duties were less productive; and the burden fell on excise and stamps. Fiscal policy was aimed at warding off income tax or reform of the land tax. Land taxes did contribute during the wars against the French, but unevenly: manufacturers and merchants got off lightly as did landowners in the north and west, whose estates were undervalued.

The other source of revenue was government borrowing. Government debt doubled during the American War of Independence; Pitt introduced a Sinking Fund in 1786 to repay national debt from tax revenue. This expansion of state capacity through issuing public debt, with interest payments financed by taxation, is also a feature of that other liberal economy, the United States. It links to the expansion of financial markets in government securities, spreading the burden of public debt relatively widely. What made this unprecedented debt sustainable, with lenders prepared to go on lending despite very high public sector debt figures by the end of the Napoleonic Wars, was the (correct) belief that the British state was still good for its debts when other European states with that kind of debt were not. This belief was founded on the capacity of the classes voting for Parliament to sustain consent and to collect taxes, which was aligned with the commitment to repay bondholders above other state creditors (6 2016). This is an argument about whose property rights took priority in terms of protection. It was the case for 18th-century Britain, as for the 18th-century United States (Edling 2014 and Chapter 6), that they honoured and prioritized their payments to bondholders, thus encouraging the development in the market in government securities, and they used taxation to finance those payments.

The other aspect of state capacity of the 18th century that O'Brien (1988) stresses is the professional and efficient bureaucracy that was created in the Commissioners for Excise, whose excise-men were educated (the basis for their selection was meritocratic), from the lower middle strata of society, and were rewarded with good salaries and bonuses, although Thomas Paine did not think so. Although, in comparison with French and Prussian bureaucracies, British bureaucratic capability was small and underdeveloped.

It was not until the post-1815 retrenchment that there was a reining in of perceived to be extravagant and wasteful public expenditures towards a recognition by elites that there needed to be a broader-based taxation system and that the war-state was too expensive (Harling and Mandler 1993). In the first half of the 19th century, the political elite were still landed and mercantile, and the role of government was to safeguard property and to protect those elites that depended on property. Fiscal reforms broadened the tax base through income taxes and took pressure off the excise tax. There was little notion that the early-19th-century state should be spending on public goods. But there was belief in removing restrictions on trade, reducing taxation and increasing government revenues, a very liberal combination.

Peel spoke to the Commons (quoted in Harling and Mandler 1993): 'It is not inconsistent with true conservative policy that we should increase the trade of the country by removing restrictions[12]...nor is it inconsistent with sound conservative policy that we should reduce the taxation of the country whilst we increased its revenue'. Harling and Mandler (1993) argue that this unique state in 19th-century Europe protected and preserved its political elite from being upturned. However, the greatest fear of radicalism from within the country was from 1818 until 1848, with the Peterloo Massacre and the Chartist movement, which represented a serious threat to the establishment; during this period, taxes did not rise much. They rose more in the second half of the 19th century, when there was less domestic radicalism. The relationship between protecting property rights and the impetus behind revolt or revolution is a complex one. Some saw the repeal of the Navigation Acts as an attack on British shipowners' property rights.

From fiscal exceptionalism and mercantilism to 19th-century reform and a liberal state

The 18th-century British state was also mercantilist. Mercantilism meant a system of nationalistic protection through giving certain interests privileges, such as the granting of monopolies, through passing Acts to protect the country's own shipping (Navigation Acts) or the country's own industries (Calico Acts). Feudal privileges were out by 1700, but mercantilist commercial privileges remained. The mercantilist state was built on rent-seeking, on gaining privileged access and on taking the surplus from that access. Interest groups got exclusionary rents, and the government taxed them. Mokyr (2012) argues that there was no systematic mercantilist policy, but that it came out of appeasing various conflicting interest groups, of the landed gentry, merchants, and manufacturers. However, there had been strategic policy in James I claiming defined zones of the sea around Britain as maritime territory and in Oliver Cromwell's western design, which were both strategic and mercantilist, with the formation of the great monopoly trading companies, one for each region, reflecting mercantilist thinking (Pincus 2009). All nations at that time played the mercantilist game of protecting their national interests at the expense of other nations.

Mokyr (2012) argues that this mercantilism shifted towards more open competition for profitable activities through 19th-century liberalism and the shift towards free trade which took place gradually during that period. Mokyr argues this shift was partly ideological and partly due to Enlightenment ideas and Adam Smith's attack on the mercantilist system. The movement towards free trade was signalled by the repeal of the Corn Laws in 1846 and the repeal of the Navigation Acts in 1849. The Bubble Act, requiring a new company to have parliamentary permission, was repealed in 1825. The restrictive labour laws of 1562, the Statutes of Artificers and Apprentices, and the Calico Acts were no longer enforced. In other words, it was seen as being advantageous to those particular groups in power to move away from protectionism and towards free trade at a stage when some in British industry wanted fewer restrictions, although it can be argued that the phase of 'free trade' lasted only until the 1870s (Marsh 1999).

The pressure on state finances receded; in 1816 income tax was abolished but indirect taxes were increased to pay off fundholders. There was pressure to reduce Old Corruption – the various privileges and sinecures attached to offices and church livings (Rubinstein 1983). The *Manchester Guardian* was founded in 1821, and the *Westminster Review* and William Cobbett's *Political Register* were founded in 1824 – all papers pushing for reform. The elites extended the franchise peacefully, without revolution, although there had been widespread violence in 1830–1832 and Parliament was alarmed (Mann 2012: 122). Lizzeri and Persico (2004) argue that both political and economic changes favoured less patronage and clientelism, which was pervasive amongst the narrow parliamentary elite of the 18th century,[13] and led the elite to acquiesce in a wider franchise and increased political competition between parties in the 19th century. This was not a smooth process, but an act in two stages: the first (of 1832) made the franchise more consistent but without much widening, and the second (of 1867) dramatically widened the franchise but against the wishes of many of Disraeli's party. This combined with economic imperatives to provide public goods to deal with poor sanitation, and sewerage systems to deal with the greater disease that had spread with rapid urbanization.

Mann (2012) puts the case for reform rather than revolution in part down to there being an absence mostly of legal privilege in Britain, unlike in France.[14] Struggles like bread riots or labour disputes did not involve the state and its reform. Economic conditions in Britain remained divorced or considered separately from political power.

In Britain, one romantic view of the role of property is particularly explicit: 'Long may Old England possess good cheer and jollity/Liberty and property and no equality' were lines from an anti-Gallican songster in 1793 (Dinwiddy in Mann 2012: 19). The Chartists did challenge the state on the basis of linking bread and jobs with political rights, but they were defeated. The trade-off that was made in Britain was in favour of individual rights over property rather than democratic civic equality. This harked back to Lockeian roots of individualism and property as the basis of political power, the role of the state being to protect that existing economic power; it did not extend to giving civic equality to the non-propertied. Economic disputes such as the Peterloo Massacre of 1819 and the Chartist movement, did not manage to overturn state authority (Mann 2012: 124).

With the 1832 Reform Act, the significance of property became even more entrenched. The £10 property franchise added 300,000 men to the electorate of 500,000 (representing 15 per cent of the adult male population of 3,300,000 up from about 1,3000,00 in 1688, according to King's (1688) estimates in Macpherson (1962)) and got rid of 140 rotten boroughs. Landowners were still the Commons majority until the 1860s, but the power of the trading and financial City-based class was growing (Mann 2012: 125).

The critical laying down of the capitalist liberal state was done in the period 1760–1820 with the giving way of the old state that had regulated wages and prices and apprenticeships, that had granted monopolies, and that had given licences for enterprises. By 1820, most of these restraints were removed and international trade was freed of monopolies (Mann 2012; Mandler 1989). Parliament was composed of merchants, bankers, landowners, and professionals with mercantile and banking interests. There were some industrialists in Parliament in 1804, but they were often people who had bought enough land to get into the system. The legislation of the elder Peel abolished guild regulation to protect apprentices, although it did enforce the Navigation Acts and the monopoly of the carrying trade in British ships.

The priority given to promoting commercial society and the freedom to enjoy its private property and its intellect – over what Mandler (1989) calls 'legislating civic equality', that is, *political* liberalization – created the liberal state in the 1820s, which was supported by a cross-class coalition between landed and middle classes. These liberal values – for a relatively 'small' state that doesn't interfere in business, for self-regulation, favouring commerce and finance over industrial capital – created deep roots for the development of British capitalism. Mandler (1989) suggests that these roots can be seen in the post-1980s British state. There are, however, profound differences between this characterization of the liberal state in the 1820s and what has emerged post-1980s. I return to this below.

Public goods, local (self-)government

In the 19th century, with the Pax Britannica, there was a changing balance between waging war and providing public goods. In outlining the nature of the British state's liberalism, which has carried through to the 21st century, the distinction made by Philip Harling (2004) between the local state and the central state is crucial. It was through the local state and local government expenditure that some areas of public goods were provided in the second half of the 19th century. In other sectors, such as ports and harbour control and the General Post Office (GPO), public good provision was centralized. The GPO was a major central provider of public goods, even more so after the nationalization of the domestic telegraph sector in 1868. The central state also undertook a great deal of regulation to ensure that public goods were provided at private expense. The inspectorates were overseen centrally.

In part, this was also motivated through self-interest by the elites in several ways: as public health became a serious concern with the rapid growth of cities and as water-borne disease affected everyone, there was greater impetus to clean up sanitation and provide various kinds of public infrastructure to do so. And as working class conditions worsened and discontent mounted in the 1830s, there were concessions made both on the political front through extending the franchise, and on the economic front through extending public goods. Expenditures on public health to regulate the quality of food and water, and high infrastructural investment were made possible by Britain's high per capita wealth. Harling (2004) says that there was a 75 per cent per capita increase in local government spending in the second half of the 19th century out of income generated from higher rates. It was, however, very uneven, with higher municipal expenditures in Birmingham, for example, and backwaters elsewhere.

Alongside this Harling (2004) stresses the greater participatory nature of politics at the local level with opportunities for women and working-class men through the local electorate on school boards, as Poor Law guardians, on local councils, as well as through voting itself with the introduction of and extensions to the local municipal franchise in 1835, 1869 and 1888. Local institutions were transformed following the 1835 Municipal Corporations Act, which established precursors to the elected municipal councils. Almost all cities became incorporated, and their rulers were transformed from being appointed to being elected (Lizzeri and Persico 2004).

Thane (1990) argues that by the mid-19th century the liberal idea of small government was established, with the state's role being to provide a framework so that society could run itself. Even though in mid-Victorian Britain the government didn't match this ideal, it was a widely held and influential view. Thane plays down the presence of a centralized bureaucracy, which was relatively small in headcount terms, arguing that it created greater flexibility and scope for negotiation and adaptation.

The mid-19th-century state did, however, have a regulatory role over the economy, working increasingly through the legal system and inspection, from the Factory Acts onwards. The sanctioning of enclosures, the building of docks, and the creation of turnpike trusts and canal companies were all done through private Acts of Parliament. The mercantilist inheritance of protecting and promoting overseas trade was maintained through tariffs and prohibitions on corn, timber and sugar.

There were lots of roles for groups of self-governing citizens, often elective but unpaid in an official capacity. These included various local government institutions. In Britain, there was not a strong bureaucratic caste group with its own interests (unlike Prussia), and there was no great expectation of what the state should be doing (unlike France). Thane (1990) argues that mid-19th-century Victorian central government had a vision of its role, but that its methods of taxing and policing were indirect and discreet. She argues that the only direct contact with the state was through the post office clerk. Against this, one can argue that this was changing with the institution of the GPO, whose charges were explicit and direct. Moreover, the founding of the Metropolitan Police in 1829 had increased direct and visible contact with the state in London. The great maritime cities, with their naval recruitment, victualling, shipbuilding and repair, had long meant close contact with the state in the defence sectors and for many people as contractors or workers. This military-industrial state did reach deep into the 19th-century economy, but was particularly built around maritime and naval affairs and procurement.

In addition, there was local administration, official and voluntary such as Justices of the Peace (JPs) and municipal boards of schools and hospitals. The powers of unpaid JPs were extensive, of arresting and punishing offenders, supervising ale-houses, punishing runaway servants and apprentices, fixing prices and wages, maintaining highways, setting Poor Law policy, suppressing nuisances, overseeing markets, appointing constables and assessing rates. The Poor Law framework was set by central government but administered by local communities. There was a growth in municipal corporations as towns grew in the 18th century that dealt with the environment and established free associations to petition Parliament. There were local bill powers to levy local taxes for street lighting, stone paving, watchmen and refuse removal. There were local improvement commissioners (Thane 1990: 7). With this level of local responsibility for local needs, there was not much intervention by central government. Yes, the courts favoured the rich over the poor, but not invariably; freedom before the law was not a myth. Severe court penalties acted as a deterrent rather than being enforced. This was changing by the 1870s. The civil service and inspectorates grew steadily in the late 19th century and became more professional, particularly in the Foreign Office, Home Office, Treasury and GPO.

Lizzeri and Persico (2004) document that public spending by local government rose from 17 per cent of government spending in 1790 to 41 per cent in 1890. They argue that increased spending on public goods, especially on health infrastructure, was desired by the elites because of high mortality in the new large cities and the inability of infrastructure to cope (Szreter 1997). This infrastructure included unfiltered drinking water, unpaved roads and little drainage, so these cities were breeding grounds for disease. Mortality was less class-specific in the early 19th century than in the 20th century.

The nature of the British state in 1850 was not *laissez-faire*, but the more interventionist laws were not enforced. There remained restrictions on joint stock companies, but alternative institutions such as trusteeships got round the lack of incorporation. Much of the internal administration was left to local authorities, such as magistrates; regulation of labour markets, justice, police, road maintenance and poor relief were all organized at the local level. Ignoring or evading rules, such as those on usury or the Navigation Acts, made Britain more of a free market economy. The Statute of Apprentices was being ignored by 1700; the Calico Acts were unable to keep out Indian calicoes; and laws preventing emigration of artisans and machinery were evaded (Mokyr 2012).

The other point to integrate here is Cain and Hopkins' (1986, 1987) argument that British capitalism was 'gentlemanly capitalism': it favoured the City, financial interests and mercantile interests over industrial interests. They divide this into two phases: from 1688 to 1850, when the landed interest predominated, and from 1850 onwards, when the financial and commercial magnates of the City and the growth of services in the southeast of England gained the upper hand.

The Financial Revolution of the 18th century (see below) was based in London, the creation of the Bank of England being part of it. It involved the creation of the national debt, the rise of the stock exchange, and the decline of Amsterdam's financial predominance. London in the 1780s was the leading financial centre with an influx of refugees from the French Wars. The Gold Standard evolved from the early 18th century and was confirmed in 1819. By 1850, other monopolies had ended, excepting the Bank of England which under the 1844 Bank Act confirmed its exclusive rights. In the second half of the 19th century, the service sector grew based on shipping, insurance, and bills of exchange. Cain and Hopkins' (1986) thesis is that the gentleman capitalists composed of the financial and merchant class always had the upper hand over the industrialists. This gentlemanly capitalism pushed for stronger protection of tradable assets than of assets associated with industrial capital.

Meso-institutions: Corporate governance – organizational forms, financing, capital-labour institutions

This section focuses on organizational forms: the formation of joint stock companies; the role of the corporation, unincorporated companies and other organizational forms such as trusts; and the centrality of the corporation in Britain's equity-based capitalism.

Joint stock companies in financing and ownership

Why did the corporation win out in the 19th century as a legal form for business organizations over the partnership or trust? As Ron Harris (2000) argues, this was not a preordained conclusion. The corporation was attached to the power of the King, whereas the trust and partnership forms were free from state interference. As one of the key questions in this book is why family-owned concentrated shareholding has persisted on the continent much longer than it did in Britain and the United States, one of the key issues is to trace when dispersed shareholding happened in Britain, the role of the corporation, the role of common law, and the use of equity markets in that process.

The trading companies of the 16th century, such as the Russia Company and East India Company, used the permanent joint stock form, although there were difficulties (R. Harris 2000: 44). Harris dates the rise of the corporation to the early 17th century, the companies relying on state monopoly and protection and the state deriving revenues from them. It was after the Glorious Revolution that the business corporation revived in importance through the big three moneyed companies: East India Company, Bank of England, South Sea Company. They became important in public finance. The joint stock feature of companies grew more popular with many new unincorporated joint stock companies forming in the 1690s promoted on a stock market.

The Bubble Act was passed in 1720 requiring parliamentary approval for setting up a company by taking out a charter. Harris (2000) argues that the Bubble Act, although seen as a turning point in the history of business organization, did not have such pivotal effects. The period from 1720 to 1810 saw great economic change but little legal change. The unincorporated company in England from the late 18th century had, to some partial extent, the four features of a joint stock corporation – transferability of assets; limited liability; managerial hierarchy; and a separate legal personality – but not enough for most entrepreneurs (R. Harris 2000). Harris' argument is that despite the legal restrictions and lack of limited liability, joint stock companies were extremely significant in 18th-century proto-industrialization. It was the needs of financing companies at the end of the 18th century that gave rise to calls for changes in the law such as the repeal of the Bubble Act in 1825, the passing of the Companies Registration Act of 1844, and the introduction of limited liability in 1856.

In the late 18th century, the limited partnership, akin to the *commenda*, was recognized and used on the continent and in England, but was not recognized by common law and only came into the English legal system in 1907. Sleeping partners in a partnership who would have limited liability had no standing in an English court. This contrasts with the post-Napoleonic introduction in France of joint stock partnerships with transferable interests, which were not recognized by English common law.

The Financial Revolution, public finance, stock markets

This section draws on Ron Harris' (2000) and on Leslie Hannah's (2015a) recent reconsideration of corporate financing data and fables, comparing institutions between the United Kingdom, the United States, Germany and France from the early 20th century. The importance of what has been called the Financial Revolution in Britain from the end of the 17th century, through the development of public credit from the Bank of England and other financial institutions, has been debated (for example, Dickson's (1967) *The Financial Revolution in England:* A Study in the Development of Public Credit, 1688–1756; Brewer's (1989) *The Sinews of Power: War, Money and the English State, 1688–1783*).

The main features that stand out about Britain's corporate financing in the 18th and early 19th centuries are the following. There was huge development of equity financing, selling shares in companies, through informal securities markets. The United Kingdom had precocious development of stock exchanges, what Hannah calls 'London's exceptional stock exchange development' (Hannah 2015a: 31). He describes the dozens of informal provincial markets where holders and brokers met in bars, matching bargains, reporting in the press. Companies made share issues out of their main headquarters. These exchanges were private, voluntary, largely unregulated associations. Harris (2000: 168–198) describes the plethora of informal, local, entrepreneurial exchanges based in the London coffee houses and elsewhere across a number of sectors where joint stock played an important role: wool milling, fishing, brewing, flour milling, shipping, mining, as well as the early canal companies of the second half of the 18th century: 'The coffeehouses of Exchange Alley soon acquired a reputation as being meeting places for specialized traders: Lloyd's for marine insurance, Tom's and Carsey's for fire insurance, Garraway's for auctioning, Jonathan's for company shares and government stocks' (R. Harris 2000: 119). This gave rise to a building being dedicated to the exchange of shares, the Stock Exchange, in 1773, and in 1801 the New Stock Exchange was constructed.

There were separate types of trading: overseas trade and high finance in the official exchanges and the more modest trading in company shares that characterized the coffee houses. Harris (2000: 122–123) gives details of the various books, *Mortimer's Everyman His Own Broker, Fortune's An Epitome of the Stocks* and *Public Funds*, which ran to many editions in the second half of the 18th century and are evidence of the widespread interest and activity in trading shares by that time.

These joint stock companies raised capital in a number of ways, some of which did not rely on any formal market. For example, the Leeds and Liverpool Canal Company was set up after a meeting in Bradford in 1766 to obtain subscriptions. After two years of raising funds in this way, it applied to Parliament for an act of incorporation to enable it to raise larger sums. It opened subscription books in a number of northern towns, but did not use any formal capital market. Harris contrasts this with the Atlas Insurance Company, which in 1807 met at Will's Coffee House in London, advertised in London newspapers and appointed five London banking houses to handle the subscription. Country bankers were involved too, and the network covered the whole country (R. Harris 2000: 125). The picture is of a vibrant corporate financing scene – 18th-century crowd-funding – that did not necessarily go through formal exchanges but was drummed up through meetings in pubs, country banks and other meeting places where shares could be traded. A capital market grew up in the second half of the 18th century that was not integrated and not efficient in the sense of one price prevailing across the market and information being easily accessed, but that was nevertheless significant in raising capital and in drawing in a wide cross-section of the wealthier part of the population, including middling sorts such as shopkeepers and skilled workers who invested their savings locally (Elbaum and Lazonick

1984: 570) and not just the large landowning gentry. Railway construction in the 1830s and 1840s was accompanied by the growth of provincial stock exchanges and the development of a more efficient secondary market in shares.

When it comes to aggregate comparisons of stock exchanges, in 1914 the London Stock Exchange (LSE) was ahead of other metropolitan exchanges in the value of its listings. The corporate bond market was also important in the United Kingdom (and the United States) especially for financing the railways. In terms of whether this implied loss of control by the entrepreneurs/proprietors, preference shares and debentures (which earned fixed interest returns but without voting rights) formed a significant proportion of securities in the UK (around 36 per cent in 1913) and US markets and suggests that there was not 'separation of ownership from control' before the First World War.

Hannah (2015b) gives us the number of corporations per million people in 1910, with the United Kingdom at 1,241 and the United States at 2,913, both way ahead of France at 306 and Germany at 403. The United Kingdom had higher capital values as a proportion of GDP, reflecting the extent of global investment especially in the pre-1914 period, whereas the United States had greater numbers. The United Kingdom had more public and more private companies than Germany in 1914 (Hannah 2015a). The colossal trading companies represented very high percentages of UK-owned investment (probably amounting to a bigger share of the world economy measured by investment than either Google or Microsoft have ever been at their respective heights) (6 2016).

Using Hannah's careful calculations, in 1913 UK corporate equities as a proportion of GDP were 110 per cent at par and 151 per cent at market values. Hannah points out this proportion was not matched by the United States until the end of the 20th century. If one counts in equities plus bonds as a proportion of GDP, the United Kingdom was 153 per cent at par and 189 per cent at market values. This was three times the pre-war ratio for the other three industrial countries.

One of the points that Hannah emphasizes is that many smaller quoted companies were not listed: 'Nearly 90 per cent of the several hundred large, independent British-owned companies with more than £1m share capital had LSE-listed securities, while less than ten per cent of smaller quoted companies were officially listed' (Hannah 2015a: 25 Footnote 60). There were more companies, and more were quoted on stock exchanges: the UK data for 1913 show that corporate capital amounted to 150 per cent of GDP; 51 per cent were listed on the LSE, 23 per cent were listed elsewhere and 26 per cent were unquoted. This shows far greater similarity to the United States, with a corporate capital ratio of 174/100, than to Germany with one of 43/100 (see Chapter 5 for a discussion of this). But it also shows a higher proportion of quoted companies than in the United States.

In 1914, the number of quoted companies in securities directories far exceeded numbers on the continent: at over 200 companies per million people in the United Kingdom compared with 25 companies per million in Germany and 28 companies per million in France in 1907 (Hannah 2015a: 33). Many thousands of these medium-sized quoted companies relied on personal reputation, trust and local networking amongst a fairly settled group of investors, often raising relatively modest sums of money. Hannah quotes Lavington's (1921: 202–204) estimates of nearly 3,000 new companies going public in 1911–1913 raising on average around £28,000 per company. The overall conclusion is that the United Kingdom (and the United States) used public markets much more extensively than did continental companies, which stuck to unincorporated forms of sole proprietorships and partnerships to a greater extent. This has continued to be the case. Figures of the number of stock-exchange-listed companies per million people in 1990 show 443 in France (excluding the Marché Libre) and 548 in Germany compared with 1,946 in the United Kingdom and 3,876 in the United States (Coffee 2004).

There was also a London junior market onto which higher-risk new IPOs (initial public offerings) could be launched. Hannah (2015a) reports two success stories of the junior market that had been refused listing on the more tightly regulated LSE: Shell in 1900 issuing £2m of shares, with the Samuel family retaining a controlling majority, officially listing in 1911 and going on to become the world's largest corporation; and Marconi raising £137,000 in capital on the junior market with no prospectus and with insiders retaining voting control, achieving huge share price increases by 1912. They are illustrative of the greater risk and diversity of opportunity that raising finance in this way offered over the more tightly regulated continental markets; there was a higher failure rate on the junior market than on the LSE or on the continental markets. However, it also encouraged a wider diversity of backers than on the continent, often local investors, trusts, agencies, or financial groups on the back of personal reputations, local networks, and trust rather than statutory regulation. Hannah also argues, however, that although ownership became dispersed in the United Kingdom faster than on the continent, family ownership and management was retained for longer there than in the United States (Hannah 2015a; Chandler 1990; and Lazonick 1984).

Regulation of securities and stock exchanges

John Coffee's (2004) work on the role of law in the rise of dispersed ownership argues that dispersed ownership in the United States and the United Kingdom did not depend on there being adequate protection for minority shareholders. What it did depend on was that the stock market in both those countries was self-regulating and that control was held by the public market itself rather than being in the hands of controlling shareholders. These were private or semi-private orderings rather than law-making being managed by the state with the government administering the market as in France and Germany. His argument is that in United States and the United Kingdom there was a separation of the market from politics, with the stock market functioning without close state control.[15] Common law was more hospitable to this type of private self-regulation than was civil law on the continent. The self-regulation consisted in ensuring that there was adequate protection from raiders into the market. Once there was a constituency of small shareholders who had entered the market, this protection became formalized into legislation. On the continent, by contrast, no such small shareholder constituency developed. The main advantage that the United Kingdom and the United States offered in the development of equity markets was a decentralized state that kept out of the market. This runs counter to La Porta, Lopez-de-Silanes, Shleifer and Vishny (1997)'s argument that it was the civil law system *per se* that failed to provide adequate protection to minority shareholders, whereas the common law system did.

This argument also runs counter to Roe's (2003) political argument that concentrated shareholding was strong in social democratic countries with left-leaning governments as a countervailing power to the power of employees backed by the government. Bebchuk (1999), in line with Roe's argument, says that concentrated shareholders will not take a company public and will not sell to dispersed shareholders in order to protect their own rents.

What Coffee (2004) does is to go through the historical sequences of events to see what did lead to the dispersal of shareholding. Securities exchanges had existed since the 17th century, but principally to trade debt securities until the early to mid-19th century. The canal and rail company stocks exploded in number and value and traded volumes by the 1830s, and the same for telegraph company stocks in the 1850s. Then, even in the presence of high private benefits of control, shareholdings were sold to small investors in the late 19th century in the United States and the mid-20th century in the United Kingdom.

The expansion of the LSE was based on different organizational principles from that of the New York Stock Exchange (NYSE): more open and *laissez-faire*, listing any security that would generate business (Michie 1987 in Coffee 2004: 43). Dispersed shareholding arrived in the United Kingdom, later than in the United States. In 1936, the median proportion of voting share of the 20 largest shareholders in the 82 largest non-financials in the United Kingdom was 40 per cent, compared with 28 per cent in the United States. In 40 per cent of UK companies, the 20 largest shareholders held an absolute majority collectively (Sargent 1961: 189). This was not separation of ownership from control. A study for 1977 found that the largest 20 shareholders held 20–29 per cent of voting stock (Scott 1986: 95). The conclusion Coffee (2004) comes to is that ownership in the United Kingdom became dispersed sometime between the 1930s and 1970s.

Capital-labour relations

Why were capital-labour relations antagonistic rather than consensual, and why did a labour voice not get incorporated into the firm's governance? The history of capital-labour relations in Britain is much more complex than the conclusion that I have arrived at of a more liberal regime of low employment protection, low union density and low employee voice in the governance of companies would suggest. I cannot do justice to this but merely touch on the history here to suggest the ways in which the liberalism outlined above fed into this area of governance.

Mann (2012), in talking about the emergence of a British working class and capital-labour relations, emphasizes that the early nature in the emergence of class relations affected its character: there was little 'class' identity from 1760 to 1832 in the build-up to the Chartist movement, and such identity as there was was based around family and community rather than around the male-dominated factory, which did not exist much at that time except slightly in cotton. There was little distinction between manufacturing and service industries, or between factory and workshop; factories or workplaces were relatively small. In 1851 on average textile firms had 100 hands, and spinning and weaving firms had 300 hands; these numbers had doubled by 1890. There were some large mines, ironworks and shipbuilding yards, but most outfits were small. The 1851 census shows that the largest employment was in agriculture and domestic service (Mann 2012: 517). The liberalizing of the 1820s and 1830s discussed above applied to working conditions as well: minimum wages were abolished, and legal protection was diminished. There was much protest in various regions and sectors: in Bradford by wool combers in 1824; of Kidderminster carpet weavers in 1828; and of London tailors in 1834 for example (Mann 2012: 519). Mann argues that the 1820s was a period of curbing workers' rights, when much collective action was seen as criminal. The Chartists were defeated, he argues, due to class unity within the capitalist class and conscious rulings in their favour, but also by their own disunity.

With the Second Industrial Revolution and the emergence of more general unions, there was broader but more moderate class organization than with Chartism. The political concessions of the Great Reform Acts, particularly in the 1860s, muted the militancy of Chartism. The rise of and recognition of general trade unions for unskilled workers had to be fought for; they became sectoral interest groups that could use their market power, when they had it, in times of rising activity and labour shortage, but such power waxed and waned with the business cycle.

One source of difference in the British labour movement from its continental counterpart was that workplace organizations had substantial local autonomy in bargaining backed by national union strength from the late 19th century during disputes. Parliament and the judiciary trying to undermine trade union strength, for instance through the Taff Vale decision, led to the creation of the Labour Party specifically to represent labour's interests and protect its rights (Elbaum and Lazonick 1984: 570). Labour interests economically had political representation. In the first half of the 20th century, British unionism consolidated its positions of control in the workplace and at the national level, but with weak managerial structures: relations between management and labour were antagonistic and strike-prone rather than corporatist and consensual, as they were on the continent (Elbaum and Lazonick 1984; Chandler 1990; Hannah 1976; Streeck 1997; Schmitter 1974). Elbaum and Lazonick and others argue that this antagonism was, in part, due to institutional rigidity in Britain: its structures had been laid down at a relatively early stage of class antagonisms in the 18th century, although the coherence of these classes was not fixed.

Is there any resemblance between the supposedly liberal British state of the post-1980s and the liberal state as characterized for the mid-19th century? The varieties of capitalism literature certainly labels the post-1980s United Kingdom a liberal market economy and characterizes its state as being 'at arm's length'. A proper discussion of this is beyond the scope of this book. But as part of its purpose is to trace historical links and test the veracity of the varieties of capitalism claims, the beginnings of an answer is necessary.

Tanner and Green (2007) make the argument that liberalism never died in England, *pace* Dangerfield's (1935) *The Strange Death of Liberal England*. Instead, it was taken up in the 'moderate' lib-lab politics of the early and mid-20th century, as stressed by Peter Clarke (1996) in referring to Hobson and Hobhouse's works of the early 20th century on liberalism.

The nature of the British state and state-business relations have undoubtedly changed fundamentally – from the mid-19th century through to the pre-1906 state, and then from liberal reformism post-1906 through to the post-1945 welfare state. The post-1980s era has also considerable continuity in forms of governance in terms of public administration, going back well into the 19th century and sometimes earlier. Independent arm's-length regulatory bodies going back to the 19th century were established for health and safety and then for railways and have continued (6 2015). 6 (2015) gives examples of tax reliefs to stimulate life insurance being introduced by William Gladstone and of the Liberal and coalition governments of 1909–1945 using private and voluntary sectors to develop social care, through partly subsidized insurance and municipal arrangements allied with charities. There is much continuity here between this and post-1980s arrangements over treatment of the welfare state: 'It would be more candid to acknowledge that the period between 1945 and 1980 was the aberration from a longer-run trend that drove developments, in Britain's case, from the 1906 election. The important discontinuity would therefore be the 1945 election, not that of 1979' (6 2015: 64).

The other main argument that 6 makes is that the post-1980s period has been one of re-regulation, of tightening up regulation after a much more lax and relatively hands-off period of greater autonomy for professionals in healthcare, education, policing, social care and local government in the post-war period through to 1980, tightening up regulation using a range of controls such as details in contracts, performance and quality targets, and auditing to get value for money (6 2015; and Hood 2006).

I want to highlight a couple of areas of further continuity which make the link between 'liberal' state-business relations in the 19th century and post-1980s, which suggest why varieties of capitalism theorists use the term 'liberal' to characterize the post-1980s British economy. The first highlights the nature of individualism in Britain, which, as I show, goes back very far into the roots of English enterprise. As I suggested in Chapter 2, Douglas (1982) couples individualism in terms of social integration with increased levels of social regulation. Focusing on the nature of individualism in the liberal market economies, compared with more emphasis on collectivities – greater group – in terms of trade unions, business associations, strength of apprenticeships, and hierarchies within businesses in the more coordinated market economies of continental Europe, would bring out a key difference between the configuration of these economies, in the nature and mode of regulation and coordination with business, rather than focusing on whether regulation *per se* exists or has increased.

The other area of continuity concerns the emphasis that I have placed on the creation and protection of tradable property rights, which goes back centuries into the construction of English and then British commercial capitalism, with its emphasis on markets and tradability both of goods and services of all sorts and then of the securitization of those markets into capital markets that traded shares in companies and government debt more successfully and from an earlier time than the continental economies did.

One could take this further and argue that in Britain (and the United States) the key mechanisms of social mobility have been through property ownership, especially land and house ownership and to some extent share ownership, more than through participating through labour in the firm. There is continuity between the liberalism of the early to mid-19th century, mass shareholding and participation in property ownership, and the reinvigoration of these trends since the 1980s. And this is consistent with participation through ownership of assets tradable in markets, rather than through voice and control within the firm or at the workplace.

Conclusions

The argument being made in all the case studies is that the property rights and the shaping of the state go together. The formation of the state – who the dominant elites in power within government and outside government were, who made the rules of the game – was bound up with property rights over land in the first instance but also over maritime assets of various sorts, which became corporate assets and financial assets. This is so in all the case studies.

However, there are some key features of the British story that are not shared with other countries (except the United States to some extent) and that, I would argue, go on to create the key distinctions in the different types or varieties of capitalism that have evolved.

Britain is *the* story of the pre-eminence of a particular type of property rights: individual private property rights based on a common law legal system. It is the story of property rights that were tradable on markets of various sorts: markets in land, financial assets of government bonds, company stocks and shares (and post-1980, the housing market). Parliament and statute law were also central in this – what Mokyr (2012) called 'a meta-institution' – in conducting enclosures and regulating chartered companies and being involved in maritime-naval industries, especially in times of war.

The process of separation of the state from the market, of making the markets in private property rights independent from the state executive (although monitored by the courts), formed one of the key constraints on the state executive and became bound up with the particular division between private and public spheres, non-state and state spheres. This needs to be distinguished from separation between the state and corporation, especially in strategically key sectors, which has been and has remained strong for several centuries.

This separation of market from state has formed a distinct and different private-public boundary from those drawn elsewhere, particularly in France and Germany and especially in more recent times in China and Tanzania. The private, non-state sphere was and is differently regulated in the United Kingdom and the United States than in France and Germany, China and Tanzania.

A further difference in Britain was the establishment of individual private property rights well before the extension of the franchise. There are arguments made that Parliament was representative of wider sections of the population than those who could vote, via petitioning, pamphlets and protests, giving some sort of 'voice' mechanism for non-voters (Mokyr 2012; Mann 1993). This is important in enabling voices to be heard other than through formal voting rights, despite major reversals during emergency periods such as the Napoleonic Wars or during the Chartist agitation, and with voices heard more vigorously in England and not much at all in Ireland. But a significant aspect about the sequencing of institutional growth was that private property rights, independent of the state executive, were established prior to mass democracy. Property rights were not often subject to change with a change in government, which is an issue in Tanzania for example.[16] North et al. (2009) gauge that by the turn of the 18th century the principle of private property rights independent of the state executive had become established. I would argue that the independence and tradability of those rights were and remain more strongly entrenched and protected from state executive interference in Britain than in continental Europe and China and Tanzania, although infrastructure and defence sectors had always been subject to state intervention. Property rights had been secured by and through the landowning propertied class in Parliament, although they were not confined to landed property but applied importantly to all types of property in commerce and manufacture. There was freedom of person and property, enforceable against even the more powerful in the state and backed by law; this led to a spread of commercialization that made those values of economic liberty more important in Britain than those of civic or political equality. I trace this thread through to the liberal state that became established by the 1820s and, with a post-war battle over the state from 1945 through to the late 1970s, from the 1980s saw its reconfiguration in the United Kingdom's liberal market economy.

Private ownership of tradable assets, including ownership of shares and government securities, was a significant mode of relatively broad participation in the economy. This affected relations between capital and labour, between employers and employees, which occurred through economic industrial confrontation in the workplace rather than with the state mandating coordination of voices in the workplace (see Chapter 5). The rule of primacy of shareholding for companies was in part protection for the small shareholder and, I would argue, in liberal fashion, took the steam out of a push for consensual workplace participation and control.

Property rights evolved gradually and incrementally over the centuries in line with the development of markets in land, in securities, and in government debt. The demise of absolutism in Britain in the 17th century and the demotion of the Crown's courts based on privileges – Star Chamber, other prerogative courts – in favour of common law courts based on property rights gave rise to a balance of power between state and non-state tilted towards the non-state, whether the state was centred on the monarchy or whether it was centred on Parliament.

In terms of the evolution of other commercial institutions such as stock exchanges, merchant banking, bills of exchange, and other financial instruments that formed the backdrop to the growth of commerce and financing of industrial infrastructure, the role of the state was indirect: to provide a legal framework through Parliament by which local companies and stock exchanges could be set up, rather than to do public provision directly. This turns out to be unusual and significant in comparison with continental Europe and other developing countries. In terms of administration of justice – local courts – and municipalities, schools, hospitals, this also was a more private (often voluntary), localized affair than in other countries until the 20th century. The private-public boundary crystallized around the creation of a liberal state (as argued by Mandler (1989), Mann (2012) and Cain and Hopkins (1987)) from the 1780s to the 1820s which, despite the Age of Reform, retained its cross-class alliances between landed and commercial (but not particularly industrial) interests in favour of a smaller state keeping out of business and intellectual interests. The balance of interest was tipped at the end of the 18th century in favour of economic 'freedoms' based on private property rather than political civic equalities based on representational rights (as in France). This was partly in reaction to what was going on in France. Both the composition of the state and the constraints on that state in Britain have consistently been economic power based outside the state vested in landed private property rights and then commercial/financial property rights diffused over landed and middle classes of the population. This recognizable entity was renewed in the 1980s – after a post-war challenge.

In Britain, much significant institutional development took place in the private, non-state sphere – from local financing, from governance of municipalities, schools, courts, and charitable foundations – through having voluntary self-appointed or community-appointed notables, as opposed to organizations with connections to the state and state-appointed officials. Countervailing powers to the state of these institutions – the CCIs – were (and remain) critical in creating a liberal, smaller state, where citizens were more concerned to preserve their individual freedoms from the interference of the state than to be more formally represented through the state. This contrasts with the French and German boundary between state and non-state institutions (see Chapter 5).

Notes

1 This is despite the fact that many of these institutions were acquired in Britain relatively late. The international slave trade was abolished long before (1807) actual slavery was (1833 Slavery Abolition Act). Catholic emancipation was begun in 1829, but it was not completed then. British rule in Ireland violated most elements in the list throughout the 19th century.
2 Scotland was much more centralized in its legal machinery (based in Edinburgh) than England was.
3 It can be argued that war itself was a public good, bringing benefits to the British trading and landed classes, as Chatham did when he argued in favour of Britain's participation in the Seven Years War.
4 Post-1689 in Scotland and Ireland, it is not a story of an independent judiciary.
5 This is truer for England, and only so for Scotland by then as the Highland Clearances were mostly over, as the violations of small crofters' property rights had been completed by then.
6 The judiciary became more independent of the state executive after the Civil War and particularly after the Glorious Revolution. See below.
7 It is hard to make this claim for Ireland, where the executive arm of the state stood behind the Ascendancy throughout (6 2016).
8 It was not the first state to do so. The Venetian Republic's huge wealth in late medieval and early modern times was built on private entrepreneurship, with an executive that did not interfere too much with business and with strong courts that enforced contracts and treated foreign and indigenous merchants in an equal fashion.
9 These look like big contrasts. But in absolute terms, in comparison with the size of farms in the Americas or east of the Elbe in Europe, these are still small farms, and differences between them in size look more modest.
10 Peasant proprietors still existed in Wales and in Ireland until the end of the Clearances in the 1820s.
11 This leaves out crucial aspects of the Weberian state such as his account of bureaucracy. In this aspect, the British state in the 18th century was much less bureaucratically developed than ancient regime France or absolutist-military Prussia (see Chapter 5).
12 This was referring perhaps to the repeal of the Navigation Acts in 1849.
13 This is not to say that jobbery or corruption was eliminated; despite the Northcote-Trevelyan reforms, much of the executive was still riddled with nepotism and patronage in the 1890s, especially in the Foreign Office (Otte 2011).
14 The Anglican Church was established, and there was royal prerogative over war-making. So there were areas of legal privilege, but fewer than in France.
15 This is true in the sense of there being a separation between the market in their stocks and the executive arm of the state. There was not a separation between the state and corporations in all cases. The great global submarine cable companies were closely involved with the state, as was the defence sector as a whole. There was oversight of the stock market from the courts, as witnessed by the increase in commercial litigation alongside the growth of the market.

16 Governments did sometimes change property rights, such as in the nationalizations of areas of the economy, from the 1868 nationalization of the domestic telegraph companies.

References

6, P. (2015) 'Governance: If Governance Is Everything, Maybe It's Nothing', in A. Massey and K. Johnston (eds), *The International Handbook of Public Administration and Governance*, 56–80. Cheltenham: Edward Elgar.

6, P. (2016) Private correspondence.

Acemoglu, D. and Robinson, J. (2012) *Why Nations Fail: The Origins of Power, Prosperity and Poverty.* London: Profile Books.

Adamson, J. (2007) *Noble Revolt: The Overthrow of Charles I.* London: Weidenfeld and Nicolson.

Anderlini, L., Felli, L. and Riboni, A. (2008) Statue Law or Case Law? Working Paper No. 2358. Munich: CESifo Group.

Austen, J. (1811) *Sense and Sensibility.* Oxford: Oxford University Press.

Bartle, I. and Vass, P. (2005) Self-Regulation and the Regulatory State – A Survey of Policy and Practice, Research Report No. 17. University of Bath: Centre for the Study of Regulated Industries.

Bebchuk, L. (1999) A Rent-Protection Theory of Corporate Ownership and Control, Working Paper No. 7203. Cambridge: National Bureau of Economic Research.

Besley, T. and Persson, T. (2009) 'The Origins of State Capacity: Property Rights, Taxation and Politics', *American Economic Review* 99(4): 1218–1244.

Bevan, G. and Hood, C. (2006) 'What's Measured Is What Matters: Targets and Gaming in the English Public Health Care System', *Public Administration* 84(3): 517–538.

Blyth, M. (2013) *Austerity: The History of a Dangerous Idea.* Oxford: Oxford University Press.

Bogart, D. and Richardson, G. (2011) 'Property Rights and Parliament in Industrializing Britain', *Journal of Law and Economics* 54(2): 241–274.

Bracton (c. 1250) *On the Laws and Customs of England* (attributed to Henry of Bratton c. 1210–1268). Bracton Online. Harvard Law School Library. Available at: http://bracton.law.harvard.edu/.

Braudel, F. (1983) *Civilization and Capitalism, 15th – 18th Century, Vol. 2: The Wheels of Commerce.* London: Collins.

Brewer, J. (1989) *The Sinews of Power: War, Money and the English State, 1688–1783.* New York: Alfred A. Knopf.

Cain, P.J. and Hopkins, A.G. (1986) 'Gentlemanly Capitalism and British Expansion Overseas I: The Old Colonial System, 1688–1850', *Economic History Review* 39(4): 501–525.

Cain, P.J. and Hopkins, A.G. (1987) 'Gentlemanly Capitalism and British Expansion Overseas II: New Imperialism, 1850–1945', *Economic History Review* 40(1): 1–26.

Chandler, A. (1990) *Scale and Scope: The Dynamics of Industrial Capitalism.* Cambridge, MA: Belknap Press of Harvard University Press.

Churchill, W. (1998 [1956]) *History of the English-Speaking Peoples.* New York: Skyhorse Publishing.

Clarke, P.F. (1996) *Hope and Glory: Britain, 1900–1990.* London: Penguin Books.

Coffee, J. (2004) Law and the Market: The Impact of Enforcement, Columbia Law School Working Paper No. 182. Available at: http://papers.ssrn.com/sol13/papers.cfm?abstract_id=967482.

Cross, F.B. (2003) 'Review: America the Adversarial', *Virginia Law Review* 89(1): 189–237.

Dangerfield, G. (1935) *The Strange Death of Liberal England.* New York: Smith and Haas.

de Soto, H. (1989) *The Other Path: The Economic Answer to Terrorism.* New York: Harper and Row.

de Tocqueville, A. (1966 [1856]) *The Ancien Regime and the French Revolution.* London: Collins/Fontana.

Dickson, P.G.M. (1967) *The Financial Revolution in England: A Study in the Development of Public Credit, 1688–1756.* London: Macmillan.

Dillon, P. (2006) *The Last Revolution: 1688 and the Creation of the Modern World.* London: Jonathan Cape.

Dincecco, M. (2009) 'Fiscal Centralization, Limited Government, and Public Revenues in Europe 1650–1913', *Journal of Economic History* 69(1): 48–103.

Djankov, S., La Porta, R., Lopez-de-Silanes, F. and Shleifer, A. (2002) Courts: The Lex Mundi Project, Working Paper No. 8890. Cambridge: National Bureau of Economics.

Djankov, S., La Porta, R., Lopez-de-Silanes, F. and Shleifer, A. (2003) 'Courts', *Quarterly Journal of Economics* 118(2): 453–517.

Douglas, M. (1982) *In the Active Voice.* London: Routledge and Kegan Paul.

Edling, M. (2014) *A Hercules in the Cradle: War, Money, and the American State, 1783–1867.* Chicago: University of Chicago Press.

Elbaum, B. and Lazonick, W. (1984) 'The Decline of the British Economy: An Institutional Perspective', *Journal of Economic History* 44(2): 567–583.

Glaeser, E. and Shleifer, A. (2002) 'Legal Origins', *Quarterly Journal of Economics* 117(4): 1193–1229.

Goodlad, G. (2010) 'Review of 1688: The First Modern Revolution by Steve Pincus', *History Today* 66. Available at: http://www.historytoday.com/graham-goodlad/1688-first-modern-revolution.

Greif, A. (2006) *Institutions and the Path to the Modern Economy: Lessons from Medieval Trade.* Cambridge: Cambridge University Press.

Hannah, L. (1976) *The Rise of the Corporate Economy: The British Experience.* Baltimore and London: Johns Hopkins University Press.

Hannah, L. (2015a) Rethinking Corporate Finance Fables: Did the US Lag Europe before 1914? Working Paper CIRJE-F-994. Tokyo: Center for International Research on the Japanese Economy.

Hannah, L. (2015b) 'A Global Census of Corporations in 1910', *Economic History Review* 68(2): 548–573.

Harling, P. (2004) 'The Centrality of Locality: The Local State, Local Democracy, and Local Consciousness in Late-Victorian and Edwardian Britain', *Journal of Victorian Culture* 9(2): 216–234.

Harling, P. and Mandler, P. (1993) 'From "Fiscal-Military" State to Laissez-Faire State, 1760–1850', *Journal of British Studies* 32(1): 44–70.

Harris, R. (2000) *Industrializing English Law: Entrepreneurship and Business Organization, 1720–1844.* Cambridge: Cambridge University Press.

Harris, T. (2006) *Revolution: The Great Crisis of the British Monarchy, 1685–1720.* London: Penguin Books.

Hayek, F. (1960) *The Constitution of Liberty*. Chicago: University of Chicago Press.

Hill, C. (1961) *The Century of Revolution, 1603–1714*. London: Routledge Classics.

Hoffman, P.T. (2015) 'What Do States Do? Politics and Economic History', *Journal of Economic History* 75(2): 303–332.

Kagan, R. (2001) *Adversarial Legalism: The American Way of Law*. Cambridge, MA: Harvard University Press.

Keay, J. (1991) *The Honourable Company: A History of the English East India Company*. London: Harper Collins.

King, G. (1936 [1688]) *Two Tracts by Gregory King. Natural and Political Observations and Conclusions upon the State and Condition of England. Of the Naval Trade of England A°.1688 and the National Profit then Arising thereby*. Edited with an introduction by G.E. Barnett. Baltimore: Johns Hopkins University Press.

Knight, R. (2013) *Britain against Napoleon: The Organization of Victory, 1793–1815*. London: Allen Lane.

Landes, D. (1998) *The Wealth and Poverty of Nations: Why Some Are so Rich and Some so Poor*. London: Abacus.

La Porta, R., Lopez-de-Silanes, F. and Shleifer, A. (2008) 'The Economic Consequences of Legal Origins', *Journal of Economic Literature* 46(2): 285–332.

La Porta, R., Lopez-de-Silanes, F., Shleifer, A. and Vishny, R. (1997) 'Legal Determinants of External Finance', *Journal of Finance* 52(3): 1131–1150.

Laslett, P. (1960) *John Locke: Two Treatises of Government. A Critical Edition with an Introduction and Apparatus Criticus*. New York: Mentor Book from New American Library.

Lavington, F. (1921) *The English Capital Market*. London: Methuen.

Linklater, A. (2014) *Owning the Earth: The Transforming History of Land Ownership*. New York: Bloomsbury.

Lizzeri, A. and Persico, N. (2004) 'Why Did the Elites Extend the Suffrage? Democracy and the Scope of Government, with an Application to Britain's "Age of Reform"', *Quarterly Journal of Economics* 119(2): 707–765.

Macaulay, T. [1848] (1968) *The History of England from the Accession of James the Second*. London: Penguin Books.

Macfarlane, A. (1978) *The Origins of English Individualism*. Oxford: Basil Blackwell.

Macpherson, C.B. (1962) *The Political Theory of Possessive Individualism: Hobbes to Locke*. Oxford: Oxford University Press.

Mandler, P. (1989) *The Strange Birth of Liberal England: Conservative Origins of the Laissez-Faire State, 1780–1860*. Cambridge, MA: Minda de Gunzburg Center for European Studies, Harvard University.

Mann, M. (1993) *The Sources of Social Power, Vol. 2: The Rise of Classes and Nation-States, 1760–1914*. Cambridge: Cambridge University Press.

Mann, M. (2012) *The Sources of Social Power, Vol. 3: Global Empires and Revolution, 1890–1945*. Cambridge: Cambridge University Press.

Marsh, P. (1999) *Bargaining on Europe: Britain and the First Common Market, 1860–1892*. New Haven: Yale University Press.

Mathias, P. and O'Brien, P. (1976) 'Taxation in England and France, 1715–1810: A Comparison of the Social and Economic Incidence of Taxes Collected for the Central Governments', *Journal of European Economic History* 5(3): 601–650.

Michie, R.C. (1987) *The London and New York Stock Exchanges, 1850–1914*. London: Allen and Unwin.

Milhaupt, C.J. and Pistor, K. (2008) *Law and Capitalism: What Corporate Crises Reveal about Legal Systems and Economic Development around the World*. Chicago: University of Chicago Press.

Mokyr, J. (2012) *The Enlightened Economy: An Economic History of Britain, 1700–1850*. New Haven: Yale University Press.

Moran, M. (2003) *The British Regulatory State: High Modernism and Hyper-Innovation*. Oxford: Oxford University Press.

More, T. (2012 [1516]) *Utopia*. London: Penguin Classics.

North, D., Wallis, J.J. and Weingast, B. (2009) *Violence and Social Orders: A Conceptual Framework for Interpreting Recorded Human History*. Cambridge: Cambridge University Press.

North, D. and Weingast, B. (1989) 'Constitutions and Commitment: The Evolution of Institutions Governing Public Choice in Seventeenth Century England', *Journal of Economic History* 49(4): 803–832.

O'Brien, P. (1988) 'The Political Economy of British Taxation, 1660–1815', *Economic History Review* 41(1): 1–32.

O'Brien, P. (2006) 'Contentions of the Purse between England and its European Rivals from Henry V to George IV: A Conversation with Michael Mann', *Journal of Historical Sociology* 19(4): 341–363.

O'Brien, P. (2011) 'The Nature and Historical Evolution of an Exceptional Fiscal State and its Possible Significance for the Precocious Commercialization and Industrialization of the British Economy from Cromwell to Nelson', *Economic History Review* 64(2): 408–446.

Otte, T. (2011) *The Foreign Office Mind: The Making of British Foreign Policy, 1865–1914*. Cambridge: Cambridge University Press.

Paine, L. (2013) *The Sea and Civilization: A Maritime History of the World*. New York: Alfred A. Knopf.

Penn, T. (2011) *Winter King: The Dawn of Tudor England*. London: Penguin Books.

Piketty, T. (2014) *Capital in the Twenty-First Century*. Cambridge, MA: Harvard University Press.

Pincus, S. (2009) *1688: The First Modern Revolution*. New Haven: Yale University Press.

Pomeranz, K. (2000) *The Great Divergence: China, Europe and the Making of the Modern World Economy*. Princeton: Princeton University Press.

Porter, R. (1982) *English Society in the Eighteenth Century*. London: Allen Lane.

Queralt, D. (2016) The Legacy of War on Fiscal Capacity, Working Paper. Barcelona: Institute of Political Economy and Governance.

Robins, N. (2012) *The Corporation that Changed the World: How the East India Company Shaped the Modern Multinational*. London: Pluto Press.

Rodrik, D. (2000) Institutions for High-Quality Growth: What They Are and How to Acquire Them, Working Paper No. 7540. Cambridge: National Bureau of Economic Research.

Roe, M. (2003) *Political Determinants of Corporate Governance*. Oxford: Oxford University Press.

Rosenthal, J.L. (1998) 'The Political Economy of Absolutism Reconsidered', in R. Bates, A. Greif, M. Levi and J.L. Rosenthal (eds), *Analytic Narratives*, 64–108. Princeton: Princeton University Press.

Rubinstein, W.D. (1983) 'The End of "Old Corruption" in Britain, 1780–1860', *Past and Present* 101(1): 55–86.

Sargent, F. (1961) *Ownership, Control and Success of Large Companies*. London: Sweet and Maxwell.

Schmitter, P. (1974) 'Still the Century of Corporatism?' *Review of Politics* 36(1): 85–131.

Scott, J. (1986) *Capitalist Property and Financial Power: A Comparative Study of Britain, the United States and Japan*. Brighton: Wheatsheaf.

Smith, A. (1970 [1776]) *The Wealth of Nations*. London: Penguin Pelican Books.

Streeck, W. (1997) 'German Capitalism: Does It Exist? Can It Survive?' in C. Crouch and W. Streeck (eds), *Political Economy of Modern Capitalism: Mapping Convergence and Diversity*, 33–55. London: Sage.

Szreter, S. (1997) 'Economic Growth, Disruption, Deprivation, Disease and Death: On the Importance of the Politics of Public Health for Development', *Population and Development Review* 23(4): 693–728.

Tamanaha, B.Z. (2004) *On the Rule of Law: History, Politics, Theory*. Cambridge: Cambridge University Press.

Tamanaha, B.Z. (2007) 'Understanding Legal Pluralism: Past to Present, Local to Global', *Sydney Law Review* 30(2): 375–411.

Tanner, D. and Green, E.H. (2007) *The Strange Survival of Liberal England: Political Leaders, Moral Values and the Reception of Economic Debate*. Cambridge: Cambridge University Press.

Tawney, R.H. (1941) 'The Rise of the Gentry, 1558–1640', *Economic History Review* 11(1): 1–38.

Thane, P. (1990) 'Government and Society in England and Wales, 1750–1914', in F.M.L. Thompson (ed.), *The Cambridge Social History of Britain since 1750 Vol. 3*, 1–62. Cambridge: Cambridge University Press.

Tilly, C. (1992) *Coercion, Capital and European States*. Cambridge: Blackwell.

Tilly, C. (1997) 'Parliamentarization of Popular Contention in Great Britain, 1758–1834', *Theory and Society* 26(2–3): 245–273.

Villaverde, J.F. (2015) *Magna Carta, the Rule of Law, and the Limits on Government*, Working Paper No. 15–035. University of Pennsylvania: Penn Institute of Economics.

5 Continental variety of capitalism

France and Germany compared with Britain

Introduction

What kind of capitalism is the continental variety, and where did it, if there is an 'it', come from? Where did the institutions underpinning the European varieties of capitalism come from? This chapter, as with the previous, is not as concerned with current formations of varieties of capitalism so much as with their historical institutional roots. I go back to the institutional origins of capitalism and state formation in those countries. As with the previous case study of Britain, the underlying questions concern the evolution of institutions: How did property rights, the legal system and the state evolve in these countries? What kinds of property rights were protected? What is the connection between that evolution and the post-1945 settlement in corporate governance? I look here at France's and Germany's institutional evolution together, emphasizing their common features, as both are classified as coordinated market economies (CMEs) (see Chapter 3). This is not to deny, however, the particularity of their institutional histories, some of which I try to convey.

The argument of this chapter is the following: France's and Germany's property rights did not evolve into individual private property rights as early as in Britain, nor did they evolve by the same processes. There were remnants of feudalism and reinforcement of feudal rights across both areas into the 18th century. The civil codes brought in by Napoleon and Frederick the Great in the 18th and early 19th centuries created a different balance between administrative and judicial power, one where power of the state administration was enhanced and that of the judiciary and the courts was lessened. The British (and US) story is one of individual property rights backed by common law courts and a judiciary that was substantially independent of the state (see Chapter 4). In France and Prussia, civil codes gave greater power of eminent domain to the state, increasing the state's power over settling property rights disputes. Whereas limited government evolved in Britain in the 17th century out of its Civil War and aftermath, absolute monarchy was strengthened in both France and Prussia, alongside the powers of centralized state administration in France and the state bureaucracy in Prussia. The 1848 Revolutions and then the unification of Germany were achieved not by a state ruled by a parliament of grandees that became a liberal state in the 19th century as in Britain, but through liberal reformers backing the Prussian bureaucratic and military state with lesser powers accorded to the *Reichstag*. Neither the French nor German states were liberal (and, therefore, more constrained) in the British mould. The powers of the central state were more extensive, and the economic spheres over which they had authority were larger, including the construction of infrastructure such as railroads and canals, and public goods such as education. Both states were more paternalistic and intrusive in economic regulation, seeing it as the role of the state to centralize (more so in the case of France) and control markets and mitigate workers' unrest through conciliatory nation-building regulation.

These features influenced greatly the organizational forms, independence, range and use of financial institutions such as stock markets, which in turn affected the nature of control over companies. The corporation, which was so important and predominant in Britain (and in the United States) was much less prevalent in France and Germany. There were alternative organizational forms – the private limited company in particular – that provided limited liability without having to be publicly-listed. This answered to the greater push to maintain closely held control over companies through concentrated, often family, shareholding blocks, without the impetus to move towards more dispersed and mass shareholding. This combined with relatively underdeveloped financial markets and greater reliance on banks and holding companies as partners that assisted in maintaining 'inside control'. In turn, the underdevelopment of financial markets can be attributable to the more centralized and regulating state that inhibited the formation of the more localized and self-regulated stock markets that were created in Britain (and in the United States).

Compared with Britain's evolution towards shareholder capitalism (see Chapter 4), where the state was liberal and kept at arm's length from the economic sphere of class-bound and antagonistic industrial relations, stakeholder capitalism in Germany and France, in their different ways, was forged through the paternalistic state becoming more involved in industrial relations in the interests of avoiding class war and enforcing industrial peace. Codetermination in Germany from the late 19th century gave workers an insider corporatist voice in the interests of consensual industrial relations. In France, the state-business-elite nexus also gave the state more of an inside voice into protecting employees and being involved in collective bargaining in otherwise antagonistic class relations.

A main link made in this argument is between the more intrusive, non-liberal, nation-building state in both continental political economies and the evolution towards stakeholder forms of capitalism, both thwarting the growth of more independent stock markets and financing and pushing company owners to retain tighter and closed control over their operations and the state to compensate in expanding its sphere of influence into areas of company operation that the more liberal states avoided.

This meant an acceptance of, indeed desire for, bigger government and a broader sphere of influence, breaking down the political-economic lines of separation that exist in the liberal economies, which are more centralized in France and more Länder-based in Germany. German corporatism – its co-opting of workers and employers, the role of state regulation, the inside nature of corporate governance – is consistent with these roots in state-building and in technological catch-up industrialization. The enhanced role of the state in France, its *étatisme*, also goes back a long way to its centralizing, state-building roots in the 17th century, but with less consensual class relations, and the state-business function being to compensate, organize, contain and pacify those antagonisms. Consistent with this bigger less-limited state, which is less respectful of private property rights, is the countervailing power of employer-owners to retain concentrated ownership and control and less transparency towards the intrusive arms of the encroaching state.

This is a very different capitalism from the shareholder primacy of Britain (Chapter 4) and the United States (Chapter 6). Shareholder democracy in Britain and the United States was the egalitarian push towards greater say in companies' affairs through the spread of shareholding in the early 20th century, the more liberal and ultimately less egalitarian route towards shareholder primacy. It also and importantly promoted the interests (and strengthened the property rights) of liquid tradable capital (based on financial sectors in the economy) at the expense of 'strategic' industrial capital fixed into firms. Continental capitalism never approached this road, lacking the financial structure, the liberalism, the strength of the corporation and the independence of the corporation from state control. Its stakeholder route in giving more inside voice to its employee-workers (rather than outside voice to a wider constituency of shareholders) also strengthened the hold and protected the property rights of strategic capital based on the 'specific' assets and processes of the firm, rather than protecting the liquid tradable assets through shares. This meant protecting different constituencies, different types of capitalists, in the two contrasting varieties of capitalism.

This chapter is organized as follows. The next sections focus on primary institutions, outlining how private property rights emerged out of feudal/seigniorial structures in France and Germany. This leads on to the nature of the respective states and their relationship with the legal system. I then look at the meso-institutions, how primary institutions influenced the organizational forms that business enterprise took, and the nature of corporate governance systems.

Primary institutions: Property rights in France and Germany compared with Britain

I deal with property rights in France and Germany together in part because property rights stemmed from the extent and state of feudalism over central Europe from the 15th century. The discussion of property rights links also to the issue of how the form of law affected property rights. The collapse of feudalism was later in France, and especially in parts of Germany, than in Britain and less complete. This had implications for land tenure, for the development of a market in land, and for agricultural improvements and productivity.

The triage – the dividing up of common lands between peasants and landlords – failed in France in the 18th century, whereas it had resulted in enclosures in England (Braudel 1983). Certain aspects of the seigniorial regime still survived: the lord having rights over woodland, owning mills and fishponds; a remnant of the *corvée* was still exacted, which was not heavy in France – amounting to two or three days a year in ploughing in 1789.

Tocqueville (1856: 53) argues that the 18th century French peasant was also a landowner, although land had been partitioned into small parcels and, therefore, landholdings were often too small for families to live on; these complaints were being made 20 years before the Revolution. Arthur Young, touring France just before the Revolution, also remarks on the extent of peasant proprietors, saying that half the cultivable land was owned by them (Young 1792). He also talks about the poverty of these French peasants, who were barely able to survive off their tiny plots of land. One can see Hogarth's caricatured paintings (in Tate Britain) of plump English yeomen fed on meat alongside scrawny French peasants surviving on gruel. Tocqueville and Young also talk about the ownership of land as an obsession with the French peasant: all savings went into buying land. This is an important contrast to the more diverse avenues for English savings in the 18th century.

Ancien régime property rights were prohibitive of economic progress; improvements were obstructed by complex and small plots of overlapping property rights, whose owners would become mired in litigation at plans for drainage or irrigation (Rosenthal 1992). They were also the product of a judicial system that protected the elite's vested interests, which did not favour reform. This compares with the earlier collapse of the feudal system in Britain, the more complete victory for large landowners in post-Civil-War Parliament and an easier passage for both enclosures and the technical improvements in land use that resulted (Braudel 1983; Landes 1998). Liberal reforms were favoured and supported by the landed gentry and merchants in England; in France and Germany, liberal reforms and the movement of property rights (suppression of common lands and customary rights in favour of enclosure and technical progress) were not supported by those with vested interests in the land.

Rosenthal's (1992) *The Fruits of Revolution* examines why pre-Revolution, *ancien regime,* 18th-century France could not carry out drainage schemes in Normandy or irrigation schemes in Provence, both of which would have yielded high rates of return. He argues that such investments pre-Revolution were prevented by the litigation arising from unclear and complex property rights. In the 17th and 18th centuries, prior to the Revolution, land reforms such as for drainage of marshes or irrigation were obstructed by judicial determination of ownership, by the mixing of common land with many of these marshes, and by the litigation that ensued. There was no mechanism to stop litigation, with much renegotiation between those affected and the state. For example, for draining the marsh of Troarn proceedings were started in the 17th century and were still going 100 years later (Rosenthal 1992: 88).

In various respects, 19th-century French property rights continued to have traces of medieval tenure. Open fields remained in places into the 20th century with scattered strips common until the Second World War (Rosenthal 1992: 13). Napoleonic inheritance laws, post-Revolution, replaced primogeniture by equal division of land, which perpetuated smallholdings. The Revolutionary settlement didn't increase the 'security' of property rights. What it did do was change the administrative/legal structure so that under the centralized administrative system and civil code it became an administrative rather than judicial matter to push through improvements that would affect property rights. Rights of veto to such measures were curtailed, and power of eminent domain was taken up by the centralized state administration under the *Préfet* and Ministry of the Interior. If anything, this points to lesser security in property rights from predation by the state. The change in process, however, unblocked the bottleneck of litigation which had created a property rights thicket. Rosenthal (1992) points to the doubling of area under irrigation in Provence between 1820 and 1860 as evidence of this.

Germany: Property rights

There was much variety across the German states, not only in tenure of land but in property rights of other types, as described for England/Britain in the previous chapter. It included the Hanseatic League of northern maritime cities with their particular property rights based on maritime trading and their sea-based economy, as for Britain. It also included the divisions between the Catholic states of Bavaria and the south, with more guild- and artisan-based production; the Protestant north, with its commercial Rhinelands; and the agrarian estates in the east, dominated by the Junker military-aristocracy. The divisions between German regions and their accommodations, through the period of the Holy Roman Empire, through the Westphalian system in the 17th century, and through the Zollverein in the early 19th century, pre-date the Prussian military dominance of the mid to late 19th century that led to German unification. A general point, made also in the other chapters, is that the formal arrangements of property rights depended and rested on the informal institutions in the area. An analysis of the interaction between and the dynamics of informal and formal institutions is beyond my scope here.

In the east, feudal ties were strengthened after the 16th-century Wars of Religion, a second serfdom in Poland and eastern Prussia. There was some peasant landownership in Germany, mainly along the Rhine, at the end of the 18th century. Elsewhere in Germany, feudal practices were more long-lived. Tocqueville (1856) finds traces of such practices as fighting with their lord, spending some time each year at court, helping with the administration of justice, and maintenance of law and order on the estate in parts of Germany in the mid-19th century.

Tocqueville (1856: 52) argues that peasants 'were still literally bound to the land, as they had been in the Middle Ages'. The peasant was indeed tied in a number of ways: he had to serve in the army; he was not allowed to quit the estate and was tracked down and brought back if he did; and he had to spend some of his working hours in the master's service, in some areas of Germany to the extent of three days a week. He could, however, be a landowner, although this was hedged with restrictions in terms of how the land was cultivated; further, the land was neither alienable nor mortgageable, and his children could not inherit the land. These provisions were in Frederick the Great's code, which was drawn up in the late 18th century.

However, Kopsidis and Bromley (2014) argue for a more nuanced and varied view of the strength of peasant property rights in Germany from the 18th century. Property rights varied between landlords and peasants, with rents depending on the balance of power between them. The legal status of the land determined the personal freedom of the peasant and the quality of peasant property rights: freedom could extend from full freedom to leave, to an obligation to remain. The range of property rights was from a simple tenancy for years without any property rights in the land, or weak ownership rights, to full peasant property rights, including the right of hereditary ownership and sale. Even east of the Elbe, by the end of the 18th century most peasants had strong ownership rights in farms (Kopsidis and Bromley 2014).

In early-19th-century Prussia, there were laws enacted in 1811 and 1821 that gave peasants stronger ownership rights. There was a law in 1821 of swift enclosure of all commons in Prussia. The 1848 Revolution furthered this process: small farmers privatized their weak holdings and redeemed remaining cases of divided property. Prussian reformers were pushing for these institutional changes, which they felt to be essential for rural development and growth in the market; the landed aristocracy were pitted against reformers. Prussia remained dominated by large landowners but carried out agrarian reforms, whereby peasants on family farms controlled most of the land (Kopsidis and Bromley 2014).

In the French-held lands further west, reforms came after the 1848 Revolution. Napoleon's civil code of 1804 reinstated the legislation of 1789 that peasants had to pay redemption money to landlords for ownership rights. In France, these could be ignored, as the seigniorial system had been abolished; but in the French-controlled Rheinbund states it acted as a tax on the *Domaine extraordinaire*, and large manorial estates fell under it, especially in Westphalia. These seigniorial agreements continued until 1848. Kopsidis and Bromley (2014: 28) argue that the Napoleonic civil code had a limited impact on German commercialization in the French-controlled Rheinbund lands, *contra* Acemoglu, Cantoni, Johnson and Robinson (2011), who argue that it was the Napoleonic civil code that boosted industrialization in the French-held lands of Germany.

Primary institutions: Nature of the state and legal systems in France and Germany

The French comparison with Britain in the 18th century is illuminating. France had been leading in terms of economic development in the 17th century: it was much more populous and much richer. Churchill (1956: 356) says that by the mid-17th century France under Louis XIV had surpassed Spain and Austria as the dominant force in Europe they numbered 20 million, four times the population of England. It was in the 18th century that British economic supremacy was established: 'This gradually developing supremacy [of England] could already be glimpsed by 1713 and the Treaty of Utrecht; it was clearly visible by the end of the Seven Years' War in 1763 and had been achieved beyond a shadow of doubt by the time of the Treaty of Versailles (1783) when England appeared (quite misleadingly) to be the defeated power, and when she was unquestionably, with Holland out of the way, the beating heart of the world economy' (Braudel 1984: 352).

Legal systems: Civil codes versus common law and their effects on property rights

France and Germany adopted civil codes, brought in by Napoleon in France in 1804 and in various states earlier in the 18th century (Bavaria 1756; Prussia 1794), that were codified by Bismarck in 1886 as part of German unification. The German civil code differed from French codification in being more technical and less accessible (Berkowitz, Pistor and Richard 2000). They both drew on Justinian codification, from antiquity, which came to be defined as 'Roman law', which influenced state-making and especially the state's role in economic development and the role of enforcement and taxation (Badian 1972).

The 'legal origins' debate (Beck, Kunt and Levine 2002; La Porta, Lopez-de-Silanes, Shleifer and Vishny 2000) discusses the way in which the legal system – meaning whether the system is predominantly ruled by common law or by a civil code – has influenced property rights and, in particular, those related to finance and corporate governance. It is argued that the common law system provides greater support for private property rights that are independent of the state judiciary. The British story in Chapter 4 is of the boosting of common law and the common law courts as a result of the Civil War and the ousting of state prerogative courts. This enhanced large landowners' power and led to enclosures and their property rights winning out over small landowners' and customary rights.

In France and Germany by contrast, civil codes became predominant from the early 19th century. The legal origins argument and its relation to property rights is that the French and German civil codes in the 19th century were constructed to solidify state power by placing the prince above the law (Hayek 1960). The civil code has been associated with state dominance of the judiciary and is argued to have produced legal traditions that focused more on the power of the state and less on the rights of individuals (Mahoney 2001). In Britain by contrast, priority was attached to private individual property rights against the rights of the state; English common law protected private property against the Crown. The other argument is one over the adaptability of the legal system, that the common law system was more adaptable and responsive to economic change than were the civil law codes.

The French civil code of 1804 was a break with previous French legal tradition, although it harked back to a much earlier Justinian 'Roman' system of codification. Napoleon wanted a legal system that empowered the state and minimized the independence of judges, with the state as interpreter of the law. The Napoleonic Code eliminated jurisprudence – law created by judges, interpreting statutes, adjudicating disputes – and imposed a stricter formalism on court processes (Levine 2005). France's legal system had evolved from the 15th century as a regionally diverse amalgam of local law, Roman law and judicial decisions; the Napoleonic Code was a movement to diminish the role of the judges, which was seen as corrupt, and to centralize and impose a more uniform interpretation of law.

Prussia's civil code was a construction of Frederick the Great, but was not brought in until the end of the 18th century. Along similar lines as the Napoleonic Code, its aim was to avoid the more decentralized interpretation of the law by judges. It was adopted by other German states in the 19th century. Bismarck, too, used codification to unify and strengthen the German state, although in the German Empire of the 1870s jurisprudence and the power of judges remained; he didn't abolish prior law or eliminate judicial discretion. Compared with British common law, the differences were in terms of jurisprudence and the balance of power between state and courts, with the state wielding greater influence in Germany whilst the courts had greater influence in Britain (Levine 2005).

It is argued that these civil codes created a more rigid but simpler rules-based legal system that got rid of the former adaptability of judges to new situations (Glaeser and Shleifer 2002; La Porta et al. 2000, 1998). According to Milhaupt and Pistor (2008), two key differences between the legal systems are the greater centralization of the continental civil codes compared with the decentralized, judge-dominated common law systems, and, related to this, the lesser contestability in civil code systems, which means less ability to bring challenges to court as individuals or through class-actions compared with common-law-dominated systems. This is in line with Hayek's (1960) view of the civil code, that it emphasized Roman law and Justinian authority as above the law, and meant that the idea of legislation protecting the individual was lost.

The argument is that civil codes gave governments greater ability to control resources against private property rights and pre-existing contracts, and also that governments could not commit to not interfering in private contracts. Posner (1973) makes the case that legislatures are more cumbersome than judges in adapting the law. It is also argued that common law systems have been more efficient, as inefficient laws are re-litigated (Rubin 1977; Priest 1977).

How do these civil codes relate to the security of property rights? The shifting of power to settle disputes over property rights (and other matters) into the administrative realm has increased the power of the state to adjudicate. In relation to state power versus the individual, I explore what this means for the concept of limited government with constraints on the state. The civil codes, compared with common law regimes, contributed to lessening constraints on the state, enhancing the absolutist nature of government. The argument made here is that civil codes as a legal system compared with common law, in their centralizing effects and in shifting power towards state administrations and away from more independent judiciaries, increased state powers, clarified property rights, but weakened rather than strengthened individual property rights while strengthening state property rights through increased powers of eminent domain.

How did the state's centralized, administrative nature link to the state's fiscal capacity, its ability to raise tax revenues? Besley and Persson (2009) argue that state legal and fiscal capacity are complementary to each other: the greater a country's legal capacity, the greater its fiscal capacity. Dincecco (2009) argues that fiscal capacity is positively related to the constraints on the state, that limited governments have been more able to raise tax revenues from their citizens because they govern with their consent. The theoretical argument is that absolutist governments cannot be prevented from spending tax revenues on projects that only the ruler desires (such as wars) instead of those that the people want (public goods), and that this hampers the state's ability to tax. I argued in Chapter 4 against this view on a number of counts: that war made or strengthened the state (Tilly 1992); that war can be considered a public good; and that war in 18th-century Britain and subsequently was supported by business in creating new markets for supplying the navy, in defence procurement, and in expanding trade generally.

Dincecco (2009) dates the French state's centralized nature from the Napoleonic era. Tocqueville (1856) characterizes the centralization of administration in France from the 17th century of Colbert and Louis XIV. Dincecco's argument is that fiscal capacity rose when states became centralized, as opposed to fragmented, and when they achieved limited government, as opposed to being absolutist. He estimates that fiscal capacity increased from around 5g of gold per capita up to the 1780s to 10g from the 1780s to 1830s, to 20g from the 1840s to the 1860s, and then to 40g from 1870 to 1913, which he argues was a period when the state had both centralized administration and limited government. As for Britain, I question this reasoning. One cannot infer that it was due to limited government that tax revenues increased.

The French absolutist state's fiscal capacity fell behind that of the British during the 18th century. Its tax base was the poorest sections of the population, with nobles, merchants and urban corporations exempt from taxation. Britain, by contrast, developed financial institutions such as the Bank of England, local securities markets, and banks, which meant that the state could issue debt to finance wars; it also taxed, indirectly, a much broader section of its population which was growing in wealth; it had 'exceptional fiscal capacity' (O'Brien 2011, see Chapter 4). In France, the consent of the three estates was bought with privileges and through exemptions from taxes and duties; France got consent through their exclusion from power but exemption from taxes. It had a centralized monarchical state elite and privileged decentralized notable parties. The 18th-century problem in France was not lack of wealth but that the tax system taxed the poorest, the peasants (Mann 2012). There was no counterpart in France to the Bank of England. France had the Company of General Farmers (tax farmers), which raised loans for the state. Mann estimates that there were over 200,000 venal offices with vested interests blocking state modernization. The French treasury was tiny, with 264 employees; the Austrian equivalent was in the thousands. The nobility and middle classes got money in non-capitalist ways from feudal dues, rents, offices and annuities. There was a lot of ennoblement between 1700 and 1789 (Mann 2012: 172). Merchants and manufacturers were also in this; there were no alternative capitalist values (as in Britain). Hobson and Weiss (1995) call this a military-agrarian type of state (compared with Britain's 18th-century military-capitalist state). The 20th-century French state has continued to be characterized as highly centralized administratively. I return to this feature and the roles that this centralized state and its *étatisme* is argued to have played in the formation of its capitalism when I discuss its corporate governance.

As in the previous chapter, I wish to highlight the need to understand the informal institutional orderings that allowed this degree of centralization of state administration to happen. The French developmental state of the Colbertian period in the 17th century, the despotic ordering of the monarch to overcome divisions of the Fronde in the 18th century, or the type of state in the Third Empire in the 19th century would not have been possible without the prevention of the kind of individualism that flourished in England. The nobility were confined to competing over status at Versailles, and the local elites were confined within tightening informal hierarchies (6 2016). These informal orderings allowed this configuration of formal institutions to take root.

German state capacity

It was Prussia that came to dominate militarily German unification from the mid-19th century. Prussia had an absolutist version of sovereignty, which was located in the relations between the king and ministers, who were representatives of the noble class. Kopsidis and Bromley (2014) describe the institutional changes in Prussia post-1807, after the defeat by Napoleon and the humiliating Peace of Tilsit. Prussian liberal economic reformers sought to catch up in order to defend the remnant of Prussia against Napoleon. There was a west-to-east gradient in German economic development, with the agrarian east much less developed than the commercial and more industrial regions of Saxony and the northern Rhineland.

But the difference between German states and that of Britain was that the urban merchants had no political power to challenge the supremacy of the landed aristocracy. The German Enlightenment of the 18th century was pushed forward by liberal administrative officials (*Beamtenliberalismus*) (Vogel 1988 in Kopsidis and Bromley 2014). German liberalism was not that of the commercial classes; instead, it was an enlightened absolutism of the bureaucracy or bureaucratic absolutism with liberal economic reforms pitched against the old landed elites. Nor was it the French statist model. The reformers saw economic reforms as more urgent than political ones. The German intellectuals were influenced by Adam Smith, one of them being Christian Jacob Kraus, who succeeded Immanuel Kant in the Konigsberg Chair of Philosophy. They favoured state-led institutional change such as uniform commercial law, relatively free markets and education for all. The bureaucrats succeeded in this due to the collapse of the German middle class from political power in the face of defeat by Napoleon. It was a defensive modernization (Fehrenbach 2008); Prussia had lost half her territory and subjects to France and was reduced to its eastern agrarian lands and forced to pay war reparations. Prussian economic liberalism sided with big business and against the nobility (Fehrenbach 2008; Kopsidis and Bromley 2014), whereas the German southwest favoured political liberalism and more localism, was more economically conservative and was composed of small farmers and artisans. Prussian catch-up, which ended up winning the day, was undemocratic; Chancellor Karl August von Hardenberg did not push for political participation (Koselleck 1967).

The key period for the creation of German capitalism coincides with the period of creation of the German nation-state. This had various consequences and continues to do so. The suppression of class relations between capital and labour was laid down in the process of the Prussian domination over the German Länder in the creation of the German nation-state, and the catch-up required by the second industrial revolution gave a greater role for the state in infrastructure, education and training, which traditions continue to the present time.

In around 1850, Prussia was on a par economically with Austria in terms of the efficiency of its agriculture and per capita industrial size. There were Prussian victories against Austria and France in wars of 1866–1867 and 1870–1871. Mann (2012) emphasizes the 'national' organization of the German economy, an economy organized within the newly national boundaries and increasingly protectionist towards the end of the 19th century.

The German Reich was founded only in 1871. The state that 'acquired the German Reich' (Mann 2012: 297) was the Kingdom of Prussia, which was relatively backward economically, although it controlled much of northern Germany. Its two rivals for forming this united state were the confederal empire of Austria-Hungary and the confederal group of other German states. The 19th century is a story of Prussia coming to dominate both Austria and the German confederation.

Despite universal male suffrage in 1867, the representative body, the *Reichstag*, was weak relative to the Kaiser and his ministers and the rule of law. There was not parliamentary sovereignty as in Britain. The *Reichstag* could not appoint ministers or debate foreign policy. The army was responsible to the Kaiser, not to the *Reichstag*. This was not a liberal representative state, and yet it had the backing of the German middle classes who had property and felt their interests best served by this conservative state. Classes were suppressed in favour of nation-building. It unified the civil code, it established the *Reichsbank*, it was ruled by laws, not by Parliament (Mann 2012: 311). The state was pro-protection, with tariffs against cheaper American grain that were supported by the agrarian Junkers. The elites were Junkers and industrialists who intertwined and intermarried. From the 1880s, there was the growth of large corporations, which formed cartels and coordinated closely with the banks. Anyone powerful owned land or an industrial or commercial company. Preserving private property was a goal of the state, and modernizing industry and agriculture for profit and state revenues was another. There was an emphasis on the military and on order, with uniforms and ranks in the bureaucracy and in industry, with duelling at universities. This was not limited government in the sense of it being constrained by representatives in the *Reichstag*.

Public/private boundaries and German state fiscal capacity

Friedrich List, the German economic theorist, argued against Adam Smith's political economy, that *laissez-faire* was a veil for British domination. Instead, his reality was of national societies that required national protectionism to bolster selective sectors and regions within that nation. German catch-up or take-off (Gerschenkron 1962) from the 1850s was built on developing German industries instead of adapting British industrial innovations. It was built on the *Zollverein* (the internal customs union from 1834) and railways (List's Siamese twins of German development) and education (Mann 2012: 302). Railways were the hero of Germany's industrial revolution (Fremdling 1983 in Mann 2012). They were state-financed and state-owned, with state planning of lines. They brought revenues to the Prussian state and strengthened the state's fiscal capacity. The railways connected the old regime core on the Prussian Junker estates to the growing towns; one line ran the length of the Saxon border. Mann (2012) describes it as deliberate that the state's railway network, like a spider's web, ran over the territories with many connections into Prussia but with few threads interconnecting the national webs, enhancing Prussian control of the territory.

The Prussian monarchy did the same with education, bringing in the middle classes and professionals inside the Prussian state. It was the first state to impose compulsory primary education and state-developed trained teachers. Its literacy rate was 85 per cent by 1850, compared with 61 per cent in France (reading only) and 52 per cent in England (reading and writing). Education encouraged a technical curriculum suited to the second industrial revolution. This is a significant continuity into the post-Second-World-War support for vocational and technical education that remains distinctive to German capitalism. The 1872 *Kaiserreich* spent as much on education as on the military – they were not seen as alternatives. This meant that the language became standardized, with all attending the same schools and universities, with the main state infrastructures set up by Prussia (Mann 2012).

This nationalist state was anti-socialist but paternalistic. Bismarck's federal legislation created social insurance in the 1880s, bringing in national sickness benefits in 1883, accident insurance in 1884 and old-age and disability insurance in 1889 (Mann 2012: 675). There were also local and provincial programmes, particularly in education. Large employers provided housing benefits and pensions graded according to income. Mann (2012) argues that this was a league of big industrialists with state elites undercutting working class movements to gain quiescence over property rights. Pre-First-World-War Germany's social insurance programmes were in advance of those of Britain, whose programmes were in advance of those of France.

Piketty (2014: 145) estimates German public capital and debt, comparing Germany with France and Britain from 1870 to 2010. German public capital has been consistently higher than that in France, with both countries' public capital higher than Britain's and with lower levels of private wealth than Britain. Piketty attributes this in part to lower values of housing stock, to rent controls and to lower market values of firms compared with the book values of their assets. This connects with greater wealth being situated in non-tradable strategic assets of firms rather than in tradable, market-valued assets such as housing or securities.

The origins of the corporate coordination that came to characterize the CME of the 1980s and 1990s are in this late-19th-century era. Iversen and Soskice (2009: 459) stress the connections between locally coordinated rural and urban economic interests in Germany represented in the local states, *Standestaaten.* This was government through groups: landowners, smallholders, guilds and church. They also stress the close integration of the countryside into urban economies on the continent (Iversen and Soskice 2009: 465). Corporate organizations proliferated, characterizing relations between businessmen and German states in the Rhineland. They included employers' organizations, cartels, pressure groups, community organizations, and choral societies. This was a more organized society than the liberal countries. The United States had lobbying by corporations, but its government was smaller. If the density of organizations is seen as an indicator of development (North, Wallis and Weingast 2009), Germany was developing fast in the last two decades of the 19th century, as well as laying down the structures through which it was coordinated.

Meso-institutions: Organizational forms and corporate governance

How did these states influence the organizational forms that companies took and their corporate governance: the financing of companies, the relations between capital and labour, and the relations between shareholders, managers and employees?

There were fewer companies and corporations in Germany and France than in the United Kingdom and the United States. Hannah (2015) gives us figures of companies per million people in 1913 of 25 companies in Germany and 28 companies in France compared with over 200 companies in the United Kingdom. Corporate capital ratios were similarly much lower: 43/100 in Germany compared with 174/100 in the United Kingdom. This went with much less use of public equity markets and less listing on the continent, with greater use of unincorporated forms of sole proprietorships and partnerships. In addition to having fewer companies, they used less equity in their capital structures. Hannah (2015) gives us the equity valuation/GDP ratios in 1913 of 109 per cent for the London Stock Exchange compared with 54 per cent in France and 44 per cent in Germany.

I link this lesser use of equity markets to less use of the corporate form of the publicly-listed company. The work of Guinnane, Harris, Lamoreaux and Rosenthal (2007) has shown that on the continent the publicly-listed corporation, which rose to prominence in the common law systems of the United States and the United Kingdom, was not favoured as an organizational form for businesses. There was much slower and later development of the publicly-listed company, the AG (*Aktiengesellschaft*), in Germany. There were very few AGs in Prussia prior to 1850. There was a flurry of creation of such companies after the 1870 victory against France, but with little regulation there was much fraud and a crash in the 1870s. In 1884, there was a new stock corporation law with tighter regulation, legal liability for fraud, and greater disclosure requirements, and at this point supervisory and managerial board functions were separated (Fohlin 2005). There was a similar story in France. Prior to 1867, corporations required government approval: only 642 corporations were chartered between 1807 and 1867.

There was an alternative corporate form, the private limited liability company, that fulfilled some basic corporate functions; it created some limited liability through keeping limited partners out of daily management whilst not giving insider management unlimited power at the expense of minority shareholders. In France, this arose out of the *société en commandite*, the limited partnership, which provided a viable alternative to being incorporated. This was descended from Colbert's Ordinance of 1673, and defined and regulated by Napoleon's Code of 1804. Sleeping partners, wealthy individuals not actively participating, had limited liability. This gradually developed into the private joint stock company, issuing transferable shares by the 1830s, a practice upheld by the courts (Lamoreaux and Rosenthal 2005). In the 1860s, the rules on corporations were relaxed, so that by 1867 they didn't need government approval, and they weren't limited in size. From 1880 to 1913, there was growth in the number of corporations at the expense of partnerships, but few were listed companies.

In Germany in 1892, the Limited Liability Company Act established the non-publicly traded limited liability company, the *Gesellschaft mit beschränkter*

Haftung (GmbH), in Germany. This allowed for joint stock to be issued but wasn't listed on a stock exchange. It was found to be more conducive for smaller and medium-sized enterprises; it avoided the more costly forms of state regulation of listed companies and allowed retention of control by family owners. In 1925, France copied the German GmbH form, creating the SARL, *société à responsabilité limitée*, mixing attributes of corporation and partnership. This was in part prompted by the recovery of Alsace and Lorraine by France after the First World War, which under German rule from 1871 had spawned many GmbH businesses. Guinnane et al. (2007) also associate the use of the private limited liability company with the civil code legal structures on the continent, arguing that the two common law countries, the United Kingdom and the United States, blocked the existence of limited partnership until 1907 in the United Kingdom and made the formation of corporations relatively easier, with falling fees and regulation in the United States during the 19th century. Meanwhile, on the continent, state regulation of corporations became tighter. German reforms in 1884, intended to protect the shareholder, strengthened the role of the supervisory board and required more detailed financial disclosure and raised the minimum size of a share tenfold (Guinnane et al. 2007).

This is the other side of thc argument made in the previous chapter that securities markets flourished in part in the common law countries because they were self-regulated with minimal direct state interference in the market; in the civil code countries of the continent, by contrast, the government administered the market, and thus regulation became more onerous and rigid and off-putting to enterprise creation (Coffee 2000).

Ownership of companies

The literature on the split in corporate governance regimes highlights the division between concentrated blockholder shareholding in Germany and France and dispersed ownership in the United Kingdom and the United States (Herrigel 2006; Franks, Mayer and Wagner 2006; Murphy 2005). The main arguments made in the literature for causing the move to dispersal of ownership on the one hand and concentration and lack of dispersal on the other are several.

Guinnane et al. (2007) link lower demand for the publicly-listed corporate form in part to the greater role of the state on the continent in owning and financing capital-intensive infrastructural projects. State financing and ownership of railroads on the continent meant that these did not give the same stimulus to the growth of equity markets as had happened in Britain and the United States. The more prominent role of state regulation on the continent and of state ownership affected also the ownership structure of companies.

There was relatively high concentration in Germany of ownership of companies. The mean number of shareholders was around 25 between 1890 and 1940, contrasting with a rising number of shareholders in the United

Kingdom. German concentration increased over that period: in 1900, 25 per cent of firms had one shareholder controlling 25 per cent of the vote, in 1910 this was 75 per cent, and by 1932 100 per cent (Franks et al. 2006). Franks et al. argue that in Germany the main holders of equity were other companies and banks, which did not become diluted into dispersed ownership (as in Britain and the United States). They argue that large numbers of firms were listed and raised equity finance, but they did so from companies and banks involved with the firm rather than from individuals.

Fohlin (2005), on the other hand, stresses the private and hidden nature of corporate ownership in Germany (and to some extent in France). The majority of the AGs were not listed on the Berlin Stock Exchange either in 1890 or in 1910. The captains of industry – Krupp, Thyssen, Stinnes, Wolff, Stumm, Kockner, Siemens and Bosch – were concerned to maintain control. There was growing use of managers and growing cooperation and concentration between firms, especially in the late 19th century, with 366 industrial cartels reported by Sombart (1954) in this period.

The pre-eminent issue was for owners to retain control of the firm. There was no separation of ownership from control: there was control by owner-managers, control by owners as supervisory board members, and control by proxy votes by supervisory board members. Voting rights shifted away from individuals and towards companies and banks, replacing insider blockholding ownership with quasi-outsider ownership. Founding family ownership was quite modest, but the concentration of those firms with a family owner was high. And the transfer of ownership from families to banks and other companies did not involve a real loss of control, as those quasi-outsiders were still connected to the firms. In Britain, by comparison, 'other financial institutions' – pension funds and insurance companies with their own independent remits – became important equity owners during the 20th century; in Britain, there were no inter-corporate pyramids. Regulation in Britain enforcing full takeovers and declaration of ownership above a 30 per cent stake meant that stealthy building up of ownership stakes was avoided.

German insider ownership was and remained throughout the 20th century through corporate pyramids and inter-corporate holdings and through proxy equity holdings by banks. These are not insiders in the sense of ownership by directors, but neither are they independent outsiders; they are insiders in terms of retaining voting control within the corporate and banking sector rather than in outside individual shareholders (Franks et al. 2006).

Post-Second-World-War concentration of ownership has persisted, but with a changing composition. Families and government decreased their shareholding, and non-financial firms increased theirs from 18 per cent in 1950 to 41 per cent in 1996. But equity ownership in the largest 100 corporations in the 1990s was still concentrated: over 50 were owned by one large shareholder, and a further 16–21 had moderate concentration with less than half of shares dispersed (Fohlin 2005). The downward trend in the number of AGs has been accompanied by continued concentration. Cross-shareholding has remained important, with non-financials holding shares in other companies. The persistence of family ownership is marked: of 274,139 enterprises above DM 2m in 1995, 3 per cent were founded before 1870, and 12 per cent were founded between 1871 and 1913. In both groups, over 70 per cent of these are family firms. Families have remained a significant force. They have the right to veto decisions at 25 per cent ownership: of the firms sampled by Fohlin (2005), in over 80 per cent of companies the leading shareholder had a blocking minority. There is evidence of pyramid-holding especially in the late 20th century.

Voting systems also have favoured maintaining control by the blockholder. There has not been a one-share one-vote regime, but one of multi-vote shares so that with a few shares and many votes the founding families could keep their grip (Fohlin 2005). Votes per share could be 20 to 250 times higher than the normal voting right. The 1965 company law still allowed multiple voting shares, although they were prohibited in 1998. Bearer shares, where the shareholders remained anonymous and where the shareholders could give banks proxy voting rights, have also been important in allowing certain groups of shareholders to retain control, with little transparency in the system. The 1965 reforms wanted more shareholder democracy and to limit the concentration of power. They enforced registered shares, restricted proxy voting and outlawed anonymous voting. They abolished the 1937 *Führerprinzip* but retained powers for the management board. The 1965 reforms heralded greater transparency on what the returns of companies were and strengthened shareholder rights over management. The 1998 reforms furthered the push towards greater openness, less secrecy and more democracy in shareholding.

Other classes of shares – depot shares or *Vorratsaktien*, untradable shares, and preferential shares or *Vorzugsaktien* – also maintained control over the company, giving preferential rights to dividend payments, but were without voting rights. They were used to raise capital without diluting control. All these features worked against hostile takeovers. Again this was reformed in 1998. Still in existence is the condition that if shares are not traded on a stock exchange, then they are not subject to the prohibition of limits on voting power. Founders, often families, have retained control (Fohlin 2005). Milhaupt and Pistor (2008) chart the pressures of liberalization, post-unification, for German ownership to become more open. It is notable that the German state has been less in favour of an open market on takeovers, blocking the adoption of the European Takeover Directive in 2000 (Milhaupt and Pistor 2008: 80). The connection I wish to make is that markets in takeovers destroy the value of assets built up inside the firm, both of skills on the labour side and of strategic capital of technology, research or machinery that is intangible and untradable. A significant feature of German corporate governance, going back into the period of the second industrial revolution of the 1880s, has been the protection of these assets, close control over which has been one of the aims of German corporate governance codes.

Corporate ownership is similarly concentrated in France. Murphy (2005) stresses the importance of historical legacy in this, arguing that a weak financial system in the 18th century and underdeveloped banking led to self-financing of companies. The importance of the patrimonial firm goes back into the 18th century, arising from the Napoleonic inheritance law. Murphy (2005) takes three strong family companies – Michelin (founded 1829), L'Oréal (founded 1909) and Peugeot (founded in the 18th century) – to illustrate their long family continuity, their adaptation and shifting into different industries, and the maintenance of family control through retaining partnership status and having dual class shares (Michelin), or through self-financing (L'Oréal and Peugeot).

Bloch and Kremp (2001) argue that the concentration of direct ownership and voting power continues to be high in France: 40 per cent of unlisted firms have as their first shareholder individuals owning the majority share of the capital. For CAC 40 firms, blockholders hold around 30 per cent of voting rights and have control. Allouche and Amann (1995) give figures for 1992 of 28 per cent of the top 1,000 industrial companies being controlled by families, with foreigners controlling 23.5 per cent and the state 28 per cent. Blondel, Rowell and Van der Heyden (2002) look at France's largest 250 publicly-traded companies for 1993 and 1998: of these, 57 per cent were patrimonial firms where families had over a 10 per cent stake. The extent of patrimonial firms has grown over the 1990s. Sraer and Thesmar (2007) calculated that of all listed firms on French stock exchanges in 2002, a third were widely-held, a third were founder-controlled, and a third were heir-controlled family firms. The founder- and heir-controlled groups outperformed the widely-held one. Data for 2002 on the 500 richest families in France demonstrated highly concentrated wealth. The presence of holding companies of large industrial groups is attributed to capital market limitations.

One strain of thought, particularly in US business history, follows Chandlerian arguments about the progression of company governance from family ownership and management through to professional management with outside investors brought in but management and ownership still firmly linked, towards larger-scale enterprises where ownership becomes detached from management, and capital requirements leading to dispersed ownership (Chandler 1988, 1990). These continental firms confound this. Roe (2003) argues for the importance of political factors in determining governance regimes: blockholding is a response to social democracy and a strong labour voice. Where there are strong forces favouring 'stakeholder over private property rights' (Herrigel 2006: 14), this leads to blockholding as a counteractive response. When states support stakeholders, in giving labour a voice, then managers are pushed to act against the interests of shareholders, and owners therefore are pushed to keep controlling stakes in their businesses.

A third line of argument is that the legal system – common law and greater protection for minority investors (in the United Kingdom and the United States) *versus* civil codes with less minority protection (in Germany and France) – accounts for the difference in governance systems. A fourth line of argument is that the split is due to timing of industrialization (TOI), that those countries catching up with Britain in industrialization – in particular Germany and Japan, although the same could be said of France – devised ways of compensating for the absence of securities markets on the continent and the consequent lack of ability of companies slowly to accumulate funds to finance investment, as had happened in Britain. Germany accelerated catch-up industrialization through developing universal banks with closer insider relationships with companies, and with enhanced roles for the state (Gerschenkron 1962; Lazonick and O'Sullivan 1997). Herrigel's (2006) overall argument is that no one particular line of explanation fully accounts for the heterogeneity in governance that has been observed across countries and within countries, and that closer and more archivally based historical analysis is required to piece together a more nuanced picture.

Role of banks and financing institutions

My overarching argument is that, compared with Britain, there was a failure to develop outsider stock markets, which were a financial innovation in Britain in the 18th century and were responsible for financing infrastructure and increasing the financial capacity of the state. Linked to the more centralized state in France, in terms of the development of financing institutions France fell well behind Britain. Credit was poorly and clandestinely organized in France. The social climate was not encouraging. The financier was a royal officeholder or a noble and maintained discretion over lending money; the borrower was afraid of publicity that would damage his creditworthiness (Braudel 1983: 389).

The British state emerged from its 18th-century wars with France victorious in part because of the development of its capital markets. French attempts, through John Law, to create a note-issuing bank and trading company to convert government securities into equity ended in collapse in 1720. Various commentators point to the relative lack of a mature capital market in France hampering mergers and the growth of industry (Levy-Leboyer 1980; Landes 1998). The French invested in government bonds or foreign securities. By 1910, over 50 per cent of French domestic savings were going abroad (Pollard 1985). French stock market capitalization as a proportion of GDP lagged significantly behind that of the United Kingdom and United States (Murphy 2005). Kindleberger's (1984: 113) verdict in the 1980s was that France lagged Britain in financial institutions and experience by 100 years or so. The *haute banque* of the early 19th century – early merchant banking – had a focus on railways, real estate, public works and insurance, but not on general industrial sectors. Crédit Mobilier of the Péreire brothers was founded in 1852 to compete with the *haute banque*; it collapsed in 1867. The *Union Générale* lasted from 1878 to 1882.

A further argument is that the continental markets in public sector debt had less credibility than their British (and US) counterparts. As outlined in the previous chapter, the ability of markets in government securities to expand rested on the belief, well-founded in the case of Britain, that the government would honour its promises to pay dividends on those securities and not to default. This was not the case with either French or German government securities. Their states never achieved such credibility in the 18th and 19th centuries or the first half of the 20th century. This too has hampered the development and use of these markets.

Murphy (2005) also points to the role of the *notaires* in France, as bankers, as contributory to France's backwardness in financing institutions. Lending activity was concentrated around the state and real estate and did not diversify into industry and commerce. The *notaires* operated as a cartel and were inherently conservative in their lending patterns. The Revolution and *assignats* of the 1790s 'embedded paranoia about paper money and banks deeply in the French subconscious' (Kindleberger 1984: 99). The *Banque de France* was established in 1800, but whereas banknotes and bank credit were central to the British economy (Thornton 1802), the French continued hoarding gold and silver into the 19th century, even as incomes grew. In 1847, the smallest denomination note of the *Banque de France* was 500 francs, greater than the annual per capita income at the time. The French economy at the end of its take-off period in the mid-19th century had the same bank density as Scotland in the mid-18th century, with fewer bank assets per inhabitant in mid-19th century than England or Scotland had had in 1770, and still lagging in 1870. Bank deposits as a proportion of M1 (the narrow definition of money supply) were 17 per cent in 1880, rising to 44 per cent by 1913, as compared with the United States and the United Kingdom, which had proportions of 88 per cent of M1 by 1913, double the density of bank deposits. Gueslin (1992) calculated that in 1937 bank deposits per capita in France amounted to 1,700 francs, compared with 12,000 francs per inhabitant in the United States and 10,000 francs in the United Kingdom. The overall picture is one of a less-developed banking sector, fewer channels for financial savings, competition of savings banks, and hoarding, which reflected the rural nature of the French economy. Only after 1966 did the banks grow.

In contrast to France, the role of the *Hausbank* in financing and being involved with enterprise governance was prominent in Germany (Edwards and Fischer 1994). Enterprises used their *Hausbank* as a provider of insider finance in Germany. Linked to tight blockholder control, the banks played a large role in developing markets for securities as jobbers on the stock exchange and promoters of securities (Emery 1898 in Franks et al. 2006). They also acquired a large role in controlling proxy voting on behalf of shareholders with their consent, but in practice banks had considerable leeway to vote on their behalf (Franks et al. 2006). Franks et al. argue that much of the legislation gave banks power when there were conflicts of interest between banks and minority investors. This power of the banks can be linked to lack of development of equity markets, absence of independent institutional investors, and absence of dispersed shareholding.

Vitols (2001), however, argues that this view overstates the role of the banks in the bank-based system, that the universal banks were not risk-takers in the investments they backed, and that there was not a total lack of equity markets in Germany. It also understates the pivotal role of state regulation of banking during the 1930s. There was more liberal regulation with a contractual approach in the United States and the United Kingdom based on rules of 'fair play' and non-intervention towards the commercial banks, whereas in Germany there was a more corporatist non-liberal approach that reinforced the position of the banks vis-à-vis markets.

Franks et al. (2006) make the point that dispersed shareownership needs to be backed by institutions of investor protection, or else minority investors stand to lose out to practices by controlling investors or by powerful managers. However, investor protection in Germany had been, if anything, stronger than in Britain in the mid-19th century. For instance, in 1861 shareholders could force an extraordinary general meeting with 10 per cent of the voting equity. But in a number of respects, individual investors were less well protected in Germany: private enforcement rights for individual investors increased in Britain during the 20th century but did not in Germany; there was no information on proxy voting by the banks until 1937; disclosure on compensation and directors' shareholdings was brought in only in 1965; and insider information and trading was made illegal only in the 1990s. German regulation fell well behind that in the United Kingdom, with little protection for minority investors (Franks et al. 2006).

In line with other features of the German state, the corporatist way of protecting small investors was taken. Dual boards, having a supervisory board as well as a management board, were seen as a way of protecting the small shareholder. Regulations in 1884 prohibited directors from having positions on both boards at the same time; information requirements to the supervisory board increased post-1870 and again after 1884. Again, this is the insider route to supervision, with various interests represented within the company structure.

Connecting with the labour side

So where did the employee voice in Germany come from? Why should Germany have created a stronger incorporated labour voice than the older industrial state Britain? McGaughey (2015) argues that the idea of the German corporation as a thing in itself, the *Unternehmen an sich*, meant that no one party had exclusive rights. Rathenau in 1919 argued that as the corporation was due to the concession of the state, so shareholder interests were not omnipotent. The emphasis was on the corporation serving the public interest, and workers counted in that. This fits with the principle behind the company itself laid out by Rathenau in 1919, the idea of it having a social obligation was established, in terms of creating jobs and in this period of nation-building, of serving the needs of the nation-state. This became the *Führerprinzip* of 1937, but it had more benign roots in the earlier period. The 1937 Stock Corporation Act downplays the interests of shareholders; the political climate was stacked against individual investors (Franks et al, 2006). This Act was not revised until 1965.

Codetermination and works councils

Codetermination – the idea that workers had a right to vote for a company board of directors and to participate in works councils – was born out of the ideals of the 1848 revolutions but wasn't implemented until 1918, strengthened by conditions in the immediate aftermath of the First World War when bargaining power of workers was temporarily greater, and due to the unity in the trade union movement in pursuing the objective of workers having a voice in corporate governance. McGaughey stresses the voluntaristic nature of the collective agreements between business and trade unions from 1918 and then again from 1945–51. McGaughey traces the continuity between the Weimar consensus and the post-war reconstruction. During Weimar, the consensus was to have direct participation rather than antagonistic class struggle with unions versus employers, which was the way things were fought over in Britain.

The Bismarck era was both highly paternalistic, caring for social welfare of workers, and highly illiberal. The Krupps family, for example, promoted the economic well-being of their workers – with a bakery, housing and other amenities – but argued trenchantly against workers having a right to participate in decision-making and broke up unionisation and anything else related to social democracy. Bismarck embodied this bifurcation, improving the lot of the workers in terms of pay and working conditions but banning any worker participation in the process as overthrowing the social order. This needs to be seen alongside Bismarck's 1883 and 1884 introduction of sickness insurance and social insurance schemes in Germany, also paternalistic and nonliberal in intent. In the late nineteenth century, collective action was suppressed. Krupp saw his obligations to the workforce in material terms alongside a denial of workers' rights to self-determination (McGaughey, 2015: 16). Krupp's philosophy was captured by Schneider (1963: 233, quoted in McCreary 1968) that he esteemed the personal freedom of his workers so little and their material well-being so highly.

In a speech to the *Reichstag* on May 9 1884, Bismarck gave his vision of social insurance, explicitly anti-socialist and bound up with the protection of the state:

> "Give the working man the right to work as long as he is healthy; assure him care when he is sick; assure him maintenance when he is old...If the State will show a little more Christian solicitude for the working man, then I believe that the gentlemen of the Wyden (Socialist) programme will sound their bird-call in vain and that the thronging to them will cease as soon as working men see the Government and legislative bodies are earnestly concerned for their welfare." (Quoted in Dawson 1890:34–35, in Krueger Princeton University Industrial Relations Section Working Paper 424 1999).

The overarching theme is the nonliberal and corporatist nature of these obligations which links in with the kind of state that Bismarck created – nonliberal in the sense that political liberalism was sacrificed to create market order.

Works councils brought in during the 1890s were voluntary and were present in about ten per cent of German firms with over 20 employees. In 1900 in Bavaria works councils were made mandatory in mining companies with over 20 employees; in 1905 in Prussia they were introduced into firms with over 100 employees. The 1918 Stinnes legislation agreement was a collective agreement. In 1919 Weimar Republic, the right of codetermination and works councils was in the constitution and there was a 1920 Works Council Act. However, just as workforce participation had been a product of post-First-World-War bargaining power in favour of workers, so in the 1930s this was eroded and conflict was suppressed with the Nazi insistence on unity and loyalty. Codetermination was abolished in 1934. Collective *laissez-faire* with independence of the unions from the state and courts was the legacy of the Nazis.

In the post-war reconstruction, there was much continuity with the Weimar themes. The unions were not interested in nationalization but wanted direct participation – socializing power without socializing ownership (McGaughey 2015: 33). Codetermination was again recreated by collective bargaining and not by law. The idea of the social state was reconstituted from the Weimar period. As McGaughey (2015) says, the Weimar principles were not torn up. There was cross-party political agreement on the principle of codetermination. In the 1952 Work Constitution Act on works councils and representatives, agreement was easier to achieve where shareholders' votes were more concentrated, which meant securing the votes of the banks. As for the 1976 Codetermination Act, the banks and corporations argued against it as a violation of the right to property and business freedom. The legitimacy of employee participation on old Weimar themes was established by 1979. There was a battle to hold on to supervisory board rights to determine directors' pay and to keep employees included. The German Corporate Governance Code of 2010 reinforces codetermination. McGaughey (2015) stresses that these rights of codetermination and worker participation through works councils were voluntary and fought for and were not granted from the top downwards. The breakthroughs were achieved – in the aftermath of the First and Second World Wars – when temporarily bargaining power swung in favour of employees. The agreements were collectively bargained rather than sanctioned by law. However, there is continuity between these post-war settlements and the Bismarckian structures of the late 19th century.

It also connects with the production system in Germany, as argued by Iversen and Soskice (2009). German industrialization in the late 19th century, with its local coordination of rural and urban economies, was built on regulated artisan systems of guilds and rural cooperatives. As industrialization shifted from local to national networks, there was a continuation of regulated artisan systems, and labour and capitalists were drawn from many quarters, maintaining their organized roots: from agriculture, entrepreneurs and financiers from the ranks of the *bourgeoisie*, state officialdom, small-scale artisan owners and independent peasant farmers. Production, especially in the south and west of Germany, became based more on skill-intensive product strategies, relying more on skilled labour (than happened in industrialization in Britain) and less on mass production, excepting some areas and industries such as the Ruhrgebiet based on large-scale iron and steel and relatively unskilled labour (Iversen and Soskice 2009: 466; Herrigel 1995: 29). This reliance on skilled labour created an alliance between insider labour, especially in exporting industries, and their management, against the more unskilled, less-exposed, auxiliary labour in non-core manufacturing and service sectors (Carlin and Soskice 2009; Dustmann, Fitzenberger, Schönberg and Spitz-Oener 2014). This dualization of the labour market, with insiders and outsiders, has maintained the coordination between insider employees and employers on which post-war German corporatism has been built (Thelen 2014; Streeck 2005).

French state-brokered labour relations

The French picture of labour relations contrasts in certain respects with the German one. Lorwin (1957) characterizes French industrial relations post-1870 as diverse. The *Confédération générale du travail* expressed support for revolutionary syndicalism in 1895 and adopted the Charter of Amiens in 1906 to promote political action through class struggle. But France was less urban, more self-employed, with a smaller proportion of its population in industry and more small and medium-sized enterprises than Britain, and also than Germany. There is much debate about whether French productivity and growth in the 19th century did or did not lag behind its competitor nations of Germany and Britain (Cameron and Freedeman 1983; Landes 1969; Maddison 1964). However, there has been more pronounced dualization of continental labour markets (than in liberal economies). This is highlighted in the literature about the post-Second-World-War period (Hancké 2001; Rueda 2005; Palier and Thelen 2010), with the state promoting national champions in the core sector, with firms or sectors perceived as non-core left outside coordinating efforts. It can be traced to earlier 20th-century roots. Government protected trade associations through cartels, against competition, enabling the survival of some less-competitive enterprises (Lorwin 1957).

Against this background, there was confrontational class antagonism, with politicized unions and non-progressive employers. Industrial elites and the unions did not look to reform and saw technical change as a menace. There were some political victories for labour accomplished through protective legislation, but the unions were dependent on the state. In the early 20th century, there were government subsidies for local labour bodies and labour-friendly policies by a socialist government in the 1930s. In contrast to Germany, neither employers nor employees self-organized for collective bargaining through employers' associations or unions. Unions were fragmented along ideological lines and decentralized (Lorwin 1957). Unionization peaked in France in 1955 at 20 per cent compared with Germany at 35 per cent in the 1970s (Palier and Thelen 2010). The state organized collective bargaining, and unions relied on strikes or government action to settle conflicts (Palier and Thelen 2010: 125). This is a picture of a more state-centred and centralized economy, with the state coordinating the various fragmented interest groups (Hancké, Rhodes and Thatcher 2007; Goetz, Mair and Smith 2013).

The state's involvement in industrial relations is mirrored in the entwining of state-business elites. One difference between French and German business relations with their respective states has been in the closeness of relations in France between elites both involved in the state administration, coming through the *Grandes Écoles*, and residing at the top of business. German elites in business have kept themselves more distinct from German bureaucracy and are more decentralized, more technically qualified and less entwined with the state administration (Granville, Martorell Cruz and Prevezer 2015).

Concentration of shareownership and the stakeholder model of corporate governance

Alongside these characteristics is the greater weight given to all stakeholders on the continent, including the voice of labour or employees in firms, as opposed to the primacy given to shareholders in the British and US system.

Roe (2003), Iversen and Soskice (2007) and Gourevitch and Shinn (2005) make the argument that concentration of shareholding is aligned with social democracy. The argument is in two parts. The first is that labour participation – summed up by codetermination, works councils, large boards, poor information flow – requires or calls forth blockholder shareholding to counterbalance it; that there was not the demand for stronger equity markets, for more dispersed shareholding, in part because this would have diluted the counterbalancing force of blockholding that was necessary in the presence of codetermination and laws giving rights to labour participation. There would be fears of closer manager-employee coalitions taking up goals that promoted the firm and its employment conditions over those of profit maximization and shareholder interests in the absence of a strong blockholder shareholder countervailing power. The second part is an observation that left-leaning social democratic governments wanting a middle way between unbridled capitalism and statist socialism correlate with blockholder shareholding. More generally, if there were organized interests – both by labour and employers – then this coordination prompted proportional representation in political parties that corresponded to more left-leaning tendencies (were more egalitarian and more redistributive) (Martorell Cruz 2016; Cusack, Iversen and Soskice 2007; Crouch 1993).

In this regard, Germany has consistently had proportional representation in its political system, whereas France has had both proportional representation and majoritarian political parties in the post-war period, despite having much less organization of interests, much lower trade union density than Germany and having more union confederations and no employers' federations in the mid-1920s (Martorell 2016; Visser 2013; Crouch 1993).

The corporatist model of corporate governance encouraged coordination between capital and labour institutions and a state mediating between them. Out of this came two-tier boards of companies, labour representation on boards, reliance on and involvement of the *Hausbank* in business financing and monitoring of management with seats on boards and control of proxy votes, and maintenance of control through private listing and blockholding by families. Alongside this, there have been internally funded pensions, less reliance on external equity markets, and less of a market for corporate control.

Vitols (2001) makes the argument that the different regimes of financing also depended on the nature of labour market regulation and, in particular, the financing of pensions, that the voluntarist system of capitalized and outsider pension funds in the United States and the United Kingdom played a part in developing and relying on securities markets. In Germany, on the other hand, companies set aside funds for their employees' pensions, which have been funded internally by the company rather than through an external pension fund. This created an inter-generational transfer and also bound workers to their corporations more closely, compared with having outsider, independent and capitalized pension funds. Provisions for pensions in German companies were, and are, retained as liabilities on their balance sheet. They involve repayment obligations at a date in the future and are therefore akin to debt. As Schneider-Lenne (1994: 295) points out, they have been seen by the company as a form of social capital, a form of equity contributed by those working for the company involving implicit obligations attached. Vitols (2001) labels this a solidaristic pension system, as it has strengthened common interests in the future of the company for all who work there.

In Germany, this has combined with the differing industrial relations systems, with greater equality of income distribution in Germany than in the liberal regimes in the United States and the United Kingdom. More unequal income distributions in the United States and the United Kingdom contributed to developing securities markets by increasing demand for securities by the rich, and hence individuals' holdings of securities were boosted in the liberal regimes.

Coordination across the reunified German economy has been challenged in the recent liberalizing era, but it has been retained in the core manufacturing and exporting sector to protect its innovativeness, with liberalized auxiliary manufacturing and service sectors (Thelen 2014; et al. 2015; Dustmann et al. 2014; Jackson and Deeg 2012; Jackson and Sorge 2012).

Conclusions

There are some resemblances between French and German property rights. In both countries, they were strengthened for the state through the mix of civil codes and the absence of strong common law courts and remnants of feudal structures. For different reasons, the state was used to standardize property rights, bringing them under centralized administrative sway. In France, this was an assertion of centralized state power against localized nobility and gentry and judicial power. In Germany, this was part of Prussian nation-building extending a more uniform code and legal practice across the disparate states.

In doing so, these states went a different route from Britain in terms of independence of property rights from the state. Whereas under common law (predominant in Britain and the United States) property rights were and are decided in the courts and the power of the judiciary against the state became significant, in France and Germany individual property rights were and are not as robust in the face of a state with stronger practices of eminent domain. This has had implications for the treatment of property rights in corporate structures and the clear tendency on the continent for (family) owners to keep control of companies through keeping them private and with concentrated ownership.

The French and German states are different from each other, however. French centralization of its state administration goes back to 17th-century pre-Revolutionary times of Louis XIV and Colbert. The French state – its *étatisme* and *dirigisme* – can be seen as compensating for the fragmentation and lack of organization of interest groups in the economy. The German state has been less centralized, but was characterized as bureaucratic and governing through law-making rather than through representative government. Economic reform and catch-up were pushed through by a paternalistic pro-active state 'owning', providing and financing key infrastructure – railroads, education, science and technology – in the face of opposition from agrarian Junker interests but in consort with large industrial interests. Post-Second-World-War, this became that mediating state – standard-creating, law-making but not directly organizing business groups which were sufficiently concentrated, cartelized and coordinated between themselves.

A common difference from the British and US liberal states is the greater spectrum of their public spheres: the realm of what was included in the public sector in terms of infrastructure, education, and science and technology was broader. It was more centralized in France, more localized in Germany, but within the public sphere compared with British and US building and funding of canals, railways and education.

These long-term historical institutional roots have shaped their corporate governances distinctly from those of Britain and the United States. The main differences are the following: there is a well-established difference between concentrated blockholder private ownership of companies compared with the more dispersed shareholding of publicly-listed companies, which are strongly intertwined with equity markets in their financing structures. German and French companies have been more reliant on their close relationship with main banks, or on raising equity finance from quasi-insiders – other companies or banks – as opposed to impersonalized outsider markets. This has led to an absence of a corporate takeover market on the continent until fairly recent developments in the opening up of companies to foreign capital. The use of privately-held joint stock companies has been a more prominent and significant organization form for the company, rather than the publicly-listed, openly traded corporation that has held sway in the United States and the United Kingdom from the mid-19th century.

There developed a broader stakeholder focus for companies on the continent, compared with a stronger shareholder primacy with no voice for labour in the United States and the United Kingdom. The roots and form of this stakeholder focus differ between Germany and France. In Germany, the stakeholder focus can be traced back to Bismarckian paternalistic anti-democratic nation-building legislation that brought within the corporate structure responsibility for employee participation and provision of pensions. Codetermination was strengthened during periods of labour's strength (immediately after the First World War and the Second World War) but with an emphasis on bringing consensus through voice inside the firm to quieten revolutionary class confrontation. This mirrors the legal position of the paternalistic state, containing labour's voice within the corporate structure. One can see concentrated blockholding and private control of companies both as a counterpart to this corporatist focus (Roe 2003) and also as a consequence of less democracy in ownership and the need for greater protection from state predation through more closed shareholding structures and from more intrusive state regulation. This contrasts with the liberal system of no labour voice or participation within the corporate structure, but a more generalized individual-ownership and shareholding-based democracy. Minority shareholding was and is more possible in the common-law liberal state regime.

I argued in the previous chapter that shareholder primacy has to be seen in the context of stronger, common-law-backed individual ownership, including ownership of shares which was broader-based (especially in the United States, see Chapter 6). And also that employers – shareholder-managers – were strongly supported through the corporation by common law judicial power. Class struggle in these liberal states occurs on a plane: through a more confrontational workplace struggle through the union movement, but confined to the economic sphere with the liberal state placing itself outside these work-based (industry-focused) struggles. It also occurs on the plane of ownership which happens through regulation. With the involvement of greater numbers and a broader spectrum of individuals in shareownership and with pensions organized through outsider institutions through independent pension funds, the issue of minority shareholder protection becomes salient, protection both from large shareholder-managers and more broadly from state incursions on private ownership. But this is in the context of a liberal state with greater overall protection and independence of private ownership, backed by common law and the judiciary, from state projects.

On the continent, individual shareholding has been less significant, and consequently the protection of tradable shares has been weaker. This goes with greater protection of strategic assets within firms which are less tradable – both the assets and the firms themselves – through being more privately and closely held, through having greater legal obstacles to takeover and less managerial autonomy. The takeover of Mannesmann by Vodafone, as analyzed by Milhaupt and Pistor (2008), highlighted the greater managerial autonomy, assumed by Vodafone but challenged in Mannesmann, over CEO compensation paid on the taking over of the firm. It also exposes the pressures which the more consensual German stakeholder system is subject to through opening up to takeovers by companies with more liberal codes of behaviour. In turn, protection of strategic assets has allowed for and has encouraged investment in co-specific skills, one of the key features and, it is argued, advantages of the coordinated market economy.

References

6, P. (2016) Private correspondence.

Acemoglu, D., Cantoni, D., Johnson, S. and Robinson, J. (2011) 'The Consequences of Radical Reform: The French Revolution', *American Economic Review* 101: 3286–3307.

Allouche, J. and Amann, B. (1995) 'Le retour triumphant du capitalisme familial', in *De Jacques Coeur à Renault: Gestionnaires et organisations*. Toulouse: Presses de l'Université des Sciences Sociales de Toulouse.

Badian, E. (1972) *Publicans and Sinners: Private Enterprise in the Service of the Roman Republic*. Ithaca, NY: Cornell University Press.

Beck, T., Kunt, A.D. and Levine, R. (2002) Law and Finance: Why Does Legal Origin Matter? Working Paper No. 9379. Cambridge: National Bureau of Economic Research.

Berkowitz, D., Pistor, K. and Richard, J.F. (2003) 'Economic Development, Legality, and the Transplant Effect', *European Economic Review* 47(1): 165–195.

Besley, T. and Persson, T. (2009) 'The Origins of State Capacity: Property Rights, Taxation and Politics', *American Economic Review* 99(4): 1218–1244.

Bloch, L. and Kremp, E. (2001) 'Ownership and Voting Power in France', in F. Barca and M. Becht (eds), *The Control of Corporate Europe*, 106–128. New York: Oxford University Press.

Blondel, C., Rowell, N. and Van der Heyden, L. (2002) Prevalence of Patrimonial Firms on Paris Stock Exchange: Analysis of the Top 250 Companies in 1993 and 1998, Working Paper 2002/83/TM. Fontainebleau, France: INSEAD – The Wendel International Centre for Family Enterprise.

Braudel, F. (1983) *Civilization and Capitalism, 15t h – 18th Century, Vol. 2: The Wheels of Commerce*. London: Collins.

Braudel, F. (1984). *Civilization and Capitalism, 15th – 18th Century, Vol. 3: The Perspective of the World*. London: Collins.

Cameron, R. and Freedeman, C. (1983) 'French Economic Growth: A Radical Revision', *Social Science History* 7(1): 3–30.

Cameron, R.E. (1958) 'Economic Growth and Stagnation in France, 1815–1914', *Journal of Modern History* 30(1): 1–13.

Carlin, W. and Soskice, D. (2009) 'German Economic Performance: Disentangling the Role of Supply-Side Reforms, Macroeconomic Policy and Coordinated Economy Institutions', *Socio-Economic Review* 7(1): 67–99.

Chandler, A. (1988) *Essays toward a Historical Theory of Big Business*. Cambridge, MA: Harvard Business School Press.

Chandler, A. (1990) *Scale and Scope: The Dynamics of Industrial Capitalism*. Cambridge, MA: Belknap Press of Harvard University Press.

Churchill, W. (1998 [1956]) *History of the English-Speaking Peoples*. New York: Skyhorse Publishing.

Coffee, J.C. (2000) Convergence and its Critics: What Are the Preconditions to the Separation of Ownership and Control? Columbia Law and Economics Working Paper. Available at: https://papers.ssrn.com/sol3/papers.cfm?abstract_id=241782.

Crouch, C. (1993) *Industrial Relations and European State Traditions*. Oxford: Oxford University Press.

Cusack, T.R., Iversen, T. and Soskice, D. (2007) 'Economic Interests and the Origins of Electoral Systems', *American Political Science Review* 101(3): 373–391.

Dawson, W.H. (1890) *Bismarck and State Socialism*. London: Swan Sonnenschein and Co.

de Tocqueville, A. (1966 [1856]) *The Ancien Regime and the French Revolution*. London: Collins/Fontana.

Dincecco, M. (2009) 'Fiscal Centralization, Limited Government, and Public Revenues in Europe, 1650–1913', *Journal of Economic History* 69(1): 48–103.

Dustmann, C., Fitzenberger, B., Schönberg, U. and Spitz-Oener, A. (2014) 'From Sick Man of Europe to Economic Superstar: Germany's Resurgent Economy', *Journal of Economic Perspectives* 28(1): 167–188.

Edwards, J. and Fischer, K. (1994) *Banks, Finance and Investment in Germany*. Cambridge: Cambridge University Press.

Emery, H.C. (1898) 'The Results of the German Exchange Act of 1896', *Political Science Quarterly* 13(2): 286–320.

Fehrenbach, E. (2008) *Vom Ancien Regime zum Wiener Kongress*. Munich: Oldenbourg.

Fohlin, C. (2005) 'The History of Corporate Ownership and Control in Germany', in *A History of Corporate Governance around the World: Family Business Groups to Professional Managers*, 223–282. Cambridge: National Bureau of Economic Research.

Franks, J., Mayer, C. and Wagner, H. (2006) 'The Origins of the German Corporation – Finance, Ownership and Control', *Review of Finance* 10(4): 537–585.

Fremdling, R. (1983) 'Germany', in P. O'Brien (ed.), *Railways and the Economic Development of Western Europe, 1830–1914*, 121–147. London: Macmillan.

Fremdling, R. and Tilly, R. (1979) *Industrialisierung und Raum. Studien zur regionalen Differenzierung im Deutschland des 19. Jahrhunderts*. Stuttgart: Klett-Cotta.

Gerschenkron, A. (1962) *Economic Backwardness in Historical Perspective*. Cambridge, MA: Harvard University Press.

Glaeser, E. and Shleifer, A. (2002) 'Legal Origins', *Quarterly Journal of Economics* 107(4): 1193–1229.

Goetz, K., Mair, P. and Smith, G. (2013) *European Politics: Pasts, Presents, Futures*. London: Routledge.

Gourevitch, P. and Shinn, J. (2005) *Political Power and Corporate Control: The New Global Politics of Corporate Governance*. Princeton: Princeton University Press.

Granville, B., Martorell Cruz, J. and Prevezer, M. (2015) Elites, Thickets and Institutions: French Resistance versus German Adaptation to Economic Change, 1945–2015, Working Paper No. 63. Queen Mary University of London: Centre for Globalisation Research.

Gueslin, A. (1992) 'Le paternalisme revisite en Europe occidentale (seconde moitié du XIXe début XXe siècle)', *Genèses* 7(1): 201–211.

Guinnane, T., Harris, R., Lamoreaux, N. and Rosenthal, J.L. (2007) Ownership and Control in the Entrepreneurial Firm: An International History of Private Limited Companies, Discussion Paper No. 959. Yale University:Economic Growth Center.

Hancké, B. (2001) 'Revisiting the French Model: Coordination and Restructuring in French Industry', in P. Hall (ed.), *Varieties of Capitalism: The Institutional Foundations of Comparative Advantage*, 307–337. Oxford: Oxford University Press.

Hancké, B., Rhodes, M. and Thatcher, M. (2007) *Beyond Varieties of Capitalism: Conflict, Contradictions and Complementarities in the European Economy.* Oxford: Oxford University Press.

Hannah, L. (2015) 'A Global Census of Corporations in 1910', *Economic History Review* 68(2): 548–573.

Hayek, F.A. (1960) *The Constitution of Liberty.* Chicago: University of Chicago Press.

Herrigel, G. (1995) *Industrial Constructions: The Sources of German Industrial Power.* Cambridge: Cambridge University Press.

Herrigel, G. (2006) 'Corporate Governance: History without Historians', in G. Jones and J. Zeitlin (eds), *Handbook of Business History.* Oxford: Oxford University Press.

Hobson, J. and Weiss, L. (1995) *States and Economic Development: A Comparative Historical Analysis.* Cambridge: Polity Press.

Iversen, T. and Soskice, D. (2007) 'Two Paths to Democracy', Cambridge, MA: Harvard University Center for European Studies.

Iversen, T. and Soskice, D. (2009) 'Distribution and Redistribution: The Shadow of the Nineteenth Century', *World Politics* 61(3): 438–486.

Jackson, G. and Deeg, R. (2012) 'The Long-Term Trajectories of Institutional Change in European Capitalism', *Journal of European Public Policy* 19(8): 1109–1125.

Jackson, G. and Sorge, A. (2012) 'The Trajectory of Institutional Change in Germany, 1979–2009', *Journal of European Public Policy* 19(8): 1146–1167.

Kindleberger, C. (1984) *A Financial History of Western Europe.* London: Allen and Unwin.

Kopsidis, M. and Bromley, D.W. (2014) The French Revolution and German Industrialization: The New Institutional Economics Rewrites History, Discussion Paper No. 149. Halle:Leibniz Institute of Agricultural Development in Transition Economies.

Koselleck, R. (1967) *Preussen zwischen Reform und Revolution. Allgemeines Landrecht, Verwarltung und soziale Bewegung von 1791–1848.* Stuttgart: Klett-Cotta.

Krueger, A. (2000) 'From Bismarck to Maastrict: The March to European Union and the Labor Compact', *Labour Economics* 7(2): 117–134.

Lamoreaux, N. and Rosenthal, J.L. (2005) 'Legal Regime and Contractual Flexibility: A Comparison of Business's Organizational Choices in France and the United States during the Era of Industrialization', *American Law and Economic Review* 7(1): 28–61.

Landes, D. (1969) *The Unbound Prometheus: Technological Change and Industrial Development in Western Europe from 1750 to the Present.* Cambridge: Cambridge University Press.

Landes, D. (1998) *The Wealth and Poverty of Nations: Why Some Are so Rich and Some so Poor*: London: Abacus.

La Porta, R., Lopez-de-Silanes, F., Shleifer, A. and Vishny, R. (1998) 'Law and Finance', *Journal of Political Economy* 106(6): 1113–1155.

La Porta, R., Lopez-de-Silanes, F., Shleifer, A. and Vishny, R. (2000) 'Investor Protection and Corporate Governance', *Journal of Financial Economics* 58(1–2): 3–27.

Lazonick, W. and O'Sullivan, M. (1997) 'Finance and Industrial Development Part II: Japan and Germany', *Financial History Review* 4(2): 117–138.

Levine, R. (2005) 'Law Endowments and Property Rights', *Journal of Economic Perspectives* 19(3): 61–88.

Levy-Leboyer, M. (1980) 'The Large Corporation in Modern France', in A.D. Chandler and H. Daems (eds), *Managerial Hierarchies: Comparative Perspectives on the Rise of the Modern Industrial Enterprise*, 117–160. Cambridge, MA: Harvard University Press.

Lorwin, V. (1957) 'Reflections on the History of the French and American Labor Movements', *Journal of Economic History* 17(1): 25–44.

Maddison, A. (1964) *Economic Growth in the West: Comparative Experience in Europe and North America*. London: Allen and Unwin.

Mahoney, P. (2001) 'The Common Law and Economic Growth: Hayek Might be Right', *Journal of Legal Studies* 30(2): 503–525.

Mann, M. (1993) *The Sources of Social Power, Vol. 2: The Rise of Classes and Nation-States, 1760–1914*. Cambridge: Cambridge University Press.

Mann, M. (2012) *The Sources of Social Power, Vol. 3: Global Empires and Revolution, 1890–1945*. Cambridge: Cambridge University Press.

Martorell Cruz, J. (2016) *One Money, Multiple Institutions: Capitalist Diversity under the Euro-Zone*. Unpublished PhD Thesis, Queen Mary University of London.

McCreary, E.C. (1968) 'Social Welfare and Business: The Krupp Welfare Program, 1860–1914', *Business History Review* 42(1): 24–49.

McGaughey, E. (2015) The Codetermination Bargains: The History of German Corporate and Labour Law, Law, Society and Economy Working Paper. London School of Economics: Law Department.

Milhaupt, C.J. and Pistor, K. (2008) *Law and Capitalism: What Corporate Crises Reveal about Legal Systems and Economic Development around the World*. Chicago: University of Chicago Press.

Murphy, A. (2005) 'Corporate Ownership in France: The Importance of History', in R. Morck (ed.), *A History of Corporate Governance around the World*, 225–238. Chicago: University of Chicago Press.

North, D., Wallis, J.J. and Weingast, B. (2009) *Violence and Social Orders: A Conceptual Framework for Interpreting Recorded Human History*. Cambridge: Cambridge University Press.

O'Brien, P. (2011) 'The Nature and Historical Evolution of an Exceptional Fiscal State and its Possible Significance for the Precocious Commercialization and Industrialization of the British Economy from Cromwell to Nelson', *Economic History Review* 64(2): 408–446.

Palier, B. and Thelen, K. (2010) 'Institutionalizing Dualism: Complementarities and Change in France and Germany', *Politics and Society* 38(1): 119–148.

Piketty, T. (2014) *Capital in the Twenty-First Century*. Cambridge, MA: Belknap Press of Harvard University Press.

Pollard, S. (1985) 'Capital Exports: Harmful or Beneficial?' *Economic History Review* 38(4): 489–514.

Posner, R. (1973) *Economic Analysis of Law*. 6th Edition. New York: Aspen Publishers.

Priest, G.L. (1977) 'The Common Law Process and the Selection of Efficient Rules', *Journal of Legal Studies* 6(1): 65–82.

Rathenau, W. (1919) *The New Society.* Translated by A. Windham. New York: Harcourt Brace and Co.

Roe, M. (2003) *Political Determinants of Corporate Governance.* Oxford: Oxford University Press.

Rosenthal, J.L. (1992) *The Fruits of Revolution: Property Rights, Litigation and French Agriculture, 1700–1860.* Cambridge: Cambridge University Press.

Rubin, P.H. (1977) 'Why Is the Common Law Efficient?' *Journal of Legal Studies* 6(1): 51–63.

Rueda, D. (2005) 'Insider-Outsider Politics in Industrialized Democracies: The Challenge to Social Democratic Parties', *American Political Science Review* 99(1): 61–74.

Schneider, W. (1963) *Essen: Das Abenteur einer Stadt.* Düsseldorf: ECON.

Schneider-Lenne, E. (1994) 'The Role of the German Capital Markets and the Universal Banks, Supervisory Boards, and Interlocking Directorship', in N. Dimsdale and M. Prevezer (eds), *Capital Markets and Corporate Governance*, 284–305. Oxford: Oxford University Press.

Sombart, W. (1954) *Die deutsche Volkswirtschaft im neunzehnten Jahrhundert.* Berlin: Georg Bondi.

Sraer, D. and Thesmar, D. (2007) 'Performance and Behavior of Family Firms: Evidence from the French Stock Market', *Journal of the European Economic Association* 5(4): 709–751.

Streeck, W. (2005) *Beyond Continuity: Institutional Change in Advanced Political Economies.* Oxford: Oxford University Press.

Thelen, K. (2014) *Varieties of Liberalization and the New Politics of Social Solidarity.* Cambridge: Cambridge University Press.

Thornton, H. (1965 [1802]) *Enquiry into the Nature and Effects of Paper Credit of Great Britain.* New York: A.M. Kelley.

Tilly, C. (1992) *Coercion, Capital and European States.* Cambridge: Blackwell.

Visser, J. (2013) Wage Bargaining Institutions – From Crisis to Crisis, European Economy Economic Papers No. 488. Brussels: European Commission.

Vitols, S. (2001) The Origins of Bank-Based and Market-Based Financial Systems: Germany, Japan and the United States, Discussion Paper FS 01–302. Berlin: Wissenschaftszentrum Berlin fur Sozialforschung.

Vogel, B. (1988) 'Beamtenliberalismus in der Napoleonischen Ara', in D. Langewiesche (ed.), *Liberalismus im 19. Jahrhundert, Deutschland im europeischen Vergleich*, 11–63. Gottingen: Vandenhoeck und Ruprecht.

Young, A. (2012 [1792]) *Travels in France during the Years 1787, 1788, 1789.* Edited by M. Betham-Edwards, Cambridge: Cambridge Library Collection.

6 The United States compared with Britain

Introduction

Far from representing the norm or benchmark in terms of institutions that Acemoglu and Robinson's (2012) *Why Nations Fail* would have us believe, the United States is exceptional in two main senses: its black-white segregation; and its shareholder capitalism that created dispersed shareholding of large corporations from the early 20th century.

Dispersed shareholding is linked to what has become known as shareholder primacy: putting the rights of the shareholder of the corporation in prime position above those of other stakeholders. Shareholder primacy is a key feature of the 'outsider' model of corporate governance, where outside shareholders and equity markets play a large role in the governance of companies. This contrasts with the 'insider model' associated with the continental European coordinated market economies, where other stakeholders such as employees, banks, suppliers, and customers of the company are taken into consideration in a company's governance.

One of the peculiarities of the United States is the transformation of the shareholder from an insider status, where shareholders were the active participants in how the firm was run, to an outsider status that is put forward in comparative corporate governance or varieties of capitalism literatures. This is a story about the shift in the early decades of the 20th century towards dispersed shareholding and comparatively mass shareholding by the late 1920s, which both distanced individual shareholders from the firms whose shares they held and created calls by the 1930s for their greater protection, both from managerial independence and from potential takeover raiders of companies. In this US framework, the other stakeholders – employees, suppliers, banks – were thought of as the outsiders to the firm. One aim of this chapter is to understand how this shift in status of shareholder happened, how shareholder primacy was constructed as a motivation, and how this relates to the United States' primary institutions of individual property rights, its constitutional set-up of separated powers in a confederation of states, its common law system, and judicial powers. Another is to relate it to the meso-institutions of the corporation as a legal entity with the backing of the judicial system, and the weak status of labour in the firm.

One cannot talk about US institutions and its capitalism without addressing what appears to be a central paradox: how the most formally egalitarian and liberal democracy, with democracy and equality enshrined in its constitution, applied this only to white men as citizens and not to non-white races. Tocqueville (1848) was impressed by the United States' democracy and equality. But this democracy has to be squared with its exclusion from citizenship of African Americans, Native Americans, and women. How are the seemingly separate issues of racial segregation and shareholder primacy connected? And how can they be traced back into the country's institutional origins? How did the United States evolve into the most liberal, shareholder-dominated and yet segregated of capitalisms?

First, I stress the centrality of slavery as property from the start of the United States, as a motivation for independence from Britain, where the abolition movement was gaining strength. Slavery was accepted as normal in both northern and southern states and, from the 18th century formed the backbone of the plantation economy. This intersected with the importance of private property rights, brought over from England, and particularly markets in property, tradable property. I bring these two arguments together in discussing the nature of relations between capital and labour. A story of a continued legacy of racial and regional segregation has intersected with shareholder capitalism, dividing the labour class both racially and geographically.

Labour in the United States was more fragmented and weaker than in continental Europe and Britain for a number of reasons; and capital was stronger. This led to labour markets being even more pro-employer than in Britain. This was combined with more employer violence, with its use by private companies (e.g., Pinkertons and Baldwin-Felts) to break strikes. The story also combines the lack of working class unity, in part due to racial segregation and differing regional interests, in part due to white male democracy coming relatively early and with no class-based political party forming to defend workers' rights.

There are four main themes to this chapter. The first is the interrelation between the evolution of individual property rights and the decentralized and contestable common law legal system. This is intertwined with the importance of judicial over administrative power, especially compared with the power of centralized state administration in continental Europe (see Chapter 5) and a 'thick' kind of rule of law bolstered by concepts of individual liberty and protection of property. These features in turn are intertwined with the nature of the state, with its separation of powers between the federal state, strongly expansionary in foreign affairs, and individual states with sovereignty over domestic affairs. This was combined with a strong power of the Supreme Court and law-making through Supreme Court decisions, both somewhat independent of and constraining the federal state and bridging relations between federal government and states. This is highly significant in underpinning individual property rights and the workings of the decentralized and powerful legal system.

The second theme is the nature of the state, which is about the balance between the individual states and the federal state, between localized power in the states responsible for much local infrastructure and administration, but with centralized power of the federal state strong in regard to 'foreign' policy, namely expansion across the North American continent during the 19th century. In the 1840s, there was a shift from states having greater power, and being 'energetic and improving' towards the federal state becoming more important and being more *laissez- faire* in the domestic economic realm. In part, this is attributable to the growth in federal fiscal capacity, which financed the expansion territorially of the United States and bailed out insolvent states, and in part the stance and role of the state became more liberal with the expansion of equity and government bond markets and the use of private capital and enterprise for financing and running infrastructure, such as the railroads, with much other government being done at the local level, as it had always been done.

Intertwined with these origins, however, are two distinctive features of US capitalism: the importance of race in shaping US institutions from the start through slavery and the protection of the plantation economy from the War of Independence through exclusion from citizenship and continued segregation into the second half of the 20th century and continued discrimination in rights. There are ample data reflecting the current relative poverty and morbidity of black America compared with white America (The Economist 2015).[1] I outline the regional and racial segregation of ownership of assets at the end of the 18th century, based on slavery and large plantations in the southern states and on smallholdings in the northern states, from Piketty's (2014) data and argue that these legacies have shaped US capitalism. In turn, race has been important in shaping relations between capital and labour, dividing the labour movement and allowing capital – in the form of corporations – a stronger voice.

The fourth theme, which the US shares with Britain to some extent but represents to a greater extent, is the importance of mass shareholding in corporations that formed the basis in both countries of the type of shareholder capitalism (as distinct from stakeholder capitalism) that distinguishes the liberal market economy from the coordinated one. The dispersion of shareholding in the early decades of the 20th century down to ownership by middling sorts of people established a constituency of owners whose rights required protection. In turn, the raising of capital via selling equity was in part a function of the early development of localized capital markets, in government bonds and raising share capital, as in Britain, from local networks of people. Aligned with this has been the importance of the corporation as an organizational form, with the status of a legal person, backed by Supreme Court decisions and independent of the state. The corporation and shareholding activities were and have remained less regulated by the state relative to more restricted banking. This shareholder democracy, largely outside the constraints of the state, with shareholders originally considered as the 'insider' controllers of the corporation shifted some time in the early decades of the 20th century to become the outsider model, with shareholders separated from (professionalized) management, who were coming to control the large corporation.

The conclusions of this chapter emphasize the importance of property rights in tradable capital, protected through the courts and by regulation upholding minority shareholder rights, which stemmed from the growth of securities markets in the 19th century and mass participation in those markets in the early 20th century. The counterpart to this emphasis on markets and tradable assets is the counterbalancing of institutions constraining the state, CCIs, to the spread of CEIs, contract-enforcing institutions underpinning markets. Greater constraints on the state took the form of a larger private sector and smaller centralized state over domestic policy, much less constrained over foreign policy. In all the chapters, I highlight the different types of property rights that are being protected and the different balances between CEIs and CCIs – between liberal economies, coordinated economies and state-dominated capitalist economies. In these liberal economies, such as the United States, the development of institutions that constrain the state, such as the 'adversarial' legal system (Kagan 2001), the role and independence of the courts and judiciary, are more heightened than in coordinated economies and state-dominated developing/transition economies. This is in line with a boundary between private (non-state) and state that enhances the non-state sector.

I am not an expert at all in any of these fields, that is, in the history of slavery, in American civil rights, or in American corporate governance. What this chapter sets out to do is to make some connections between the outlines of these stories and in doing so to draw out some comparisons between the United States and United Kingdom in terms of what the former drew from the latter, but also in terms of how it differed from the United Kingdom and, more conventionally, what both those liberal market economies drew from their institutional histories in distinguishing them from the continental European countries in the previous chapter. In doing so, I want to draw attention to the much greater nuance that is required if one is to argue, as do Acemoglu and Robinson (2012) building on a host of mainstream institutional economics work, that US institutions form the norm and benchmark against which to judge other, mainly developing, countries' institutions. It also sets the scene for some comparison between customary property rights in the United States colonies and their evolution into formal common law property rights and the path of property rights evolution in Tanzania in the following chapter from colonial and customary rights into state-vested rights. It enables also a comparison between the nature of state power and state capacity and constraints on that capacity, which forms a central part of the story in Sub-Saharan African states from the late 20th century, as it does in that of the United States in the 19th and 20th centuries.

This chapter is organized as follows: after this Introduction, the next section looks at primary institutions of property rights and the common law heritage and legal system, and then looks at the nature of the state, meaning particularly the post-Revolution constitution, separation of power between federal and state power, and evolution towards the liberal state. Then I move onto connecting with meso-institutions on the nature of the corporation, its legal status as property-owner, its backing by the courts, and into the balance of power between capital (corporations backed by law) and labour (unincorporated and seen as a collective force and therefore illegal), as well as the evolution of shareholder primacy out of shareholder democracy rather than any sort of stakeholder stance.

Primary institutions: Property rights and the legal system

Let us go back to the beginning of US institutions (Hughes 1977). In terms of property rights, one can distinguish two routes into formal private property rights: through colonization and the chartering of corporations and the issuing of land rights that were private, capitalistic in the sense of being tradable, and protected by law; and the extra-legal route of gradual conversion of squatting, informal occupation into formal private property rights, especially as the United States expanded westwards (de Soto 2000). This second route can be linked to the aggressive expansion of the United States – by war, by purchase, by treaty – that was intent on ousting previous occupiers of the land and remaking 'unsettled' territories into freehold farms (Edling 2014: 8).

Hughes (1977) stresses that formal institutions were capitalistic from the outset and that these initial institutions go some way in defining the nature of US capitalism. As outlined in greater detail in Chapter 2, Douglas (1986) argues for a two-way shaping between institutions and individuals' thinking in a society: that institutions shape and legitimize the structures that individuals recognize and that in turn individuals' thinking creates those institutions. As Tocqueville, writing in 1848 in *Democracy in America*, says, when you look back at a person or a country's history, you can see the characteristics there from the outset.[2] The United States inherited from Britain a liberal ideology of possessive individualism, emphasizing the importance of property and individualism and their protection from others in civil society and from the state.

Route 1 to formal private property rights: Colonization

Private property rights were bound up with colonization. Two significant features of this colonization stand out: the corporate form was often used for colonization, highlighting the centrality of the corporation in US capitalism, and formal white and Christian private property rights displaced American Indian land rights, which did not transition into individual private property rights.

In terms of ownership of the land, the colonists were considered English subjects and the colonies were considered English land. King James' Charter of 1606 said of colonists going to Virginia that they 'shall have and enjoy all

Liberties, Franchises and Immunities, within any of our other Dominions… as if they had been abiding and born, within this our Realm of England' (Hughes and Cain 2011: 12). Conquest of non-Christian non-white occupiers of land was considered a legitimate transfer of ownership to white Christians. If no non-Christian owner was identified, then discovery conferred ownership.

Colonization was done as a private venture through companies, and shares were bought in those companies that conferred ownership rights on the land colonized. This varied between colonies. For Virginia and Plymouth, land rights were given on a per share basis. In Virginia, large blocks of land were also granted for subscriptions in cash, without full membership of the company. Headright grants of land were given to each man, woman and child crossing the ocean as an incentive to entice people in and land to be settled.

Formal American tenure was of 'free and common socage' or fee simple that was inherited from England. This form of tenure was perpetual, not limited in time, directly heritable by will, all obligations on it were fixed and certain and the land was alienable, could be sold by the owner; and the owner had rights to minerals, timber, water, oil or other resources on or under the land. There were fixed rents payable to the donor, which became known as quit rents, which evolved into local property taxes (Hughes and Cain 2011). American land was a commodity; there were active markets in land from the start; and there was speculation in land. Most of the exploitation of coal, oil, iron and minerals was done by private owners when industrialization took off. The commercial intentions were there from the beginning; for instance, the granting of the colony to the Virginia Company in 1606 was done through a patent, as was done for other commercial companies like the East India Company, settling a site that would serve as a trading post. As Hughes and Cain (2011: 14) say: 'Colonial land ownership contained the seeds of the American capitalism that was to come'.

The Massachusetts Bay Company is an example of a company-based, commercially oriented settlement. In the early 1620s, a group of Puritan refugees were granted a patent by the Council for New England; this folded and was re-formed as the New England Company, which got a Royal Charter on the land between the Merimac and Charles Rivers and changed its name to the Massachusetts Bay Company in New England. It was the company that ruled – it had 'full and absolute power and authority to correct, punish, pardon and rule' over all English subjects within its jurisdiction. The company stood in the role of the state, as the Charter stipulated that it had to protect the colonists from any invaders. These Puritans wanted to establish a Church and commonwealth on Calvinist principles, tying together religion and state. The colony of Maryland established by Lord Baltimore in 1634 was set up as a safe haven for Catholics (Hughes and Cain 2011: 14). There was also purchase of land from the colonial governments. For instance, William Penn in Pennsylvania had a grant of 47 million acres and tried to sell most of it. This practice of land sales for cash was extended to other colonies.

The legal status of the various colonies needs to be seen in the context of the wider British empire: 'Whenever a new colony or conquest was added to the expanding empire, its particular constitutional status had to be determined – or relitigated, decades later. Newfoundland was not deemed a legal settlement, but a mere fishing outpost…South Carolina, Pennsylvania and Maryland were granted to private proprietors under charters that…gave the lords proprietary a wide ambit in organizing and governing the new colonies….Overall, the legal result was that the empire was a constitutional and administrative patchwork, under which the applicability of common law or British statutes and the prospect of conciliar review were highly irregular and often unclear – as contemporaries saw'(Bush 1993: 462–463). Amar (2006: 41) stresses how very different the various colonial settlements were; comparing Virginia and New England, there were 'diverse weather zones, sects, labour systems and local temperaments'. The federalist aim of creating a *united* states was far-reaching.

Route 2: Extra-legal squatting rights into formal private property rights

The practice of settling lands and then claiming ownership built up from the third quarter of the 18th century, when there was movement into the empty lands westward. These were squatter settlements of people who had cleared land and then claimed ownership. These rights were resisted by government in New England but not in the middle and south colonies.

De Soto (2000) describes the extra-legal squatter rights of new settlers, such as the miners' rights following the California gold rush of the 19th century. His argument is that gradually, during the 19th century, the extra-legal property rights of settlers, which operated through claims' groups with their own courts and which solved complex disputes over property rights, were incorporated into a formal legal system. The great achievement of the United States was, according to de Soto, the creation of meta-rights – the rights to legal property rights.

De Soto (2000: 99) argues that formal English property law was not suited to handle cases of land with uncertain title, leading to 'open trials of title in the county courts', where all parties could testify and the court decided. There was much variation and extra-legality, far away from England, for instance in surveying. De Soto talks about squatting – occupying land without a title, which the local governments tried to prevent, and tomahawk rights, cabin rights and corn rights, which were names for various extra-legal social-contract-based property rights (de Soto 2000: 100–104). De Soto argues that the key breakthrough in formalizing and making property rights adaptable to capitalist development was the doctrine of pre-emption, that those who settled on and improved their land acquired the legal right to buy it.

In 1784, the Northwest Ordinance gave the Northwest Territory the same rights and privileges as the original 13 states. The federal government tried to sell these lands, but at such high prices that migrants could not afford them; there was much squatting and extra-legal settlement (De Soto 2000: 110). The government raised revenue by issuing land scrip to soldiers – paper redeemable in land – giving rise to a market in land scrip. The government also gave land for the railroad, either to private companies or to states. With the Louisiana Purchase (1803), the United States was extended by 500 million acres, with the Florida Purchase (1819) by 43 million acres, the Gadsden Purchase (1853) by 19,000 acres, and the defeat of Mexico (1848) by 334 million acres.

By the 1820s, there was an array of property rights: extra-legal squatting mixed with legal. In the first half of the 19th century, there was a raft of occupancy laws recognizing rights to land if improvements had been made to them (de Soto 2000: 115–116). The backlash against the Supreme Court decision Green v Biddle in 1821, which had declared Kentucky's occupancy law illegal, illustrates the pressure that the legal system was under from mass immigration to accommodate extra-legally acquired rights. Green v Biddle, and another Supreme Court decision like it, were overturned, and the tide turned and came to recognize and legitimate occupancy and improvement. As the United States extended westwards, new states adopted occupancy laws; this was recognized by a pre-emption law in 1830 which was consolidated during the 1830s (de Soto 2000: 120–121). De Soto also talks about claim associations and miners' organizations as extra-legal groupings that came together to defend their property rights in the Midwest and California according to their own drafted rules and constitutions. These were eventually recognized and legitimated by Congress in the 1860s. De Soto (2000: 95) says that the Homestead Act of 1862 allowing settlers 160 acres of free land was legalizing a *fait accompli*, that Americans had been settling and improving their lands outside the law for decades.

Edling (2014) puts a different slant on this expansion. There was a lot of rhetoric claiming the Republic as peaceful, coming from Thomas Jefferson, Andrew Jackson and Henry Adams. But this was not what the neighbours in Mexico or Canada felt: 'Its rise to greatness was due not to liberal institutions and enterprise but its use of state-sanctioned and state-directed aggression and violence' (Edling 2014: 4). The federal state was neither peaceful nor weak in foreign affairs. It fought three major wars in the early 19th century, including the Civil War, and between 1783 and 1867 expanded from an area of 820,000 square miles to 3,400,000 square miles – by war, purchase and negotiation underpinned by threats of violence. With the American Indians, there were over 300 treaties regulating land cessions (Edling 2014: 8), clearing the land and pushing them westward, removing them from agricultural land and eventually putting them on reservations. Edling paints the picture that the United States had the objective of occupying the whole continent from the outset. Without it, it would have been a country shaped like Chile, confined to the eastern seaboard and one of many nations on the continent, which would have included British, French, Russian, as well as Native American lands – a model not unlike Europe with its continuous wars and rebalancing of powers. Instead, the conversion of extra-legal to legal property rights can be seen as part of this imperial expansion of the 19th century, concerned to convert white settler land rights into American freehold. Mann (2012: 59) considers the settlement of the American continent by white settlers an imperialism that constructed a racial hierarchy that has endured to the present: 'civilized whites on top, then decadent Latinos, then primitive African Americans, then savage Native Americans'.

In part, this is important for the comparisons in Part III, with Tanzania and China. Rather than seeing customary, extra-legal property rights as something relating only to African countries or post-communist countries in their movement to create capitalist institutions, this argument brings out the commonalities between political imperatives behind the creation of legal property rights in early US settlements and the political nature of land rights in Tanzania and China, with extra-legality defined as not having political backing through their legal systems (Chapters 7 and 8). The United States did not seamlessly create capitalist property rights. One distinction though between the expanding United States of the 18th and 19th centuries and 21st-century developing transitioning countries is that the United States was more of a legal wilderness, reliant on social contracts between smaller groups, than are Sub-Saharan African countries in the 21st century.

Tocqueville (1848: 52–54) has an interesting section in *Democracy in America* on the influence of laws of inheritance, of land in particular, in which he contrasts the influence of primogeniture (such as in England), where estates were kept intact and pride and attachment to that estate were strong, with inheritance laws that ordained equal shares, as in parts of the United States. Through breaking up landed estates, the building up of fortunes became detached from the land and hastened investments in company ventures, and it prompted sons of wealthy landowners to go into trade, the law, medicine and further dissolved hereditary rankings in that society. He comments on how great the appetite for money-making was in the United States and how this also increased social mobility: 'Most rich men began by being poor' (Tocqueville 1848: 55) and how rapidly fortunes waxed and waned. One can associate this with the development of financial markets and entrepreneurship, which became signatures of American capitalism.

The peculiar institution: Slaves as assets

Capitalists saw slaves as assets, very valuable ones. The slave economy was entrenched from the start, especially on southern plantations, linked to the English slave trade. The trading of slaves was a very well-established business. Between 1492 and 1820, five times as many Africans went to the New World as did white Europeans. The discovery of America and its settlements led to a resurgence in the slave trade (Thomas 1997: 794).

This was a land where labour was scarce and which developed in the south plantation agriculture in tobacco and subsequently in cotton. Labour shortage or scarcity, apparent from the start in US economic history, combined with abundance of land should, according to economic rationales, have given greater power to labour rights over capital. But this ignores the history and politics of the southern states particularly. The decentralized power of the state (see below) increased the power of employers, and they had a freer hand in their use of violence than in a more centralized state. It was at such times of labour shortage that the push for slavery and indentured labour increased. Tocqueville (1848: 35) distinguished between the north and south, with the southern settlements like the one in Virginia introducing slavery as soon as the colony was established (Tocqueville 1969: 35), which distinguished its character from the New England settlements.

Likewise, in the political set-up: in the Proclamation of the Rights of Man, there is an insistence on carrying over English freedom and common law alongside the legality of slaveholding. Bush (1993) talks about the strange silence on the question of slave law in the colonies. Whereas common law had been carried over for the most part from England to the colonies, in the question of slaves as property there was almost no case law under common law on this. He explains the silence and lack of a body of slave law as the colonial adoption of prerogative law answerable to the Crown, which had been abolished in England but was convenient to adapt and use in the colonies. It was convenient because by the mid-17th century plantation labour was central in the Caribbean and Chesapeake colonies for cotton, tobacco and sugar, and this allowed the law under which slaves were treated to be a matter of private law rather than public common law. A doctrine of prerogative governance allowed plantation owners to retain local customs like slavery: ‘With its origins in local custom, its legal authorization based on an autonomous status within the Empire, and its supporting doctrines in the patchwork of received common law, an incomplete colonial American slave law could serve the needs of slaveowners’ (Bush 1993: 51). Horne’s *The Counter-Revolution of 1776* and Hadden’s *Slave Patrols: Law and Violence in Virginia and the Carolinas* both argue that fear of abolition was one of the motivations for independence, so that the United States would be able to protect and continue its slave-based economy in the southern states. The northern states were implicated too, as Jefferson (1785) said in talking about the Declaration of Independence, that ‘our northern brethren also I believe felt a little tender under those censures; for tho’ their people have very few slaves themselves, yet they had been pretty considerable carriers of them to others’.

Property rights in labour were legal. There are various decisions that demonstrate that African Americans could not formally be considered citizens and could be held as slaves. An early 18th-century dictum of Chief Justice Holt was: ‘Negroes are merchandise and hence within the Navigation Acts’ (Hughes 2014; Cobb 1858). As Frederick Douglass said in Rochester, New York, on July 4 1852, ‘This Fourth of July is yours, not mine. You may rejoice, I must mourn’ (Joyce 2016).

The infamous Dred Scott v John Sandford decision of 1857, a Supreme Court decision, reinforced the notions of slaves as property and of former slaves as non-citizens. It states: ‘A free negro of the African race, whose ancestors were brought to this country and sold as slaves, is not a "citizen" within the meaning of the Constitution of the United States'. The upshot of that decision was that the Missouri Compromise, of Congress banning slavery in lands that were not part of the United States territory in 1787, was made unconstitutional. So the federal government could not free slaves brought into federal territories. This is a landmark decision, as African Americans, whether slaves or free, could not be American citizens. It argues for the moral lawfulness of treating these people as property and holding them as slaves (Scott 2016).

Post-Civil-War, segregation replaced slavery in the progressive era with Jim Crow laws enforcing segregation in southern states. The Plessy v Ferguson decision of 1896 legalized racial segregation and the concept 'separate but equal'. And a connection was made in 1992 by Justice Scalia between the Dred Scott decision and Roe v Wade, who argued that they both rested on substantive due process in the Supreme Court. As Dread Scott (2016) says, slavery's 'horror and brutality...was as commonplace and natural then as ten per cent of young Black men imprisoned is to many people now'. Even after the Civil Rights Movement 100 years later, current economic data for black America can be linked with the shortfall in political rights highlighted in the *Black Lives Matter* campaign deriving from this legacy of no institutional rights for African Americans.

Slavery in the southern colonies was the bedrock of plantation agriculture and large-scale landholding. Common law primogeniture in the south gave rise to much larger landholdings than in the northern states. In the middle colonies and New England, there was equal division with double portion for the eldest son, and daughters received shares equal to younger sons. The southern colonies had higher percentages of black slaves in their populations in 1770: 45 per cent in Georgia, 60 per cent in South Carolina, 42 per cent in Maryland compared with 1 per cent in New Hampshire and 2 per cent in Massachusetts (Hughes and Cain 2011: 34). European immigrants went to northern and middle colonies, avoiding the south.

According to Piketty (2014: 159), the number of slaves increased from 400,000 in the 1770s to 1 million in the 1800 census. This number quadrupled to 4 million by 1860. In 1800, slaves formed 20 per cent of the US population: 1 million out of 5 million; in the south, this proportion was 40 per cent: 1 million slaves to 1.5 million whites. This proportion remained at 40 per cent in 1860 with 4 million slaves to 6 million whites. Piketty (2014: 161) stresses the importance of slaves as assets in southern wealth, which was more concentrated and unequal than in the north. Piketty estimates the value of slave capital in the period 1770–1810 at one-and-a-half years of national income. The market price of a slave in the antebellum United States was 10 to 12 times a free worker's wage. Piketty gives the average price of a male slave in 1860 at $2000, with the average wage of a free farm labourer at $200. The price of individual slaves varied widely (Piketty 2014: 162).

The point I wish to make is that slavery and the slave economy were entrenched from the time of the early settlements, that they were embodied in the constitution, in the systems of representation, and that respect for due process of law through the Supreme Court and for property rights was paramount. Madison argued that 'no power is given to the general government to interpose with respect to property in slaves now held by the states' (Amar 2006: 113). The federal government lacked such authority to alter property rights, or so the argument went. This is significant in the argument that liberal states were constrained when it came to powers of interference in property rights.

Mann (2012) makes the point that slavery and the treatment of non-whites as inferior was not exceptional to the United States. European colonizations did the same, and civil rights movements in the United States coincided with the end of European colonies in the 1960s. The big difference was that in the United States this was a domestic issue, whereas slavery and colonization was an imperial issue for European countries.

Mann (2012) argues that the century 1783–1883 can be seen as one of continental empire within the North American continent. The extension of the Republic to the Pacific coast was the intention of the founders (Dunbar-Ortiz 2014). It is germane to this institutional argument because one of the chief planks of the Acemoglu camp is arguing that the difference between the North American and other Anglo colonies is that the colonizers 'settled' and stayed in the areas and constructed 'good institutions', whereas those colonizations which were inhospitable (in Latin America and African countries) and where the northern Europeans did not or could not settle instead plundered and extracted rather than creating institutions: 'Historical and econometric evidence suggests that European colonialism caused an institutional reversal: European colonialism led to the development of institutions of private property in previously poor areas while introducing extractive institutions or maintaining extractive institutions in previously prosperous places' (Acemoglu, Johnson and Robinson 2002), or: 'Europeans adopted very different colonization strategies with different associated institutions. In one extreme, as in the case of the US, Australia and New Zealand, they went and settled in the colonies and set up institutions that enforced the rule of law and encouraged investment. In the other extreme, as in the Congo or the Gold Coast, they set up extractive states with the intention of transferring resources rapidly to the metropole… The colonization strategy was in part determined by the feasibility of European settlement' (Acemoglu, Johnson and Robinson 2001).

What does this mean, more precisely? Yes, where colonizers could settle, they did and over time created institutions of individual property rights and common law brought over from the British system. But Mann (2012: 59) stresses the viciousness of the continental American conquest, which killed 95 per cent of the 4 million to 9 million native inhabitants, most from disease but some from killing: 'Settlers almost everywhere were more lethal than colonial or church authorities were – the more the *de facto* self-government by settlers the greater the killings by settlers' (see also Mann 2005: 70–110). In other words, this colonization of settlement was not benign in its institution-building; it was vicious in its displacement and extermination of previous inhabitants. More than that, the sanctity of private property rights itself was not benign, although it was certainly capitalist. Mann also points out that the United States became the main home of slavery, apart from Africa, once it was abolished in the British Empire in 1833. This generated a strict racial hierarchy that continued formally until the Civil Rights Movement of the 1950s but which continues to the present. Racial segregation has affected capital-labour conflicts and the capitalism that grew up there (see below).

Common law heritage

How important was the use of English common law in differentiating the United States and the United Kingdom in their variety of capitalism from continental Europe? Hughes (1977) goes into the institutional foundations of the US colonial state. The charters of the colonies had stipulated that the legislative acts of colonial assemblies must conform to the laws of England. From 1696 to 1776, such acts were reviewed by the Board of Trade lawyers and some were thrown out. So contract, judicial review and the whole common law of England came over to colonial America: the laws on land, labour, trade controls and business practices were all transplanted.

Law-making was more important than administration; it was the mode by which key institutional decisions were made. This marks the United States out from the continental countries, where legislatures and administrative modes of law-making under civil codes were and are stronger, and it also marks it out from the United Kingdom with the its greater balance between common case law and statutory law (Anderlini, Felli and Riboni 2008).

Villaverde (2015) makes a similar distinction between the US and UK 'thicker' versions of rule of law, imbued with implicit and sometimes explicit ideas of individual liberty (associated with common law), and the 'thinner' more formalistic interpretations of rule of law in the '*droit administratif*' regimes in continental Europe, concerned with due process but less with individual and particularly economic freedoms. Villaverde argues that the early-17th-century settlements, such as the Massachusetts General Court in 1641, upheld 'liberties, immunities and priveledges…no man's goods or estaite shall be taken away from him nor any way indammaged under colour of law….No monopolies shall be granted or allowed amongst us' (Villaverde 2015: 11–12). In other words, the 17th-century legal systems in the United States entwined individual liberty with protection of private property and ideas of 'economic freedom' associated with competition and against monopolies and privileges.

Milhaupt and Pistor (2008: 52) stress that the decentralized and contestable nature of the legal system in the United States related to the protective function of property rights in this system, and that the role of what they call 'the private attorney general' is more substantial in the United States than elsewhere. Kagan (2001) calls this tradition *Adversarial Legalism* which gives individuals through the courts the means to protect their rights against the state.

Milhaupt and Pistor (2008) discuss this in the context of 21st-century corporate governance issues, such as those illustrated by the scandal over Enron, but they date the argument to the Berle and Means (1932) analysis of the separation of ownership of companies from control of those companies. The federal securities laws of the 1930s made it clear that it was down to the legal system and the law to protect dispersed minority shareholders of corporations and that they should be able to take legal action, individually or through class actions, to protect their assets. My argument here is that I date this decentralization and contestability of the legal system and also the functions of this legal system to protect private property rights back to its institutional roots: local (decentralized) judges and juries were more important than (centralized) state administrators in deciding disputes of all sorts, including property rights, through the roles of Justices of the Peace and Courts of Sessions. Property rights backed by common law were paramount. One of the earliest post-Revolution decisions, Dartmouth College v Woodward in 1819, upheld the charter of the college, asserting that the Revolution did not upset property rights. Marshall 'considered the idea monstrous that a successful revolution would upset arrangements already set in place by the government that had been overthrown' (Hughes and Cain 2011: 142). The American Revolution was not a revolution in that sense, of overturning social structures; it firmly insisted on maintaining the principles of protection of individual property rights carried over from the English. Mann (2012) makes the point, however, that the Revolution was also a civil war, with those loyal to Britain having their property expropriated and having to flee. So to some extent, the new constitution, whilst upholding the principles of the sanctity of property rights and previous contracts, did alter them pragmatically in favour of the winners.

Judicial review itself became a key mechanism of power against the federal government. Marbury v Madison 1803 established the principle of judicial review at the federal level with the Supreme Court overturning an action of the federal government. The sanctity of contracts was maintained in the constitution: no state shall pass any law impairing the obligation of contracts. The process of common law decision-making, with the Supreme Court as final arbiter, highlights the importance of law as an institution above the administration.

The role of law and judicial interpretation had its greatest impact between 1780 and 1880. With the power of eminent domain, the state could take property as long as it compensated and used due process of law. The law and courts backed capitalist development. There was huge power of the courts to encourage economic entrepreneurial activity through the interpretation of cases, with decisions on property rights favouring some over others. There was a move from prescriptive rights to priority rights, which allowed change: favouring tree-cutting, river-damming, mine-digging, factory-building, even when this affected neighbours. In 1838, Parker v Foote in New York, the judge notes that one can't apply the doctrine of ancient light in growing cities and villages (Hughes and Cain 2011: 138). Fortunes were made, and they were not required to compensate other property owners unless negligence was proved in court. These changes in property rights were done through private law cases. There was still sanctity of private property rights, but the meaning of rights changed with the needs of economic development. For instance, Van Ness v Pacard 1829 ruled that improvements to rental property made by the tenant did not belong to the landlord; the tenant needed to be compensated.

Those rights were strengthened that the courts wanted developed and those weakened that they did not. This was done through the courts rather than directly by the states. Just as the English Parliament post-1688 reflected the interests of the landowning and merchant classes, in the United States judges' law-making reflected the interests of capitalist enterprise and its growth and development rather than the status quo of existing landowners. As Horwitz (1977) argues, the push for American law to adapt came from rapid economic growth in the early 19th century. It transformed English common law principles in favour of a strong judiciary pushing forward economic change. The laws promoted a competitive commercial capitalist economy. For example, in challenging the mill acts which had defended the mill owner in preventing adjacent land being developed (Horwitz 1977: 51), American courts and judges supported entrepreneurs and limited restrictions on economic development.

Similar dismantling of older legislation applied to changing the nature of contracts. Old ideas of natural justice dictating that equality between contracting parties had been needed had excluded children, the mentally impaired, and often women from making contracts. It had also provided an argument for collective bargaining in contracting between factory workers and the corporation, to equalize their respective strengths. This gave way to the idea that the role of the government was not ensuring equity but enforcing willed transactions, 'the meeting of wills', as long as the contract was made between free and legal persons. Factories could contract with masses of employees on working conditions and wages (Hughes 2014).

The law was made in favour of entrepreneurs, of economic growth. Pro-business judges instructed juries towards the pro-economic answer, giving re-trials to overturn jury decisions and dismissing juries. Horwitz (1977: 143) argues: 'The subjugation of juries was necessary not only to control particular verdicts but also to develop a uniform and predictable body of judge-made commercial rules'. For example, in the Charles River Bridge case, the Massachusetts Court and the Supreme Court upheld the competitive development of another bridge that challenged the prescriptive claim of the older bridge proprietors. Horwitz's argument is that emerging contractual and commercial law was bent towards favouring decisions that promoted competition and economic growth at the expense of individual justice. This transformation, it is argued, was a response to the impulses of economic growth: the legal system was propelled by the requirements of an expanding capitalist society. It required judicial freedom to reinterpret common law in favour of stronger, dynamic and more powerful factions over weaker groups. It sanctioned the use of a free market in wages and prices, escaping from notions of natural justice. For instance, the dangers of work were assumed to be reflected in the wage, which reduced the employer's liability. What Parliament did for British emergent capitalism the Supreme Court and judiciary did for that of the United States.

The overall picture is one of law and property rights adapting to employers' wishes through Supreme Court decisions ruling in an increasingly liberal fashion from the mid to late 19th century. They were what Scheiber (in Hughes and Cain 2011: 139) termed 'intangible contributions' to economic growth done through the courts in private law cases.

Primary institutions: Nature of the state

One major difference that stands out between the liberal US and UK political economies and the continental European ones (as argued in Chapter 4) is that the private-public boundary is placed significantly increasing the private realm and diminishing the public/state realm. Libertarian values supported a smaller state and a larger private sector. People were suspicious of government. Both liberal economies have this character, but their routes to it differ. When did this come about and why? As argued in Chapter 4, this 'liberal' aspect crystallized in Britain in the 1820s. When did it happen in the United States?

In 1760, 2 million people in America were British, but Americans had their own decentralized governments with elected assemblies, police, and tax authorities. Formally, there was a governor representing the Crown, but in practice Americans ruled themselves. There were local judges, governors and staffs with salaries set by local assemblies, not by Britain (Mann 2012: 137–138).

The 13 states, plus the national government in the United States when they declared independence from Britain, all had sovereign powers. This was made explicit in the state constitutions, the Articles of Confederation and the federal constitution of 1787 (Wallis 2004). The separation of powers – between the presidency, two houses of congress, 13 states and local governments, and a separate Supreme Court – arose from a desire to avoid having concentrated power in any one place, to prevent despotism by a monarch or disorder from the mob. Amar (2006) emphasizes that this set-up of separated powers gave significant power to individual states in counterbalancing federal executive power.

The system centred on the constitution as the rule of law and the Supreme Court as the federal court with independent judiciary, which could veto legislation and government action alongside other lesser courts. The Supreme Court and federal constitution were agreed to by sovereign states that had their own legal systems. This is what Milhaupt and Pistor (2008) characterize as a decentralized and contestable legal system. Mann (2012: 129–166) stresses the legal profession as the main regulator rather than the administration.

The state was and remains more decentralized and regionalized than Britain's, and its central state control of violence – the police and army – was weaker, over domestic affairs, than for more centralized states. There were private militias, such as Pinkertons, that were used by employers to break strikes, for example.

Individual rights – to bear arms, to be tried in court, to remain silent in court, for example – were protected in the constitution and enshrined in the individual libertarian values of the 18th century. Mann (2012) contrasts the strength of both US and British states in foreign policy with their relative constrainedness in their domestic spheres.

In Britain, the sequencing of institutional development was that property rights independent of the state came well before any real democracy in the form of the extensions of the franchise in 1832 and 1867. In the United States, democracy in the form of local assemblies and participation was there from the start, as argued by Tocqueville, with different characters according to the nature of the colonization. Tocqueville (1848: 75) argued that the absence of rules of hierarchy increased the power of law, that elected officials made greater use of judicial punishments as weapons of administration, as illustrated in Arthur Miller's *The Crucible.*

Tocqueville contrasts the United States, from the vantage point of the 1840s, with his observations of France and their contrasting balances between structures of state administration and judicial power in the two countries. Whereas power in France stemmed from the highly centralized state, with the government lending officials to the township (Tocqueville 1848: 66), in New England the township was sovereign and lent officials to the government. He points to the township in the United States as a strong corporation having legal status and power in itself. He contrasts the decentralized and powerful legal system in the United States implicitly with the much more centralized and larger role for state administration and lesser role for the judicial system in France: 'In no country in the world are the pronouncements of the law more categorical than in America, and in no other country is the right to enforce it divided among so many hands' (Tocqueville 1848: 72).

By the 1820s, there was universal white male suffrage in most states. Extending the franchise did not threaten the rule of property. In the Anglo-American tradition, political rights came with property rights. Property ownership qualifications for free white male adults were removed in 1860. State by state, there was gradual white enfranchisement from the 1820s; non-property-owners needed to pay rent above a certain level, do militia service or pay a fine. This was designed to ensure that people were local and permanent, and it excluded labourers. The newer Western states were more liberal with the franchise (Mann 2012: 129–166).

Taxation and fiscal capacity: Of states and federal government

This system retained its decentralization. Most state functions of education, health, police and public works were devolved to the states. But foreign affairs and westwards expansion were directed and financed by the federal state. Edling (2014) charts the 'extraordinary fiscal expansion' in the post-confederation, federalist period. The federal government assumed the debt of individual states and paid them with federal public bonds, transferring $74m worth of domestic and foreign debt into long-term federal bonds in 1790, representing about 30 per cent of gross national product (GNP) (Irogoin 2015). The states in turn gave the tariff by the Impost Acts of 1790 to the federal government. This, along with customs revenues, made up over 80 per cent of federal income in the mid-19th century. The federal state's fiscal capacity expanded through these two routes: of issuing public debt and taxation through customs duties. Edling (2014) argues that this fiscal capacity formed the basis for the territorial expansion westwards, building up the military capacity of the army and navy. One can characterize this federal state as stronger 'abroad' than domestically, although even domestically, for an African American, this was not a weak central state. By taxing through customs duties, direct taxes were kept light. Taxation and public loans were also perceived to be voluntary, through indirect taxation and the buying of public bonds, and this, as for Britain, fitted with the anti-*étatisme* stance. It made the US state stealthily strong (Edling 2014) compared with European states that raised finance through requisitions and defaulted on their loans.

From protectionism to greater liberalism

The early-19th-century federal government was protectionist; there was no free trade. The growing of markets was negotiated by treaty, and trade routes were policed by the American navy (Edling 2014). The aggressive expansion across the continent, securing access to the Pacific with its trade routes into Asia, increased trade, which in turn increased customs duties. The federal tax burden per capita did not rise due to the huge expansion in population and GDP, so taxation was perceived as being relatively light and was less heavy than in Britain during this period. In the late 18th and early 19th centuries, most states' taxes came from direct taxes in property and persons. In the south, the land tax and slave tax were the most important (Edling 2014: 54). Customs taxes were significant particularly for states with busy ports.

The argument of Larson (2001) is that the early-19th-century states were interventionist and regulatory, an 'energetic government'. From the 1780s to the 1840s, there were experiments in public works such as canal-building. Wallis (2004) charts the struggles in a democratic state to find fair ways to raise taxes to fund infrastructure that was not going to benefit all the states' citizens equally.

By the 1820s, there was growth in states-level government investment in banks and transportation infrastructure such as canals, roads and bridges. This was financed through issuing debt and chartering corporations. This was also a way of raising taxation; in Massachusetts, taxation on bank capital in the 1830s contributed 50 per cent towards state revenues. But this gave special privileges to political allies and powerful families. In the Jackson era, there were cries of corruption and anti-democratic manipulation, that this was an exchange of privilege for revenue (Wallis 2004).

Most of these infrastructural investments were made by the states' governments, not the federal government. The power to incur debt by government was inherited from the British example; bridge, road and turnpike companies were given subsidies, stock was purchased in them or bonds were issued. Some of these were profitable, such as the construction of the Erie Canal by New York, which was completed in 1825. States spent $183m on banks, canals and railroads; $13m of this was in bonds issued in New York and Ohio (for their canal constructions) that were repaid by the early 1830s out of profits.

Wallis (2004) attributes major changes in the balance between states and the federal government to the financial crisis in individual states in the 1840s. There were constitutional reforms in the 1840s in 12 of the states, with new procedures for issuing debt and for chartering corporations in 11 out of 12 of them (Wallis 2004). Constitutional reform involved limiting the extent to which states could issue debt and included provisions for taxes to service debt. At the same time, there were restrictions made on special incorporation (Wallis 2004: 27). States altered taxation so that infrastructure could not be financed through special tax arrangements but had to be financed through general taxation throughout the state, typically through *ad valorem* taxation for all property (Wallis 2004: 28).

The result of the 1840s fiscal crisis in many states led to a fundamental shift in attitudes towards state investments in general. Madison, Hamilton and Jay's *Federalist Papers* raged against the corruption of 'oligarchic rule: standing armies, patronage and public debts' (Pocock 1977: 145 in Wallis 2004: 30). The new Indiana constitution, for example, required general incorporation laws banning special incorporation and prohibited state investment in private corporations (Wallis 2004: 33). This was repeated across most states. Here is the turn towards liberal, *laissez-faire* government and distrust of state intervention. The attitudes are well envisaged in this quote of Mr. Morrison of Marion County, Indiana (Wallis 2004: 33): 'The state has been aptly compared to a goose, and according to the saying, he was a fool who did not pluck her'. After the 1840s, state borrowing and spending was on a smaller scale and more local, such as in public utilities, public health and education, and it was funded by local taxation; larger infrastructural projects were left to private corporations to build.

Larson's (2001) point is that the private capital market did not triumph until the 1840s, driven by the idea of markets as more unbiased arbiters of conflict between different interests than democratic governments susceptible to corruption, and that the invisible hand of competition was fairer in a democratic society. This coincided with *laissez-faire* liberalism taking hold in Britain by the mid-19th century. In the United States, *laissez-faire* meant a triumph for the monopolies and big business backed by the courts, and the stockholders behind them, against farmers, artisans and small businesses.

From the mid-19th century, there was a push for greater freedom from government control and for deregulation; New York in 1846 abolished many of its police power controls. Control over public utilities was continued through special franchise monopolies, especially with the development of canals and railroads up to 1860. But most controls were done at the local government level, not at the federal or states government level. Local government granted privileges through regulation such as creating entry barriers into the Massachusetts legal profession.

The early decades of the 20th century saw an increase in government regulation pushed by the Progressives. There was a raft of state interventionist reform on maximum working hours, restricting child and women's labour, as well as racist laws, such as those restricting Asian migration. The origin of the minimum wage legislation is illustrative of the 'illiberalism' behind these laws. Leonard (2016) argues that the push for minimum wage laws came from the desire to protect white Saxon workers from being priced out by undesirables in the labour market including African Americans, women and the 'feeble-minded'. The eugenics movement fed into racism. Leonard highlights the sterilization case in 1927 Buck v Bell, which was written up by Oliver Wendell Holmes Jr, a much-respected Justice in the Supreme Court, who saw it as natural and obvious to intervene and sterilize a young woman deemed to be feeble-minded to prevent procreation of this sort of person from weakening the white race.

The trust problem and concentration versus competition

The 'trust problem' concerned the perceived growth in power of large enterprises, through holding groups and cartels, that in effect were anti-competitive (through price-fixing, for instance) and stole from the consumer (Wells 2009).

The states had liberalized rules on incorporation, making it available to any business group. Business colluded; there was price-fixing and merging of firms into trusts. This gave rise to populist resentment at the huge increase in industry concentration: in 1880, 1,900 firms made farm implements but the top 4 made 65 per cent of them. By 1890, the copper industry was dominated by a few giants. By 1879, Standard Oil refined 90 per cent of US pumped crude oil and owned 80 per cent of US pipelines.

There was protest against these forces of concentration and monopoly power. The Granger Cases and Populist movements represented farmer protest against the railroads, which were seen as private property that should be treated as public property due to their new uses. The railroads became subject to government regulation, with 25 state railroad commissions by 1886. The role of government was to protect competition in the market in the public interest.

The Anti-Trust Acts were a further attempt to regulate monopoly power in favour of competition. The 1890 Sherman Anti-Trust Act states: 'Every contract, combination in the form of trust or otherwise or conspiracy, in restraint of trade or commerce among the several states or with foreign nations is hereby declared to be illegal' (Hughes and Cain 2011: 375). The Clayton Anti-Trust Act of 1914 amended Sherman, but was in the same spirit. In particular, it was used against organized labour, seeing labour unions as illegal combinations or conspiracies in restraint of trade. The Federal Trade Commission was set up in 1914 to enforce the anti-trust laws. It partly reflected popular opposition of farmers and small business, which had been losing out to big business since the end of the 19th century. In restricting the power of trusts or cartels, they promoted full mergers that increased concentration.

As with Britain, this is a particular interpretation of what constitutes a 'liberal' state: it combined government intervention in terms of regulation such as the anti-trust laws or sterilization case cited above, which in one sense are far from liberal, with a certain type of *laissez-faire*. The difference in comparing these states – the United States (and Britain) – with continental European ones is that these interventions were done through law-making and the use of the courts rather than by the state executive. And such intervention was allied to anti-statism in terms of the executive state's stance towards private business and markets.

There was distrust of government and its privileges and strong pressure to restrain government in favour of self-regulating markets. Coffee (2001) argues that the rise of equity and stock markets in the United States (and the United Kingdom) as privately, self-regulated markets separated from politics, distinguished them as institutions from public control over stock markets in France and Germany, with the government administering the market. Coffee argues that in the United States (and the United Kingdom) the common law system was more hospitable to the private decentralized self-regulation of the market that encouraged private initiatives. A constituency then developed that needed protecting, which gave rise to shareholder protection legislation. By contrast, on the European continent, the state monopolized law-making initiatives over the market, and civil law was more hostile to private law-making, inhibiting a constituency of individual shareholders from emerging. Self-regulation for financial markets has been linked, I would argue, to the strength of and support for the financial sector and tradable assets and its interests in the liberal economies. The pressures in favour of smaller government came also from regional, sectoral and racial divisions. Southern states were agrarian and populist (so pushing for regulation of big business), but also racially segregated and conservative, distrustful of big government (Mann 2012).

Meso-institutions: Nature of companies and incorporation and the law

The final section links the above to corporate governance issues and organizational forms: the use of corporations and joint stock companies and the development of equity markets, and the question of how ownership of companies became widened and dispersed in the first half of the 20th century.

The corporation

The chartering of corporations by the sovereign was taken from British custom; the use made of it in the United States was new. The corporation was treated in the law as a legal person with perpetual life and limited liability. Dartmouth College v Woodward 1819 upheld the college's charter of incorporation against New Hampshire. Richard Sylla (in Becht and DeLong 2005) argues that, from the 1790s to the 1850s the United States developed the business corporation as a form of competitive enterprise to a greater extent than Europe. US federalism played a large role in this, with state governments as well as the federal government being able to charter corporations (Wallis 2004). Americans created many more corporations than was done in Britain from the 1790s onwards:

> We have in our country an infinite number of corporations aggregate which have no concern whatever with affairs of a municipal nature.... There is a great difference in this respect between our own country and the country from which we have derived a great portion of our laws. What is done in England by combination, unless it be the management of municipal concerns, is most generally done by a combination of individuals, established by mere articles of agreement. On the other hand, what is done here by the cooperation of several persons is, in the greater number of instances, the result of consolidation effected by an express act or charter of incorporation.
>
> (Angell and Ames 1831, quoted in Wallis 2004: Footnote 4)

Hurst (1970), also quoted in Wallis (2004), states that there was no legal experience for using corporations for business in the 1780s, when their use began to be developed. Charters were granted and used by small groups of people to build a bridge or a canal (Maier 1992 in Wallis 2004).

In 1790, there were 40 American corporations. Between 1790 and 1800, 300 new charters were issued. Each charter required a new act of state legislature. The federal government could also charter companies, but was reluctant until the First World War. From 1811 onwards, New York allowed incorporation without special charter. Connecticut did the same in 1837. The British Parliament was much more cautious in allowing limited liability in England; American incorporation law, according to legal historian Hurst, did not owe much to the British system.

The use of the corporation also was more prevalent than in continental Europe. The number of corporations was far higher than in France in the first half of the 19th century. Lamoreaux and Rosenthal (2004: 5, 6, 10) compare 642 corporations charted in France between 1807 and 1867 with 3,200 in New England between 1800 and 1843 and 3,500 between 1844 and 1862. In 1920, there were 314,000 corporations operating in the United States. Lamoreaux and Rosenthal (2004) argue that the dominance of the corporate form in United States under common law (whose only alternative in the United States was the limited partnership form, which was encumbered with various restrictions) favoured majority over minority shareholders. Early general incorporation laws, such as New York's 1848 statute, required corporations to issue financial statements. But requirements became laxer over time, so it was harder for small stockholders to monitor management. They could not assist in decisions over whether to buy stock – only existing stockholders had the right to examine books, although in practice this was hard to do. Not until the Securities and Exchange Commission in 1934 was there protection for minority shareholders. But this gave protection only for publicly-traded, large corporations, and not for small enterprises. It was only in the second half of the 20th century that protection for shareholders in non-public corporations was strengthened, making them more similar to the French SARLs and limited liability partnerships.

What stands out for the United States is the power of the corporation backed by the judiciary and common law. It did much of what in continental Europe was done by the central state, such as technological development and research and development.

Conceptions of shareholder capitalism

The varieties of capitalism debate links the ideas of liberal capitalism with shareholder primacy, meaning that the rights of the shareholder come first and above those of other stakeholders in the firm: managers, employees, customers, suppliers, banks. But that association of the rights of shareholders as prime with what has come to be called 'outsider models' or 'market-oriented models' of capitalism is relatively recent, since the 1980s and 1990s, and is contrary to the initial conceptions of shareholder capitalism which saw shareholders as insiders to the corporation. How and when did that transition occur?

Even in the 1820s, it is argued that many corporations in New York had more shareholders than could have been actively involved in management: the average corporation had 74 shareholders, and a few had several hundred (Hilt 2008). Hilt notes that this was not managerial control but minority control by managers holding a large enough stake to free them from accountability to other shareholders. Harwell Wells (2009) traces the shifting conceptions of what shareholder capitalism meant from writers such as William Z. Ripley (1927) in *Main Street and Wall Street* writing of corporate governance issues in the United States from the turn of the century through to Berle and Means' (1932) *The Modern Corporation and Private Property*. First, the rise in dispersed shareholding in the last decades of the 19th century is noted, and the birth of what may be called mass shareholding. The largest holdings in 1900 were in railroads and a few industrial companies. Of the largest US railroads in 1900, only the Union Pacific and Pennsylvania had more than 10,000 stockholders, and of industrial companies, American Sugar and US Steel had more than 10,000 stockholders each (Navin and Sears 1955; Means 1930). Means' study showed that the three largest US corporations trebled the number of stockholders between 1900 and 1917. There was then a real explosion in ownership of stocks in the 1920s when millions of Americans invested in companies (Ott

2008). In terms of numbers of Americans owning shares, that rose from a few hundred thousand pre-First-World-War (3 per cent of US households) to an estimate of 8 million by 1929 (a quarter of households) (Ott 2009). Utilities companies, for example, became widely held; Ripley estimated that 1,307,000 customers of utilities were also shareholders (Wells 2010: 1279).

The concern then was about the loss of active ownership and participation through shareholding and that control was being wrested from shareholders, not by managers but by financial intermediaries such as J.P. Morgan, who was organizing the selling of shares. This often happened with turn-of-the-century mergers, when owners of smaller enterprises were bought out and they sold on their shares in the newly merged enterprise (Wells 2010: 1254). Another concern was about the division between voting stock and non-voting stock and the maintenance of control by a small group of shareholders holding voting stock with the mass of shareholders receiving non-voting stock (Ripley 1927: 121).

Brandeis (1914) was concerned both with the power of management and that of the bankers. He argued that corporations were too large to be managed and that the public and other small proprietors would be injured (Wells 2010: 1257; Urofsky 2009: 397). Alfred Sloan, writing in 1926 of General Motors' shareholding composition and whether there could be too many stockholders to enable monitoring of the management, argued that they had found a happy medium, of 70,000 small shareholders owning 40 per cent of the stock, with the rest held by a small group of mainly the DuPont family, who were actively involved in the company and its welfare (Wells 2010: 1278).

The direct responsibilities of ownership were stressed and the concern that the growth in dispersed ownership severed active involvement with the firm (Ripley 1927: 94). But a transition was going on seeing shareholding as part of investment, with shareholders not actively engaging with the management of the company whose shares they owned. This is a transition from the rights and role of shareholders as an insider model of governance towards what is now considered to be an outsider model.

Another interesting feature of these writings of the 1920s is that smallholdings of shares were thought to solve the labour problem by turning smallholders into small capitalists (Carver 1925: 112; Brookings 1925: 9). The widening of shareholding shifted attention onto the welfare of those shareholders, where previously there had not been any concern for them. It is also pointed out that the concerns of labour are not mentioned (Tsuk 2003). The growth of employee stockownership in the 1920s furthered this view that labour's involvement in the corporation was through holding stock rather than through direct voice in the running of the firm (Brandes 1976). Ripley (1927: 100) argues that it was through the campaigning of small shareholders that the 12-hour workday at US Steel was abandoned, although Wells (2010: 1275) says that the fight for that was more complex than the version portrayed by Ripley.

An important shift was from pre-1920s conceptions of corporate governance concerned with the corporation's relationship to groups outside the corporation –

customers, competitors, the public – and which was called the trust problem, towards the concerns of the corporation's relationship with its shareholders from the 1920s. Wells puts this as a shift from a concern with outsiders towards a concern with insider issues of corporate governance (Wells 2010: 1284) or, as Lasswell (1928: 658–659) put it, a distinction between the trust problem and the corporation problem, from concerns about business gouging the consumer and the public to concerns for the small investor. Alongside this is the accompanying shift in conceptualizing the shareholder from being an insider to the corporation – as considered up to the 1920s – towards being an outsider and functioning through incentives provided by the market, which predominated at least after the Second World War. What Berle and Means (1932) contributed to the debate was not only a much closer statistical scrutiny of what was happening in shareholding in leading companies, but also a closer investigation of what 'control' meant, how it was shifting, and how that caused a reinterpretation of the nature of property.

Corporations, equity markets and dispersed shareholdings

Another part of this story of dispersal of shareholdings and growth of equity markets is the role of the market itself in encouraging or enabling this transition. What made blockholder family owners of large corporations – the robber barons of the 1870s – sell out to small shareholders? And what made small shareholders buy shares in the absence of legal protection for minority investors and in the presence of substantial private benefits of control?

From the large shareholding families' perspective, the question is why they sold out and lost control of their corporations when they need not have done so. As Becht and DeLong (2005: 615, footnote 3) put it: 'The real puzzle of the US corporation then [meaning in the first decades of the 20th century] is how and why professional managers managed to wrest control from the former owners – who could have stayed in control had they taken steps to set up devices to do so'. The story is one where owner families sold out and diluted control because they were made offers on the back of buoyant and developing equity markets that they couldn't refuse and believed that they could maintain control through representation on executive boards.

Dispersed shareholding came about at the turn of the 20th century, under the influence of bankers like J.P. Morgan, in persuading families that they could diversify their shareholdings and retain control of companies. This resulted in a lack of blockholding from the 1930s and the demise in control of companies by the grand families, which stands in stark contrast to the blockholding in Europe through pyramids, holding companies, and proxy control through banks and institutional shareholders. This helps to explain the growth in use of equity markets and the relatively restricted nature of the banking system, which was hemmed in by state regulation like Glass-Steagall.

Galbraith (1967) had been amazed at the speed at which US capitalism had become detached from its founding families (in Becht and DeLong 1991):

'Seventy years ago the corporation was the instrument of its owners and a projection of their personalities. The names of those principals – Carnegie, Rockefeller, Harriman, Mellon, Guggenheim, Ford – were known across the land....The men who now head the great corporations are unknown... and own no appreciable share of the enterprise....They are selected not by the shareholders but in the common case by a Board of Directors which narcissistically they selected themselves'.

Becht and DeLong (2005) look in detail at the transition from owner-controlled US corporations – still the main form at the end of the 19th century – to the point when Means (1930, 1931) and Berle and Means (1932) talk about separation of ownership from control. By 1929, only 11 per cent of the 200 largest corporations in the United States were controlled by large blockholders; 44 per cent were controlled by incumbents with reduced ownership. In another 44 per cent, management was alleged to have taken control. Becht and DeLong's argument is that dispersion of ownership happened a generation earlier, around the turn of the century, is related to the trust movement and anti-trust policy, and was encouraged by investment bankers like J.P. Morgan's ability to sell off shares to a wider public. The big owners – Vanderbilt, Carnegie, Guggenheim – sold out in the early 20th century. A further argument was that the family could maintain control if the ownership was dispersed enough – made by Morgan to Vanderbilt and others.

Coffee (2004) inserts into this story the nature of private or semi-private ordering or self-regulation of the public equity market, the greater hospitality of common law to that private ordering of the equity market, and argues that this self-regulated market gave sufficient protection – through disclosure rules – to small shareholders in that it did not allow raiders to enter the market and build up stealthily holdings of companies such that they could then steal the private benefits from those companies.

The initial push towards the growth of public securities markets was the financing requirements of the railroads in the 19th century, creating a huge demand for capital. This impetus was then transferred to the financing of other large-scale industries – steel, the auto and the telephone industries in the next decades. Much of the capital for the railroads was foreign. It required the intermediation of the investment bankers as agents by their taking seats on boards to protect public investors from raiders. Coffee stresses the role of investment bankers such as August Belmont, Rothschild's agent in the United States, and J.P. Morgan, a representative of an Anglo-American investment bank. They added equity securities onto debt securities that they were marketing. The Erie War of the 1860s between Commodore Vanderbilt and Jay Gould and Daniel Drew was over the manipulation of stock for control over the Erie Railroad (Coffee 2004: 29). Judges were bribed by one side; the New York state legislature was bribed by the other to prevent Vanderbilt from taking over control. There was no federal regulatory authority, so battles moved from one jurisdiction to another. There was no corporate law or enforcement mechanism, and there was huge corruption. These were what Coffee (2004: 31) calls 'legally primitive conditions' combined with a need for foreign capital from foreign investors who could not monitor what was going on. So investment bankers took seats on their clients' boards. All the US railroads had close ties with a US investment banking firm. J.P. Morgan held 23 directorships in 13 banks; First National Bank had 14 directorships in other banks. The presence of these bankers on boards created value to the firms' stock (DeLong 1991).

Coffee (2004) argues that these investment bankers were not active monitors of management, as they would have lost their positions on the boards had they done so. But what they did do was defend the corporation from incoming raiders stealing their wealth. The raider in the late 19th century did not need to announce their bid; the investment banking firms were well placed to detect such dealings. Coffee cites examples of such protection going on: by Kidder Peabody and Barings over the Santa Fe Railroad fought off Jay Gould; by J.P. Morgan organizing a merger to fight off Gould again from taking over the Albany and Susquehanna Railroad by merging it into the larger Delaware and Hudson. These tactics enabled a public equity market to develop, as the founders could sell into the market without losing control to a rival.

Coffee (2004) argues that this did not happen either on the European continent nor in the United Kingdom because the (smaller) investment banks did not want to underwrite equity securities and did not represent the group of public shareholders as did US investment banks. The merger wave in the United States in the 1890s, spurred on by the Sherman anti-trust legislation, which prohibited collusion and price-fixing, also led to a dilution of shareholdings, for instance, in the creation of US Steel out of 8 competing steel companies. British courts were less vigilant in preventing cartels, and so there was not an equivalent merger wave.

The other institutional propulsion towards growth in equity markets came from the nature of the regulation of the New York Stock Exchange (NYSE). The NYSE was more active than the London Stock Exchange (LSE) or continental bourses; it was also not the leading equities securities market, as the Boston Stock Exchange was the dominant market in the late 19th century, so the exchanges were competing for business. In addition, it was a more closed market, not allowing new members. This encouraged larger, more diversified financial services firms. Its smaller size of membership meant that it created a high-quality part of the equities market more suitable for wider-spread public ownership. The NYSE firms could raise capital from outside their firm, which the LSE members could not. And the NYSE had fixed brokerage commissions, which the LSE did not. Overall, then, the NYSE was organized and structured differently from the LSE and in the process encouraged more exclusive, lower-volume trading in higher-quality stocks, which itself encouraged the greater holdings of those stocks. The NYSE was more conservative and risk-averse in which stocks it would list, which again encouraged public holdings of those stocks. The NYSE, therefore, had higher listing standards and requirements in terms of disclosure and reporting standards, which it monitored itself, and it rejected lower-quality applications (Coffee 2004: 42). Coffee calls these the twin pillars – the monitoring capacity and the bonding mechanisms of US underwriters to attract foreign capital – in the development of liquid equity markets, which can be dated from around 1900. The legal framework did not follow until 1934.

Why capital was strong and labour weak in the United States

This leads to consideration of the capital-labour relationship and in particular Sombart's (1906) question of why there has never been a strong socialist labour movement or working class labour party in the United States, which is distinct from the situation in Europe and Britain. The argument made here is twofold: race has beaten class as a unifying force, or rather it has dissipated such class-based unity as led to working class parties being created in Europe and Britain (Mann 2012); and political judicial power has been pro-business, backing the power of the corporation and has been pitted against both governmental power and working class power.

Mann's basic argument is that race trumped class, that labour or worker unity in having collective action against employers or capitalists was not managed, as there were severe racial segregations and regional divisions that prevented any cohesion. Werner Sombart's (1906) *Why Is there no Socialism in the United States?* contrasted the United States with Germany. But Mann compares the United States to Britain and the other Anglophone countries which all had working class labour parties representing workers in government.

In the United States, labour combining could be construed as conspiracy and injurious to others. Commonwealth v Hunt 1842 ruled that secondary boycotts during strikes were prohibited although strikes themselves came under free speech, and so were legal. In 1880, a very low percentage of the labour force was in a union. Mann (2012) puts this down to the structure of the labour force, with more independent businesses than workers in industry, and to almost three quarters of the population being rural. Naidu and Yuchtman (2016: 18) stress the role of the courts and judicial backing of the corporation and judicial interpretation of the common law of employment that was influential in weakening labour: 'Differing from Britain, American labor law stayed in the hands of courts in the late 19th century: indeed, Forbath (1991) points to the difference between "judicial supremacy" in the United States and "parliamentary supremacy" in Britain as crucial to the diverging labour movements in the two countries'. The law – injunctions – was used against individuals like labour leader Eugene Debs. Yet, the American Federation of Labour was a large organization, and there was a high strike rate (Mann 2012).

Mann (1993: 635–659) puts forward the conjunction of reasons that combined to keep labour weak relative to employers: the strength of employer militias (such as Pinkertons or Baldwin-Felts) used to break strikes; the backing of the courts for employers' property rights but not workers' rights of combination; and there was no political party that represented labour's interests, partly because there was already democracy for white males, which lessened the type of worker unity that occurred in Germany through its struggle for democracy. This stance is consistent with the overall argument made here that emphasizes the power of the legal system in adjudicating disputes. Similarly, state regulation was weak on working conditions until the New Deal. Leonard (2016) argues that the wave of reform in the early decades of the 20th century was more concerned to protect white male rights against immigration and lower-wage sections of the labour market than with liberal reform. Liberal labour market conditions were a consequence of all these structures that weakened and fragmented the labour force.

Conclusions

The overall thesis of this chapter is that the property rights of fee simple and common law carried over from Britain were combined with a post-Revolution constitution and separation of powers that gave substantial powers to judges and judicial decision-making, and that regulation was done through states-level law-making rather than centralized administration – almost the opposite of France. The nature of the state was a decentralized confederation with strong centralized state capacity on military matters. There was a shift in the 1840s from the 'energetic government' involved in internal improvement and infrastructure, taking a liberal turn from the mid-19th century towards an anti-statist, liberal, small-government stance on capitalistic economic matters. Big business won out over small business and agrarian interests. Corporations were powerful and had property rights, as legal entities, that were equivalent to individual property rights. But collective rights were weak, and so labour unions were always suspect and under attack. Judges and law-making was pro-business. Similar to the British story, the expansion of financing through securities markets, both of equity markets for private enterprise and also of markets for government securities financing public debt, played a big part in consolidating the private-public boundary to encompass a larger private sector that financed and owned large-scale infrastructure.

The American institutional story is one of white capitalism from its inception (Roediger 1991; Roediger and Esch 2012). From its colonization in the 17th century, and in tracing the structures of this capitalism, Mann (2012: 140) points to the evenly spread property-holding by the white population with no opposing white non-propertied class. Democracy for whites and capitalism went together from the start; racisms and the exclusion of non-whites was also there from the start in the expropriation of land from the Native Americans and in the justifications of slave-owning. Saxton (1990) argues that the theories of white racial superiority themselves originated from the rationalization and justification of the slave trade, slavery and the expropriation of land from non-whites, and that they occupy a central place because they met the needs to justify the ruling groups. Roediger (1991) makes the link between racist brutality and white egalitarianism, not ironic or paradoxical but with a coherent logic linking the two.

State capacity needs to be understood as shifting from decentralized states' power and fiscal capacity based on financing through chartering companies towards the combination of local government financing based on taxation of local property, with the rise of private capital markets for large infrastructure such as the railroads. The state became more liberal, as the power of the courts and judiciary increased at the expense of the administrative apparatus of the federal state in settling disputes and creating law and priorities in terms of property rights and corporations. Linked to this was the power of corporations backed by law rather than the power of government and the state.

The shift from plutocratic shareholding towards more dispersed shareholding with managerial control arises out of the turn of the (20th) century regulatory battle against the power of the trusts through the Sherman and Clayton Acts. The concern to break up monopoly power and promote competition stemmed from the more democratic pro-competition impulse in the United States. The irony is that the broader spread of shareholding did not in itself mean more democratic control of companies but rather more concentrated managerial control (Berle and Means 1932; Mizruchi and Hirschman 2009).

The story is one of the power of capital, shareholder rights, that comes out of the clash of anti-trust and pro-competition law versus big business and a combination of reasons why labour – as a collective force, as an unincorporated force, as a racially divided force – did not have political power. This is not to deny that there were unions, strikes, working class action in the early 20th century, but that these unions have not had formal political representation as they have in Britain and Europe, and they have not been formally incorporated into governance through representation on boards or works councils as in Germany. Out of this weakness of labour and the move towards dispersed and mass shareholding of the larger corporations came the assertion of shareholder primacy in the 1930s as the constituency that needed protection.

One major difference that stands out between the liberal US and UK political economies and the European ones is that the private-public boundary has been placed significantly increasing the private realm and diminishing the public/state realm. The US stance towards the state has been both anti-trust and pro-competition in reaction to large-scale business power. But this has been combined with a profound anti-statism and liberal small-government stance in comparison with European states and with my developing states of Tanzania and China.

Notes

1 *The Economist* of 9 May 2015 constructs some rankings for 2013 of 'If black America were a country': there is a $25,000 gap between black and white median incomes; the wealth gap is larger with the median white family having net assets of $142,000

compared with the median black family's assets of $11,000. Black America would rank 130 on the homicide rate compared with 60 for white America, 23 for Britain, 25 for China. Life expectancy at birth ranks black America at 65, below Sri Lanka, and infant mortality at 60, below Tonga.

2 'Go back; look at the baby in his mother's arms; see how the outside world is first reflected in the still hazy mirror of his mind; consider the first examples that strike his attention…Only then will you understand the origin of the prejudices, habits and passions which are to dominate his life. The whole man is there, if one may put it so, in the cradle. Something analogous happens with nations. Peoples always bear some marks of their origin. Circumstances of birth and growth affect all the rest of their careers' (de Tocqueville 1848: 31).

References

Acemoglu, D. and Robinson, J. (2012) *Why Nations Fail: The Origins of Power, Prosperity and Poverty*. London: Profile Books.

Acemoglu, D., Johnson, S. and Robinson, J. (2001) 'The Colonial Origins of Comparative Development: An Empirical Investigation', *American Economic Review* 91(5): 1369–1401.

Acemoglu, D., Johnson, S. and Robinson, J. (2002) 'Reversal of Fortune: Geography and Institutions in the Making of the Modern World Income Distribution', *Quarterly Journal of Economics* 117(4): 1231–1294.

Amar, A.R. (2006) *America's Constitution: A Biography*. New York: Penguin Random House.

Anderlini, L., Felli, L. and Riboni, A. (2008) Statue Law or Case Law? Working Paper No. 2358. Munich: CESifo Group.

Angell, J. and Ames, S. (1831) *A Treatise on the Law of Private Corporations Aggregate*. Boston: Hilliard, Gray, Little and Wilkins.

Becht, M. and DeLong, B. (2005) 'Why Has there Been so Little Blockholding in America?' in R. Morck (ed.), *A History of Corporate Governance around the World: Family Business Groups to Professional Managers*, 613–666. Chicago: University of Chicago Press.

Berle, A. and Means, G. (1932) *The Modern Corporation and Private Property*. New Brunswick, NJ: Transaction Publishers.

Brandeis, L.D. (1914) *Other Peoples' Money and How the Bankers Use It*. New York: Stokes.

Brandes, S. (1976) *American Welfare Capitalism, 1880–1940*. Chicago: University of Chicago Press.

Brookings, R. (1925) *Industrial Ownership: Its Economic and Social Significance*. New York: Macmillan.

Bush, J.A. (1993) 'Free to Enslave: The Foundations of Colonial American Slave Law', *Yale Journal of Law and the Humanities* 5(2): Article 7. Available at: http://digitalcommons.law.yale.edu/yjlh/vol5/iss2/7.

Carver, T.N. (1925) 'The Diffusion of Ownership of Industries in the United States', *Proceedings of the Academy of Political Science in the City of New York* 11(3): 39–46.

Cobb, T. (1858) *An Inquiry into the Law of Negro Slavery in the United States of America*. Athens, GA: University of Georgia Press.

Coffee, J. (2001) 'Convergence and its Critics: What Are the Preconditions to the Separation of Ownership and Control?' in T. McCahery, P. Moreland, T.

Raaijmakers and L. Renneboog (eds), *Corporate Governance Regimes: Convergence and Diversity*, 83–112. Oxford: Oxford University Press.

Coffee, J. (2004) Law and the Market: The Impact of Enforcement, Columbia Law School Working Paper No. 182. Available at: http://papers.ssrn.com/sol13/papers.cfm?abstract_id=967482.

DeLong, B.L. (1991) 'Did J.P.Morgan's Men Add Value? An Economist's Perspective on Financial Capitalism', in P. Temin (ed.), *Inside the Business Enterprise: Historical Perspectives on the Use of Information*, 205–236. Chicago: University of Chicago Press.

de Soto, H. (2000) *The Mystery of Capital: Why Capitalism Triumphs in the West and Fails Everywhere Else.* New York: Basic Books.

de Tocqueville, A. (1969 [1848]) *Democracy in America.* London: Penguin Classics.

Douglas, M. (1986) *How Institutions Think.* London: Routledge.

Dunbar-Ortiz, R. (2014) *An Indigenous Peoples' History of the United States.* Boston: Beacon Press.

Edling, M. (2014) *A Hercules in the Cradle: War, Money and the American State, 1783–1867.* Chicago: University of Chicago Press.

Galbraith, J. (1967) *The New Industrial State.* Princeton: Princeton University Press.

Hadden, S.E. (2003) *Slave Patrols: Law and Violence in Virginia and the Carolinas.* Cambridge, MA: Harvard University Press.

Hilt, E. (2008) 'When Did Ownership Separate from Control? Corporate Governance in the Early 19th Century', *Journal of Economic History* 68(3): 645–685.

Horne, G. (2014) *The Counter-Revolution of 1776: Slave Resistance and the Origins of the United States of America.* New York: New York University Press.

Horwitz, M. (1977) *The Transformation of American Law, 1780–1860.* Cambridge, MA: Harvard University Press.

Hughes, J. (1977) 'What Difference Did the Beginning Make?' *American Economic Review* 67(1): 15–20.

Hughes, J. (2014) *The Governmental Habit Redux: Economic Controls from Colonial Times to the Present.* Princeton: Princeton University Press.

Hughes, J. and Cain, L. (2011) *American Economic History.* 8th Edition. New York: Pearson.

Hurst, J.H. (1970) *The Legitimacy of the Business Corporation in the Law of the United States, 1780–1970.* Charlottesville, VA: University of Virginia Press.

Irogoin, A. (2015) Representation without Taxation, Taxation without Consent: The Legacy of Spanish Colonialism in America, Economic History Working Paper No. 64804. London: London School of Economics.

Jefferson, T. (1998 [1785]) *Notes on the State of Virginia.* London: Penguin Classics.

Joyce, F. (2016) 'Are You Ready for Some Hard Truths about the Birth of our Nation? Brace Yourself', *Alternet*, 3 July. Available at: www.rawstory.com/2016/07/are-you-ready-for-some-hard-truths-about-the-birth-of-our-nation-brace-yourself/.

Kagan, R. (2001) *Adversarial Legalism: The American Way of Law.* Cambridge, MA: Harvard University Press.

Lamoreaux, N. and Rosenthal, J.L. (2004) 'Legal Regime and Contractual Flexibility: A Comparison of Business's Organizational Choices in France and the United States during the Era of Industrialization', *American Law and Economic Review* 7(1): 28–61.

Larson, J.L. (2001) *Internal Improvement: National Public Works and the Promise of Popular Government in the Early United States.* Chapel Hill, NC: University of North Carolina Press.

Lasswell, H.D. (1928) 'Review of *Administrative Justice and the Supremacy of Law in the United States*', *American Journal of Sociology* 33(6): 1006–1008.

Leonard, T. (2016) *Illiberal Reformers: Race, Eugenics and American Economics in the Progressive Era*. Princeton: Princeton University Press.

Maier, P. (1992) 'The Debate over Incorporations: Massachusetts in the Early Republic', in C. Wright (ed.), *Massachusetts and the New Nation*, 73–111. Boston: Massachusetts Historical Society.

Mann, M. (1993) *The Sources of Social Power, Vol. 2: The Rise of Classes and Nation-States, 1760–1914*. Cambridge: Cambridge University Press.

Mann, M. (2005) *The Dark Side of Democracy*. Cambridge: Cambridge University Press.

Mann, M. (2012) *The Sources of Social Power, Vol. 3: Global Empires and Revolution, 1890–1945*. Cambridge: Cambridge University Press.

Means, G. (1930) 'The Diffusion of Stock Ownership in the United States', *Quarterly Journal of Economics* 44(4): 561–600.

Means, G. (1931) 'The Separation of Ownership and Control in American Industry', *Quarterly Journal of Economics* 46(1): 68–100.

Milhaupt, C.J. and Pistor, K. (2008) *Law and Capitalism: What Corporate Crises Reveal about Legal Systems and Economic Development around the World*. Chicago: University of Chicago Press.

Miller, A. (1953) *The Crucible*. New York: Viking Press.

Mizruchi, M.S. and Hirschman, D. (2009) 'The Modern Corporation as Social Construction', *Seattle University Law Review* 33(4): 1065–1108.

Naidu, S. and Yuchtman, N. (2016) Labor Market Institutions in the Gilded Age of American Economic History, Working Paper No. 22117. Cambridge: National Bureau of Economic Research.

Navin, T.R. and Sears, M.V. (1955) 'The Rise of a Market for Industrial Securities, 1887–1902', *Business History Review* 29(2): 105–138.

Ott, J.C. (2008) 'When Wall Street Met Main Street: The Quest for an Investors' Democracy and the Emergence of the Retail Investor in the United States, 1890–1930', *Enterprise and Society* 9(4): 619–630.

Ott, J.C. (2009) 'The Free and Open People's Market: Political Ideology and Retail Brokerage at the New York Stock Exchange, 1913–1933', *Journal of American History* 96(1): 44–71.

Piketty, T. (2014) *Capital in the Twenty-First Century*. Cambridge, MA: Harvard University Press.

Pocock, J.G.A. (1977) *The Political Works of James Harrington*. Cambridge: Cambridge University Press.

Ripley, W.Z. (1927) *Main Street and Wall Street*. Boston: Little, Brown and Company.

Roediger, D. (1991) *The Wages of Whiteness: Race and the Making of the American Working Class*. New York: Verso Books.

Roediger, D. and Esch, E. (2012) *The Production of Difference: Race and The Management of Labor in U.S. History*. Oxford: Oxford University Press.

Saxton, A. (1990) *The Rise and Fall of the White Republic: Class Politics and Mass Culture in Nineteenth-Century America*. New York: Verso Books.

Scott, D. (2016) *Fragments of the Peculiar Institution*. CPInprint. Available at: www.critialpractices.org.

Sombart, W. (1976 [1906]) *Why Is there no Socialism in the United States?* London: Macmillan.

Temin, P. (1991) *Inside the Business Enterprise*. Chicago: University of Chicago Press.

The Economist (2015) 'If Black America Were a Country', *The Economist*, 9 May.

Thomas, H. (1997) *The Slave Trade: The Story of the Atlantic Slave Trade, 1440–1870*. London: Simon and Schuster.

Tsuk, D. (2003) 'Corporations without Labour: The Politics of Progressive Corporate Law', *University of Pennsylvania Law Review* 151(6): 1861–1912.

Urofsky, M. (2009) *Louis D. Brandeis: A Life*. New York: Pantheon Books.

Villaverde, J.F. (2015) Magna Carta, the Rule of Law, and the Limits on Government, Working Paper No. 15–035. University of Pennsylvania: Penn Institute for Economic Research.

Wallis, J.J. (2004) 'Constitutions, Corporations and Corruption: American States and Constitutional Change, 1842–1852', *Journal of Economic History* 65(1): 211–256.

Wells, H. (2009) 'The Modernization of Corporation Law, 1920–1940', *University of Pennsylvania Journal of Business and Law* 11(3): 573–629.

Wells, H. (2010) 'The Birth of Corporate Governance', *Seattle University Law Review* 33(4): 1247–1292.

Part III

7 Institutions debate for development

Theories, concepts and institutional development in Tanzania

The book turns now from historical case studies to development. I am looking at the same underlying institutions – property rights, the nature of the state and how they influence corporate governance – but with a different emphasis. The focus in the next two chapters is on property rights, the role of law and legal system in development and on the entanglement between property rights and nature of the state in Tanzania and China and how they affect organizational forms and governance, with a focus on cooperatives in Tanzania and on listed firms in China.

The two countries in Part III are China (Chapter 8) and Tanzania (Chapter 7). China is here for several reasons. As a transition country, from socialism to capitalism, it allows us to look at a different evolutionary route into the institutions underpinning markets. It makes us disentangle the idea of markets and market incentives and how they operate within an officially non-capitalist institutional framework. In particular, it allows us to examine incentives underpinning market development, such as the use of the price mechanism over segments of the market and freedom to produce what individuals choose to produce once quotas are fulfilled (what used to be called market socialism) (Brus and Laski 1989). The route into capitalism from socialism also highlights the role of the state, which moves from one of extensive control via planning over production towards a gradual but very partial distancing from business. This is very different from a liberal ideology of separation between state and business affairs, and different also from the role of the state in nation-building coordinated capitalist economies. China is here also for the challenge it poses to prevailing ideas of what good institutions are and which institutions are necessary to foster capitalist enterprise and growth of markets.

Chapter 8 uses the North, Wallis and Weingast (2009) limited access order (LAO) framework to consider the nature of the state in the transition from planned non-market economy towards a market, capitalist economy. The discussions in the state versus market literature of Chinese institutions appropriate for this transition treat China as a 'normal' case of transition requiring the shopping list of market-supporting institutions. This approach was badly misguided for Russia; for China, which takes less notice of Western ideologies and international bodies, it leads to a lack of understanding as to how the Chinese political economy has made the transition and what its institutional underpinnings are. The literature has not taken into account the nature of the Communist Party, how it works at its different levels of government, and how far it has been flexible and permeable in being 'inclusive', an assessment of how that institution has functioned to absorb dynamic elements. And this requires an assessment of what kind of balance has been created between the political settlement of the dominant elite and the economic settlement, allowing a private sector and foreign investment sufficient security of property and contract to enable them to flourish. The LAO framework is appropriate for this kind of assessment, as it weighs up the trade-offs between different power groups in thinking about how such security and contracting is or is not supported. This requires the historical context in order to get at the shifting elites within the power structures.

Tanzania is also here for several reasons: it represents a basic LAO where control of violence and stability has been established by the state but where civil society is relatively fragile in terms of independence from the state, largely based around agricultural collectives such as cooperatives; and state fiscal capacity for spending on public goods is low. The challenge to capitalist development is to understand how institutions of particular types of property rights and rule of law/legal capacity favour certain groups over others and can inhibit market and enterprise development. In the context of post-1990s liberalization and exposure to international trade in commodities, there are tensions between individual, customary and state-vested property rights and the ability of agricultural groups to raise loans and develop enterprises. The argument made in Chapter 7 is that a basic LAO with low state fiscal capacity and high state intervention and control of agriculture – through various structures of pricing, selective support for cooperatives, marketing boards – where state-vested property rights have superseded customary property rights, and where individual property rights are tainted with their colonial legacy and are associated with foreign enterprise, building capitalist enterprise out of rural agriculture is fraught with obstacles. I also highlight the differences between capitalist development based on individualist structures – as illustrated particularly strongly in the cases for Britain and the United States – and that based on more collectivist structures such as cooperatives. The tensions between cooperatives establishing their own enterprise structures and governance and being dominated by state measures of control are brought out here, as well as the tensions between individual farmers and cooperatives.

I contrast the case of Tanzania with the argument of Chapter 8 on China where, despite highly skewed land rights favouring urban development against rural farmers' property rights and despite weak private property rights overall, rural (capitalist-type) enterprise expanded in the 1980s (being largely individualist and private despite being called town and village enterprises (TVEs)), sanctioned by state economic decentralization and local officials' incentives guaranteeing rights of enterprise that brought growth and employment. In both countries, contract enforcement and the rule of law have been subservient to the state executive, much more so in China than in Tanzania.

The other aim is to relate some of these current issues of development to the historical parallels in Western Europe pre-their transition to open access orders (OAOs). The thread developing here, mentioned in North, Wallis, Weingast and Webb (2013), is that institutional development in developing countries does not have the equivalent agenda as the Western trajectory had. I want to bring this theme out. This is in part due to the sequencing of institutional development. The history of colonialism, post-colonial independence and the move from state-led socialistic independence movements and governments giving way after a time to more market-driven and foreigner-friendly economic initiatives needs to be taken into account in understanding institutional evolutions. I wish to draw the comparison to the settlement of the United States, which was also a colonial settlement, and assess the argument made by Acemoglu, Johnson and Robinson (2001) that it was those colonies being settled with imported institutions that led to their successful adoption of capitalism and growth along European capitalist lines. This is too simplistic. The context of post-colonial relations and the issue of industrialization and catching up in a more internationalized world dominated by Western institutions are surely relevant.

So what is a limited access order?

I highlight two theoretical frameworks that are used in Part III: the North et al. (2009) and North et al. (2013) framework that characterizes the state in developing countries as an LAO and the Levy and Fukuyama (2010) framework on the sequencing of institutional governance patterns in the face of development constraints in poor countries.

The North et al. (2013) framework is an adaptation of the North et al. (2009) framework discussed in Chapter 2, but particularly focusing on the relevant aspects of the LAO for developing countries to think about how to adapt the LAO – in particular the middle areas of the basic LAO – to make it more relevant and have more traction with current development issues.

The logic of the LAO is built on the creation and structuring of rents, with rents making behaviour more predictable. Limiting access – there being a dominant coalition that has power – creates rents which may be stabilizing. Local monopolies and restrictions hinder entry and growth, but may also solve problems of violence. This is critical to coordinating powerful members of the dominant coalition. Rents limit violence, if violence destroys rents. The dominant coalition sees stability as a price worth paying for rents; it is better to allow some costs to the economy, to curb civil and political rights in order to create stability. Eliminating these rents would lead to disorder and violence, not to a competitive market economy. Rents are seen as a symptom of the development problem, not as a cause of it. There is a need to avoid instability and violence from competing groups.

This framework is forced to consider the dynamics of rent allocation: are new rents good or bad for economic growth? Do they sustain coordination or not? The solution to violence may impede long-run economic development through limiting access and competition. One question here is how the building of state capacity has contributed to limiting access – through extracting surpluses from agriculture and through restricting enterprise-building – in the interests of quenching violence and maintaining stability. A question for the China chapter concerns the knife-edge balance between expanding the private sector and guaranteeing sufficient security without the Chinese Communist Party being forced to give up political control.

There are different types of LAOs – fragile, basic, mature – depending on their control of violence and stability. Fragile LAOs have violence potential that has not been centralized into the state, and there are multiple sources of violence; instability of the state is a major problem. The concern in this book is not with the fragile LAO, but with the nature of the basic LAO and the mature LAO. The basic LAO is defined as having a well-established government/state, which is stable and which controls the main sources of violence potential; it has control of military and police. It is characterized as when the state or government is the main durable type of organization and there is a relative paucity of or lack of density in non-state civil society organizations. Elite privileges and organizations are strongly identified with the state. The mature LAO has greater development of civil society and perpetually-lived private organizations outside the state. In basic LAOs, there is still a threat of violence from outside the state; mature LAOs are more stable, and the government controls organizations with violence potential. In basic LAOs, political organizations are controlled by the state – often a one-party state – and there are rarely opposition parties. Mature LAOs have many political organizations and may have democratically elected parties. A mature LAO has courts or bureaucracy that enforce public law. Private organizations outside the state are developed and pressure government to keep commitments. Complex public sector institutions mean that there are courts, independent of government, and that private sector organizations can prosper. There can be regions within LAOs that are mature and regions that are basic. Some LAOs bring more violence capacity within the state – it is not necessarily the case that the state has a monopoly of violence, but the state can allocate rent activities to motivate organizations with violence capacity to refrain from violence, buying them off. North et al. (2009) argue that increasing the scope of the rule of law covering all public relations comes quite late in the maturation process; some aspects of the rule of law become universal before others. There is increasing reliability of government providing support for organizations and enforcing agreements. The strengthening of organizations – executive, legislature, military, police, political parties, unions and organizations in the private sphere, such as the creation of private firms – is part of becoming mature. This framework argues that independence from the state needs strength and coherence to hold the state accountable for its commitments.

LAOs compared with OAOs

How does the LAO differ from the OAO? OAOs foster organizations – economic, political and social – that defend their interests in response to government policies. Strong private organizations help check military and police control by the government. There is a fine balance here between the basic LAO, where there are constraints on the state due to private armies existing, and OAOs, where constraints on the state subject the state itself to the rule of law. (Employer armies such as Pinkertons in the United States suggest that the United States in the 1920s was not an OAO). In OAOs, entry is open to all meeting impersonal requirements, and the rule of law is impartially enforced. During the transition from LAO to OAO, impersonal exchange amongst elites expands and increases access. The movement is from having credible commitments to sustain rights for elites, which are defined impersonally, which are then extended to wider circles, for example, the case of property rights and their extension to wider impersonal rights. This involves defining and enforcing legal rights as societies develop private elite organizations.

The doorstep conditions of being on the cusp of becoming an OAO are that the rule of law applies to elites; that there are perpetually-lived elite organizations, public and private; and that there is consolidated political control of organizations with violence capacity. The rule of law for elites – adjudicating disputes amongst elites – needs to become formalized into the machinery of government and justice, and become operational for elites. Property rights – whose rights and what kinds of rights – and legal systems, say North et al. (2013), define elite privileges in the LAO. Perpetually-lived organizations create the possibility to limit entry and generate rents, especially for the government (North et al. 2009: 23). The establishment of laws and courts regularizes relations amongst elites. The key points in the case studies of LAOs in North et al. (2013) are the centrality of violence management; the central place of organizations of all sorts, private and public; the use of rents to organize political and economic coalitions; and the source of rents, which are privileges provided by the dominant coalition. It matters whether those rents are compatible with growth or not. The kinds of privileges that are talked about here are monopolies, advantageous political appointments, or control over resources.

The lessons I take from North et al. (2009; 2013) are that developing countries have their own social dynamic, which is different from now-developed countries. The problem of control over violence in order to gain stability is central. This affects the nature of property rights, which are not independent of the LAO state; LAOs are organized to prevent violence, and property rights in these states are subordinated to this logic.

An example of rents in Sub-Saharan African (SSA) countries are where groups enjoy privileges; monopsonistic marketing boards extract rents from farmers producing export crops to keep food prices low (Bates 1982). Those with power receive rents, and those without are exploited. Does such rent creation create stability in Tanzania? Would removing these institutions destabilize and create violence?

In other words, I need to think about the dynamics of institutional development: key organizations with violence potential can be satisfied so they remain in the ruling coalition, and yet there may be space for dynamic parts to open up. But this is not a foregone conclusion; things can progress or regress. Banks and stock markets may fail to pool savings in LAOs, and loans may be given to insiders and elites and not to outsiders. There may be rule of law and courts on paper, but in practice they may be corrupt. There may be rents for dominant elites and constraints on competition: the question North et al. (2009) ask is this: is it a zero-sum game or does it open things up? For example, with limits to access to a state's telephone monopoly, how much can rents be reduced without destabilizing the government?

Economic progress creates new areas for rents, and the issue is whether rents are distributed according to impersonal rules. So does the redistribution of ownership and control over property lead to growth? Does the process of privileges becoming impersonal lead to growth, or is there redistribution to dependencies, which reduces growth? In terms of land reform, is this an economic opportunity, or is land held by the politically powerful? North et al. (2009) compare the distribution of rents in industry in Korean *chaebol* which, they argue, gradually lessened in importance with government gradually trimming privileges, opening up opportunities; they contrast this with China where, they argue, the power of foreign companies has been linked to the political party, with no opening up. They also highlight the importance of organizations of all types, which are independent of government, in the context of single-party governments. The difficulties in forming a business or getting a licence matter, and that depends on how impersonally both government agencies and banks operate towards outsiders.

Democracy and elections are different in LAOs from OAOs; they are useful even if not free and fair. But moving quickly to democracy can lead to instability due to highly personal patron-client relations, with clients trading votes for privileges. Adjustments in power through elections need to occur peacefully. The relationship between elections and growth is unclear; in Korea, there has been a slow move towards democracy.

In reducing violence, does the state have a monopoly of violence, and how should it get there? Strengthening the military can be counterproductive. There needs to be incentives for organizations not to use violence. There needs to be a balancing of powerful interests, along with a recognition of who they are, to be able to limit military power, as well as the military having a monopoly of violence. The history of state capacity in Europe arose out of military capacity. It is questionable, even for OAOs, whether civilian politics controls military power in many countries. I do not manage to answer these myriad questions in Chapters 7 and 8, but I place them here so that they inform the considerations of property rights and their entanglement with the nature of the state.

The other framework I wish to juxtapose here is that of Levy and Fukuyama (2010), which highlights the importance of the sequencing of institutional measures integrating governance and growth. It considers state capacity building, the reshaping of political institutions, the transforming of civil society, and what they call 'just enough governance' in order to think about the dynamic interconnections between these different ways of entering into the development process. From our historical stories, I saw that Britain had a different development sequence from Germany, from France, and from the United States, and this issue of sequencing is important for the developing and transition country development process. As a way of historicizing the North et al. (2009) framework, it is a matter of historical contingency which type of transformation occurred first and how they linked together. I need to think of the development process in developing countries in a similar historical light.

Levy and Fukuyama (2010) suggest a four-pronged framework for thinking about unlocking the institutional obstacles to growth and development in poor countries. These four prongs are: state capacity building, meaning improving public sector performance and increasing investor confidence that way; transformational governance, which means a wholesale reshaping of the country's political institutions which increases accountability and reduces arbitrary action; just enough governance, which focuses on growth itself and tackling institutional obstacles as and when they are reached; and bottom-up development strategies that look at civil society organizations, increasing non-public-sector organizations as a way of pressurizing public sector institutions to reform themselves. The back and forth between institutional reform and growth, in poor countries today and in historical terms for our now rich countries, happened in a variety of sequences. This framework highlights the different routes or entry points, as they argue, and also the importance of the interactions – one unlocking leading to another unlocking – that characterize the development process. Thinking about these dynamics using this framework brings a historical contingency element into the developing country studies.

On the sequencing of economic and political reform, writers on the authoritarian transition (Moore 1966; Huntingdon 1968; Zakaria 2003) argue that the liberal rule of law comes more often before democracy, with the causal connection running from economic growth to democracy, as it did in Western Europe and the United States. So how do I think about the sequencing issue in the building of civil society, state building, and of liberal democratic political institutions including the rule of law and electoral democracy? How are they related to one another?

The role of the rule of law needs to be considered broadly; there are different conceptions of the legal system. Previous chapters considered the different balances between judicial and administrative power alongside the degree of independence from the executive of judicial power. One question that is levelled in assessing the status of rule of law is whether the rule of law applies equally to the executive as to the rest of society. On another level though, it is a question of the philosophy of law, the role that the rule of law plays, where 'it' comes from.

In *How Institutions Think,* Mary Douglas (1986: 6–8) sets up a thought experiment about a group of people trapped in a cave without food debating whether to kill one of their party in order to survive. It is set up as a story, 'The Case of the Speluncean Explorers', in a court of law, with different judges deciding whether to convict the survivors of murder. She contrasts the hierarchical order, which would gently debate which of their members should be sacrificed – the leader, the youngest, the eldest; the sectarian group, which would await death singing hymns; and the individualists, who would play a game of dice to decide who should be sacrificed. The judges themselves have differing views of the rule of law: they cannot agree because 'they are using their institutional commitments for thinking with' (Douglas 1986: 7). The commitments to the role of the rule of law come prior to how the law operates. This ties in with the extent of individualism, extent of collectivism or hierarchical groupings within the structures of each society.

For China and Tanzania, the individualist view of the rule of law as above and separated from the executive is contested. For both countries, periods of one-party socialist rule demoted the rule of law to dependence on the executive. For Tanzania, as for other SSA post-colonial states, in part this represented a reaction against colonial rule. For China, this was part of the legacy of the Maoist period. How much and in what ways has this mattered? How has it impeded capitalist development? Routes to capitalist development depend less on prior institutionalizing of private property rights, independence of rule of law and judiciaries from the state, and independence of business from the state than the institutionalist literature supposes. This is not to say that anything goes.

Tanzania's variety of capitalism and limited access order

Does Tanzania have a variety of capitalism? How can I integrate ideas about Tanzania's LAO and the intertwining of property rights and state capacity to analyze its capitalism? In continuing themes from Chapter 6, the aim of this chapter is also to make a contrast with the early origins of the post-colonial United States – that archetypal capitalist economy and also former colony.

Part of Acemoglu and Robinson's (2012) argument is that colonial origins shaped the formation of institutions underpinning capitalism either positively (for the United States and other British colonies such as Australia and New Zealand) or negatively (for most African countries). The effort in the previous chapter was to nuance those arguments and understand the shaping of underlying institutions in the United States and their influence on capitalist institutions of corporate governance, such as the use of equity markets and companies' ownership structures in terms of which types of property rights became most protected.

It might seem strange to juxtapose the evolution of the United States into capitalism with the Tanzanian transition, but one point of this book is to emphasize the roots from which capitalism grew in the West – their particularity, the uncertain processes that were undergone in the formation of the institutions that came to signify 'market-building capitalist institutions' – and to show that similar pathways, debates, struggles between different groups characterize current transitions in the poorest countries.

Some key institutional features that I emphasized for the United States in Chapter 6 included the gradual winning of individual property rights and their legitimation, meaning the translation of squatting rights, extra-legal rights, into formal legal rights. The United States in its expansion evolved towards strengthening individual property rights, backed by common law, independent of the state executive but shaped by Supreme Court decisions. The United States had by design a relatively decentralized state with separated powers, with states' sovereignty balanced against federal government power – a relatively weak central federal state in domestic matters compared with states' sovereignty and the judiciary's powers through the Supreme Court. However, US federal fiscal capacity was strengthened through the institution of its creating public debt and funding that debt through taxation and customs duties. This strengthening of fiscal capacity played a key part in financing the expansion of the United States in the various purchases and wars. Stemming from the relatively weak central state, race and racial difference institutionalized themselves in the basics of institutions: non-whites did not have property rights but were property, were not full citizens until the 20th century, and remain discriminated against into the 21st century. The centrality of the corporation, as a legal (and individual) person backed by common law decision-making with the support of the Supreme Court, was independent of the federal government and hugely significant in forging the US variety of capitalism. It contributed to giving substantial power and autonomy to employers against employees through the corporation and through employer violence and private armies. The US state did not have the monopoly of violence; other institutions and individuals armed themselves.

This chapter places Tanzania against these characteristics of the early United States and its expansion and growth of capitalism. Tanzania has a quasi-typical SSA history – typical in the sense of having a colonial history (under Germany and then Britain), which was followed by the post-colonial creation of an Africanized one-party socialist state under a charismatic leader, Julius Nyerere, who forged Tanzanian identity and independence from Western powers, and then a post-socialist liberalization of institutions in the 1990s. It is also relatively land-rich and dependent on land and agriculture (Platteau 1992).

The nature of its property rights is central to Tanzania's variety of capitalism. Tanzania is relatively peaceful, not violent in the ways that 19th- and 20th-century United States was: the state has a greater monopoly of violence; employers do not have independent means to suppress workforces; it is not expansionary, fighting wars and extending its borders. The argument made here is that individual market-based property rights, independent of the state, were associated with colonial rights of foreigners and have not been favoured as a goal for development. A strong centralized state with few constraints emerged in the 1960s both to counter foreign power and to suppress inter-ethnic violence coming from attachment to customary rights to the land. Customary rights have been transformed into statist user property rights, with strong links maintained between the state and government in power and the rights to settle or resettle particular districts with state-backed in-migrants.

State-vested property rights have bolstered state-led urbanization and industrialization policies keen to promote large-scale and foreign investment. The promotion of these rights has led to land conversions from smallholder agriculture towards more industrial uses. It is a continuation of policies from the 1960s of extracting agricultural surpluses for use in state-led projects. The weakness of farmer land rights has excluded the rural poor from participating in rural enterprise.

The strong centralized state has, by and large, quashed and quietened ethnic divisions within the country. As argued below, there have been tensions through state-vested user property rights in favour of particular ethnic groups backed by the state and against other ethnic groups with stronger customary claims in specific regions, but these ethnic tensions have not escalated to a national level, and ethnic difference has been subdued by the overriding strength of centralizing state political power.

In terms of meta-institutions, the focus here is on agricultural structures and rural enterprises associated with agriculture. I look at agricultural cooperatives in coffee and tea, on their relationship with the state and on the tensions between different enterprises in the agricultural value chain.

Agricultural enterprise has been dominated by cooperatives, which themselves have a long (collectivist) tradition and particular history. These structures have gone through a period of being completely under state control, particularly in the 1970s, through to liberalization in the 1990s. I argue here that, despite liberalization, cooperatives remain dominated by the state through its involvement not only in regulatory matters but in their internal governance, such as vetting the selection of members of primary society boards and auditing their financial affairs. Mixed in here is an attitude of strong paternalism by the state towards the cooperative members, which is shared by some of the farmers themselves. I suggest that these pulls of traditional collectivist structures also may inhibit individuals' capacity to break away in more individualistic capitalist modes, which is compounded by their weak entitlement in terms of land rights and access to external finance.

The other meta-institutional governance issue touched on here is the complex relationship down the value chain from tea-growing farmers in a tea association into ownership of a tea-processing company with further links into branding and direct selling to Western companies. Again, it is not clear that farmers have sufficient clout in the value chain to influence the terms of trade they receive for tea in their favour. There are, however, opportunities for some to work in those factories further down the value chain.

Context

Tanzania is typical of poor agricultural Sub-Saharan Africa with goals of economic growth and poverty alleviation. By 2013 figures, 68 per cent of its population were living below the level of $1.25 per day (UNDP 2013); 36 per cent of its population in 2012 were assessed as below the basic needs poverty line. Real per capita GDP increased from $304 in 2002 to $647 in 2012, despite growth in GDP of 6.8 per cent per annum between 2007 and 2012, which is above the SSA average of 5.2 per cent (Planning Commission 2013). Agriculture as a share of GDP has been declining, from 30 per cent in 1998 towards 20 per cent in 2012, according to the Tanzanian Planning Commission, although the Food and Agriculture Organization of the United Nations (FAO) estimate places it closer to 30 per cent; but agriculture still accounts for around 80 per cent of employment (FAO 2013). Agriculture's average growth rate was 4.2 per cent per annum 2002–2012.

Sutton and Olomi (2012) give us an enterprise map of Tanzania after a decade of substantial growth: agriculture grew by a factor of 1.5 and manufacturing by 2.2, and the foreign direct investment/gross domestic product (FDI/GDP) flow averaged 3.2 per cent per annum over 2001–2010. They chart the diverse industrial growth that has taken place since 2001 across different industrial sectors, from agribusiness, manufacturing and construction. Enterprises are a mix of cooperatives, multinational corporations and local private firms. Since the mid-1990s, there has been substantial privatization. Of the 50 largest industrial companies, 29 are domestic private companies and the rest are foreign or government-owned. Of the 29 domestic companies, 14 are start-up ventures and 12 are pre-existing trading firms built on the long tradition of trading and knowledge of markets. However, these firms are still relatively few in number and fairly concentrated: 22 firms account for half of Tanzania's exports, so growth has been led by a small number of leading firms (Sutton and Olomi 2012).

Sutton and Olomi highlight poor infrastructure and unclear property rights inhibiting enterprise development. The inability to get hold of raw materials has affected volumes and scaling up. Many of these challenges relate to insufficient public expenditure and low fiscal capacity: poor infrastructure, poor distribution, lack of power supply, and inability to scale up due to failure to get access to inputs such as raw materials or capital. In addition, various issues relating to property rights are identified as challenges to enterprise growth by Sutton and Olomi (2012): restrictions on access to land, lack of clarity over land title, difficulty in transferring title, and administrative delays are all obstacles to industrial enterprise. Why has economic development and poverty reduction not taken place through industrialization processes, building up diffuse rural and urban enterprise, diversifying away from reliance on agricultural commodities, in the way managed by China (see Chapter 8)?

Boone's (2014) argument is that the obstacles to development cannot be understood without seeing the institutions of property rights and their entanglement with African states: 'The architecture and political character of rural property regimes have been invisible and untheorized' (Boone 2014: 3). They have made most of rural Africa governable but in their institutional underpinnings have created or perpetuated dependency by the rural poor and have prevented their escape from subsistence agriculture.

This chapter examines the underlying institutional foundations in terms of the intertwining of different types of property rights of different groups and their traction with the dominant elites within the apparatuses of government. The basic argument is that the rural poor, overwhelmingly smallholder farmers, have had and continue to have weak *de facto* land rights which are customary in type over their lands, held in villages and organized often through cooperatives. In the struggles between different types of property rights – customary *versus* state-vested *versus* individual private property rights – despite some formal legal protection for customary land rights, *de facto* customary land rights have lost out in the privatization of land rights via state-vesting of those rights, which is done to encourage large-scale and mainly foreign investment. Typical of many SSA countries, including Tanzania, has been the faith the state or government has placed in large-scale investment, often foreign, to create development opportunities through industrialization of agriculture to reduce poverty (German, Schoneveld and Mwangi 2013).

The power given to state-vested user property rights is a continuation of a longer history of post-colonial vesting of powers in a centralized state and its bureaucracy. This operated for around 30 years (1961 to the early 1990s) through more formal state-owned and state-directed highly concentrated industrialization projects, which were financed through control over pricing and marketing of agricultural commodities such as coffee and sisal produced by farmers. Post-1990s, with liberalization, there has been encouragement of private ownership and investment opened up to outsider, foreign, larger-scale investors. Despite liberalization, there is still substantial state control over agricultural prices through marketing boards and through state agents – district commissioners, extension officers – having influence over policies, personnel, and enforcement of regulation in agriculture.

Imagine yourself a farmer in a coffee cooperative or tea association in Tanzania. Land is allocated by the village primary society. There is a board of the primary society for which you have a vote. The board of the primary society settles property disputes within the village. It is likely that some of the hierarchical structures of electing elders to the board remain. There is diversity between older and younger generations, with the younger on average being more literate, better educated, more able to keep accounts and more likely to use services provided by the state, such as extension officers, more likely to use fertilizers and pesticides and newer tools, and more able to monitor prices of coffee or tea and to choose between buyers – whether to market through the cooperative and marketing board or market directly to outside buyers. They are also more likely to have a bank account. This chimes with Collier, Radwan and Wangwe's (1986) observations of inequality within villages in Tanzania. But farmers are very unlikely to be able to raise money for loans for investment. Surpluses are small, and there is no formal written title to their land. They are able to monitor prices of crops closely but will not have sufficient capital to move out of traditional crops. Diversifying into other crops, such as avocados, and operating on a larger scale, is done by foreign investors buying up land with more secure title and with state backing (observations from field trip in August 2011). Nyerere (1968) himself in The 1967 Arusha Declaration emphasized the divisions in his country between urban dwellers and rural dwellers and said that 'the real exploitation in Tanzania is that of the town dwellers exploiting the peasants' (Nyerere 1968: 376).

To get at this story, I use Boone's (2014) analysis of conflict over land rights through different types of property rights and how the strength of a particular form is linked to who is in power in the state. I link her arguments to the North et al. (2009; 2013) framework, outlined in the introduction to Chapter 7, to flesh out Tanzania as a basic type of limited access order. Restricted access to property rights and narrowly-based state capacity underpin development that itself is narrowly-based, reliant on larger-scale investments requiring access that only domestic and foreign elites have.

The chapter is organized as follows: the next sections focus on primary institutions and set out Boone's analysis of different types of property rights and uses it to analyze the disposition of land rights in Tanzania historically since independence in 1961 through to the post-liberalization of the 1990s to 2012. I then analyze the nature of the Tanzanian state using the parameters of North et al. (2009; 2013), incorporating various of the measures used by Levy (2004, 2013) and Bates (1982, 2014) and setting these in historical context. I discuss this as elite capture of the rule of law (German et al. 2013) and suggest contrasts with the institutions of early US capitalism, a most unlikely comparator from the perspective of the 21st century, but closer in structure if comparing formative post-colonial states and how property rights and state fiscal capacity were constructed in the creation of a unified nation-state. The final section takes a closer look at the meso-institutions, organizational forms such as cooperatives, particularly coffee cooperatives and tea associations. This examines how their (more collectivist) governance structures have worked, squeezed between state influence and the pulls of the market. In outlining their history to the present day, I argue that state involvement in these cooperatives has continued to be substantial and perpetuate indirect ways in which rural surpluses have continued to be siphoned off towards urban industrial development and in which rural enterprise has been restricted.

Property rights and land reform: Conflicts between three types of rights

The big institutional issue shaping capitalism and development in Tanzania, alongside other SSA countries, is that of land tenure, the nature of property rights and land reform. In Tanzania, 80 per cent of the population continue to depend on agriculture (FAO 2013). The context for considering different types of land rights is one of increased acquisition of SSA farmland by large-scale investors (German et al. 2013; World Bank 2011). German et al. (2013: 2) argue that 'strengthening customary land rights may conflict with investment promotion as policy objectives'. Boone (2007, 2014) contrasts market-based property rights regimes of individualized private property rights, tradable through markets in land, with hierarchical systems of land rights, customary, neo-customary and state-vested user property rights. These latter systems are hierarchical in the sense of deriving authority through either the state as hierarchy or the family/village/elder as customary authority.

Boone (2014: 4) links the nature of land tenure with the nature of the state in Africa: 'Land tenure regimes are property regimes that define the manner and terms under which rights in land are granted, held, enforced, contested and transferred'. Perry Anderson (1974: 404–405) used the term 'regime' to signify the system of rules in which property rights are operated: who has access to rights, who assigns them, who transfers them, who enforces them, adjudicates disputes and the procedures for doing so (Boone 2014: 4). Boone's argument is that land rights – their type, access to them, adjudications of them and support for them – are highly politicized in SSA states, with support for particular forms of land rights associated with support for particular groups in a region. Her case studies across SSA countries illustrate that within any one country there are areas where the state supports indigene groups (for example the Ashanti Region in Ghana, or Central Province in Kenya), in-migration is low, and authority over land disputes is relatively decentralized at the local and family levels (Boone 2014: 85). She contrasts these areas of strong neo-customary rights with those where statist rights predominate (such as the Rift Valley in Kenya, the Kiru Valley in northern Tanzania, or eastern Rwanda). These statist-dominated areas give priority to in-migrants at the expense of ethnic insiders (indigenes). The tying of particular governments to support of particular forms of property rights makes elections tense, as land rights for a group are associated with a particular party in power. Boone (2007: 560) argues that mass enfranchisement has come before rather than after the general consolidation of a market-based property regime and that this makes African countries' different from Western Europe's histories.

Early US history shows a similar sequencing of democracy before the settling of land rights (see Chapter 6). The difference there was that, with a weaker central state and stronger corporations, extra-legal land rights became legalized through a more decentralized common law system in favour of individualized private property rights. De Soto (2000), for example, and the World Bank (1989) see private formal registration and titling of land in poor agrarian countries as a way of increasing efficiency and productivity in agriculture. They argue that it is the uncertainty and negotiability of customary tenure that inhibits improvements in agricultural resources (German et al. 2013).

Boone (2007, 2014) argues that the way the African state has been created has been through interpretation and enforcement of rural land rights, protecting the power of allies, promoting commercialization of agriculture, which has fixed some rural populations to the land whilst promoting the mobility of others. The idea behind state user rights was to break down old customary rights, to bring new land into productive use. Under these user rights, small farmers are not freeholders as the state is the landlord holding final rights to the land.

History of land rights

Before colonialism, landholding in Tanzania was based on customary laws of the 120 different tribes. Title to land was based on traditions and customs. Ownership was communal, land being owned by the family, clan or tribe. Chiefs, headmen and elders had powers of land administration. Since 1963, chiefs have been replaced by elected village councils.

German (1884–1916) and later British (1917–1961) land tenure declared all land to be Crown and public land. By a German imperial decree of 1885, all land – occupied or not – was treated as unowned Crown land, vested in the Empire, excepting claims of ownership by private persons which could be proved. There was a distinction between claims of occupancy and rights of occupancy. Claims had to be proved by documentary evidence; occupation by fact of cultivation. Settlers doing plantation agriculture such as sisal or tea and who could prove title had security of tenure; indigenous people who couldn't prove ownership had only permissive rights of occupancy. By British land tenure legislation, the Land Ordinance of 1923, all lands, occupied or not, were public lands except those lawfully acquired before the ordinance. Rights of occupancy were either granted or deemed: granted rights were statutory and subject to law, whereas deemed rights were customary and governed by administrative policy. During 44 years of British rule, 3.5 million acres were alienated from native lands in favour of settlers.

The Government of Tanganyika in 1961 inherited the vesting of land in the state as the ultimate landlord, and until 1995 the Tanzanian government kept these basic premises with the president holding radical title and occupancy rights. State-vested property rights underpinned strong charismatic one-party rule from independence through to the mid-1980s. Tanzania has a user rights property rights regime, where land use over time confers citizenship and access rights. This is mainly for farming households, the moral basis to the land claim resting in their labour (sweat equity). This confers huge rights to the state in terms of allocation of land rights and settlement of disputes. The state is the mediator in exchange in user rights regimes: the state's endorsement is required to acquire land. This is very different from a private property rights regime where land is commoditized and under market allocation rather than state allocation (Boone 2007: 50). This is also different from a regime of customary rights where local groups reallocate property rights and have the political sovereignty to do so.

In Tanzania, the 1967 Arusha Declaration led to villagization, *ujamaa*, a form of collectivization of cooperatives into more directly controlled communal farms. This challenged existing land rights and allocation, carrying out relocation and resettlement on a massive scale in the 1970s and involving 50 per cent of the national population, with between 5 million and 8 million people being relocated to 8,000 new villages (Boone 2014: 41). This involved the forced movement of farmers into collective villages (Collier et al. 1986). Agricultural productivity stagnated, and it left a legacy of suspicion and fear of state interference in agriculture. State agents have continued to play a hands-on role in resource allocation and dispute resolution in defiance of traditional communal rights. The 1990s structural adjustment programmes, aiming to get states to withdraw from input-distribution (of seeds, credit and tools) nevertheless allowed the connection between land tenure and the state to remain.

There have been a number of land law initiatives since 1992: the 1995 National Land Policy; the Land Act and the Village Land Act of 1999; and the Land (Amendment) Act of 2004. The National Land Policy in 1995 recognized the need to accommodate changes and conflicts in land use and increases in the population, and it wanted to encourage prospective investment with liberalization as well as getting over the heritage of the villagization programme of the 1970s.

There has been considerable dispute in Tanzania over the kind of property rights regime that should be adopted (Tsikata 2001). The user rights principle has won out, and the law has strengthened the power of the central state (Shivji 1998). Through the two land bills, the Ministry of Lands and through the Ministry the commissioner have powers over ownership, control and management of village land. The commissioner has even greater powers over reserved and general land. The bottom-up role of more elective bodies, such as village assemblies, has been reduced (Shivji 1998). A user rights regime does provide some constraint on the central state expropriating land without recourse to due process of law, but it nevertheless gives huge redistributive power to the state in terms of reallocation of land rights. It then becomes a question of whose rights prevail.

There are pressures for land reform and clarity over land rights: but all reform has been in the direction of vesting land rights in the state, institutionalizing user rights rather than promoting private property rights or reinforcing community rights (Boone 2007). There is some dispute as to whether formalizing customary rights strengthens or weakens those rights. Herbst (2000: 186–187) argues that state recognition of customary tenure has been disruptive. Others argue that state recognition helps preserve these rights. Green (2006) argues that institutionalization of collective land rights in Uganda has curbed the power of the central government to expropriate land and has stemmed the flow of outsiders and foreign investors.

A user rights strategy calls for land registration and titling to stabilize land access, securing rights, making expropriation less easy and making investment and technological change less risky for the small farmer. But Boone (2014) argues that the political implications of a user rights strategy go against customary rights. Users are not community members; they are usually 'ethnic strangers', outsiders to the traditional community, with state rights boosting in-migration to an area. Boone calls them protected clients of the state, such as in the case of the Kiru Valley in the Manyara Region of Tanzania. Tsetse used to infest the valley until the colonial government eradicated it in the 1940s, after which the lands were owned by European settlers, with some in-migrant farm labourers allowed to own a few acres. The lands were then expropriated by the state in 1967 and leased out to foreign companies by the state. In the 1990s, the lands were then leased out to large landholders, often Tanzanians of Asian descent, against the objections of smallholder farmers. The state has backed outsider investors against 'indigenous' small-scale farmers (Boone 2014: 347). It also goes against private property rights, as the state continues to be involved in land exchange and allocation.

Another Tanzanian case that Boone reports is in the Babati District in northern Tanzania. This again is a case of a sparsely populated area until cleared of tsetse fly in the 1940s and 1950s. It was then populated by in-migrants purchasing land from the Gorowa Native Authority. *Ujamaa* resettled these villages, with farmers being allocated new lands by the government. In 1992, pre-*ujamaa* land rights were abolished by the government and in-migration was continued. Land administration is settled by the local courts and tribunals. There are no competing customary claims in this area, which would not be recognized by the statist local courts (Boone 2014: 347–348).

The Mbulu District in the Iraqw homeland in northern Tanzania on the edge of the Rift Valley has intensive agriculture, with high competition for land. Customary claims are strong at the village level in this region, but the strong statist regime means that disputes are sent to the national land administration bodies rather than being tried locally (Boone 2014: 348). A contrasting area reported by Boone is of the Giting Ward in Hanang District, where pastoralists were pushed out in the 1950s by the colonial administration, creating a 'yeoman' class or commercial farmers with large holdings. These were then broken up by the *ujamaa* policy and redistributed to smallholders and landless who migrated into the region. There is competition in the area between erstwhile large landholders trying to regain lands against smallholders. The former customary pastoralist claims have been extinguished by statist law (Boone 2014: 349).

There are supporters of a non-statist private property rights regime. The World Bank has advocated land registration and titling programmes to promote capitalist farming (World Bank 1989; de Soto 2000). Turning arable land into private property with formal property rights means land can then be mortgaged, sold or used as collateral for loans. Women's movements also support a private-rights-based approach to landownership as a way of escaping the hierarchical, patriarchal customary rights that discriminate against women having ownership of land. But the World Bank's idea of land titling would gradually transfer land use and rights away from small farmers with little capacity to invest in land and into the hands of richer capitalist farmers, a version of the kulak problem. There are protests against this sort of land reform for the adverse effects it has on the land rights of small producers (Myenzi 2005).

German et al. (2013) look at how land rights are processed and dealt with on the ground across four SSA countries (Tanzania, Ghana, Mozambique and Zambia) with differing formal emphases on customary rights and statist rights. They look at provisions to protect customary rights, what types of land rights are offered to investors, what kinds of initiatives there are guiding the allocation of land, consultation processes with customary users, local representation mechanisms, the roles of intermediaries and who they are, whether there are compensation mechanisms and requirements to mitigate impact, the monitoring of procedures, and finally what the mechanisms are for resolving disputes. They find Tanzania more protective of statist rights and less so of customary rights than Ghana in particular. Although there are formal provisions for consultation, representation and mitigation for customary rights, in practice the dice are stacked against customary users and in favour of outside larger-scale investors.

The overall picture is of statist land rights, administered at the district and national level, being the predominant form of property rights in Tanzania. This contrasts with various other SSA countries – Ghana, Rwanda, Côte d'Ivoire and Senegal – where in regions customary rights are stronger. There is a patchwork of different and shifting land rights over many SSA states. What unites them thematically is their close ties to the political regime in government: land rights are politicized and not independent of the state.

Tanzania's limited access order and state capacity

The legacy of colonialism in Tanzania has been the creation and support for a more centralized and strongly enforcing, unifying Africanizing state than occurred in the United States in the post-colonial late 18th century. The creation of this state suppressed ethnic rivalries, uniting around Nyerere, around Swahili and suppressing private property. The elites were less concerned with containing state powers and constraints on the state.

I argue here that post-independence Tanzania fits into the categorization of basic limited access order (LAO). It has suppressed inter-ethnic violence. Violence capacity organizations are part of the government. The state is the main organization in society; political organizations are controlled by the state; and private elite organizations are closely tied to the dominant coalition. This conforms to North et al.'s (2013: 14) conception of the basic LAO. But what kind of basic LAO? What are its characteristics? The nature of the basic LAO in North et al. is rather thinly theorized, as pointed out by Levy in North et al. (2013). This is the area that many low-income developing countries are in and in particular Tanzania. Levy (2013) points to a trade-off within the basic LAO space between those states whose resources are concentrated on building up stronger state capacity and bureaucracy and those states whose state capacity is weaker but whose non-state organizations and constraints on the state are more developed. In determining where Tanzania fits into this schema, I look first at its post-colonial history to gauge who have been and are the dominant elites in Tanzania. This question has to be seen in terms of who have been insiders within the state and which groups have benefitted from the particular state policies adopted. Seen in terms of power and rent extraction, the small-scale rural farmer in cooperatives is excluded from the dominant coalition. According to North et al. (2009), change, transition, happens when the dominant coalition widens to allow more of the excluded in to reap rents. Has this happened and is it likely to?

From independence in 1961, Nyerere combated fragmentation and created a national identity through charismatic one-party leadership, Africanizing and strong enforcement of state control. Foreign-owned firms were taken over, and Tanzania became a one-party LAO, fusing economic and political power under state control. The civil service became a key source of patronage. It grew rapidly, becoming the largest employer in the country.

On independence, the legacy in terms of governance was a strong shell of formal institutions, political and bureaucratic, but mostly just a shell with a mix of colonial legacy and aspirations of independence (Levy 2004). The mode of governance shifted from formal checks and balances to what Levy and others call the neo-patrimonial system of rule, meaning strong central state control, reliant on allies loyal to the regime (Dia 1996; Lewis 1996; Levy 2004). With autocratic political leadership, there was a decline in the quality of bureaucracy, affecting policy and performance. Neo-patrimonial rule meant giving privileges and rents to allies of the ruling party. According to Levy (2004), this meant a disruption of markets, rising costs of doing business, protectionism, urban bias and a rentier relationship between government and business, with the business class dependent on government. Measuring the relationship between private firms and government in 1986 and 1996 and asking whether government was obstructive or helpful, Tanzania comes out as obstructive in both years, but less so in the later year (Levy 2004).

Price controls were imposed on the purchase and sale of food crops and on other products. The economy was centralized and managed through parastatals during the 1970s. The *ujamaa* villagization policy between 1973 and 1976 forced the movement of many farmers and illustrates the extent of state power at the expense of rural small farmers. The one-party state excluded many people, especially the rural poor. The central tool was distribution of patronage to the elite, the economy subordinated to maintaining the elite and allocating rents towards them.

Bates (1982, 2014) has charted the history of such policies against agriculture, pro-urban development, pro-highly-concentrated industry that gave out monopolies to favoured elites. Newly independent states, like Tanzania in the 1960s, seeking development and with socialist and independence ideologies, sought to industrialize. The policies for this were, and still are to some extent, taxing or extracting revenues from the primary exporting crops – coffee and sisal – and from the rural sector as a whole. The way this was done was through state institutions, the marketing boards, corralling all crops through it, paying the farmers a lower price than that on international markets, and taking as revenues the difference between those prices. These marketing boards are part of the state apparatus; they were established before independence with an original mandate to use the revenues for the farming community. But the state sequestered the revenues – either through borrowing at favourable rates of interest, or directly through control of the marketing agencies. The boards are 'faithful servants of governments' (Bates 1982: 15). The marketing boards were the main vehicle for appropriating funds from farmers.

Over time, borrowing shifted to taxation of farmers. Investments were made in the urban sector, with the urban population at 10 per cent receiving 30 per cent of public expenditure in the 1970s (Clark 1978). Investment policies for industrial development included the state securing low prices of raw materials from the farmers. Bates (1982) gives examples of coffee and sisal in Tanzania, with the Crop Authority buying coffee from farmers at under half the world market price in 1975–1976. For sisal, grown on large estates, the state subsidized six major spinning mills so that by 1980 Tanzania could process over 90 per cent of sisal production in order to increase the value of textile exports. The Sisal Authority sold to domestic sisal producers at a price well below the world market price and bought from the farmers at a reduced price. In 1976, the Tanzanian Sisal Authority sold 36.072 tons of fibre to local mills at TZS 1,984 per ton compared with an export price of TZS 3,007 per ton. Sales to spinning companies were subsidized, and the producers bore the brunt of the subsidy. The interests of farmers were sacrificed to building up industry. But in addition, plant location was on the basis of political advantage, maintaining labour forces for political advantage rather than profitability.

So the dominant elites were state civil servants and allies in monopoly industrial positions, and the smallholder farmers were outsiders, who did not favour industrial development especially when exports of agricultural goods were diverted to domestic urban use. The building up of state capacity through bureaucracy was another feature. With weak constraints on the state, the costs of marketing, storage, transport, disposal, careless contracting and growth in staff members and their perquisites soared (Bates 1982: 27; Kriesel, Laurent, Halpern and Larzelere 1970).

In this way, surpluses were extracted from farmers and agriculture, and transferred towards the growth of urban centres, towards growing industry, albeit in highly concentrated form. With few checks and constraints on the state, policy was captured by vested interests. With the state as the main employer, curbing unrest meant keeping down the cost of living, which meant keeping food prices low and controlling or forbidding exports of food. The Turner Commissions in Tanzania and Zambia on labour unrest in the 1970s focused on the urban demands for higher standards of living and the efforts of the governments to keep down prices of wage goods, food, to appease those demands. These states' wage bills included not only civil servants and bureaucrats but those operating ports and harbours, railways, transport systems and nationalized firms. One way to pacify urban interests was co-opting labour leaders onto government boards and public enterprises and giving them perquisites. Another was repression: using state capacity to jail labour leaders and dissolve unions. The link between urban unrest and agricultural policy was tight.

Further evidence of elites as urban and industrial at the expense of farmers can be seen in statements from the Bureau of Marketing and Research of the Tanzanian Ministry of Agriculture in 1977: 'Retail prices for the main cereals have not been increased for three years' (quoted in Bates 1982: 39). The government of 1971–1976 offered farmers between one-fifth and one-half of world food prices. Farmers marketing produce outside official channels were then subject to legal action. There was persistent conflict between farmer and bureaucrat in rural markets, with joint gains to corruption, as the bureaucrat could help the farmer evade market controls in exchange for bribes.

Post-liberalization position

Stevens and Teggemann (2004), in Levy and Kpundeh's *Building State Capacity*, compare Tanzania, Zambia and Ghana. They argue that the public sector in Tanzania has been run by elites beholden to various interest groups. Tanzania's political environment, with relative civic peace, unity and stability, owes much to the dominance of a single party (Kiragu and Mukandala 2004). Under the socialist system, there was a single ruling party – originally the Tanganyika African National Union, which later became the *Chama Cha Mapinduzi* (CCM). There was limited party competition, with broad popular support for CCM into the 1990s and 2000s in parliamentary and presidential elections. Trade unions stayed acquiescent. There was an uncompetitive pluralism and political stability. During the liberalization of the 1990s, there was a revival of the multiparty system and a re-emergence of the unions, and pay reform became a political issue, with a proliferation of allowances favouring senior civil servants. So, as Levy (2007) argues, there has been stability and bureaucratic capacity but dominated by a single-party state with much weaker civil society checks on state power through an independent judiciary or free press. Political order was achieved at the expense of spreading rights widely.

Levy (2007) highlights Tanzania's relatively strong bureaucratic capability. This idea of bureaucratic capability has more to do with the quality of the civil service, its administrative capability, than how far the state reaches into society. Levy contrasts this with constraints on the state, which comprise non-governmental organizations, the independence of the legislature, the judiciary, and features of civil society and media such as scrutiny by a free press, free elections and other institutions outside the immediate executive running government. Levy measures these checks and balances by amalgamating various world indices – the University of Maryland Polity IV database of executive constraints and Kaufmann-Kraay's rule of law and voice and accountability. He argues that Tanzania has weak constraints on its state power compared with Zambia.

How far has there been competitive clientelism in Tanzania, with competing elites as opposed to state dominance (Levy 2014)? How permeable are the boundaries between insiders and outsiders? Levy argues, based on these indicators, that Zambia has stronger checks and balances institutions than Tanzania, with more outside scrutiny and influence on insiders, but with weaker state capacity than Tanzania, and less public investment (at levels of 6 per cent of GDP). Tanzania's reported public capital investment figures give proportions of 9 per cent of GDP in 2012.

Tanzania is one of a group of low-income countries with strong bureaucracies and weak checks and balances institutions. Levy emphasizes the different types of elite bargain between insiders and outsiders. Tanzania has relatively sharp boundaries between insiders and outsiders, with higher payoffs for insiders than outsiders, in contrast to Zambia's more diffuse boundaries and payoffs between insiders and outsiders. Levy suggests that at low levels of income insiders in Tanzania have an incentive to consolidate their authority by building state capacity rather than investing in constraining institutions. These sharp boundaries between insider elites and outsiders map onto the urban-rural divide.

Tanzania's meso-institutions

Collectivist rather than individualistic organizational forms

Rural Tanzania is also a highly developed capitalistic agrarian economy in various respects. Alongside subsistence crops – of bananas and grain – are cash crops of tea, coffee, sisal and tobacco. These have complex organizational forms but not based on Macfarlane-style individualism. Rather than enterprises for cash crops being individual farms, they are organized into cooperatives. This overlaps with anthropological issues: relations between groups, be they tribes or clans, and the individual, and the role of leadership within groups and of patronage and obligation within groups. Who is chosen to represent farmers on primary society boards and on what grounds, and how decisions are made and debates conducted, especially when there are conflicts between members, are potent issues (Prevezer 2012: 32).

I look at the governance of cooperatives, which as an enterprise form has been important since the 1920s and has revived in significance in the

Tanzanian economy, and in particular cooperatives in cash crops, coffee and tea. These comments are based on Sutton's (2014) unpublished PhD thesis, fieldwork observations from a 2011 field trip, Prevezer (2012) and Prevezer and Sutton (2013). In particular, that work looked at the operation of Fairtrade Standards in the context of these cooperatives, which illustrate the structures of these enterprises. I look here at their internal governance structures – in terms of their issues of representation and voice for farmers within them – and their external governance, seen as their interface both with state agencies and structures such as district commissioners, marketing boards and technical extension officers, and their relationship with 'the market', the competition between what farmers receive at auction, through the marketing boards, and from selling directly to (international) companies.

These organizational forms are built up from individual farms and are complex organizational forms with elected representatives into primary societies – often collections of 2 or 3 villages – which are then organized into secondary unions, an example being the Kilimanjaro Native Cooperative Union (KNCU). In 2011, there were 70,000 producers in the KNCU with 67 primary societies. These large unions have a degree of control over pricing, the use of marketing boards, and the provision of training and equipment.

History of the cooperative as an organizational form in Tanzania

An important element of Tanzania's cooperative evolution since independence in 1961 has been a history of harnessing these cooperative structures first for socialist development from the mid-1960s to the late 1980s, and then for capitalist development since the cooperatives' liberalization from state control in the late 1980s. According to Bee (1996), Tanzania's cooperative history can be classified into six main periods, as outlined in Table 1. In 1967, 97% of agricultural exports were channelled through the cooperative movement, making Tanzania the cooperative giant of Africa (Livingston in Chambo 2009) and third largest cooperative movement in the world in terms of market share of agricultural exports (Maghimbi 2010). Maghimbi has figures of 62 primary societies in 1948 rising to 857 in 1961 at independence, to a peak of 2,500 in 1974, which fed into 38 secondary unions in 1961, reducing to 21 unions by 1974. Membership was around 331,000 people in the early 1960s, rising to 600,000 by the late 1960s.

For example, in 1925 the Kilimanjaro Native Planters Association (KNPA) was created in order to bulk and market Chagga coffee in the Moshi District and, according to the Tanzania Coffee Board (2010) (TCB), to protect the interests of small farmers. This was the first indigenous association of African coffee farmers and was created in order to address the monopoly of the crop by European settlers (Develtere 2008). In 1933, as a result of the 1932 Cooperatives Ordinance, the KNPA became the KNCU and was divided into primary societies. With independence in 1961, Nyerere praised cooperatives for their contribution to African socialism and provided coffee cooperatives

Table 7.1 Overview of Tanzania's cooperative history

Period	***Classification***
1925–1961	Growth of indigenous cooperatives
1961–1967	Nationalistic period: Expansion of cooperatives
1967–1976	Infusion of the *ujamaa* ideology into cooperation
1976–1984	Dissolution of cooperatives and parastatalization
1982–1991	Reinstatement of cooperatives and retreat of the parastatal sector
1991 onwards	Deofficialization of cooperatives and privatization

Source: Bee (1996)

with virtual monopoly status. But this came at a price of lessening their independence.

The laws setting up cooperatives in the 1960s gave the government a huge part to play. It had a strict supervisory and regulatory role over operational procedures: the registrar appointed by the state had the power to register and manage cooperatives, to amalgamate, deregister, approve budgets, authorize borrowing and expenditure, audit accounts, monitor financial performance, and replace elected members. All employment issues were within the commissioner's mandate (for example, remuneration, salary, hiring and firing) (Delvetere 2008). In the conflict between government and cooperative leadership, the government took responsibility for both external and internal governance (of cooperatives' unions dealing with markets and of their dealings internally with and within primary societies). Cooperatives lost their autonomy, their democratic control and their business efficiency, and membership of cooperatives fell.

In economic terms, there were benefits to cooperatives from their local monopoly positions through the absence of competition, the assuredness of a market, the fixing of prices, in other words the benefits of being part of state planning mechanisms. But the costs of those planning mechanisms were in terms of limitations to cooperatives' capacity-building, their access to markets, with no room to diversify and with costs of bureaucracy and attendant corruption.

In the 1967 Arusha Declaration, Nyerere stressed the role of cooperatives as an important tool for achieving the self-reliance that his party sought. While African cooperatives were ostensibly member-run organizations, many retained government-run features following independence: they were still large, had inflexible governance structures, and were based on administrative regions (Tallontire 1999). In the early 1970s, controversially Nyerere moved the majority of the country's population to farms in a forced villagization programme. This 'collectivization' was against the wishes of many producers, and production fell.

The 1975 Villages and Ujamaa Villages Act declared these villages to be multi-purpose cooperatives, but in 1976 the government abruptly announced the disbandment of all cooperative unions (Bryceson 1983). Nyerere justified this with claims that cooperatives could not cope with his 'quick march to socialism', as they were capitalist organizations (Birchall and Simmons 2010). All land became common property managed by the state, and from 1976 to 1982 cooperatives were replaced with crop authorities responsible for marketing agricultural produce directly from the villages. Cooperatives in effect became parastatals, losing their assets and disbanding their formally independent structure. The early 1980s were characterized by a crisis in production, which was in part due to external factors such as weak international demand for agricultural products and deteriorating international terms of trade, and in part due to public overspending and excessive government intervention (Ponte 2002). Six years following their dissolution, marketing cooperatives were reinstated by the Tanzanian parliament in a 1982 act, but they remained essentially government institutions in a monopoly marketing system (Tallontire 1999: 185).

After Nyerere stepped down in 1985 after five terms as president, as part of liberalization, structural and economic adjustment programmes were negotiated with the International Monetary Fund (IMF) and the World Bank (Ponte 2002). The 1991 Cooperative Societies Act made cooperatives autonomous from the government. Private curing companies were established to replace the parastatal companies of Tanzania's Coffee Marketing Board system, and the cooperative unions lost much of the coffee curing market share (Ponte 2002). Private traders, both local and foreign, entered the market and eroded the dominance of cooperatives in the marketing of agricultural products. These private companies were able to go straight to the coffee farm to buy, and farmers could sell to these private buyers rather than to the cooperative.

The period 1991–2003 saw more formal liberalization through the withdrawal of the state and a greater degree of management autonomy at the level of the union. Managerial autonomy in the secondary unions increased, which has resulted in conflicts between central management of cooperatives in the secondary unions and the members of primary societies. Chambo (2006: 6) talks also about the tussle between government and cooperatives, with the government seeing itself as protector of the governance of cooperatives 'so that it does not fall prey to unscrupulous individuals who may use the cooperative to exploit the lot of the members into continued poverty'. The government has talked about empowering members of cooperatives, but without giving the wherewithal to achieve this. There has been continued suspicion since 2003 of government control, that the government will take over again or disband the cooperative movement. with continuing suspicions that cooperatives still belong to the government. The cooperative policy document of 2004 emphasized the weakness of cooperatives, their low capital, poor leadership, derailed governance, low member participation, high degree of embezzlement, and poor trading (Chambo 2006).

The new policy sought to rejuvenate the cooperatives by placing them into new competitive markets, giving them greater freedom; encouraging competitive, member-based, ground-up governance; and emphasizing the centrality of the primary society as the engine of cooperative development. But the legacy of state control has remained in various ways: through the export crop strategy, linked to particular cash crops such as coffee, through the structures such as the state marketing boards and the auction whereby coffee is channelled through into exports. Cooperatives remain subcontractors, agents or affiliates of the powerful marketing boards, rather than having independent marketing strategies. The issue of interference or control by the state therefore remains. This manifests itself in continuing discontent within cooperatives over perquisites for managers and divisions between executive or management of secondary unions and primary societies.

Modern-day structures in the coffee sector

The transition to a capitalist economy is not complete, and the cooperatives are caught in the middle of this transition. They continue to be seen as agents of the state and state policy. The state's role vis-à-vis cooperatives is unclear: it has a regulatory and law-making role, but it also influences cooperative structure, processes and attitudes in more direct ways. This is endorsed by some general managers of the unions, who feel that cooperatives cannot run themselves without government supervision and direction.

In the early 21st century, Tanzania's coffee cooperatives come under the Ministry of Food, Agriculture and Cooperatives, which supervises the agricultural cooperative sector (see Figure 1). The Cooperative Development Department (CDD) is the main external contact for most primary and secondary cooperatives, and it oversees the Tanzanian Federation of Cooperatives (TFC), which is the umbrella body for all cooperatives in Tanzania. The TFC is an independent non-governmental, non-partisan umbrella body that promotes and coordinates all cooperative societies in Tanzania, and it is a member of the International Cooperative Alliance (ICA) (TFC and CDD 2006).

There is a registrar of cooperative societies, appointed by the government, who oversees the implementation and enforcement of cooperative laws and rules. The registrar's duties include registering, promoting, inspecting and advising cooperatives; in other words, this individual is quite highly involved in the societies' activities. The registrar has representatives, including district cooperative officers (DCOs) at the district level and assistant registrars at the regional level. The DCOs visit primary societies at least once a year and are involved in selecting individuals eligible to run for board elections. In an interview, a Bukoba DCO told Sutton (2014) that this situation is longstanding, although the number of DCOs has been greatly reduced since the country's period of socialism. The Moshi DCO told Sutton (2014) that her role involves supervising all cooperative activities, including registering new cooperatives, attending meetings, overseeing day-to-day activities, and

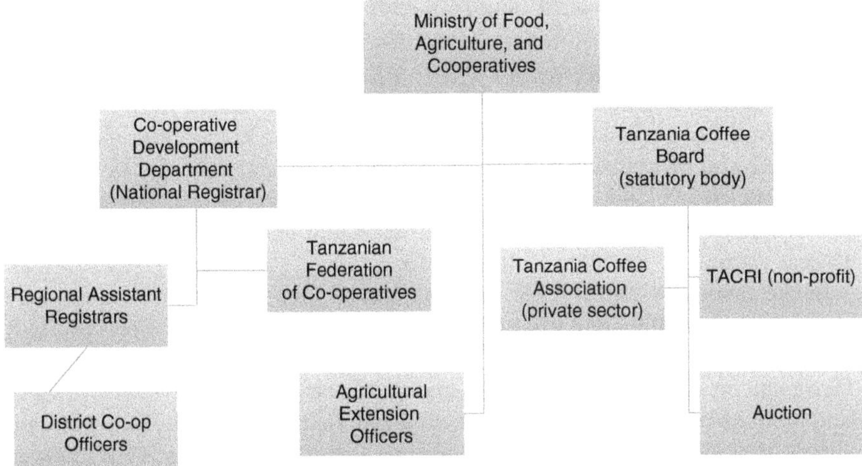

Figure 7.1 Tanzania's coffee structures

auditing the financials, as well as educating members, the board and employees. This level of government involvement was felt to be necessary because of the low level of education and capacity deemed to exist amongst farmers. The government sees itself in a paternalistic fashion as there to advise and guide farmers.

DCOs are heavily involved in selecting members of the board at the primary society, while the registrar fulfils the same role for the union. They play an active part in interviewing and screening individuals for cooperative management posts. There are rigorous procedures in place for those wishing to run for board elections. The 2003 New Cooperative Societies Act limits board tenure to three terms of three years each (United Republic of Tanzania 2003: 37). According to the country's cooperative laws, AGMs must be held once a year, two months before the financial end-of-year, and there must also be a mid-year meeting. These individuals must have been active members for a minimum of three years and must meet minimum qualifications based on cooperative education and formal schooling. The government claims that the country's cooperatives of the past were poorly managed because leaders remained in their position for overly long periods of time and made decisions without involving everyone (TFC and CDD 2006). A government body, COASCO, conducts external audits of the unions; while annual audits are mandatory, unions pay for this service and have the option to hire an alternative auditor.

Tanzania's government aims to maintain an overall regulatory function of the coffee industry while at the same time minimizing state involvement (Pirotte, Pleyers and Poncelet 2006). This is achieved through the TCB. In its latest incarnation, the TCB is a government organization that was created through a 2001 Act of Parliament. Originally established under the Coffee Ordinance in 1961, the TCB's original purpose was to act as an agent of the unions for the purpose of selling their coffee. The TCB over time began to take on more activities requiring deductions, or levies from the export price, providing inputs for disease control and collecting an export tax (Moshi 1980). Following the dissolution of the cooperative unions, the Tanzania Coffee Board was renamed the Coffee Authority of Tanzania in 1977. This structure lasted eight years until, after 1982 and the reinstatement of cooperatives, it became the Tanzania Coffee Marketing Board and oversaw auction purchases by private buyers (Baffes 2003). This board eventually became a marketing agent, reverting back to its original name, the Tanzania Coffee Board.

In the early 21st century, the TCB is a government body whose mandate is to regulate the coffee industry in Tanzania, including all matters pertaining to coffee production and marketing. It oversees all coffee-related activities in Tanzania, providing export licences and organizing the weekly coffee auction held in Moshi every Thursday. The auction is mandatory, and the TCB possesses a great deal of power. There is disagreement over whether the TCB's powers are too strong and restrictive, or whether collective and state institutions such as the auction should be strengthened in order to restrict direct exports.

Liberalization has created both opportunities and threats for the unions. Until the liberalization of the 1990s, smallholders could only sell their coffee crops through the cooperatives. This changed, and with the resulting increase in competition many producers are both members of the cooperative and sell to private buyers (Tallontire 2000). Private traders, both local and foreign, have eroded the dominance of cooperatives in the marketing of agricultural products in Tanzania. Private traders offer farmers the entire payment up-front, and for this reason many farmers opt to sell to them instead. This is especially tempting when market prices are high.

Can groups break away from both the cooperative and from state structures? It is very hard for poor farmers to negotiate this. There have been various breakaway groups leaving the secondary union KNCU. We came across a breakaway group in the primary society in the area of Kahawa Shamba that was selling coffee directly at a higher price to a foreign (Swedish) farmer, who was lending them equipment and helping them with marketing, whilst they kept one foot in the KNCU camp by selling 20 per cent of their coffee to it via the primary society (Prevezer 2012: 32). This is precarious, however, for the group, and it also endangers the KNCU, which loses control over some of its most productive farmers. It appears that breakaway groups have occurred more where there were smaller, more homogeneous, more productive groups than when there were larger more diverse cooperatives or associations which were more susceptible to hierarchical control by the secondary union over their primary societies (Prevezer and Sutton 2013).

Farmers still belong to cooperatives out of loyalty and belonging to something, part of family tradition. Also, it is felt that smallholders in Tanzania cannot succeed or scale up their coffee business on an individual basis without joining forces with others. Tallontire (1999) argues that many farmers have continued to sell to the cooperative because this is what they have always done.

Cooperatives are therefore not independent of the state. The Cooperative Reform and Modernization Program (CRMP) of 2005–2015, which was overseen by the CDD, aimed to promote good governance, defined as 'a framework for promoting transparency, accountability and predictability in organisations', as well as to empower members (United Republic of Tanzania 2005: 13). This programme identified problems of poor management, inappropriate cooperative structures, corruption, lack of cooperative democracy, weak supporting institutions, and a general inability for Tanzania's cooperatives to compete in a liberalized economy (Bibby 2006).

An illustration of governance issues in a tea association

Tea illustrates a different organizational model, also based around a collectivist form – the association of tea growers – but involving forward integration down the value chain into the processing, packing and branding of their tea. There appears to be less of an issue of direct state interference and more contestation between different parts of the value chain, with farmers appearing to lose out to larger processing, packing, branding and buying companies, despite technically holding shares in the processing company.

I take the example of the Rungwe Smallholder Tea Growers Association (RSTGA), which represented 15,000 farmers in the Rungwe area of the 50,000 tea families in Tanzania in the early 2000s (Baffes 2003: 1), which means that it was a large collective and influential in the Tanzanian tea industry. In tea, smallholder farmer small producer organizations (SPOs) are distinguished from hired labour workers on larger plantations. SPOs have a General Assembly for dealing with collective issues like how to spend the Fairtrade premium. Larger plantations have a Joint Body representing labour and the management of plantations. The relationship between farmer and cooperative for tea is also a complex one with a long history (Prevezer 2012).

The RSTGA smallholder tea growers have moved into tea processing through part ownership of the tea processing company. This used to be a state-owned company, part of the Tanzanian Tea Authority (TTA). This was privatized in 2000 to become the Wakulima Tea Company (WATCO). RSTGA owned 25 per cent of the shares of WATCO, with the Tatepa tea packing company owning 75 per cent of the shares. The branch manager of WATCO was involved with the TTA and continued to help run WATCO. WATCO owned two tea estates, Kymbila and Rungwe, which contributed 20 per cent of the tea that WATCO processed, with 80 per cent coming from RSTGA. There has been much updating of equipment and renovation of the tea estates.

The ownership share by RSTGA in WATCO increased to 30 per cent in 2011, and was contracted to rise to 49 per cent by 2012. So the tea growers have a share and some say in their tea processing company. Tanzania Tea Packers set up the Tatepa tea packing company and developed the Chaiborn tea brand, which was invested in by the Commonwealth Development Corporation, an investment bank set up by Department for International Development

(DfID) in the United Kingdom. Tatepa launched an initial public offering on the Dar Stock Exchange in 1999. WATCO has had an agreement with Cafédirect to supply tea for its Teadirect brand. The Teadirect premium fund has financed local development in the Rungwe area. WATCO has been expanding into a second tea factory. There have also been direct buyers for RSTGA, the main ones being Cafédirect, Finlay and Tonkin Trading. Trading has not, however, been through long-term contracts. What this illustrates is the intertwining of company structures in different parts of the value chain. But how far has this benefitted farmers?

Shares by RSTGA in WATCO have been paid out of deductions at source from the per kilo price paid for green leaf to farmers, first without their explicit consent and then requiring farmers to consent. Ownership of shares by individual farmers in the tea factory has been managed for the first few years through RSTGA. Failures to pay regular dividends have caused complaints by farmers. The price of tea paid to farmers has been 30 per cent of the market price, with the remaining 70 per cent going into running the company, investment, profits and dividends. Farmers have wanted more paid in the direct price to them.

The issues of the relationship between group and individual are still potent: who is chosen to represent farmers on primary society boards, how decisions are made, and how conflicts are resolved remain difficult issues. There is disquiet over cooperative management salaries, which are paid by farmers (Prevezer 2012).

The issue of banks and loans for tea farmers is also illustrative of a broader question of access to external finance for growth. There were SACCOs (Savings and Credit Cooperative Societies) in operation, with a branch in Tukuyu servicing the RSTGA farmers. About 20 per cent of the farmers in RSTGA had a SACCO account, with a divide between those who did and those who did not. If farmers did have access to credit, they could take out loans for equipment and fertilizers. This correlated with literacy and account-keeping, with great diversity between farmers in this respect. The workers in the tea processing factory all had bank accounts and were better off there than being a smallholder farmer, although in practice factory workers were also farmers (Prevezer 2012).

Conclusions: Linking primary institutions to meso-institutions

This chapter has been looking at Tanzania's institutional development through a limited access order lens, asking about the institutional underpinnings to capitalist development, namely the institutions of property rights and the nature of the state.

This is a basic LAO, as violence is under the control of the state. Control of violence has meant suppressing ethnic groupings so that disputes do not get settled at the national level: there is strongly centralized state capacity in this sense. But there is low state capacity in terms of the narrowness of the fiscal base and ability of the state to tax and issue public debt and, therefore, invest in infrastructure and public goods, which are necessary for enterprise development.

Statist user property rights have dominated customary property rights and have also dominated individual private property rights. In terms of Milhaupt and Pistor's (2008) framework (see Chapter 2), this makes Tanzanian property rights highly centralized and under the control of the state and poorly contestable. Despite formal protective procedures for consultation, representation and mitigation, in *de facto* terms customary rights are weakly protected and the avenues for bringing cases to local tribunals in the case of disputes over land are difficult, making these property rights relatively incontestable by non-elites outside the state apparatuses.

We can see this illustrated in the state's relations with cooperatives. Despite moves towards liberalization and freeing cooperatives formally from state control, in practice and informally and with endorsement from members of secondary unions and some in primary societies the state has a very hands-on role in the running of cooperatives. It does this not only through its formal regulatory structures, such as the TCB, but through the involvement of the DCOs in the selection and running of primary societies and in the operation of marketing boards and extension officers. The justification for this is seen in terms of protecting cooperative governance from unscrupulous or poorly educated individuals. In practice, as well as stifling independence in governance of cooperatives, it might well be contributing to stifling the ability of individuals to establish rural enterprises.

The tea example illustrates not so much the influence of state regulation as the complexity of governance of the value chain, with the tea association buying shares in the tea processing company to which they largely sell their tea. However, ownership shares in the tea processing company and links with packing and branding companies do not guarantee farmers receiving either a good price for their tea, or a voice in the decision-making of the processing company. These are areas of discontent in the running of the RSTGA.

How do I link these meso-institutions of tea and coffee governance structures back into the primary institutions of property rights and nature of the state? It illustrates how weak and negotiable private property rights are. Strong state property rights have underpinned state authority, especially over agricultural cooperatives and have given agencies of the state powers reaching well beyond the regulatory powers of a liberal state. It is very hard for farmers to escape – either from cooperatives to which they owe great loyalty and from which they derive also benefits, or by extension from the 'grabbing hand' of the state.

Given that the majority of the population are farmers in villages, weakening customary rights excludes farmers from participation in the state; they are the non-elite outsiders. The elites or dominant coalition are based within the state, through political offices of president, the Ministry of Lands, district commissioners and further down the hierarchy of regulatory bodies and state offices; the elite includes the civil service or bureaucracy associated with the political apparatus and also political allies in the development and running of industry, both domestic and foreign investors. The boundaries between insiders and outsiders are sharply drawn: it is not easy for the farming non-elite to become insiders to the state and have access to the privileges and rents of the elite.

There are various contrasts with the institutionalization of early US capitalism. Capitalism in the United States was more decentralized, anchored on individual private property rights with a weaker and less centralized state. 'Customary' or extra-legal property rights were gradually legitimized and became more widespread rather than exclusive rights, more inclusive of non-elite groups and more independent of state power. In the United States' expansionary spread into new lands, the powers of existing elites diminished. The Tanzanian state has not been expansionary in this way, but nor have the powers of elites diminished and become more inclusive.

US state capacity was extended through the issue and securitization of public debt, which meant extending the use of the market more broadly into the population; taxation being indirect, largely based on customs and excise, was also quite broad-based and included taxing elites as well as non-elites. Tanzanian state fiscal capacity has remained low, drawing on extracting surpluses from the poor agrarian population through pricing and marketing controls. Its anti-colonial legacy has made it more autarkic and inhibited in issuing public debt, which (in this era of more integrated capital markets) would expose the Tanzanian state to control by foreign investors.

Following Atkinson (2014), I suggest that property rights based on state user rights, favouring bureaucratic elites and monopolistic industry have been based on greater inequality, particularly related to agriculture and negatively related to growth (Atkinson 2014). Since liberalization in the 1990s, and particularly over the last decade, there has been growth in the number of enterprises and greater complementarity between legal and fiscal capacity more positively related to growth especially in industrial capacity. But smallholder agriculture and farmers remain outsiders.

Looking at development paths through the lens of these power balances, despite the cooperative movement and the sophistication of their structures and claims for empowerment, capacity-building and giving democratic voice, given state dominance and state-vested property rights the lot of the smallholder farmer continues to be squeezed with few avenues to prosper.

References

Acemoglu, D., Johnson, S. and Robinson, J. (2001) 'The Colonial Origins of Comparative Development: An Empirical Investigation', *American Economic Review* 91(5): 1369–1401.

Acemoglu, D. and Robinson, J. (2012) *Why Nations Fail: The Origins of Power, Prosperity and Poverty.* London: Profile Books.

Anderson, P. (1974) *Lineages of the Absolutist State.* London: New Left Books.

Atkinson, A.B. (2014) The Colonial Legacy: Income Inequality in Former British African Colonies, Working Paper No. 45. Helsinki: UNU-WIDER.

Baffes, J. (2003) *Tanzania's Coffee Sector: Constraints and Challenges in a Global Environment*. Washington, DC: The World Bank.

Bates, R.H. (1982) *Markets and States in Tropical Africa: The Political Basis of Agricultural Policy*. Berkeley: University of California Press.

Bates, R.H. (2014) 'The New Institutionalism', in I. Sened and S. Galiani (eds), *Institutions, Economic Growth and Property Rights: The Legacy of Douglass North*, 50–65. Cambridge: Cambridge University Press.

Bates, R.H., Block, S., Fayad, G. and Hoeffler, A. (2013) 'The New Institutionalism and Africa', *Journal of African Economies* 22(4): 499–522.

Bee, F.K. (1996) *The Impact of Trade Liberalization on Agricultural Marketing Cooperatives in Developing Countries: The Study of Tanzania*. Tokyo: Tokyo Institute of Developing Economies.

Bibby, A. (2006) 'Tanzania's Cooperatives Look to the Future'. Available at: www.andrewbibby.com/pdf/Tanzania.pdf.

Birchall, J. and Simmons, R. (2010) 'The Co-Operative Reform Process in Tanzania and Sri Lanka', *Annals of Public and Cooperative Economics* 81(3): 467–500.

Boone, C. (2007) 'Property and Constitutional Order: Land Tenure Reform and the Future of the African State', *African Affairs* 106(425): 557–586.

Boone, C. (2014) *Property and Political Order in Africa: Land Rights and the Structure of Politics*. Cambridge: Cambridge University Press.

Brus, W. and Laski, K. (1989) *From Marx to the Market: Socialism in Search of an Economic System*. Oxford: Clarendon Press.

Bryceson, D.F. (1983) *Second Thoughts on Marketing Co-Operatives in Tanzania: Background to their Reinstatement*. Oxford: Plunkett Foundation for Co-operative Studies.

Chambo, S.A. (2006) National Policy Environments: Some Reflections on the Co-Operative and Modernization Programme. Paper presented to the National Thematic Seminar on Improving Governance and Performance of Tanzania SACCOS.

Chambo, S.A. (2009) Agricultural Cooperatives: Role in Food Security and Rural Development. Paper presented to the Expert Group Meeting on Cooperatives.

Clark, E. (1978) *Socialist Development and Public Investment in Tanzania, 1964–73*. Toronto: University of Toronto Press.

Collier, P., Radwan, S. and Wangwe, S. (1986) *Labour and Poverty in Rural Tanzania*. Oxford: Clarendon Press.

Delvetere, P. (2008) 'Cooperative Development in Africa up to the 1990s', in P. Develtere, I. Pollet and F. Wanyama (eds), *Cooperating Out of Poverty: The Renaissance of the African Cooperative Movement*, 1–37. Geneva: International Labour Organization.

De Soto, H. (2000) *The Mystery of Capital: Why Capitalism Triumphs in the West and Fails Everywhere Else*. New York: Basic Books.

Dia, M. (1996) *Africa's Management in the 1990s and Beyond: Reconciling Indigenous and Transplanted Institutions*. Washington, DC: World Bank.

Douglas, M. (1986) *How Institutions Think*. Syracuse, NY: Syracuse University Press.

FAO (2013) *Food and Agriculture Organization of the United Nations Statistics*. Rome: United Nations.

German, L., Schoneveld, G. and Mwangi, E. (2013) 'Contemporary Processes of Large-Scale Land Acquisition in Sub-Saharan Africa: Legal Deficiency or Elite Capture of the Rule of Law?' *World Development* 48: 1–18.

Green, E. (2006) 'Ethnicity and the Politics of Land Tenure Reform in Central Uganda', *Commonwealth and Comparative Politics* 44(3): 370–388.

Greif, A. (2006) *Institutions and the Path to the Modern Economy: Lessons from Medieval Trade*. Cambridge: Cambridge University Press.

Herbst, J. (2000) *States and Power in Africa: Comparative Lessons in Authority and Control*. Princeton: Princeton University Press.

Huntingdon, S.P. (1968) *Political Order in Changing Societies*. New Haven: Yale University Press.

Kiragu, K. and Mukandala, R. (2004) Tactics, Sequencing and Politics of Public Service Pay Policies in Developing and Middle Income Countries: Lessons from Sub-Saharan Africa, Draft report. Washington, DC: World Bank.

Kriesel, H., Laurent, C., Halpern, C. and Larzelere, H. (1970) *Agricultural Marketing in Tanzania: Background Research and Marketing Proposals*. East Lansing, MI: Michigan State University.

Levy, B. (2004) 'Governance and Economic Development in Africa: Meeting the Challenge of Capacity Building', in B. Levy and S. Kpundeh (eds), *Building State Capacity in Africa: New Approaches, Emerging Lessons*, 1–42. Washington, DC: The International Bank for Reconstruction and Development/The World Bank.

Levy, B. (2007) *Governance Reform: Bridging Monitoring and Action*. Washington, DC: The International Bank for Reconstruction and Development/The World Bank.

Levy, B. (2013) 'Seeking the Elusive Developmental Knife Edge: Zambia and Mozambique – A Tale of Two Countries', in D. North, J. Wallis, S. Webb and B. Weingast (eds), *In the Shadow of Violence: Politics, Economics, and the Problems of Development*, 112–148. Cambridge: Cambridge University Press.

Levy, B. (2014) *Working with the Grain: Integrating Governance and Growth*. Oxford: Oxford University Press.

Levy, B. and Fukuyama, F. (2010) *Development Strategies: Integrating Governance and Growth*, Research Working Paper No. 5196. Washington, DC: World Bank.

Lewis, P. (1996) 'Economic Reform and Political Transition in Africa: The Quest for a Politics of Development', *World Politics* 49(1): 92–129.

Macfarlane, A. (1978) *The Origins of English Individualism*. Oxford: Blackwell.

Maghimbi, S. (2010) Cooperatives in Tanzania Mainland: Revival and Growth, Coop Africa Working Paper No.14. Geneva: International Labour Organization.

Mann, M. (2012) *The Sources of Social Power Vol. 3: Global Empires and Revolution, 1890–1945*. Cambridge: Cambridge University Press.

Milhaupt, C.J. and Pistor, K. (2008) *Law and Capitalism: What Corporate Crises Reveal about Legal Systems and Economic Development around the World*. Chicago: University of Chicago Press.

Moore, B. (1966) *Social Origins of Dictatorship and Democracy*. London: Penguin Books.

Moshi, E. (1980) *Peasants Participation under Kilimanjaro Native Cooperative Union (KNCU) and Coffee Authority of Tanzania (CAT)*. Dar es Salaam: University of Dar es Salaam.

Myenzi, Y. (2005) *Implications of the Recent Land Reforms in Tanzania on the Land Rights of Small Producers*. Paper prepared for internal discussion at the Land Rights Research and Resources Institute in Dar es Salaam, Tanzania.

North, D., Wallis, J. and Weingast, B. (2009) *Violence and Social Orders: A Conceptual Framework for Interpreting Recorded Human History*. Cambridge: Cambridge University Press.

North, D., Wallis, J., Weingast, B. and Webb, S. (2013) *In the Shadow of Violence: Politics, Economics and the Problems of Development*. Cambridge: Cambridge University Press.

Nyerere, J. (1968) 'Those Who Pay the Bill', in T. Shanin (ed.), *Peasants and Peasant Societies*. London: Penguin Books.

Piketty, T. (2014) *Capital in the Twenty-First Century*. Cambridge, MA: Harvard University Press.

Pirotte, G., Pleyers, G. and Poncelet, M. (2006) 'Fair-Trade Coffee in Nicaragua and Tanzania: A Comparison', *Development in Practice* 16(5): 441–451.

Planning Commission, President's Office (2013) *State of the Tanzania Economy*. Dar es Salaam, Tanzania: J.K. Nyerere Conference Centre.

Platteau, J.-P. (1992) Land Reform and Structural Adjustment in Sub-Saharan Africa: Controversies and Guidelines, Working Paper No. 107. Rome: Food and Agriculture Organization of the United Nations.

Ponte, S. (2002) *Farmers and Markets in Tanzania: How Policy Reforms Affect Rural Livelihoods in Africa*. Oxford: James Curry.

Prevezer, M. (2012) 'Fairtrade Governance and its Impact on Local Development: A Framework', in B. Granville and J. Dine (eds), *The Processes and Practices of Fair Trade: Trust, Ethics and Governance*, 19–42. London: Routledge.

Prevezer, M. and Sutton, S. (2013) The Relationship between External and Internal Governance in Tanzanian Coffee Cooperatives, Unpublished Working Paper. Queen Mary University of London: Centre for Globalization Research.

Shivji, I. (1998) *Not Yet Democracy: Reforming Land Tenure in Tanzania*. London: International Institute of Environment and Development.

Stevens, M. and Teggemann, S. (2004) 'Comparative Experience with Public Service Reform in Ghana, Tanzania and Zambia', in B. Levy and S. Kpundeh (eds), *Building State Capacity in Africa: New Approaches, Emerging Lessons*, 43–86. Washington, DC: The International Bank for Reconstruction and Development/The World Bank.

Sutton, J. and Olomi, D. (2012) *An Enterprise Map of Tanzania*. London: International Growth Centre.

Sutton, S. (2014) *Voice, Choice and Governance: The Case of Tanzania's Fairtrade Coffee Co-Operatives*. Unpublished PhD Thesis, Queen Mary University of London.

Tallontire, A. (1999) Making Trade Fair? An Examination of the Relationship between Cafédirect and a Coffee Cooperative in Tanzania. Unpublished PhD Thesis, University of Bradford.

Tallontire, A. (2000) 'Partnerships in Fair Trade: Reflections from a Case Study of Cafédirect', *Development in Practice* 10(2): 166–177.

Tanzanian Coffee Board (2010) Tanzania Coffee Board Annual Report, 2009–2010. Moshi, Tanzania.

TFC and CDD (2006) *Cooperatives and Development in Tanzania: A Simplified Guide to the Cooperative Development Policy and the Cooperative Societies Act of Tanzania Mainland*. Dar es Salaam: Tanzania Federation of Cooperatives and Cooperative Development Department.

Tsikata, D. (2001) Land Tenure Reforms and Women's Land Rights: Recent Debates in Tanzania. Paper prepared for the UNRISD Project on Agrarian Change, Gender and Land Rights at the Institute of Statistical, Social and Economic Research (ISSER) at the University of Ghana.

UNDP (2013) *2013 Human Development Report*. United Nations Development Programme.

United Republic of Tanzania (2003) The Cooperative Societies Act 2003. Dar es Salaam, Tanzania.

United Republic of Tanzania (2005) The Cooperative Reform and Modernization Program, 2005–2015. Dar es Salaam, Tanzania.

World Bank (1989) *From Crisis to Sustainable Growth – Sub-Saharan Africa: A Long-Term Perspective Study*. Washington, DC: The World Bank.

World Bank (2011) Conflict, Security and Development. World Development Report 2011. Washington, DC: The World Bank.

Zakaria, F. (2003) *The Future of Freedom: Illiberal Democracy at Home and Abroad*. New York: W.W. Norton.

8 China in its institutional transition to capitalism

Introduction

The China chapter complements that on Tanzania. It illustrates transition from planning to market under a highly interventionist central and local state apparatus, which resembles to an extent the state machinery in Tanzania. But in other respects, there are contrasts, not only in the decentralization of the state in China and its elaborate control by the centralized Chinese Communist Party (CCP), but also in the success that China has had in enterprise creation. The scale and level of development of the two countries are of course completely different from the perspective of 2016. However, in 1980 China's per capita GDP was $1,061 compared with Tanzania's $601. By 2010, the gap between them was immense: $8,032 for China in per capita GDP compared with $804 in Tanzania, a tenfold difference (using Maddison's World Bank data, 1990 GK dollars, see Table 1 in Chapter 1). In part, this chapter is about understanding China's success story compared with Tanzania's relative failure.

This book is about institutions underpinning *capitalism*. So why is China included? How capitalist is China? There is huge controversy over this, of course. Yasheng Huang (2008) argues strongly that the growth and success of capitalism in China is attributable to the liberalization of rural institutions that prompted rural entrepreneurship in the 1980s and access to Western legal and financial institutions in Hong Kong, especially when it came to scaling up more capital-intensive enterprise. He also argues that the rural private sector was the motor behind growth in the 1980s and that there was more liberalization in the 1980s and less gradualism than others have argued. The contrary view is that Chinese institutions underpinning capitalism have been peculiarly 'with Chinese characteristics', which is to say that the Chinese state was and has been pervasive and that capitalism has been policy-driven and reflects not the strength of market institutions but the adeptness of policy choices in knowing which enterprises to support and which to allow to fail, which has been done via gradualism and experimentation. My argument straddles a middle-ground. I am interested in understanding the way in which markets have grown: not via straightforward underpinning by Western-style rule of law and protective property rights, but by more roundabout routes of joint incentives to local officials and entrepreneurs; by the use of market-building incentives using the price mechanism and yardstick competition between regions; and in the role of the CCP as a sort of 'meta-institution' pulling the strings of economic liberalization when it suited its political aims, not uniformly or consistently but highlighting the mixed pattern across the regions and over time of legal and capitalist institution-building.

China is the one country in my sample that is a transition country, meaning that it has been shifting, since 1978, from institutions of communism and state control towards institutions of capitalism and markets (although post-colonial Tanzania was a socialist one-party state for 30 years, with strong central direction related to building up industry). How do I analyze the creation of capitalist market-building institutions coming from the direction of diminishing state planning, growing out of the plan (Naughton 2007)?

In shifting from planning to market, from socialism to capitalism, China has been using the market and market incentives. For market incentives to work, markets have conventionally been thought to need such institutions as protection and security for private property rights and freedom from expropriation by the state. Chinese institutions do not follow Western orthodox conventional wisdom of protecting private property rights, enforcing contracts, separating government from business, and having strong rule of law. China has none of these and yet has had fast and sustained economic growth based on quasi-private, or non-state, enterprise since the early 1980s. Formal constitutional protection of property rights did not come about until 2004; the government was and remains entwined with business; contract enforcement and the rule of law are very weak and not independent of the state (Xu 2010); the judiciary is not independent of the executive. Yet there has been private enterprise and investment – both domestic since the early 1980s, and foreign since the 1990s, delivering economic development and growth. How has this been done? That is the China puzzle.

The story is about market-building incentives given out by the CCP. The politics of this has been more complex, with many CCP leaders in the 1980s being against economic reform and market incentives; Huang (2008: 104) says that there was no agreement in favour of markets. Rather, they were 'context specific innovations, local knowledge and experimentation' (Naughton 1996; Rodrik 2007).

In building markets, there have been winners and losers in property rights, with the rural sector advancing largely in the 1980s and then losing out in the 1990s to urban and state-promoted development. There has been centralization of political control combined with decentralization of economic incentives, co-opting entrepreneurs and the middle classes into exchanging political rights for economic growth or siding with what Dickson (2003) calls the 'non-critical realm'. The CCP has been a meta-institution (similar to Parliament's role in England), adapting and shaping institutions including itself and its composition to achieve its aims of economic growth and to sustain itself in power. I support Huang's (2008) argument that there was much greater institutional liberalization in the 1980s that favoured the rural enterprise sector, which was then retracted in the 1990s with greater urban development favouring the state sector and promoting foreign investment. Constraints on rural credit and greater insecurity for rural private enterprise pushed rural farmers into seeking jobs in the cities as migrants, the great migration of over 160 million migrant workers moving from rural to urban areas. My point is that, in terms of institution-building, these changes were both instrumented by the thrust of CCP policy, dependent on changes in leadership, from the leadership of Zhao Ziyang and Wan Li in the 1980s favouring rural reforms to the urban state-favouring Jiang Zemin and Zhu Rhongji era of 1989–2001, which took in the events of Tiananmen, after which policy was recalibrated against liberal and rural reforms. The post-2002 era of Hu Jintao saw more reform, but the 2012 era of Xi Jinping appears to signal a resumption of the government reasserting its grip on economic levers (The Economist 2016).

As in the other case studies in this book, I am influenced by Milhaupt and Pistor (2013, 2008) in their approach to the relationship between the legal system and economic development. They argue that looking simply at the formal legal origins or formal legislation does not tell us enough about the importance of the rule of law and legal system in a country. The function of the legal system in relation to economic development and capitalist development in particular is not only to protect property rights but to perform various other functions such as coordination, signalling and credibility enhancement; different countries give more weight to some functions than others (Milhaupt and Pistor 2013: 330 and see Chapter 2). To recap, the coordination functions of the legal system, which are stronger also in the continental European countries than in the liberal economies, is to give parties with a possible claim to property rights a seat at the bargaining table. As Milhaupt and Pistor (2013: 330) argue, 'it [the legal system] is not unprotective but places greater emphasis on participatory over individually enforceable rights and interests'. The signalling function of the legal system, which is highly significant in China, is to send out a message of policy intentions and principles that are going to be followed. By credibility enhancement, Milhaupt and Pistor mean the use of the legal system to strengthen belief in policies that are signalled by legal measures, which is also highly significant in China.

In tracing the ways in which property rights and relatedly the legal system or rule of law has evolved in China, I argue that property rights in China since the 1978 opening up have not conformed to individual 'Western' common-law-based protectionist rights; but nor have they been non-existent, and the legal system has evolved in an iterative fashion under the state apparatus. Rather, property rights and the legal system and rule by law have been used by those in charge of the state – the CCP and state bureaucrats at various levels, central, provincial, local – to protect certain property rights to assist economic development. The groups that have been protected have varied over time and between regions.

The settlement of property rights is always a distributional issue: Kennedy (2013) argues that where one group's property rights are strengthened another group's are weakened. In China (as with our other case studies), there are different types of property rights and different groups of people with claims to those rights: rural land rights versus enterprise property rights; rural property rights versus urban developmental rights; official-backed and run state-owned enterprise ownership rights versus private enterprise rights. These types of rights have shifted over time: different groups have come into favour and then fallen out of favour in how far the regime has backed their rights. Below, I mesh the progress of different kinds of property rights onto the evolution of the variety of capitalism that China has been building since the late 1970s.

The second, but related, theme of the chapter is to understand the nature of this state. I am using North, Weingast and Wallis' (2009) limited access order (LAO) framework to think about the issues of elites and the nature of the state in the context of an elite Communist Party. What is the relationship between the CCP and state cadres, and how has the composition of the CCP changed over time? What are the incentive structures used to control local officials' behaviour and tie them in to market expansion? It explores how the CCP has maintained control using a combination of decentralization over economic incentives for local officials and centralization of control over political careers, which are dependent on yardstick competition in economic results. CCP and local official backing for local non-state enterprises have been the sources of economic growth, first in the 1980s through the household responsibility system (HRS) and rural non-state (largely private) township and village enterprises (TVEs), and then through the accommodation of official-backed private enterprises, both domestic and foreign.

The development of the market means non-state activity, private sector, so including TVEs and the HRS. But it means more than the enterprise forms: it includes the use of the price mechanism, competition and economic incentives which include career incentives such as promotions and pay within the state career ladder. Use of these 'price mechanisms' are market-supporting in the sense that they harness the use of individual knowledge of capabilities, demands, energies which are or were only available at the local level to individuals knowing the context of their own capacities (Hayek 1945). The paradox has been that these types of incentives have been heavily used within the CCP and state apparatus to give 'high-powered incentives' to cadres to use initiatives in the promotion of economic development, which was set as a local target post-1978.

State policy towards enterprises has provided relational 'good enough' property rights (Coase and Wang 2013), security of the proprietor (Huang 2008) rather than secure individual private property rights *per se*, to foster spectacular growth of those enterprises, initially coming out of poorer inland provinces. The CCP has adapted and shifted through 'gradualism and experimentation', in a similar fashion to the way the meta-institution of the 17th-century English Parliament did, both in its policies towards fostering markets and in its own composition, replacing ideologically Communist Party members with more technical expertise and ensuring that the 'non-critical' realm of new property owners, managers, and the growing middle class would stay supportive of the regime in their own interests. It has eschewed the 'double balance' espoused by North et al. (2009) that argues that markets and capitalism in the economic sphere need to be accompanied by a move towards representative democratic politics.

The third theme that is explored in this chapter relates to corporate governance, China's variety of capitalism. It examines the corporatization of both state-owned enterprises (SOEs) in the interests of raising equity, and access to broader sources of finance coming through listing on the newly created stock markets of Shanghai and Shenzhen. Relatively strong state control of management of these listed firms has been maintained by the state, continuing to hold blockownership of the bulk of shares in those companies and controlling who the top management of these firms were. There has been an absence of independent legal enforcement of discipline on managerial behaviour – very poor financial disclosure, few market-driven takeovers, and little legal punishment against misappropriation. To counter this lack of institutions, and to provide some information flows, the quota system of local officials choosing which companies can be listed, with ranking of companies for listing based on their performance, has mitigated to some extent the lack of an effective legal framework, argue Pistor and Xu (2005). Although it is argued that more viable companies become listed, there is then an incentive not to reveal their weaknesses, resulting in misappropriation, tunnelling, and asset-stripping by managers with relatively little in the way of state will to detect and punish these crimes. Workers' rights in this erstwhile socialist regime have been disregarded, as capitalist market growth has let rip, with surpluses of labour kept in check only mildly by the *hukou* registration system, which in turn has served to create a dualization in the labour market around more privileged urban workers, on the one hand, and rural migrants lacking official status and welfare support, on the other. The combination of lack of either market or state discipline over management combined with lack of worker rights has promoted a political capitalism without the market checks and legal protections afforded by decentralized individualized property rights backed by the legal system of the liberal market economy and without the labour protections and coordination mechanisms of the coordinated market economy.

The rest of the chapter is organized as follows. The next sections on primary institutions look at the nature of property rights in China and their relationship to the legal system, and they explore the nature of the state, the dominant coalition of elites, examining the relationship between the CCP and the state apparatus, the CCP's relation to institutional development, and its changing composition. I then look at the meso-institutions of organizational forms of enterprise and corporate governance, focusing on the corporatization of SOEs, the launching of stock markets in the early 1990s and the governance relationships between the state as owners, managers and employees. I conclude with thoughts about China's variety of capitalism.

Primary institutions: Property rights and the legal system

As in previous chapters, I am building on Milhaupt and Pistor's (2008) framework (see Chapter 2) analyzing the relationship between property rights and legal systems. There are three main dimensions of differentiation of property rights systems according to how centralized or decentralized the legal system is, meaning whether law emanates from the centre with strong state influence or is created in a more dispersed fashion – both geographically and in terms of power structures. This is aligned with how contestable property rights are, meaning whether individuals or groups can bring cases through the courts, challenge decisions, bring class actions, and whether they have access to lawyers; and the influence that lawyers and judges have on the system (in turn related to their numbers, their status, their education and therefore influence). The third dimension is assessing the various different functions that property rights systems provide, distinguishing between their protective function, their coordinative function giving different groups a place at the bargaining table, and their signalling function to provide a lead on the direction that policy is taking. I add to this a fourth dimension, which I have been highlighting in previous chapters, concerning the type of assets that are being protected through the legal system: tradable assets of investors based around ensuring fair market trading and protection of minority investors (in the liberal Britain and United States); protection of strategic assets of more closely-held firms with a strong coordinative function to property rights and the state as regulator (in continental Europe); or where the legal system and property rights support the state/party elites' interests with a stronger role for the state as coordinator and in the maintenance of order (in Tanzania and China). Which assets are protected bears a strong relation to which groups form the elites in each society.

This chimes with David Kennedy's (2013) argument, outlined in Chapter 2, that legal systems of property rights always have distributional implications; property rights – whether they are private or public legal regimes, or playing off formal rules against discretionary standards – are always decided or clarified in favour of particular groups and in doing so harm other groups. Identifying who those groups are at particular points in time is a theme of this chapter.

Property rights in land for small farmers were initially strengthened between 1949 and 1956 (Prosterman 2013). As Prosterman says, the Chinese Revolution, led by the CCP, was supported by the 60 per cent of the rural population, who were poor tenants paying rents to landlords. Farmers were issued land certificates and titles to land. Post-1956, individual rural property rights disappeared and have remained weaker than rights accorded to urban development. With collectivization from 1956, individual rural land rights disappeared with disastrous results of falling production and famine and up to 30 million deaths between 1956 and 1962.

From the period of opening up in the late 1970s, there are the beginnings of the use of market incentives, which heralded a sort of capitalism. There were no formal individual property rights protecting private property until the property law in 2007, although post-2004 private property rights were recognized. But this has been a process of recognition of property rights of those who will deliver economic growth through private enterprise. Property rights have been informally recognized or tolerated rights backed by local officials.

Given the incentives of the CCP, those groups which through enterprise development could foster economic growth and results – through GDP, exports, employment – at the local level were recognized as legitimate. They have extended – through the HRS – to giving incentives to rural farming households. But in any contest between rural farm and urban enterprise development, it is the latter that has won out.

In China, both clarity of property rights and the notion of individual liberty are not concepts that have the same resonance as in the West. The United States enshrines liberty to include property rights. Zhang (2008) quotes Western jurisprudence on liberty and property, 'You can't give up one without losing the other', with property rights as the cornerstone of liberty, the right to own private property being an essential human right as well as the basis for economic growth. Western ideas of liberty mean both the right to private property and to freedom from government interference (the possessive individualism talked about in Chapters 4 and 6; Macpherson 1962; Laslett 1960), and in particular governments may not interfere with property rights without the process of law. In China, it is different. The notion of inalienable individual rights is much weaker. If rights are recognized, they are deemed to have been given or granted, and can therefore be taken away as well. Having said that, in 2004 the National People's Congress (NPC) amended the constitution to protect the individual, 'freedom of the person', and the 'personal dignity of citizens as inviolable' (Constitution of China 2004).

Private property rights were not fully acknowledged until the 2004 amendment to the Constitution. Under Article 13 of the Constitution, as amended in 2004, citizens' lawful private property was declared 'inviolable'. This became the property law in 2007 granting legal protection to private property rights. It placed private property on equal footing with public property for the first time.

What I am interested in is the period up to that point in 2007, when economic reforms and private enterprise grew up in the absence of such legal recognition and protection of private property. How secure was private property and contracting and private enterprise that produced goods for the market? And how were those property rights secured? There remained a stigma against the term 'private', as it was deemed to signify 'capitalist' in an era when official ideology remained socialist. The superiority of public ownership had been enshrined in the 1954 Constitution in Article 6. The 1975 Constitution added 'socialist public property is inviolable', and the 1982 Constitution read 'sacredly inviolable'. Under the 1982 Constitution, the state owned urban land, whereas the collectives owned rural land administered by local officials (Volberda et al. 2011: 673).

In the 1982 Constitution, there was the shift from pure public ownership to multiple ownerships – recognizing that the market, to the extent that there could be a socialist version, required a broader notion of property ownership. Getting rich, which was endorsed as legitimate at this time, required at least non-public ownership and a need to respect private rights. The 1986 Civil Code – General Principles of Civil Law of China – had the purpose of protection of lawful civil rights, whilst not calling them private or individual rights. The 1988 Amendment to the 1982 Constitution allowed the private sector to exist as a supplement to the public economy. It protected the lawful rights and interests of the private sector and allowed the transfer of the right to use land. It did not use the terms private property or private ownership, but the term private economy as a supplement, with state powers to guide, supervise and control the private economy. The 1988 Amendment was a legal watershed. Private property was recognized in the 1980s, but was not as strongly protected as public property.

Whose property rights? Rural agricultural land rights versus urban development

Property rights are a bundle of rights: the rights to control, the rights to derive income from property, the rights to transfer property even in the absence of full ownership (Oi and Walder 1999). Rural land rights did not include rights to transfer ownership: in the 1990s, farmers were granted 30-year leases, but could not use the land as collateral for loans or sell it. They could rent it out, but paid a fee to the local administrator for doing so (Volberda et al. 2011: 669). This compares with urban residential leases, which were for between 40 and 70 years. Farmers' land was not secure from seizure by the state; compensation to farmers was for its agricultural value, a tenth of its market value, with the village administration taking a cut. The government did not want a free market in rural land, with farmers selling holdings. This compares with urban private property, which individuals have used as collateral for loans and have been able to trade, creating huge wealth for themselves. In 1998, rural land rights were reformed somewhat: farmers were issued land-use contracts, and in 2003 there were restrictions introduced on collectives reassigning land within villages and strengthening farmers' rights to transfer land between themselves for farming (Volberda et al. 2011: 672–673). This contrasts with more liberal urban rights; the urban housing market was privatized in 1998, and workers could buy their houses.

Enterprises in the 1980s, security of property rights, and capitalist incentives

The nature of property rights and contract enforcement need to be understood in the context of the growth in various forms of the private economy or non-state sector from the 1980s onwards. The growth of these enterprises was closely related to the stimulus of market incentives allowed by the state. In other words, being allowed to keep surpluses, selling above the quotas onto a market, constituted a form of private property right that had not been allowed previously, a right over resources sanctioned and protected by official dictum.

There were four forms of private enterprise: private farming and the household responsibility system (HRS); town and village enterprises (TVEs); special enterprise zones (SEZs); and *Geti* (individual urban) enterprises (Coase and Wang 2013). In agriculture, the institution of the HRS adopted in 1982 gave households the ability to keep the residual once their plan quotas were fulfilled. The state had formal ownership of land and controls over pricing. But households replaced team contracts and could buy means of production. Agriculture took up 71 per cent of the labour force in 1983.

The TVEs represented rural industrialization with non-farming jobs for peasants, coming out of old commune and brigade enterprises which employed 28 million peasants in 1978. The 1984 No. 4 Resolution renamed these as TVEs – so named because of their location rather than their ownership. TVEs grew to employ 135 million people in 1996, with the share in GDP growing from 6 per cent to 26 per cent of a growing GDP. The 1980s saw a flourishing of rural entrepreneurship – the setting up of private businesses especially in the poorer provinces (Huang 2008: 50–108). This is the period when private enterprise was often disguised as red-hat (Tsai 2006). The private economy was still held in contempt: parents would not allow daughters to marry men in the private sector. There were three noes for the private sector: no promotion, no publicity and no ban. So these enterprises were tolerated for the tangible economic benefits they were bringing, but had second-class status in terms of formal recognition and protection.

Property rights and contracting were not guaranteed by law but by power structures, agreements between officials, and local family structures (Mann 2013: 229). Officials and local families reached agreements; there were mutual synergies between local governments and local economies; and investments were channelled into favoured projects (Shamburgh 2008: 17). The role of local officials was critical in the security of property rights, they had decentralized authority with incentives to obtain regional growth. This was an iterative process between experiment on the ground delivering economic results, this being recognized as beneficial by local officials, and the official line adapting to reflect and acknowledge practice. There was also corruption and rent-seeking: what Shamburgh terms 'organized dependence' between the Party/state apparatus and citizens (Shamburgh 2008: 20). So state socialism in the urban sector was counter-balanced by the more dynamic and productive household-centred small rural businesses in the rural sector, with poorer provinces in the vanguard in the 1980s (Huang 2008).

Who owned the TVEs? Xu (2011) says the community governor was the *de facto* owner and that property rights were vague. Huang (2008: xiv) argues that 10 million out of 12 million TVEs in 1985 were completely privately owned. How secure were these property rights in the opening up period? Huang (2008) talks of the security of the proprietor rather than the security of property, and that it became less dangerous to open an enterprise compared with the Cultural Revolution period. One example that Huang (2008) gives is of the watermelon-seed seller, Nian Guangliu in Anhui Province, who became a millionaire. But Deng Xiaoping had to speak out for him in 1984 and 1992 to defend him from imprisonment. Others suffered assaults on private business. In 1982, there were 16,000 cases of economic crime and 30,000 people arrested. Many private businesses were disguised as red-hat enterprises or survived by bribing state enterprises to be part of them (Tsai 2006). 'Rural enterprise, that's our second treasury', said a local official (Mann 2013: 230).

Township governments provided infrastructure, financing land and training labour. In exchange, TVEs had access to resources. Official recognition overcame weak legal protection and weak contract enforcement. There was a mixing of enterprises with officials: in Jiangsu Province, large manufacturing plants employed local village labour and were run by local officials; officials assisted in steering enterprises towards cheap state credit, how to qualify for funds, arguing for tax breaks, inflating the size of the workforce. There were tight relations between local officials and enterprises. Regional administrative measures acted as substitutes for law and law enforcement (Xu 2011). Pistor and Xu (2005) argue for the movement in China from *de facto* to *de jure* rights, claiming that laws developed after business practice. The roles of the municipal governments of Taizhou and Wenzhou of Zheijiang Province, where the private sectors were ahead of the legal framework, catalyzed the legalization of private property rights (Du and Xu 2008).

There was variety between regions. Prototypes were tried out in Anhui, Sichuan and Guangdong, with land and output quotas contracted out from local governments to households. This was then rolled out. So in 1981, 45 per cent of households participated; 80 per cent in 1982, and then 99 per cent in 1984. Households kept their residual incomes; control rights of allocation and management of land resources were kept by local officials. Jiangsu Province had a long history of entrepreneurship; the Sunan model in southern Jiangsu gave a leading role to community government. The Guangdong model was linked to the SEZs and foreign direct investment (FDI) from Taiwan, Hong Kong and the diasporas. In the Wengzhou model, in the poorer mountainous region, local officials were key entrepreneurs, labelled red-hat with protection, with regulatory remedies for lack of property rights. Administrative provisions for registered operations gave private business in Wenzhou a legal identity. For example, there were local clusters of footwear firms with distributed but coordinated ownership, with government owning land and buildings. In Zheijiang Province, 60 per cent of the province's output was private by 2000 with local government support (Xu and Zhang 2009).

Huang (2008) emphasizes the upsurge in the 1980s in the creation of enterprises: village party secretaries became capitalist bosses (Chen in Huang

2008); private cooperatives grew with government credit; the military set up enterprises; prison camps set up enterprises. Urban control over rural areas was abolished in the 1980s: collective production in communes was replaced by the contract responsibility system whereby farmers could market their surpluses out to nearby urban areas. Rural industrial firms were emerging as competitors to the state sector. Xu (2011) says that agricultural output increased by 61 per cent between 1978 and 1984, with 78 per cent of the increase attributable to the institution of the HRS according to McMillan, Whalley and Zhu (1989). Coase and Wang (2013) argue that it was the poorer provinces that were in the vanguard. TVEs accounted for four-fifths of output of the non-state sector by the early 1990s. Between 1981 and 1990, industrial output of the TVEs grew 28 per cent per annum compared with that of the state sector, which grew at 7.7 per cent per annum.

SEZs were regions of private enterprise. This was part of state policy – that of having designated SEZs that were containment areas for the market economy and particularly for FDI. FDI was negligible in 1978; it was driven by the institution of the SEZ. In 1985, 37 per cent of FDI was in SEZs; by 2005, this figure was 93 per cent, accounting for a similar proportion of exports. SEZs were initiated by local governments; the first four were in Shenzhen, Zhuhai and Shantou in Guangdong Province and Xiamen Fujian in 1980. In 1984, they were rolled out to 14 cities, and reached 342 cities by 2005.

Privatization of SOEs was gradual, carried out by regional governments at their discretion. They would not do it if it hurt growth. It was done from the mid-1990s, a *de facto* privatization through the leasing of SOEs whereby firms paid subnational governments a proportion of their profits. In Zhucheng in Shandong Province, loss-making SOEs were sold to employees. The policy was to retain the large (large firms in strategic industries), release the small. Privatization increased after 1997 through share issues, joint ventures, sales to outsiders (Gan, Guo and Xu 2008). *De facto* ownership was turned into *de jure* by the mid-2000s; in 2005, regional governments still owned 31,000 SOEs, whereas the central government had control of 166 firms. This was still state ownership, but was on the way to privatization; regional governments sold land for development to raise revenue, taking property away from agriculture.

The flipside of property rights being at the behest of regional governments with law-making and contract enforcement under their control was that property rights of the agricultural population were weak. Regional governments favoured urbanization and urban development, and they ignored the land quota system controlling the conversion of arable land to non-arable land. Arable land was *de jure* collectively owned by the commune and village. Rights of use and income were assigned to farm households in the early 1980s. But farmers and village authorities could neither alter nor transfer land usage; they were subject to the whims of local governments in the question of land conversion. Kung, Xu and Zhou (2013) argue that conflicts between local officials and farmers have been the outcome.

Rule of law in China

There are two sorts of argument put forward here in considering what role the rule of law has had in Chinese economic development. The first point of view stresses the subservience of the rule of the law to the CCP, the lack of independence of the judiciary (through low status and poor educational standards) from the political system and the CCP. The second viewpoint (Milhaupt and Pistor 2008; Pistor and Xu 2005) stresses the difference in functions of the legal system from its independent protective function in the West, having more to do with coordination, signalling and credibility of policy than protection of investors. Again, I want to tread a conciliatory middle ground: the legal system is weak, is non-Western, and is subservient to political processes and CCP policy; but it has evolved and is evolving and has grown in stature and independence. The judiciary remains, however, fundamentally less powerful than it is in Western liberal systems. I deal with each argument in turn.

The legal system in China was created by the CCP, which abolished the previous laws, decrees, judicial systems of the Kuomintang government in its September 1949 common program (Keyuan 2006). The first constitution of 1954 established the socialist legal system. The Cultural Revolution destroyed this legal system, smashing the structures of public security, Procuratorate, courts. Post-1978, the legal system had to be rebuilt. The third plenum of the eleventh central committee of the CCP in December 1978 declared its purpose to strengthen the socialist legal system so that democracy was systematized and written into law. Formally, the law was elevated and the equality of all people before the people's laws, denying anyone the privilege of being above the law.

Rule of law, the constitution and the CCP

The Chinese system is less bounded in terms of what can be made law than the Western system: the law is not independent from what the CCP can create, and the constitution is used to enshrine principles and policies by which the CCP wishes to operate. The rule of law has been created by the CCP and is not independent of it. It can therefore be interpreted and unmade by the CCP. The rule of law was incorporated into the 1982 constitution (Keyuan 2006).

The Party constitution and state constitution have a close relationship; the Party directs what is to be adopted, and measures made in the Party constitution are adopted into the state one. Constitutional changes follow changes in the Party constitution: amendments in the Party constitution were in 1987, 1992, 1997 and 2002; amendments in the state constitution were in 1988, 1993, 1999 and 2004.

For example, the state constitution adopted in 1982 embodied the principles of the 1954 constitution of all citizens being equal before the law, with the people's democratic dictatorship replacing the proletarian dictatorship; it also enshrined the policies of economic reform, seeing the construction of modernization as a national task (Keyuan 2006). This process has continued: the 1988 amendment to the 1982 constitution legitimated the existence of the private economy, giving a constitutional basis to the commercial transfer of land use rights and constitutional protection to different forms of non-state ownership. The rule of law and its status therefore falls within the political sphere of power; it is seen as something political rather than as an independent institution, and in the 1980s the rule of law was set as a political priority in terms of political development.

The Party decides policy and then makes the law. Any law of major principle has to be reported to the CCP central committee for approval. The Party has discretionary power to intervene, especially on economic, administrative and political laws. And it has control over appointments to the National People's Congress, the legislature. CCP members account for over 70 per cent of NPC representatives, and so it is therefore regarded as a rubber stamp for Party policy. The chairmanship of the NPC is taken by the Party secretary general. In 2003, 22 chairmanships of provincial People's Congresses were filled like this. The CCP therefore will not allow laws in conflict with it. When the Tiananmen Square protests happened, martial law was passed hastily. Keyuan (2006) sees this as a way for the CCP to legitimate itself through the use of process and rule by law. For example, administrative procedural law gives the right to citizens to bring Party members or organizations to court. But at the same time, the CCP has been clear to retain control over legislation, despite using legal procedure.

The status of law has shifted in different periods according to political priorities. The early 1980s was a period of discussion of democracy and the rule of law. From 1996, Jiang Zemin at a law lecture for the CCP committee made it an objective requirement to rule the country in accordance with law; it was seen as a symbol of civilization and a guarantee of stability. Post-2001, there has been an emphasis on rule by virtue, meaning belief in communist ideals and collectivism, with legal and ethical norms going together.

The relationship between the state and the rule of law is critical to determining how China fits into the North et al. (2009) framework. They argue that open access orders have a series of conditions relating to the rule of law: impersonality of the rule of law, that it does not matter who you are, you will be treated equally before the law; independence of the judiciary from the state; a legislature creating law that is independent of government; and government bound by the rule of law (North et al. 2009).

China has a different take on what is meant by the rule of law in Western institutional terms. The Chinese rule of law does not match up to these Western ideals. The CCP has used the rule of law to legitimate its processes: the Party is above the law, but there is recognition that there is need for law. Despite constitutional declarations, there is not equality before the law, or stability of law; in this sense, China does not fulfil the North et al. conditions to be an OAO. For example, in dealing with corruption the Party investigates corruption ahead of the judiciary (Manion 2004).

Milhaupt and Pistor (2008) assert that Western-style indicators of rule of law are not the appropriate measures to consider how the Chinese legal system has worked. This goes against La Porta, Lopez-de-Silanes, Shleifer and Vishny (1998) and La Porta, Lopez-de-Silanes and Shleifer (2008), who argue that China's formal legal system is weak, politicized, controlled by the CCP. The Milhaupt and Pistor (2008) framework (see Chapter 2) has two leading dimensions: how decentralized or centralized the legal system is and how contestable the legal system is. The legal system in China is a peculiar mix of centralized and decentralized: law-making has followed centralized CCP policy-making, but enforcement of law has been decentralized to the regions. Formal law expanded over the 30 years since 1978. Focusing on central government law misses what is going on at the regional and local levels: for example, for the SEZs a specially designated set of rules was designed to attract foreign investment and stimulate exports. Regional company laws, securities laws and bankruptcy laws were decentralized. The system has not been contestable in that it has been difficult for plaintiffs to mount cases. In the late 1980s, laws were passed making litigation against government agencies possible; the 1989 administrative litigation law allowed individuals to sue government agencies. The legal system has not been about legal protection for investors, although there have been actions taken by investors according to Milhaupt and Pistor (2008). It has not been easy to litigate, and only 20 per cent of possible litigation during 2001–2006 was pursued. People's Courts have heard one million plus cases; plaintiffs win 30 per cent of them.

The point Milhaupt and Pistor are making is that the function of law has been evolving, that the legal system is a living dynamic system. The Chinese state set out to use the law to coordinate and as an instrument of state control but also to signal the direction of policy. However, the legal system takes on a life of its own, and the government can't control the law entirely.

How independent is the judiciary from the CCP?

It is quite clear that the legal system in post-1978 China is not set up on a parallel basis with Western liberal systems, despite officially being modelled on the civil law systems of Germany and France. As with property rights, we have to distinguish between official pronouncements and practice on the ground, both of which have been changing.

First, the judicial system was not conceived as being independent from political control. President Xiao Yang in 2007 said 'the power of the courts to adjudicate independently doesn't mean independence from the Party. It is the embodiment of a high degree of responsibility vis-à-vis Party undertakings' (Yang 2007); the judiciary is not independent of the Party, and its loyalty is a requirement.

The intertwining of judicial and political authority has meant that alongside the construction of the 1980 organic law of the People's Courts and the 1982 state constitution, there were established four levels of courts and adjudication committees for courts at every level to review cases, find errors and interrogate judges. There are special courts for military, transport and forestry, which are more explicitly political, dealing with plundering, bribery and sabotage. It is a highly centralized structure under the SPC having four tiers; in 2004, it had 3,500 courts and 220,000 judges (against 70,000 in 1988). If branch courts are included, there were over 10,000 courts in 2004 (Cabestan 2005; Grimheden 2006).

The political legal committee of the CCP was founded in 1980 and was put in charge of big issues. On it were the heads of the SPC, the Supreme Procuratorate, the Ministry of Public Security and the Ministry of Justice. It gave instructions to courts on the handling of cases. It could issue legal documents; it could strike hard *yanda* campaigns on crimes by mafia gangs, for example the 1993 *yanda* against kidnapping of children and women, and the 2000 *yanda* against gangs. Punishment could bypass normal legal procedures, with courts following Party instructions. The CCP Discipline Inspection Committee, whose remit is to safeguard the Party constitution and rules, interferes with judicial work and is an alternative to using the courts. For example, in 2002 the Party discipline inspection committee listed 861,917 cases for investigation and punished 846,150 persons. It handed over to the judiciary only when the cases had been through the discipline committee (Keyuan 2006: 91). Cheng Weigao, the Party Secretary of Hebei Province, was accused of accepting bribes, and his two personal secretaries were sentenced to death. He was brought to the discipline committee and expelled from the Party, and his case did not go to the judiciary. This is an overtly politicized legal system; the Party mechanisms are seen as alternatives to the judicial system. Only 0.5 per cent of lawbreakers are punished, says Zou Keyuan, and only 0.056 per cent are punished for corruption. The influence of the CCP over the judiciary is huge. There are certain Party documents – red-dotted documents – that are above the law. In 2003, Zhang Yinghong, a cadre in the Party organization of Hunan, published an essay on how the political legal committee hampers judicial independence; this was condemned, and he was pushed out.

However, there are signs that this predominance of the CCP over the judiciary has begun to change. This attitude has in 2012 been officially softened. There have been more recent reforms in 2011 and 2012 prohibiting self-incrimination, barring illegally obtained evidence, and speeding up trials for suspects. The 2012 state council paper on judicial reform does not mention the subordination of the judicial system to the CCP (Lubman 2012). So things are changing. It is nevertheless a highly centralized and incontestable legal system, hard for individuals or class actions to be taken up independently against either other individuals or against the state.

Low status and poor education of Chinese judges

Judges have been seen as political animals (The Wall Street Journal 2014). Many are leaving, fed up with time wasted on political study, on transmission of attitudes, reflecting on important speeches (Liu Shibi, veteran court judge, on Weibo). It is unusual for judges to speak out, but there is much discontent and many are leaving.

There has been recent attention paid to promoting the rule of law and fighting corruption under President Xi Jinping. They are not aiming to create a Western legal system. They protect Party authority over politically sensitive issues. But there are many disputes, strikes and protests – over 100,000 per year. Ting Shi (2014) reported that on average 67 judges per annum have resigned from the Shanghai courts since 2009. Making judges more independent of local officials is one aim, by transferring power over local court budgets to provincial authorities.

Compared with the Western judiciary, judges' education levels are extremely basic. Judges in 2014 come to courts from law school and are on the bench after a couple of years as clerks. Ten years previously, in 2004, they had no legal training. Ai's (2008) survey on judges' educational levels stresses the poor level of training and qualifications in 2004. Their pay has been low, which has made them open to corruption. They have been pushed to consider issues of social stability when deciding cases. Courts are seen to be the weakest point of Chinese government (Cohen 2014).

Primary institutions: Nature of the state

I talked about the relationship between the state and rule of law and property rights in the previous section. I cannot consider how centralized/decentralized and how contestable property rights and rule of law are in this system without understanding the structure of the state administration. This section talks about the structure of the state: its regional decentralization and the relationship between Party and state. It is also looking to answer the question of who the elites in China have been and are and whether they are within the state, the Party or in civil society.

I divide this section on the nature of the state into two themes: regional decentralization and the relationship between the central state and provincial governments and how the centre has maintained control over the provinces despite regional autonomy over expenditure; and the relationship between the state bureaucracy (cadres) and the Party in terms of administrative structures and incentives and changing composition over time.

Regional decentralization and state incentives

A key ingredient in the contribution of 'institutions' to Chinese development has been the structure of incentives – structure in terms of geography and organizational structure. China has had a peculiar mix of decentralization of authority to provinces, municipalities and prefectures whilst maintaining a centralized control over the careers of its state cadres. Chenggang Xu (2011) calls this a regionally decentralized authoritarian regime with a combination of regional decentralization and political centralization. Xu argues that this structure is responsible for the success of the HRS and non-state enterprises. This is how regional economies have worked: they are self-contained in the sense that subnational governments have been responsible for initiating and coordinating reforms, providing public services, and making and enforcing laws, giving these local governments huge powers over land resources. The 1958–2002 average for local government expenditure was 55 per cent of public expenditures, well above the figure for the average democracy of 25 per cent decentralization of expenditures (Landry 2008). Xu (2011) gives a higher figure for 2006, stating that subnational governments have been responsible for 70 per cent of public expenditure, compared with 46 per cent in the United States, 40 per cent in Germany, and 38 per cent in Russia (Xu 2011). China has had one of the lowest proportions of central fiscal revenue (World Bank 1990). Fiscal reforms of 1993–1994 recentralized somewhat, with a clearer institutional separation between central and local tax bureaux. Relative to Western economies, such as the United States and Germany, a far higher percentage of expenditure has been devolved to the regional level.

Competition between regions has been an important incentive, with economic reform built into the incentives of officials, and a ranking between provinces, municipalities, and cities according to various measures of economic performance. Regional governments have been controlled by the central state through the rotation of governors (Xu, Wang and Shu 2007). Various forms of competition have been used as incentive mechanisms, such as performance targets with target responsibility contracts with superiors, ranking of officials by lists, for township officials, for governors of provinces, and using rotation and promotion of governors as a reward and incentive mechanism. Xu likens the governance structure of government to an M-form hierarchy: regional governments were granted autonomous powers but were controlled through appointments by the central state or CCP. Between 1978 and 2005, 80 per cent of provincial regions had rotation of governors imposed by central government (Xu et al. 2007).

Competition between the regions has had a particular structure. At each level – provinces, municipalities, counties and townships – careers have been linked to performance, measured in terms of various types of economic growth such as GDP total or per capita, growth rate, FDI attracted and where that unit is in the rankings. The upgrading of counties to municipal levels, an advantage in terms of resources, has been based on performance. This has been helped by regional lack of specialization, with each region as a self-sufficient unit with a mix of industries. This has weakened interdependence between regions and has fostered competition. This contrasts with the industrial structure in the Soviet Union, where there was specialization and high interdependence between regions.

Xu (2011) calls this tournament competition between regional officials, where regional officials' promotion has been related to the performance of the jurisdiction relative to the national average: if the average growth rate was higher by one standard deviation, this raised the probability of promotion by 33 per cent. If the growth rate was lower by one standard deviation, this increased the probability of termination by 30 per cent. These incentives have had an impact; provincial growth has mattered for governors and officials. The upgrading of cities, which gives municipal governors greater authority, has been dependent on higher growth rates. This has created an endogenous cycle of career promotion, upgrading authority, attracting FDI and domestic investment leading to faster growth and further career promotion. Xu argues that this process has worked better with simpler non-conflicting targets such as economic growth and led to ditching more complex redistributive targets such as lessening inequality. Local officials have balanced their raising of revenues against giving incentives to non-state players through the HRS, land tenure, the SEZs and TVEs. To the extent that enterprises and private ownership brought in taxes and fulfilled economic targets – in terms of employment, numbers of enterprises, economic growth – this relationship (between officials and the private sector) has been symbiotic.

Party control over state capacity and state structure

The Chinese economy was decentralized in structure with authority for expenditure at the provincial level. But this gave rise to a fear of local elites and their independence. This was countered and controlled by the structure of the Party administration. Higher authorities had leverage over their subordinates; locally managed enterprises remitted a portion of their revenues to the county-level bureaux. This created a form of control from above over local revenues (Blecher and Shue 1996). The political capacity of the central government is not captured by the degree of fiscal centralization. Institutional control has been maintained through Party administrative incentives. The mechanism of control is through the selection of leaders by the CCP at all levels – national, intermediary and local (White 1998). There is a dual state structure of state cadres and CCP members and a linkage between the cadre management system and political control over the elites. There is a Party web of veto points throughout the cadre hierarchy: Party approval was and is needed for access to offices at all levels of central, provincial, municipal, county and township officialdom. No cadre was appointed without the assent of the CCP committee.

The CCP used the appointment system to get responsiveness to policy from the provinces. The one-level-down system of cadre management was a mechanism for decentralizing but not giving local autonomy; this was how the CCP dealt with the idea that 'the sky is high and the emperor is far away'. Although expenditures were devolved to the local level, control over local elites was maintained using the incentives of getting economic growth and rewarding officials for it (Yin 2001: 39). Personnel policy controlled by the CCP has been used as a critical intermediary variable. The cadre responsibility system meant that the central government steered local leaders and held them accountable using promotion, dismissal and transfer to enforce their authority. Performance contracts were used whereby Party secretaries and township officials signed contracts pledging to reach targets and were held responsible for them. There was a ranking of different targets into soft, hard, priority or bottom line. If the township did not make its priority targets, this would cancel out all other work performance.

The elite, the CCP

Shamburgh (2008) talks about the changing nature of the communist party state from its mobilization phase under Mao towards its bureaucratic phase, a move from a totalitarian regime towards an authoritarian regime. The government's rationale has been to hold onto power and to adapt itself and adjust in order to do so, what Shamburgh calls both atrophy and adaptation. There is division over how strong or coherent the CCP is. It has relied on its capacity to deliver economic growth (Hutton 2006). Others have emphasized the predation and corruption of the CCP, the rent-seeking of officials and rural discontent, what Minxin Pei (2006) calls a trapped transition. Optimists have emphasized the benefits of economic reforms in strengthening state capacity.

What is clear from the reflections on the nature of communist states at the fall of communist parties in Eastern Europe from 1989 and with the disintegration of the Soviet Union in 1991 is the reflexivity of the process; that the CCP learned lessons from the failure of these communist parties and resolved to adapt itself in order to hold onto power. Shamburgh (2008) talks of the CCP view that within the socialist system the market could and should be used, that there had been too little emphasis on agriculture in the Soviet Union and too much emphasis on industrial economies of scale, on the state monopoly of property rights, there was over-centralization and too low a tax base. A Central Party School member, Zhao Yao, in criticizing Gorbachev, implicitly thought it possible to have market-like economic reforms whilst maintaining political authority and not going down the bourgeois democratizing route (Shamburgh 2008: 170). Stability was thought to be paramount, and Party leadership over the state apparatus was core. Evolutionary gradual change was thought to sustain this. This fits with the limited access order framework of North et al. (2009), placing stability and lack of violence at the centre of concerns.

Who are the elites in this system?

The hub of the CCP structure was and is the Organization Department, in charge of personnel, the first department under heaven (Landry 2008: 136; Shamburgh 2008: 141). It was and continues to be in charge of retiring and replacing old ideological revolutionaries and recruiting younger, more technocratic and meritocratic members to the CCP. It was secretive, with no public phone number, no sign on the building near Tiananmen Square, with highly confidential and detailed dossiers, handling high-level personnel decisions secretly. Its incentives were aligned with economic growth: to foster growth, create employment, attract FDI, control social unrest and achieve targets (Hoffman and Wu 2009). In terms of incentives for local officials, if they managed to promote growth in their region, they could keep the surplus for reinvestment and would be more likely to be promoted from local to central officialdom. Shamburgh (2008) has an estimate of more than 70 million party members in 2003, with three levels of privilege: the *nomenklatura* system for the top 2,500 party officials at minister level and governor and party secretaries in the 31 provinces and four centrally controlled municipalities; the *bianzhi* system, which is the system of the state bureaucracy administered by the state council and which numbered 33 million personnel in 2004; and ordinary Party committee assignments to the 168,000 Party committees.

The Organization Department has processed several thousand cases a year to give approval to appointments, and has been in charge of the *nomenklatura* system since 1949 (Burns 2006). There was greater openness in the 1980s about the role of the *nomenklatura* and then more secrecy in the 1990s following Tiananmen. Since China entered the World Trade Organization (WTO) in 2001, greater openness has been required. Patronage extends to jobs, tendering, and licensing requests. Economic development and the market system have been a challenge to the *nomenklatura* system, with individuals accumulating resources outside Party control. The CCP stress on performance has been undermined by corruption and nepotism too. There have been moves to reform the bureaucracy, for it to become more meritocratic, with no life tenure, to raise its education levels and to punish corruption.

State and CCP structures

How does the Party structure mesh with the state bureaucratic structure? Local government is a nested hierarchy under the state council with three tiers of provinces, counties and townships. There are some exceptions such as the autonomous prefectures responsible for the same things as municipalities, where the supervision of officials is weaker, or the central cities which are managed directly by the counties. There are also local people's congresses (LPCs) elected by representatives. All levels above the county have bureaucratic authority over the next level down. The strength of the LPCs and the rule of law have been limited. This structure runs in parallel with the CCP structure, with the CCP replicating the state's hierarchy at each level and asserting authority over the state via Party committees (Landry 2008: 57). This is a highly complex administrative structure with dual accountability to both government and to the Party. Local cadres have some ability to take local decisions, but the higher state hierarchy is monitoring them and Party officials above and outside the locality are monitoring the state officials.

The Party trumps state cadres. To be promoted, an official needs to be a CCP member as part of the route up. Village Chairmen and the Party

Secretary are often the same people. As a snapshot in 1998, state cadres numbered 40 million, CCP members 60 million; of the 40 million state cadres, 25 million were non-Party and 15 million were Party. Of the 60 million CCP members, 15 million were state cadres and 45 million were outside the state cadres (Walder 2006). Walder estimates the CCP political elite to have been 0.5 million, with a state bureaucracy of 40 million and 45 million Party members outside the state cadres. If all groups stick together, then there is cohesion. Defections in May 1989 threatened the hold of the CCP. Challenges to the elite can come from both within and outside the state and Party membership. Underperforming cadres are not pushed out, but are kept in post and in the Party to control their opposition.

Composition of the CCP

In terms of who the elites are, I am interested in the social characteristics of Party members and the composition of the Party. Hong Yung Lee (1991) talks of the change in the CCP from revolutionaries to technocrats. Dickson (2003: 31) talks of the red *versus* expert debate. Landry (2008) says that there has been a shift from class credentials to being more educated. Dickson (2003: 31) says that post-1978 the period of class struggle was over; there were reconciliation policies with new goals of economic modernization creating new elites. They needed to include these new groups or be threatened by them. Lee (1991) reports on increasing proportions of college-educated members, with a large peaceful elite turnover. In 2001, on the 80th anniversary of the CCP, there were 64.5 million members, which amounted to 5 per cent of the population; 17 per cent were women, 6 per cent were ethnic minorities, 50 per cent were under 45 years old. This was a squeezing out of the proletariat. A 1990 study of 30,000 workers in 50 enterprises found 18 per cent had been Party members in 1982, which had fallen to 8 per cent in 1990 (Dickson 2003: 33). The Tiananmen period was an interlude of the Party losing cohesion. From 1994, there was a renewed recruitment of workers and farmers as well as a push towards technical and entrepreneurial people and those in universities. Dickson (2003: 35) says that 40 per cent of college teachers and administrators were Party members in the mid-1990s. In general terms, it has helped the career to be a member of the Party.

The Party has had different influences on rural and urban populations. The Party is less present in rural areas, with a declining membership. In rural areas, the Party branch committee supervises the village administration, controls the promotion of Chairmen to Party Secretaries; if there are candidates for election, it selects out anyone it sees as a troublemaker such as local activists (Landry 2008: 234). There is more direct Party influence on urban committees, with voters having less say than in villages. The relations between the CCP and enterprises have changed over the decades; Party thinking has shifted from seeing private enterprise and entrepreneurs as class enemies towards harnessing their economic benefits and recruiting them into the Party. There was a ban on entrepreneurs being in the Party from 1989 to 2001, which was then lifted (Dickson 2003).

Tensions between development and democracy, market and CCP

Does economic development lead to civil society and lead to democracy? The relationship between development and various freedoms, one of which being democracy, is not straightforward, nor is it a causal one (Robinson 2006; Sen 1999; Lipset 1959; Dahl 1971). The extension of markets means the dispersal of power, greater competition, choice, and private citizens and firms having bargaining power through their resources and through their position in civil society, acting as a counterweight to state power. Walder (2006) argues that the market system has eroded the institutional pillars of the communist system, cutting out the mediation of the Party. Just as the legal system has had a life of its own in terms of escaping from control by the Party, so markets too have evolved beyond the reach of Party control.

China has confounded the North et al. (2009) idea of a double balance – that inclusiveness and development in the economic and political spheres necessarily go together. China has combined greater openness and market development in economic terms with no move towards democracy in political terms; the CCP has retained its hold on the political system. This process of economic liberalization without political democratization has created shared interests between middle classes and state officials (Dickson 2003: 13). Entrepreneurs have supported the regime by and large; they have benefitted from it and fear that political change would threaten their property interests. The symbiosis between local officials and entrepreneurs, talked about above, has created joint interests. Officials are partners in enterprises; they get fees for joint ventures; and they tax farmers and firms.

Dickson (2003: 19) argues that civil society is not counterposed to the state in China but is embedded within the state; it is not outside the state system, but rather inside it. The system is defined by the state, and civil society is not antagonistic to it (White, Howell and Xiaoyuan 1996). Dickson (2003) distinguishes between what he calls the critical and the non-critical realm. The critical realm includes outsiders to or non-beneficiaries of the system, protesters, and some intellectuals; the non-critical realm includes entrepreneurs, managers, and professionals who are anti-political in character and not engaged in political activities. For instance, they did not support the protesters in Tiananmen. The non-critical realm is crucial; if the critical and non-critical are not joined, the state supports the market dynamic but represses the political dynamic. State policies have been inclusive towards the non-critical realm. Entrepreneurs have not been interested in political power; they have solved issues of property rights and contract enforcement through clientelism, with a state that is sympathetic to local business views. This can be seen as a corporatist framework that binds state-society relations together. This contrasts with Western civil society based on pluralism with the state as an independent actor (Dickson 2003: 24). For example, the organization law of 1989 made every organization register with the government, supervised by the Party or government unit, creating limits to the autonomy of civil society organizations.

Has the CCP itself been changing?

As the CCP has been less in absolute control, there has been the need for it to work through other organizations (Dickson 2003; March and Olsen 1989) with the recognition of the need for mediation through market institutions. The CCP itself has been dependent on the growth of the private sector and the use of market forces, which themselves have undermined the status of the CCP: the working classes have become more independent of the state, there has been greater occupational and geographical mobility, challenging the Party's ability to monitor and control. In response, the CCP has moved towards co-opting businessmen, technocrats and professional classes. This has been done by ditching social goals and ditching the rural farmers. Huge inequalities have opened up – between provinces (especially coastal versus inland provinces), within provinces, and between rural and city areas (Dickson 2003). The CCP has pushed the interests of employers over workers and of urban development over rural farmers' interests. I turn now to how this gets worked out in terms of Chinese corporate governance.

Meso-institutions: Corporatism, organizational forms and corporate governance institutions

The Party/State (Mann 2013) has created a corporatist framework as part of state-society relations to bind society together (Dickson 2003: 24). In this corporatism, unlike the West, labour-side interests are not represented; it is corporatist on the business side.

The path of institutional development has been therefore very different from that taken in the liberal democracies. It is a more extreme version of the coordinated corporatism of Germany and France. The emphasis has been on institutionalizing the participation of key groups, achieving consensus and common goals (Dickson 2003: 62). Corporatist structures have substituted for coercion, propaganda and central planning of the former era, as the state's grip lessens. Every organization has had to register with the government and be sponsored by a state unit, with one organization for each profession or activity, so that they do not compete with each other. Leaders of such associations have been in the CCP, the Party not liking organizations to be outside its control (Dickson 2003). Corporate groups are therefore not independent in the sense of acting as checks and balances on the state. Unger and Chan (1996) compare this process with that in Japan, South Korea and Taiwan, which transitioned from state to societal corporatism, where groups acquired autonomy from the state as a consequence of democratization. Dickson's (2003: 37) survey of business associations in

China concludes that they are not agents of the state, but nor are they autonomous.

As to how inclusionary or exclusionary the Chinese state is, Dickson (2003: 68) argues that it is selectively inclusionary, incorporating some individuals and groups but excluding others. The CCP's corporatism excludes the critical intelligentsia. It includes technocrats and entrepreneurs of the non-critical realm. The entrepreneurs in Xiamen disapproved of the student demands of 1989, placing stability above democracy (Wank in Dickson 2003: 96). In the 1990s, there were ways of getting round the ban on private enterprise – through disguising them, through co-opting entrepreneurs into the Party. In the late 1990s, the legality of private enterprise was established. By the 2000s, there were special classes and programmes for entrepreneurs given by the Party. In return for official discretion and protection from competition, entrepreneurs were expected to contribute to the local community schools and roads, and ward off jealousy of them, labelled red-eye disease. Guanxi and the corruption that went with it were diminishing; there has been greater reliance on laws and regulation. But there has not been a growth in liberal faith in parliamentary democracy; reform has been initiated by the Party rather than by society. In terms of political culture and beliefs, enterprises and beneficiaries of development would rather have those interests protected and see them and their prosperity better protected by the existing political system than by any democratizing principle.

I follow Aguilera and Jackson's (2010) interpretation of corporate governance as 'the study of power and influence over decision-making within the corporation'. As Aguilera and Jackson say, the corporation is itself an institution with the rights and responsibilities of different parties linked to law and politics. There are diverse parties associated with the firm: owners, managers, employees, state, and these have different structures and roles across countries. For example, dispersed individual shareownership contrasts with concentrated blockholder ownership; the role of institutional investors varies across countries; and the role of employees varies – whether formally represented on boards or having works councils within firms or representation within trade unions or very few rights and representations. And the role of the state varies – from being hands-off with very little remit to interfere except through regulation, to being involved as a coordinating agency between parties, to being a blockholder owner and immersed in the politics of certain firms' decision-making.

In making comparisons between Chinese capitalism and Western capitalisms, as in the previous chapters, I look at organizational forms. Chapters 4, 5 and 6 contrasted the pre-eminence of the corporation in Britain and the United States – as a legal person, backed by common law, independent of the state and held through dispersed shareholding tradable in markets – with the more closely-held, concentrated holdings, unlisted and less-tradable organizational forms in continental Europe that had the effect of protecting the strategic assets within those firms rather than protecting investors' rights through shareholding of those firms. Where do Chinese companies sit in this spectrum?

In addition to the non-state enterprises described earlier, there has been a transition of SOEs into enterprises listed on the newly created stock exchanges of Shanghai and Shenzhen in the early 1990s. Liu (2006) gives data of 1,400 firms having made initial public offerings between 1992 and 2002, raising $100bn with market capitalization of $500bn and with 130 securities firms, 100,000 practitioners, and 70 million investor accounts (CSRC website in Liu 2006: 421).

The 1994 company law was designed for corporatization of SOEs, to impose some discipline on management despite the state retaining ownership of the majority of shares of listed companies. Thousands of companies were incorporated. Some 1,300 SOEs were listed on the two stock exchanges by 2004. This enabled them to raise equity finance from investors rather than relying on banks (Pistor and Xu 2005).

Despite listing on stock markets, these firms remain heavily influenced by the government in various ways. These data show that these listed firms have concentrated ownership, and the majority have a parent company, often an SOE. Liu (2006) calculates that the controlling shareholders for over 80 per cent of listed firms are central or local governments. Listed companies are not by and large private companies. There is limited independence of boards from political and state-controlling owners. Chen, Fan and Wong (2004) argue that 80 per cent of directors on boards have some connection with the state. There are different classes of shares – state shares, legal person shares and public shares – with only public shares being tradable, the transfer of the other two types being controlled by the government.

This is different from the publicly-owned and traded corporation of the liberal economies and also from the privately-owned and less traded GmbH-type company. I have argued that the coordinating and signalling functions have been stronger than the protective function of property rights in China, especially than protecting individual investor assets. There has been instead much stronger protection via control of state assets, restricting trading, influencing boards and changing top management in favour of politically approved managers. I would argue that these listed companies are not 'private' in the Western sense.

Relation between law and corporate governance

Formal legal shareholder protection and regulatory quality for instance by the La Porta *et al.* (1998) indicators show Chinese formal protection to be below the average for transition economies (Pistor and Xu 2005). Shareholder protection has been weak and private enforcement very weak. In 2001, courts were unable to hear cases brought by investors whose rights had been infringed by misrepresentation of accounts, insider trading or asset stripping. Public enforcement was done by the China Securities Regulatory Commission

(CSRC) and the Chinese Supreme People's Court (SPC). They have vetted which litigation is permissible. Gradually, more litigation has been allowed by the private securities litigation rules, issued in 2003, to allow joint litigation but only where the defendant company is registered. The Pistor and Xu (2005) data for 2001–2004 reported that no civil law case resulted in a court imposing a liability. Public enforcement has also been weak.

In China, corporate governance as an issue has been debated more closely in relation to the governance of companies listed on the Shanghai and Shenzhen stock exchanges from 1990. Between 1990 and 2005, the Chinese stock market grew to be the 8th largest in the world by number of firms and market capitalization (Liu 2006). Listed firms nevertheless accounted for less than 5 per cent of large and medium-sized firms in China and a small fraction of GDP (Allen, Qian and Qian 2005). Liu (2006) argues that listed firms' governance has operated in a similar fashion to that of non-listed firms, under the norms of administrative governance. The listing of former SOEs was seen as a way of raising equity, rather than of distancing the state from direct control over the levers of management. The state has maintained blockholder ownership of the majority of listed companies. Liu (2006) names the model of governance over listed firms a control-based model, where controlling shareholders – usually the state – use governance mechanisms to continue to control the firm. Thus ownership structures have remained concentrated and often linked, through pyramids, to non-listed SOEs (Ning 2015). Boards have been constructed that were friendly to management, with little financial disclosure to the public and lacking an active takeover market (Liu 2006). The careers and turnover of top management of listed firms have been influenced by the CCP and state administration (Ning, Prevezer and Wang 2014).

This represented, then, a change in manner of control by the state, from direct state/Party management towards indirect control. This goes hand-in-hand with the continued ownership stake by the state in publicly-listed companies. Around 70 per cent of shares on the Chinese stock market remain owned by the state, and a controlling interest is kept in leading enterprises (Mann 2013: 233). Ownership structures of listed companies are not transparent: the state often has acted as a holding company structure with branches of the company listed on stock exchanges to raise capital from private and foreign sources but with the state maintaining strategic control through pyramidal ownership (Sutherland and Ning 2015). This mirrors the kind of pyramid control structure found in other countries (in continental Europe, Latin America), where control is often maintained by a family through pyramid structures.

The CCP has less control and influence in purely private enterprises; there is weak Party-building in both private and foreign-owned sectors (Dickson 2003: 42). The enterprise law gives stockholders the authority to hire and fire board members and management; if the enterprise Party committee has no shares in the firm, it cannot control hiring and firing. Party committees can influence standards for selection and approve decisions of owners and shareholders, but can't directly remove managers and others. There has been resistance in Shenzhen to taking on unproductive Party people. Instead, Shenzhen has a private enterprise association, a new form of Party organization.

Status and role of workers/labour/employees in the firm

Since 1978, the status of workers in Chinese firms and in the economy in general has declined. The reforms in the SOEs have reduced the status and power of workers (Yongshun 2006). Since the reform, there has been greater disrespect and falling in consultation, in perks and in authority. Under Mao, in the SOEs there was job security, subsidized prices for essentials, egalitarian wage policies, welfare benefits and housing. This was not a question of labour autonomy: under Mao, labour was controlled through state-run unions; there were Party members in each factory; and workers were encouraged to join the Party. But there was the iron rice bowl, a basic level of welfare provision organized by the work unit (Mann 2013: 220). Since 1980, these worker-oriented rights have gone. With priority given to economic growth and much greater precedence given by the Party to non-state activities, the reform of inefficient SOEs has meant layoffs and diminished power of the workers. Disrespect and weak rights are reflected in things like poor treatment in cases of injury or healthcare, long working hours and the flouting of labour laws: 'We were the master but we are not now. In the 1950s when we walked in the street with uniforms, even the police would show their respect to us and we felt proud of ourselves; but now if you walk in the street with your uniform, even the salesperson is reluctant to talk with you, and we feel inferior to others' (Yongshun 2006: 174).

Ching Kwan Lee (2007) contrasts the old SOE-dominated northern city of Liaoning with the booming coastal industries. In the former, there was unemployment as SOEs collapsed; in the booming areas, there was low wages, abuse of migrant workers, and working six sometimes seven days a week: 'Workers and peasants appeal to the law, and the bourgeoisie – employers and officials – flout it (Lee in Mann 2013: 239). No-one wishes to be a worker with its low social status and widening income gap, with 70 per cent of enterprise workers having below average salary in the mid-1990s (Yongshun 2006: 176).

The role of trade unions in communist states has always been difficult with the state supposed to be on the side of the worker and therefore unable to tolerate independent trade unions. In the reform period, membership in trade unions fell; political activists in SOEs were the first to be laid off. For example, there was a fight over forcing workers to buy shares and sacking them if they did not; the interviewee was sacked.

In terms of formal rights, workers' councils used to have decision-making powers in enterprises, but since the 1980s these have become powerless. They lack knowledge; they are threatened with punishment by management if they object to plans; they are not the legal owners; and their approval for reforms is no longer sought. The Party is no longer constrained by socialist ideology in its dealings with workers. Are the trade unions moving towards social representation in China? Are they agents of the state or of their members? Yunqui Zhang (1997: 125) and Dickson (2013: 62) argue that they are both, having a dual role, wanting both autonomy and embeddedness.

Changing role of management

In terms of manager-worker relations, the reforms have brought increasing management autonomy, formalized in the MRS, the management responsibility system. This is equivalent to the HRS for agricultural households, but here allowing SOEs the freedom to dispose of surpluses over quotas. In terms of Party representation, the manager in charge under the leadership of the Party committee gave way to the MRS starting in the early to mid-1980s. The Party committee became secondary in terms of types of decision-making in enterprises, demoted from financial affairs and key strategic decisions. The enterprise law of 1988 legalized the status of manager. In the 1990s, the Party was still in control of selecting managers in theory, but in practice managers were selected by higher-level (Party) authorities, with the priority of economic development and generation of surpluses. Coase and Wang (2013) talk about the chaos of the MRS, with managers each negotiating different prices and tax rates. The tax reform of 1994 and the contract system reform of 1993 led to a simplification of taxes with a uniform 17 per cent value-added tax to manufacturing. It was a centralization under a national tax administration and ended the tax negotiation between central and provincial governments. Coase and Wang argue that this fostered regional competition between regions rather than there being regional fiefdoms.

Conclusions: Nature of China's variety of capitalism

China's development has been predicated on the survival and development of the Party hierarchy, on economic expansion, on the expansion of the numbers of the college-educated and on slow privatization. It has legitimized capitalism. Stability has been at its core and mostly lack of violence. Walder (2006) stresses the huge expansion of college-level education, transforming the urban elites, with faster growth in college students than economic growth. From 1949 to 1979, there were 3 million graduates per year; since 1979, 12 million per year. The privatization of state assets has been very slow compared with Eastern European counterparts; the private share in GNP in China in 1999 was 55 per cent compared with Poland's 65 per cent, Russia's 70 per cent and Hungary and the Czech Republic's 80 per cent (Walder 2006: 18). Correspondingly, the elite turnover has been higher in former communist countries compared with that in China.

So what is China's variety of capitalism? Does it resemble at all the liberal market economy or the coordinated market economy? It combines a curious mixture of highly liberal labour markets with low employment protection and labour rights and with high coordination masterminded by the CCP – at least in the non-private areas. Even in the private sector, owners and managers require good relations with state officials and are subject to their coordinating pressures.

How far does the primacy of shareholder value of the LME hold in China? This is not a model that supports shareholder primacy. The shareholder is not king; the state is. Minority shareholders are not protected; the stock market does not accurately reflect values of companies. How far does the autonomy of the CEO of the LME hold? The CEO of the non-private enterprise has much less autonomy than in the LME, being subjected to pressures from the state. So this in various respects is not an LME. Is there coordination through the state along the lines of the CME? The stakeholder model, enshrining rights of labour along German/CME lines, does not hold in China. This is not a classic CME with its stakeholder model of bringing all parties to the table to negotiate conditions.

I concur with Naughton and Tsai (2015) that China's variety is a form of state capitalism – a political market economy borrowing some features from the LME in the diminishing of worker/employee rights and protection and in increasing managerial autonomy, but very different from both the LME and CME in the role of the state-management nexus. Naughton and Tsai (2015) call it state capitalism; Mann (2013) calls it a capitalist party state but demurs from calling it capitalism. The role of the state/Party has shifted from having direct Party involvement in enterprise decision-making through having leadership positions on the board to a more indirect hands-off control through shareownership, through higher Party-level monitoring of managerial careers but greater managerial autonomy and responsibility for strategic decisions in the enterprise. A politicized but not a direct state control. Above all, state-owned and state-controlled assets are protected in a variety of means: through dominance over the legal system, over the stock market, over management and over careers in enterprises. But non-state assets are also selectively protected via the relationships cultivated between private entrepreneurs and the political class.

References

Aguilera, R. and Jackson, G. (2010) 'Comparative and International Corporate Governance', *Academy of Management Annals* 4(1): 485–556.

Ai, J. (2008) What Do Chinese Judges Maximize? Economic Analysis of Law in Empirical and Comparative Perspectives, Working Paper. Nanjing: Nanjing University.

Allen, F., Qian, J. and Qian, M. (2005) China's Financial System: Past, Present and Future, Working Paper No. 05–17. University of Pennsylvania: Wharton Financial Institutions Center.

Blecher, M. and Shue, V. (1996) *Tethered Deer: Government and Economy in a Chinese County*. Stanford: Stanford University Press.

Burns, J. (2006) 'The Chinese Communist Party's Nomenklatura System as Leadership Selection Mechanism: An Evaluation', in K. Brødsgaard and Z. Yongnian (eds), *The Chinese Communist Party in Reform*, 33–58. London: Routledge.

Cabestan, J.P. (2005) 'The Political and Practical Obstacles to the Reform of the Judiciary and the Establishment of a Rule of Law in China', *Journal of Chinese Political Science* 10(1): 43–64.

Chen, D.H., Fan, J. and Wong, T.J. (2004) *Political Connected CEOs, Corporate Governance and Post-IPO Performance of China's Partially Privatized Firms.* Mimeo: Chinese University of Hong Kong.

Coase, R. and Wang, N. (2013) *How China Became Capitalist.* New York: Palgrave Macmillan.

Cohen, J. 2014, 'Struggling for Justice: China's Courts and the Challenge of Reform', *World Politics Review*, January 14, 2014.

Constitution of China (2004) The National People's Congress of the People's Republic of China.

Dahl, R. (1971) *Polyarchy: Participation and Opposition.* New Haven: Yale University Press.

Dickson, B. (2003) *Red Capitalists in China: The Party, Private Entrepreneurs, and Prospects for Political Change.* Cambridge: Cambridge University Press.

Du, J. and Xu, C. (2008) 'Market Socialism or Capitalism? Evidence from Chinese Financial Market Development', in J. Kornai and Y. Qian (eds), *Market and Socialism: In the Light of the Experience of China and Vietnam*, 88–109. New York and London: Palgrave Macmillan.

Gan, Y., Guo, J. and Xu, C. (2008) 'A Nationwide Survey of Privatized Firms in China', *Seoul Journal of Economics* 21(2): 311–331.

Grimheden, J. (2006) 'The Reform Path of the Chinese Judiciary: Progress or Stand-still?' *Fordham International Law Journal* 30(4): Article 2.

Hayek, F. (1945) 'The Use of Knowledge in Society', *American Economic Review* 35(4): 519–530.

Hoffman, B. and Wu, J. (2009) Explaining China's Development and Reforms, Working Paper No. 50. The Commission on Growth and Development: International Bank for Reconstruction and Development/The World Bank.

Huang, Y. (2008) *Capitalism with Chinese Characteristics: Entrepreneurship and the State.* Cambridge: Cambridge University Press.

Hutton, W. (2006) *The Writing on the Wall: Why We Must Embrace China as a Partner or Face it as an Enemy.* New York: Simon and Schuster.

Kennedy, D. (2013) 'Law and Development Economics: Towards a New Alliance', in D. Kennedy and J. Stiglitz (eds), *Law and Economics with Chinese Characteristics*, 19–70. Oxford: Oxford University Press.

Keyuan, Z. (2006) 'The Party and the Law', in K. Brødsgaard and Z. Yongnian (eds), *The Chinese Communist Party in Reform*, 77–102. London: Routledge.

Kung, J., Xu, C. and Zhou, F. (2013) 'The Social Consequences of Changing Fiscal Incentives on Local Governments' Behavior', in D. Kennedy and J. Stiglitz (eds), *Law and Economics with Chinese Characteristics*, 1–29. Oxford: Oxford University Press.

Landry, P.F. (2008) *Decentralized Authoritarianism in China: The Communist Party's Control of Local Elites in the Post-Mao Era.* Cambridge: Cambridge University Press.

La Porta, R., Lopez-de-Silanes, F. and Shleifer, A. (2008) 'The Economic Consequences of Legal Origin', *Journal of Economic Literature* 46(2): 285–332.

La Porta, R., Lopez-de-Silanes, F., Shleifer, A. and Vishny, R.W. (1998) 'Law and Finance', *Journal of Political Economy* 106(6): 1113–1155.

Laslett, P. (ed.) (1960) *Locke's Two Treaties of Government*. Cambridge: Cambridge University Press.

Lee, C.K. (2007) *Against the Law: Labor Protests in China's Rustbelt and Sunbelt*. Berkeley and Los Angeles: University of California Press.

Lee, H.Y. (1991) *From Revolutionary Cadres to Party Technocrats in Socialist China*. Berkeley: University of California Press.

Lipset, S.M. (1959) 'Some Social Requisites of Democracy: Economic Development and Political Legitimacy', *American Political Science Review* 53(1): 48–57.

Liu, Q. (2006) 'Corporate Governance in China: Current Practices, Economic Effects and Institutional Determinants', *CESifo Economic Studies* 52(2): 415–453.

Lubman, S. (2012) 'Reading between the Lines on Chinese Judicial Reform', *Wall Street Journal*, 28 October. Available at: http://blogs.wsj.com/chinarealtime/2012/10/28/reading-between-the-lines-on-chinese-judicial-reform/.

Macpherson, C.B. (1962) *The Political Theory of Possessive Individualism*. Oxford: Oxford University Press.

Manion, M. (2004) *Corruption by Design*. Cambridge, MA: Harvard University Press.

Mann, M. (2013) *The Sources of Social Power, Vol. 4: Globalizations, 1945–2011*. Cambridge: Cambridge University Press.

March, J. and Olsen, J. (1989) *Rediscovering Institutions: The Organizational Basis for Politics*. New York: The Free Press.

McMillan, J., Whalley, J. and Zhu, L. (1989) 'The Impact of China's Economic Reforms on Agricultural Productivity Growth', *Journal of Political Economy* 97(4): 781–807.

Milhaupt, C.J. and Pistor, K. (2008) *Law and Capitalism: What Corporate Crises Reveal about Legal Systems and Economic Development around the World*. Chicago: University of Chicago Press.

Milhaupt, C. J. and Pistor, K. (2013) 'The China Aviation Oil Episode: Law and Development in China and Singapore', in D. Kennedy and J. Stiglitz (eds), *Law and Economics with Chinese Characteristics*, 329–357. Oxford: Oxford University Press.

Naughton, B. (1996) *Growing out of the Plan: China's Economic Reform, 1978–1993*. Cambridge: Cambridge University Press.

Naughton, B. (2007) *The Chinese Economy: Transitions and Growth*. Cambridge, MA: MIT Press.

Naughton, B. and Tsai, K. (2015) *State Capitalism, Institutional Adaptation, and the Chinese Miracle: East Asian Government, Politics and Policy*. New York: Cambridge University Press.

Ning, L., Prevezer, M. and Wang, Y. (2014) Top Management Turnover and Corporate Governance in China: Effects on Innovation Performance, Working Paper No. 53. Queen Mary University of London: Centre for Globalisation Research.

North, D., Wallis, J.J. and Weingast, B. (2009) *Violence and Social Orders: A Conceptual Framework for Interpreting Recorded Human History*. Cambridge: Cambridge University Press.

Oi, J.C. and Walder, A.G. (1999) *Property Rights and Economic Reform in China*. Stanford: Stanford University Press.

Pei, M. (2006) *China's Trapped Transition: The Limits of Developmental Autocracy*. Cambridge, MA: Harvard University Press.

Pistor, K. and Xu, C. (2005) 'Governing Emerging Stock Markets: Legal vs Administrative Governance', *Corporate Governance: An International Review* 13(1): 5–10.

Prosterman, R. (2013) 'Rural Land Rights in China', in D. Kennedy and J. Stiglitz (eds), *Law and Economics with Chinese Characteristics*, 214–235. Oxford: Oxford University Press.

Robinson, J.A. (2006) 'Economic Development and Democracy', *Annual Review of Political Science* 9: 503–527.

Rodrik, D. (2007) *One Economics, Many Recipes: Globalization, Institutions and Economic Growth*. Princeton: Princeton University Press.

Sen, A. (1999) *Development as Freedom*. Oxford: Oxford University Press.

Shamburgh, D. (2008) *China's Communist Party: Atrophy and Adaptation*. Washington, DC: Woodrow Wilson Center Press.

Shi, T. (2014) 'Scholars Press China to Embrace Judicial Independence'. *Bloomberg*, 19 October. Available at: http://www.bloomberg.com/news/articles/2014-10-19/scholars-press-china-to-embrace-judicial-independence.

Sutherland, D. and Ning, L. (2015) 'The Emergence and Evolution of Chinese Business Groups: Are Pyramidal Groups Forming?', in B. Naughton and K. Tsai (eds), *State Capitalism, Institutional Adaptation, and the Chinese Miracle: East Asian Government Politics and Policy*, 102–153. New York: Cambridge University Press.

The Wall Street Journal (2014) 'China Tries to Hold On to Judges by Offering Freer Hand', *The Wall Street Journal*, 21 October. Available at: www.wsj.com/…/china-tries-to-hold-on-to-judges-by-offering-freer-hand.

Tsai, K. (2006) 'Adaptive Informal Institutions and Endogenous Institutional Change in China', *World Politics* 59(1): 116–141.

Unger, J. and Chan, A. (1996) 'Corporatism in China: A Developmental State in an East Asian Context', in B. McCormick and J. Unger (eds), *China after Socialism: In the Footsteps of Eastern Europe or East Asia*, 95–126. Armonk, NY: M.E. Sharpe.

Volberda, H., Morgan, R., Reinmoeller, P., Hitt, M., Ireland, R. and Hoskisson, R. (2011) *Strategic Management: Competitiveness and Globalization*. Boston: Cengage Learning.

Walder, A. (2006) 'The Party Elite and China's Trajectory of Change', in K. Brødsgaard and Z. Yongnian (eds), *The Chinese Communist Party in Reform*, 1–32. London: Routledge.

White, G., Howell, J. and Xiaoyuan, S. (1996) *In Search of Civil Society: Market Reform and Social Change in Contemporary China*. Oxford: Clarendon Press.

White, L.T. (1998) *Unstately Power, Vol. 2: Local Causes of China's Intellectual, Legal and Governmental Reforms*. Armonk, NY: M.E. Sharpe.

World Bank (1990) China. Available at: http://www.worldbank.org/en/country/china.

Xu, C. (2010) The Institutional Foundations of China's Reforms and Development, Discussion Paper No. DP7654. London: Centre for Policy Research.

Xu, C. (2011) 'The Fundamental Institutions of China's Reforms and Development', *Journal of Economic Literature* 49(4): 1076–1151.

Xu, C. and Zhang, X. (2009) The Evolution of Chinese Entrepreneurial Firms: Township-Village Enterprises Revisited, Discussion Paper No. 854. Washington, DC: International Food Policy Research Institute.

Xu, C., Wang, X. and Shu, Y. (2007) 'Local Officials and Economic Growth', *Economic Research (Jingji Yanjiu)*, September.

Yang, X. (2007) 'A Correct Concept of Judicial Authority Is the Proper Meaning of Rule of Law', *China Court Daily*, 18 October.

Yin, W.-q. (2001) 'Causes for China's Local Market Fragmentation', *China and World Economy* 6: 27–33. Available at: http://caod.oriprobe.com/articles/24859939/causes_for_china_s_local_market_fragmentation.htm.

Yongshun, C. (2006) 'The Weakening of Workers' Power in China', in K. Brødsgaard and Z. Yongnian (eds), *The Chinese Communist Party in Reform*, 173–191. London: Routledge.

Zhang, M. (2008) 'From Public to Private: The Newly Enacted Chinese Property Law and the Protection of Property Rights in China', *Berkeley Business Law Journal* 5(2): Article 4.

Zhang, Y. (1997) 'From State Corporatism to Social Representation: Local Trade Unions in the Reform Years', in T. Brook and M. Frolic (eds), *Civil Society in China*, 124–148. Armonk, NY: M.E. Sharpe.

9 Conclusions

This book set out firstly to explore the historical routes into the varieties of capitalism, distinguishing between the liberal economies of Britain and the United States and the continental capitalisms of France and Germany. The aim has been to do this through the debate on primary institutions, in particular the institutions of property rights and legal systems and what I have called in short-hand 'the nature of the state'. In other words, one aim was to establish and make the connections between the varieties of capitalism debate, which focuses on the meso-institutions of corporate governance and labour markets, and the primary institutions underlying corporate governance and labour markets, namely those of property rights and legal systems and the nature of the state.

The other significant question the book set out to answer was asking how well the 'good institutions' template – of clear property rights, a legal system with rule of law that is independent of the state, an effective but constrained state – has fitted with the institutional evolutions of the now mature economies of Britain, the United States, Germany and France, and to compare those with the developing and transitioning economies of Tanzania and China. This has meant unpicking and elaborating on the concepts of property rights, on the 'natures' of different states, on the concept of constrained states and their effectiveness, through legal and fiscal capacities, and on the different structures and functions of legal systems and their relationships to the states they operate in.

It also means thinking along Mary Douglas' (1986) lines that these institutional evolutions – choices made at any point in time – are governed by the prior shaping of institutions, with formal institutions subject to the dynamics of their interaction with informal institutions. If the country has a long history of settling an area or administering an enterprise through chartering corporations which have legal status and in which shares can be bought, this creates a tradition, a choice for followers in setting up enterprises to take this route. Markets for trading assets – be they land, goods, slaves, shares, government bonds – are not a question of culture; they create the conditions through which choices are made, they present themselves as the parameters by which to fulfil whatever purposes people in those places at that time have. Stressing the histories here means, therefore, emphasizing the connections between one set of institutions – markets in tradable assets and corporations – and another set of institutions – the superior status of common law – a more decentralized and contestable form of law-making – over civil codes, for example. Through a Douglasian lens, the institutions themselves do the thinking. What Douglas meant by 'doing the thinking' was that strong or weak social regulation and strong or weak integration (hierarchy or individualism) is replicated in strong or weak cognitive regulation and integration of people's thought-styles, which then cultivate the framing, preferences and linkages with the formation of formal institutions (6 and Richards 2017).

I have not paid sufficient attention to the role of informal institutions, which is beyond my scope here. Informal institutions matter hugely in creating these thought-styles (Douglas 1982, 1986; 6 and Richards 2017). The individualism of 15th-century England, the importance of group and hierarchy in pre-Revolutionary and then 19th-century continental Europe, the significance of collectivist forms such as cooperatives in 21st-century Tanzania arise from informal institutions.[1] Informal orderings set the preconditions that allowed the formation of the more formal institutions to take root. The dynamics of this complex interaction is a subject for future research.

There are three sets of conclusions that emphasize the evolution and connections between institutions. The first is on property rights, distinguishing between types of property rights, whose property rights and the functions of property rights and how they link into the different legal systems. This conclusion emphasizes the difference between protection of tradable property rights (Britain and the United States), protection of strategic (private) property rights (Germany and France) and protection of state-controlled property rights (Tanzania and China), and how these link into more decentralized, contestable legal systems in Britain and the United States, as opposed to the more centralized, less-contestable legal systems in the other countries. And how the functions of the legal systems themselves differ between being more protective against state power in the liberal economies on the one hand, whilst being more coordinative and having signalling and credibility functions in continental Europe and in China and Tanzania on the other hand.

The second set of conclusions is on the nature of the state. This means making the connection between effectiveness of the state and its fiscal capacity, on the one hand, and the form that constraints on the state have taken, on the other. There are significant differences between the constructions of constraints on states' power, leading to differences between how constrained states are – in one sense more constrained for liberal states, less so for coordinated European states and significantly unconstrained for emerging economies. But this also requires considering how liberal states' fiscal capacity and particularly capacity to raise public debt has been linked with their credibility in financing that debt and protecting those property rights holding debt, which credibility is in turn linked to their promise to honour that debt and not to default, especially in wartime periods. So whilst liberal states seem most constrained directly over protecting property rights, they also have had more leeway, less constraint, in foreign affairs especially during wartime and expansionary periods due to their ability to incur and service significant public debt.

This also involves linking the relationship between type of state and legal systems outlined above: the status of the rule of law, the balance between judicial and administrative power, and how independent of the state the judiciary is. And it means connecting type of state and ideology, which in turn links to how constrained the state is. Those states with ideologies that sanctioned state intervention had less-constrained states, and conversely those ideologies that emphasized constraining the state had institutional formations that did constrain the state.

The third conclusion is on organizational forms and shareholder/stakeholder capitalism, outlining for liberal economies the emphasis on the corporation, listed on markets and backed by common law and judiciary, leading to dispersal of shareholding and shareholder democracy, managerial autonomy, and shareholder primacy. This was accompanied by a deal with labour that meant that labour acquiesced in weaker protective rights in exchange for investment globally that would sustain demand for labour's services domestically. It also means integrating the role that race and slavery have played in the evolution of the US state and the shaping of shareholder capitalism. This contrasts with countries with other private corporate forms, tightly-held firms controlled by families, by the state, by business groups which have been less tradable, with greater coordination of interest groups, with or without state involvement in that coordination.

Conclusion 1 Property Rights: Which rights became protected, and connections to legal systems

Property rights and clarifying property rights are not straightforward concepts. Questions about property rights have emerged that this book tries to answer – whose property rights were clarified, what type of property rights assets were clarified and what have been the functions of those property rights? Whose property rights were clarified depended on who, which group(s), were the dominant elites in the period when those rights were institutionalized.[2] The type of property rights that became protected is linked to whether and when markets formed that traded those assets, such as landed property and slaves, shares in companies, and government securities, or whether company shares were not tradable as companies, were not listed, and the assets in those companies were more protected from being taken over through markets and trading. This led to a different kind of asset being built up within companies, based more on untradable values such as skills or strategic assets. The functions of different property rights regimes have also varied, with liberal regimes emphasizing protective functions and others placing greater weight on coordinative and signalling functions.

Table 9.1 Property Rights (PRs): Which rights are protected, unprotected/weakly protected, and how protected

	Strongly protected PRs	*Unprotected/ Weakly protected PRs*	*How protected – Which mechanisms and by whom*
Liberal economies – Britain and US	Landed, mercantile, financial, corporations, tradable assets Slaves up to mid-19th century	State assets, industrial assets, unincorporated labour skills	Courts, judiciary, rule of law Markets, trading mechanisms Lawyers, judges, information through stock markets and legal rules
State – centralized, coordinated France and Germany	State PRs Mittelstand Strategic assets of closely held firms Insider/coordinated employer and employee rights	Auxiliary sectors Service sectors in unprotected part of dualized labour market	Administration/ bureaucracy State regulation Obstacles to trading – strategic and structural
Emergent capitalisms China and Tanzania	State PRs Urban, industrial enterprise PRs	Farmers Customary PRs, cooperatives Rural land rights in poorer provinces Non-state enterprises not supported by officials	Local state officials Central state officials Administration and regulation

Property rights in liberal capitalisms

The liberal capitalisms (Britain and United States) grew up on the back of the recognition and protection of tradable assets. Tradable assets belonged to the landed and trading elites, and these assets were shaped into the mercantile and financial sectors in the liberal economies.

The growth in tradable assets, through shares in trading companies from the 16th and 17th centuries, was linked to the expansion of trade, to the colonization of the United States and elsewhere through private companies, and formed the longstanding institution of trading shares in joint stock companies. There were also markets in land linked to private property rights. This trading was locally organized and increasingly unregulated by central government.[3] Out of this arose local stock exchanges, important in financing railways and banks in the middle quarters of the 19th century in the liberal economies. One can see a direct link between the early use of joint stock companies for trading enterprises and the protection of the tradable nature of property rights in all sorts of assets – land, goods, slaves – and markets developing in tradable shares in those companies and securities. The link between them is the alienability of the assets, their tradable nature.

It matters how those property rights were arrived at and whether they were settled prior to democracy, coeval with democracy or after it. In Britain, property rights became individualized because they were settled by a state apparatus in the late 17th and 18th centuries that gave power to large landowners, merchants and commercial people, whose interests were to have individual property rights independent of the state,[4] and at a time when ideologies of liberalism and possessive individualism underpinned these ideas. Liberalism and possessive individualism came at a period of time, during the 17th century after a turbulent civil war, the settlement of which gave power to Parliament to limit absolute monarchy. Parliament at that time was composed of the propertied class.

In Britain, there was an alliance between landed and financial interests, in turn linked to the growth of the City, with financial interests trumping industrial interests. This is what Cain and Hopkins (1986, 1987) dubbed 'gentlemanly capitalism', linked to trading and imperial interests more than to protecting domestic capital and its skills. One key distinction between Britain and continental Europe is the relative power and prominence of its financial centre and capital compared with its industrial capital. Chapter 4 argued that the landed/mercantile and financial interests banded together and were more represented in Parliament than was industrial capital. I trace also the 'liberal turn' in Britain in the 1820s and in the United States in the 1840s, when the central state shifted somewhat from protectionism, from 'energetic improvement' towards a more *laissez-faire* stance domestically, with infrastructure financed by private capital. The importance of localized stock exchanges used to finance such infrastructure can be linked (see below) to the development of shareholder capitalism.

Legal systems and their relationship to capitalism are also varied, with different kinds of legal system evolving in each country. I connect here with the literature on the spectrum of legal systems according to how centralized or decentralized and how contestable legal systems are. This builds on the division between common-law-based systems and civil code legal systems. The former have more prominent places for lawyers and juries, more lawyers per capita within their population, greater emphasis on courts and less place for the state administration in settling disputes. Legal systems with a prominent place for lawyers, with many lawyers, with relative independence of the judiciaries and the running of judiciaries from political processes, are argued to be both more decentralized and more contestable – operate diffusely across the countries – and are more accessible to individual and class actions being taken through using lawyers, challenging legal precedent and evolving over time in response to social and economic change. These are the arguments of Milhaupt and Pistor's (2008) *Law and Capitalism* and Kagan's (2001) *Adversarial Legalism*.

The decentralized contestable legal system arose out of the victory of common law and statutory law, using Parliament and courts, over prerogative law during the English Civil War in the 17th century. Common law (along with individual property rights) was transported to the US colonization, enshrined in the constitutional structures that separated judicial powers as a counterbalance to the executive government, where Supreme Court decisions steered a path creating a pro-capitalist, pro-corporation and pro-slavery economy. The legal and financial sectors were prominent and powerful, which enhanced contestability of the law: lawyers were relatively numerous, prominent and able to prosecute cases. The function of property rights in these systems has been protective: to protect assets of investors in markets, and particularly minority investors without insider power. The growth of powerful legal and financial sectors has been linked to the development of equity markets and the demand for decentralized expertise – the private attorney general.

I highlight, too, a significant difference in institutional set-up between Britain and the United States over racial segregation. The United States institutionally shares some features with Britain: common law, possessive individualism and individual liberty, and the importance of individual property rights were formative in the United States' Declaration of Independence. But there are also differences. Plantation capitalism based on slavery was fought for in the War of Independence in the setting up of the United States, and slavery in the southern states was institutionalized from its inception.[5] The more formal decentralization and separation of powers in the constitution was designed as a constraint on the build-up of power. This decentralization allowed the regional and, with that, racial segregation to become and remain entrenched. The United States was like two different countries on the racial/economic front: Piketty's (2014: 161) figures for capital or wealth in the United States around 1770–1810 illustrate the relatively egalitarian north, with capital not worth very much because land was abundant and cheap and because immigrants did not have much accumulated capital, compared with inequalities in the south, where ownership of slaves as capital was greater than ownership of landed capital.

When I square this with the institutional set-up of the United States, liberal, democratic codes applied only to white men, and not to African Americans, Native Americans, or to women, none of whom were recognized as full citizens.[6] Individual private property rights were for white male citizens at the expense of Native Americans and imported and then native African American slaves. The American Republic expanded imperially westwards from sea to shining sea, formalizing land rights into private rights for white settlers.

Segregation was not fully amended until the civil rights movement in the 1960s, and even then only through tremendous struggle; its results continue into economic divergence between black and white and violence against the black population, particularly in southern states, as evidenced in the current *Black Lives Matter* campaign (Scott 2016).

More coordinative capitalisms (Germany, France)

The French intertwining of settlement of property rights and state power bears the marks of (not surprisingly) a very different history. It combines both

17th-century pre-Revolutionary administrative centralization through absolute monarchy asserting itself over the dispersed nobility and their law courts (the story of the *Intendants* who became the post-Revolutionary *Préfets*) with post-Revolution Napoleonic triumph of the *Code civil*, and administrative over judicial power. The civil code legal systems in continental Europe have had more centralized state administrations, the legal system has had more rules-based statutory regulation rather than case law, and the system is argued to have been less contestable in the sense that disputes were less likely to be challenged through the courts and more likely to be settled through administrative processes. The centralized state and its administration has had greater power over reassigning property rights in the interests of state-led and state-financed projects than the British state has ever had. The French state has also been instrumental in coordinating and centralizing fragmented interests, geographically and politically, which has been significant in its involvement in corporate governance. The encompassing nature of collective bargaining agreements despite falling union density in the current period (Martorell Cruz 2016; Granville, Martorell Cruz and Prevezer 2015) is testament to the pervasive nature of state regulation in the post-Second-World-War period, which dates much further back.

The German state was created out of Prussian-led nation-building in the 1860s and 1870s and has remained a more decentralized collection of *Länder* than the French or British states. Its representative body, the *Reichstag*, was weaker than the British Parliament, with greater sovereignty vested in the Kaiser and his state bureaucracy and army than the equivalent in Britain or France. As Mann (1993) argues, it was not a liberal state in economic affairs, in the British sense of favouring small government. It saw its role as central in the catch-up in infrastructure, education and technology required to promote the German Reich to British status. In terms of property rights and the balance of administrative and judicial power, the German situation sits somewhere between the French and British, with greater balance between independent judicial and state administrative power and greater decentralization and independence regionally of the various states from the central bureaucracy.

The property rights that were more protected were strategic assets of more closely-held shares in companies, whose shares have been less tradable. The protective function of the legal system in relation to property rights was less prominent and was balanced by a more enhanced coordinative function of bringing significant parties to the bargaining table. There has been less contestability in the legal system: it has not been easy to bring actions to defend individual rights, there were not the equivalent numbers or powers given to lawyers and financial sector expertise, fighting individual or class actions through the legal system was not as supported.

Centralized state administration and bureaucracies have been more powerful. In these capitalisms, the realm of the public sector has been greater (compared with liberal capitalisms), and state regulatory power has been more centralized and more pervasive. These countries did not go down the route of developing strong localized equity and government bond markets, and stock exchanges, and legally backed corporations, but continued to have companies more closely-held in blockholdings with greater reliance on debt and insider financing, rather than publicly-raised financing through listed companies and more broadly-held shareholding. The relationship between stronger state regulation and the non-development of dispersed market-based finance is unclear but possibly connected.

Hand-in-hand with protecting strategic assets has been the coordinative function of corporate governance, building in codetermination and works' councils (and a raft of protective insurance legislation) to co-opt workers away from class-aligned socialist protest and towards more consensual coordinated bargaining. This has to be seen as interdependent with the state-led bargain over Bismarck's pension and insurance offer in exchange for political quiescence about property rights; the one was dependent on the other. If the assets of those companies are more protected – through prevention of trading, through cross-shareholding, through blockholding, holding companies, there is a complementarity, noted in Hall and Soskice (2001), between the interests of capital/managers/owners of those companies and a coordinated consensual workforce.

Emergent capitalisms: Which kind of property rights, whose property rights and how protected?

Neither China nor Tanzania has states in power that have favoured backing individual property rights, for different reasons. In Tanzania, private property rights have been associated with foreign colonial investors, and state-vesting of property rights has been a reaction to this threat. In China, private property rights were seen as antithetical to socialist Party ideology, and there has been a reluctance, until very recently in 2007, to put private property on an equal footing with public property. It has been state assets that have been most strongly protected in these countries. Their legal systems have been less independent of their states' executives, which in turn were less constrained than those in coordinated developed economies. The legal systems themselves have served as a signalling and coordinating system, rather than in protecting assets from either the state or large blockholders, who have had close connections with each other. This has made property rights vulnerable to the will or policies of those in power in the state, which has more overtly politicized the settlement of those property rights. The state has protected urban rights more strongly than rural rights, and has encroached on the rights and independence of cooperatives in Tanzania and of listed firms in China.

Conclusion 2 On the nature of state: Links between property rights, type of state, state fiscal capacity and constraints on the state

State fiscal capacity – the ability of the state to raise taxes – affects the state's effectiveness, its ability to spend on public goods domestically or to finance foreign wars and expansion. The liberal states – Britain in the 18th century and the United States in the early 19th century – both achieved 'exceptional' fiscal capacity. How? Britain's ability to tax arose from the spread of its commercialism and the reliance on indirect taxation – customs and excise – taxing an increasing proportion of the expanding population across a wide range of goods. This in turn financed the expansion of the navy and the victory in wars for Britain, the increase in its empire, in turn bringing in further revenues to the state. The United States' federal fiscal capacity was similarly based on customs revenues, given over to the federal state when this central state assumed responsibility for individual states' insolvencies in the 1840s. In both liberal states, this ability to tax was allied with an ability of the central government to issue public debt, to sell that to the wider public in the market and to be able to finance that debt out of taxation revenues. The United States was what Edling (2014) calls 'a stealthy strong state', strong enough to finance its westwards expansion.

It is important to stress the relationship between war and wartime emergencies in the making of the state (Tilly 1992). In this, there was a critical link with the ability to issue public debt and the liberal states' relationship in protecting tradable property rights. These states were able to override peacetime protection with the support of business that favoured the opening up of new markets both in war materials procurement and as a result of victory in war. The (liberal) governments of Britain and the United States were able to issue debt with a credible promise that they would not default on these debts. By offering tradable state debt (government securities) with a stronger commitment not to default than France or Germany, Britain and the United States were able to sell tradable, valuable and low-risk assets within their own countries, denominated in their own currencies, by which they could offer a *quid pro quo* for temporarily overriding their property rights during wartime. The German Reich during the Great War was not able to do this, as its promises to stand behind its debts were not as credible; this affected its capacity to mobilize resources from its domestic economy for war purposes, despite its economy being in many respects more productive than the British one at that time. Both the British and US governments were able to sustain this 'domestic bargain' – the British state from the 1650s through to the collapse of Bretton Woods in 1971 and the US government from 1873 through to the present – in an affordable way, with public debt being paid off very gradually. It took a century to bring down the national debt ratios from 1815 in Britain and 35 years to do the same after 1945 in the United Kingdom.

I draw two conclusions from this. Fiscal and financial capacity of the liberal states was (and has continued to be) not transparent, largely invisible, and was constructed through, and in itself helped to create, the expansion of financial markets trading securities, and was broadly based over their populations with large numbers participating in these markets. And this capacity was used more in foreign policy areas rather than to finance domestic public goods, was used for war and investment abroad rather than to build railways or canals domestically.

How is this linked to constraints on the state?

Constraining the state has been a more significant trope in the liberal economies since the 17th century than in continental European economies, and one can trace this idea back to the 13th century in England through *Magna Carta* and the push against absolutist government. Britain's story is of individual property rights backed by common law becoming predominant through the Civil War, triumphing over prerogative courts and kingly authority, constraining the monarchy. The state was conceived post-1688 as the King in Parliament, limited monarchy; the large landowners gained power through Parliament, and it is they for whom property rights were strengthened and clarified and made independent of the state. The US state was similarly constrained by construction of separated powers, with a relatively independent Supreme Court counterbalancing the executive powers of the federal government.

And how does constraining the state link in to property rights?

In all countries, there has been the suppression or disappearance of customary communal property rights in the wake of capitalist development in favour of either individual property rights or state-vested property rights.

Property rights can be divided along a spectrum according to how independent of the state they are.[7] At one extreme are individual liberal-based property rights backed by common law courts, adjudicated by a judiciary that is largely independent of the state executive (Britain and the United States). Individual private property rights and their protection, coupled with decentralized contestable legal systems, formed the bulwarks of what constrained the domestic state. The state was not allowed to infringe these private property rights. These states were (and remain) significantly less constrained in the foreign policy arena. Why? These states needed discretion in foreign policy because they were genuinely insecure. This applies to all states, including developed ones, and is a point stressed by North, Wallis, Weingast and Webb (2013) in their consideration of developing country states. In the liberal states, there was acquiescence in the temporary infringement of property rights during wartime emergencies on the understanding and belief, which was not without foundation, that these rights would be protected in peacetime.

This configuration of stronger constraints on the state domestically for liberal states contrasts with more centralized administrative legal systems, particularly France since the 17th century and more strongly post-Revolution, where legal disputes were settled through administration and regulation rather than in the courts, and where judges and judiciary were by design less independent of the political executive and the states were less constrained, with a stronger power given to the state administration and bureaucracy in adjudicating property rights than to the judiciary (France) or with a balance between administration and judiciary (Germany). These property rights have been more vulnerable to state powers in peacetime as well as wartime.

At the other end of the spectrum, there are property rights that are openly vested in the state, with a rule by law but with strong political state involvement in law-making, not an independent rule of law and with lack of independence of the judiciary, with the state able to allocate and reallocate rights according to political preferences (Tanzania and China). These states are even less constrained, standing over their legal systems with a politicized rule of law and the allocation of state-vested property rights, dependent on the will of the government.

There appears also to be a difference between liberal states and other states in terms of whether elites are part of the state, in the sense of being within the bureaucracy or connected with leading businesses that themselves have strong ties to the state, or outside it. The public-private divide emerges from this history, with Britain's and the United States' elites being more distanced from the state bureaucracy and acting as constraints on the state, whereas German and French elites have been within or attached to the state or government to a greater extent.[8] France's and Germany's stories are ones of state-building through nation-building, with greater roles for the administration and bureaucracy attached to more centralized civil law systems and more subservient judiciaries than in the liberal economies.

In the emergent capitalisms in Tanzania and China, the history of and creation of these relatively unconstrained states have to be seen in the context of post-Second-World-War independence from colonial control and institutions for Tanzania and post-Second-World-War communist forging of Chinese paths of economic development via a disavowal of capitalist institutions of private property and market expansion, which called on the state/Party to control all institutions including property rights, the legal system and rule of law, the judiciary, and cultural institutions such as the media, control of ideology and thought processes.

I have attempted to link ideas about these emergent capitalist states to the North, Wallis and Weingast (2009) limited access order framework in order to build on their theory. I conclude that they are both LAOs – a basic LAO in the case of Tanzania and a mature LAO in the case of China. Tanzania is a basic LAO because of the low density of organizations not attached to the state. Its richly organized cooperatives and associations have been, and continue to be, subjected to strong state influence and direction. China is a mature LAO because of its richer organizational landscape, including private business, but lacking independence of the rule of law from the state. North et al. (2009) and Levy and Fukuyama (2010) posit a trade-off between growth of state capacity and the development of civil society. Both these states – Tanzania and China – have gone the route of stronger, more centralized states and weaker civil societies, with fewer constraints on those states.

A further aspect to note about whose rights and assets are protected is the rural-urban divide in both countries, with rural rights considerably less protected than urban; this goes for rural property rights, rural incomes and rural pensions, for example the lower pay and fewer rights of Chinese migrant workers (Li 2016) or the weak rights of Tanzanian farmers in cooperatives vis-à-vis state agencies (Prevezer and Sutton 2013). The United States' black-white racial divide is reproduced here in a rural-urban divide.

In both cases, there has been a strongly empowered central state and government apparatus, with insufficient constraints on it to prevent bureaucracies and officials from unleashing their powers on business and agriculture, in the absence of constraining institutions such as rule of law, courts, judiciary, media and opposition parties, which would have prevented or damped down corruption.

The other conclusion to draw from the developing countries' institutional evolution is to stop seeing the double balance – the parallel development of political with economic institutions – through the liberal lens. Democratic rights are desirable for their own sake. But to see a double balance between economic development and political development as essential for economic growth is a mistake. There are some trade-offs that strong states have made – quelling fragmentary violence and achieving unification of the country across relatively disparate groups, ethnically, linguistically, economically, at the expense of curbing political rights and expression. However, without effectual democracy and equal rights, this will perpetuate the segmentation of the country across rural/urban divides.

Conclusion 3 Shareholder capitalism versus stakeholder capitalism: Where do they come from?

Linked to the decentralized nature of both the judiciary and importance of local government in what functions it covers in the liberal economies have been local self-regulating equity and bond markets, the rise of corporations as an institutional form for enterprises, supported by the judiciary upholding legal property rights of those corporations alongside individuals' property rights.

The precocious, decentralized and relatively unregulated development of financial markets for equity and public securities is an integral part of this story and connects with both the different types of fiscal capacities between liberal and other economies and also with the different boundaries between private and public sectors. Joint stock companies and publicly-listed companies on local stock exchanges financed railways, banks and other infrastructure within the private sectors in the liberal economies, whereas large-scale infrastructure such as the railways was financed and owned by the public sector in continental economies and later in developing and transition economies.

The liberal state kept out of regulation, particularly of the stock market and financial sector, although it was pro-competition in industrial sectors and heavily pushing anti-trust laws, particularly in the United States. Coffee (2004) argues that it is because these markets were self-regulated that a constituency of smaller shareholders came into being and a demand for their legal protection also arose. My argument is slightly different: financial markets were self-regulated because the landed/mercantile/financial groups who controlled these markets were better represented in Parliament and were more powerful than the industrial magnates. This was combined with a liberal ideology in both Britain and the United States against state intervention in particular areas of the economy. It is notable that liberal state intervention has been more pronounced on issues such as industrial structure, anti-trust and competition than on regulating their financial sectors in the provision of services to industry.

The prominence of financial markets also links into the story of organizational forms, with many more publicly-listed and eventually diffusely-held companies in the liberal economies in contrast to the more closely-held and concentrated, private ownership of companies elsewhere. I connect this with the different emphases given to shareholder primacy in the liberal economies in contrast to the stakeholder emphasis on the Continent and to the state-dominated stories for our transition and developing economies. These are mediated by very different ideologies of the state, and I trace the institutionalization of the liberal (and illiberal) state, more constrained domestically in the liberal economies, contrasted with the formation of more 'regulating' or 'compensating' states in the continental economies and more 'pervasive', less-constrained and more politicized states' apparatuses in our developing and transition economies.

This leads us on to the important characteristic of what one may call shareholder capitalism that was significant in the United States and Britain. There was, relatively speaking, widespread shareholding amongst the population down to quite middling types, with typically middle-class single women or second sons living off their holdings of stocks and government securities from the 19th century. One can look at the novels of Jane Austen, Elizabeth Gaskell or Anthony Trollope to get an idea of the importance of these sources of income for particular groups of people. I speculate that this mass shareholding was more widespread institutionally in the United States and Britain than in continental European capitalism, although more comparative research needs to be done to establish this.

From the development and wide use of local equity and bond markets, particularly in the late 18th up to the late 19th centuries, came in the early 20th century the development of dispersed and relatively widespread shareholding, the call for investor protection of those smaller shareholders and the split between shareholders and managers.

This could be seen as one facet of liberal democracy, that it was linked to the power of capital rather than of labour, and tradable capital rather than strategic capital, that relatively small shareholders gained rights as owners of tradable capital. The type of property rights that have garnered protection have been tradable and financial property rights, geared towards investor (small shareholder) protection of tradable liquid financial assets at the expense of protecting the more fixed strategic assets within firms.

To some extent, the debate about the separation of ownership from control that followed from Berle and Means (1932) work has been a red-herring, in that the debate became concerned with the separation of interests of shareholders and managers, ignoring Berle and Means' emphasis on the growing power of concentrated managers vis-à-vis the lessening power of more dispersed shareholders. The ideals of shareholder capitalism were to protect the interests of the small shareholder. Instead, shareholder primacy has been interpreted more recently in the early 21st century as upholding the interests of outsider shareholders against other stakeholders, seen as insiders to the firm. In the early 20th century in the United States, it was other stakeholders who were seen as outsiders to the firm rather than the insiders that 'insider' capitalist models portray them as. This is revealing: stakeholders were outsiders to the liberal corporation, shareholders were the insiders.

Corporate governance: Capital-labour relations

Property rights of capital and particularly property rights in tradable capital became more strongly protected than property rights of labour in liberal economies. The rights of shareholders were emphasized, and other stakeholders, such as employees, were not given a coordinating role at the table. Iversen and Soskice (2009) stress the formative times for institution-building of these capitalisms being the late 19th century, when in liberal economies there was relatively unskilled labour who had migrated to the cities, there was low cohesion amongst different types of labour and uncoordinated trade unions. The liberal state was not corporatist; it saw its role as keeping out of business. And employers were not coordinated into strong business associations. Capital-labour relations were antagonistic, with businesses seeking autonomy over production processes and workers/employees seeking to protect and control their job content to prevent being displaced by unskilled labour or by machines. In the United States, racial segregation domestically led to and links with shareholder capitalism through a different route than that of Britain. The absence of strong working class solidarity in the United States was partly due to racial segregation. It was also contributed to by stronger employer violence in putting down worker protests and a weaker federal state in legislating for worker rights (compared with Britain). The racial tie-in with British institutions and its capitalism is that the slave trade was more invisible within Britain and was abolished earlier, although British shareholding of shares in slave-trading companies, such as the Royal African Company, contributed to the importance of protecting those shareholding rights.

The emphasis on managerial autonomy and rights has driven a path from the late 19th century towards deskilling of labour, capital-intensive mass production, with more violent and antagonistic class confrontation in terms of relations between capital and labour. It has also led to much higher top executive pay in recent decades than in the coordinated economies.

This contrasts with a different argument in more coordinated capitalisms with an alliance between strategic capital within firms dependent on skilled labour. Employer interests in heavy capital-intensive industries (engineering, machine tools, and chemicals) were better served in protecting skilled labour and the skilling processes through apprenticeships and firm-specific training, and skilled labour was better served by consensual agreement and coordinated discipline. There have been weaker rights for outsider unskilled workers, giving rise to a more marked dualization in continental labour markets than in liberal ones.

In the emergent capitalisms, corporate governance has been skewed towards state-manager alliances, with labour rights unrepresented and suppressed, and particularly so in rural areas. It is notable that the status of the worker is the least protected in the Chinese variety of capitalism, just as the rights of the state are strongest. In Tanzania, the rights of smallholder farmers, rural labour and their cooperatives are the least protected from and by the state.

Final thoughts

This book has attempted to draw out the multiple linkages within the paths of the different institutional evolutions, with an emphasis on their key historical periods when these configurations were laid down in each country. The fundamental institutions of property rights and legal systems connect with the creation of very different types of state. In turn, these configurations created the distinct varieties of capitalism that are in evidence today. In the post-referendum world of Brexit, the strength and durability of these institutional legacies have reasserted themselves. Without connecting back into their formative periods, these political impasses cannot be understood.

Its contribution lies in bringing together disparate literatures – on varieties of capitalism, on institutional economics, anthropological and historical material – in order to get them to speak to each other more and to gain greater nuance in considering the role that different institutional evolutions have played in shaping the very different varieties of capitalism around the world. It has taken representative examples of liberal, coordinated and emerging economies to highlight their commonalties (within each category), but also their distinctiveness from each other. It shows that we need a keener insight into each country's history in order to make sense of its institutional development, rather than implementing a one-standard policy-making that does not take account of each country's particularity. Having said that, it does also show some patterning in the protection of different types of property rights through differently structured legal systems and by differently constituted states, between liberal, coordinated and emerging capitalisms. This tension between cross-country theory-building and historical analytic narratives at the country level is a useful one in understanding the relationships between those constituencies with power (and how they are supported) and those without.

This kind of insight is particularly relevant in identifying, for example, the gainers and losers in 21st-century Britain underpinning the vote for Brexit. Outsiders have been the less-skilled, less internationally competitive who have been squeezed out in an increasingly globalized economy lacking manufacturing jobs and where services jobs demand educational qualifications. It is Britain's liberalness, with its emphasis on international competitiveness, that does not protect its indigenous people or companies who fail to make the grade, in comparison with continental capitalism, where they do to a greater extent. Levelling the playing field between insiders and outsiders, as liberal economies do to a greater extent, punishes outsiders. Hence Brexit and Trump, with their rhetoric of redressing the balance. Understanding the sources of these power imbalances in the kinds of property rights that are protected and the kinds that are not is essential.

I made some references to the kind of research necessary to understand further the dynamic interplay between informal institutional orderings and the formation of formal institutions, without at all doing justice to these themes. This requires more careful piecing together the histories through which these informal/formal dynamics have played out. A huge area for further work.

Notes

1 For example, without significant prior development in England of individualism following the Black Death and the greater economic power this gave to tenants, and without the seaborne trade and maritime cities, and the naval state's procurement and supply chain, England's formal institutions of property rights would not have been shaped as they were.
2 This is oversimplified to make the point that it mattered who was 'in power' when the 'rules of the game' were being made. But it was critically about the interaction with the mix of informal institutions in play at the time and how conflicts were resolved between those informal institutions and the formal institutions. Again, the elaboration of these interactions is beyond the scope of this book.
3 Although one has to qualify this by remembering that the Bubble Act was a major piece of legislation in the early 18th century and that the Navigation Acts were in force from the 1650s through to the 1840s. But these were being repealed by the third decade of the 19th century as Britain became more liberal.
4 I stress the importance of the late 17th century and the settlement with Parliament, although individualism had been present in England since the 15th century and private property rights included not only landed property but very importantly property associated with the maritime economy and the rise of the maritime cities, which predates the parliamentary settlement.
5 This is not to deny the importance of the slave trade and slave economy in Britain, particularly through the triangular trade, with Britain dependent on US cotton. The institutional order in the United States sustained Britain as well. This was less visible, however, in Britain than in the United States.
6 Parallels can be drawn between US internal treatment of non-citizenry and the British treatment of Ireland, and of India under the East India Company until 1857, and with its colonies in Africa during the 'scramble for Africa'. The difference was that for Britain, its raw material base came from afar compared with the United States' relations with its southern plantations.
7 One could see this independence of property rights from the state as a sort of self-denying ordinance not to override them in peacetime except in dire emergencies or with widespread consent, which might be interpreted as a particular form of dependence on the state rather than independence. North et al. (2009: 104) talk about this, however, as property rights being independent from the state.

8 One needs to qualify this with consideration for Britain of how patronage in civil service appointments lasted until the 1870s officially and much longer in parts of it like the Foreign Office. Also the East India Company and those who ran it were not independent of the state. The army and navy preserved fast-track entry for aristocrats into the first half of the 19th century and likewise the higher echelons of the judiciary. But again, this depended from the second half of the 19th century more on informal links and patronage than on direct official sinecures. This takes us to the need for greater elaboration of dynamics between informal and formal institutions, which is beyond my scope here.

References

6, P. and Richards, P. (2017) *Mary Douglas: Explaining Human Thought and Conflict*. New York: Berghahn.

Berle, A. and Means, G. (1932) *The Modern Corporation and Private Property*. New Brunswick, NJ: Transaction Publishers.

Cain, P.J. and Hopkins, A.G. (1986) 'Gentlemanly Capitalism and British Expansion Overseas I: The Old Colonial System, 1688–1850', *Economic History Review* 39(4): 501–525.

Cain, P.J. and Hopkins, A.G. (1987) 'Gentlemanly Capitalism and British Expansion Overseas II: New Imperialism, 1850–1945', *Economic History Review* 40(1): 1–26.

Coffee, J. (2004) Law and the Market: The Impact of Enforcement, Columbia Law School Working Paper No. 182. Available at: http://papers.ssrn.com/sol13/papers.cfm?abstract_id=967482.

Douglas, M. (1982) *In the Active Voice*. London: Routledge and Kegan Paul.

Douglas, M. (1986) *How Institutions Think*. London: Routledge and Kegan Paul.

Edling, M. (2014) *A Hercules in the Cradle: War, Money and the American State, 1783–1867*. Chicago: University of Chicago Press.

Granville, B., Martorell Cruz, J. and Prevezer, M. (2015) Elites, Thickets and Institutions: French Resistance versus German Adaptation to Economic Change, 1945–2015, Working Paper No. 63. Queen Mary University of London: Centre for Globalisation Research.

Hall, P. and Soskice, D. (2001) *Varieties of Capitalism: The Institutional Foundations of Comparative Advantage*. Oxford: Oxford University Press

Iversen, T. and Soskice, D. (2009) 'Distribution and Redistribution. The Shadow of the Nineteenth Century', *World Politics* 61(3): 438–486

Kagan, R. (2001) *Adversarial Legalism: The American Way of Law*. Cambridge, MA: Harvard University Press

Levy, B.and Fukuyama, F. (2010) *Development Strategies: Integrating Governance and Growth*, Research Working Paper No. 5196. Washington, DC: World Bank.

Li, D. (2016) The Returns to General and Vocational Education Qualifications – Evidence from Urban and Migrating Workers in China. Paper presented to PhD Symposium, School of Business and Management, Queen Mary University of London, 22 September.

Mann, M. (1993) *The Sources of Social Power, Vol. 2: The Rise of Classes and Nation-States, 1760–1914*. Cambridge: Cambridge University Press.

Martorell Cruz, J. (2016) *One Money, Multiple Institutions: Capitalist Diversity under the Euro-Zone*. Unpublished PhD Thesis, Queen Mary University of London.

Milhaupt, C.J. and Pistor, K. (2008) *Law and Capitalism: What Corporate Crises Reveal about Legal Systems and Economic Development around the World*. Chicago: University of Chicago Press.

North, D., Wallis, J.J. and Weingast, B. (2009) *Violence and Social Orders: A Conceptual Framework for Interpreting Recorded Human History*. Cambridge: Cambridge University Press.

North, D., Wallis, J., Weingast, B. and Webb, S. (2013) *In the Shadow of Violence: Politics, Economics and the Problems of Development*. Cambridge: Cambridge University Press.

Piketty, T. (2014) *Capital in the Twenty-First Century*. Cambridge, MA: Harvard University Press.

Prevezer, M. and Sutton, S. (2013) The Relationship between External and Internal Governance in Tanzanian Coffee Cooperatives, Unpublished Working Paper. Queen Mary University of London: Centre for Globalization Research.

Scott, D. (2016) *Fragments of the Peculiar Institution*. CPInprint. Available at: www.critialpractices.org.

Tilly, C. (1992) *Coercion, Capital and European States*. Cambridge: Blackwell.

Index

References in **bold** indicate tables and those in *italics* show figures.

Acemoglu, D. and Robinson, J. 20, 87–8, 194
Acemoglu et al. (2001) 18, 19
agency theory 57–8
Aguilera, R. and Jackson, G. 56, 57–8, 59
America *see* United States of America (USA)
Anglo-American system 56, 59; *see also* liberal market economies (LMEs)

Bank of England 101, 102, 126, 127
banks: Bank of England 101, 102, 126, 127; bank-based financial systems 137–8; Banque de France 137; Hausbank 137
Bates, R.H. 206
Becht, M. and DeLong, B. 175, 176
Besley, T. and Persson, T. 92, 126
Bismarck, Otto von 139
Boone, C. 39, 198, 199, 200, 203
Braudel, F. 33, 34–5, 84
Britain: capital markets in 104–5, 153–4; capital-labour relations 108–10; centralization of power in Parliament 81, 86, 87, 88–9, 93–4; and colonization in America 156–7; common-law-based property rights 87–90, 112; company ownership data 53–4, **54**; company ownership structures 133; constraints on the state 93–4, 265–6; contract-enforcement institutions (CEIs) 94; corporate financing mechanisms 103–6; emergence of the working class 108; English individualism 32, 79, 110; evolution of institutions 77, 80–1; Financial Revolution 101, 102; fiscal capacity 78, 93, 95–6, 126–7, 264–5; fiscal revenues and military expenditure 94–5; formal property rights vs. customary rights 91–2; free trade, movement towards 97–8; 'gentleman capitalism' in 102, 260; independence of the rule of law 80; joint stock corporations 103, 104; land enclosures 83–4, 85, 91; land ownership and the Civil War 84–6, 87–8; landownership 83–4, 90–1; as liberal state 78–9, 80, 99, 109–10, 260–1; local state/central state distinctions 99–102, 112; London Symphony Orchestra 68–69; management ideologies 60–1; maritime institution development 32; maritime property rights 38, 81; mercantilism 96; national football team 68, 69; nineteenth-century reform 98–9; openness of football league 68–9; per capita GDP (1990) **5**; prerogative law 88; primogeniture 85–6; private individualist property rights 82–4, 86–7, 111–12, 260; private self-regulation of the financial markets 106–7; property rights 81–2; property rights and Parliamentary Acts, seventeenth century 91; rise of the corporations 63, 102–3, 105–6; Russell Group universities 69; shareholder capitalism 106–7, 112, 268–70; shareholder democracy 120; skill formation (labour) 60; social orders 91; state capacity and bureaucratic capabilities 96; state capacity and government debt 96–7, 136–7, 265; state-business relationships

109–10; statute law 88; stock exchange development 104, 105, 107; trade unions 108, 109; tradeable property rights 7, 90, 92, 110, 112; transition to open access order 46

Cain, P.J. and Hopkins, A.G. 101, 260
Canada **54**
capital markets: in Britain 104–5, 153–4; in continental economies 24; in France 136; in liberal economies 23; in market-based economies 59
capital property rights 58–9
capitalism: in China 223–4, 250–1; definitions of 33–5; evolution of in America 194–5; fixed capital formation 34; 'gentleman capitalism' in Britain 102, 260; property rights and evolution of 38
Chen et al. (2004) 247
China: Beijing-Shanghai high-speed rail route 21; capitalism in 223–4, 250–1; corporate governance institutions 247–9; corporations in 245–7; corporatization of state-owned enterprises (SOEs) 227, 233, 247, 249; economic development and democracy 244; enterprise creation 232–3; entrepreneurs in 246; expansion in college-level education 250; fiscal capacity 239; household responsibility system (HRS) 226, 229, 231; individual liberties 229; institution-building in 225; judicial system 236–8; labour markets 227, 249–50; legal systems 234–6; liberalization of rural enterprises 223, 225; limited access order framework and 187–8, 267–8; local elites 240–2, 243; manager-worker relations 250; market-building incentives 224, 226, 229, 231; nature of the state 238; per capita GDP **5**, 223; property rights and the legal system 228–30; property rights in 224, 225–6, **259**; public vs. private ownership 229–30; regional decentralization 238–40; role of the rule of law 194; rural property rights 24, 228, 230; shareholder protection 247–9, 251; special enterprise zones (SEZs) 231, 232, 233; state bureaucracy and the Party structure 242–3; state capacity and Party control 226, 240–1; state constitution 234–5; state-society relations 244–5; township and village enterprises (TVEs) 226, 231–2; trade unions in 249; urban property rights 230
Chinese Communist Party (CCP): changing status of 241, 245; composition of 243–4; and judicial independence 236–8; market-building incentives 224, 226, 229, 231; as meta-institution 224–5, 226; Organization Department 241–2; Party constitution 234–5; and the rule of law 234–6; and the state bureaucratic system 242–3; and state capacity 226, 240–1
civil codes: contrasted with common law systems 125–6, 261; in France 118, 124–5, 262; in Germany 118, 124–5; and property rights 126
coercion-constraining institutions (CCIs): and constraints on the state 37; and property rights 35, 67; public-/private-order CEI relationships 36, 37
Coffee, J. 106–7, 176, 177
collectivist societies 36, 37
colonization: and the development of institutions 19, 162; extractive states 18, 19, 162–3; and formal property rights in America 156–7; neo-European 18, 19, 162–3; settler mortality rates 19
company law 62–3
comparative corporate governance: agency theory 57–8; as coalitions 56–8; institutional theory 57, 58
continental European system: coevolution of property rights and the state 23–4; corporate governance models 56, 135–6; labour markets in 59–60; nation-building states 119; stakeholder capitalism 119, 120, 268–70; *see also* coordinated market economies (CMEs)
contract-enforcement institutions (CEIs): in Britain, 15th century 94; and constraints on the state 37; designed 35; organic 35; organizations as 37–8; overview of 35; private-order CEIs 35–6, 37; and property rights 35, 67; public-order CEIs 35–6, 37; and township and village enterprises in China 231–2; variations within 28
coordinated market economies (CMEs): capital-labour-management relations 67; company ownership data 54;

comparative corporate governance in 56; contrasted with liberal market economies 53–4, 55, 68–71; corporate coordination within 130; equity markets in 54; overview of 2, **26**; protection of property rights 24, **259**, 262–4; state-business relationships 55; trade unions in 53; *see also* continental European system; France; Germany
corporate governance institutions: capital and property rights 58–9; China 227; continental systems 135–6; and legal systems in China 247–9; political approaches to 61; role of labour 59
corporations: in America 63, 172–6; in China 245–7; corporate financing in Britain 103–6; corporate forms of land ownership in colonial America 156–7; in France 63, 106, 131, 134–5, 173; in Germany 63, 106, 120, 131, 132–4; joint stock corporations 103, 104; legal concept of 62–3; non-profit corporations 63; ownership models 63; rise of in Britain 63, 102–3, 105–6
Curtin, P. 19
customary (traditional) property rights: customary vs. formal property rights in Britain 91–2; defined 39; state vs. customary/rural land rights in Tanzania 24, 195–6, 198–9, 201–4, 217

De Castella, T. and Westcott, K. 20
de Soto, H. 38, 157–8
Deakin, S. 62, 63
democracy: and economic development in China 244; and the liberal rule of law 193; in limited access orders 192; in United States of America (USA) 152
Dickson, B. 243, 244, 245–6
Dincecco, M. 41–2, 94, 126
dominant coalitions 43–4
Douglas, M. 21, 29–31, 32–3, 155, 194, 256, 257

economic development: and democracy in China 244; and geography 17–18; and institutions 4–6; and legal systems 225; and property rights 198; sequencing of institutional measures 193; and trade 17–18
economic performance, concept of 24, 28
Edling, M. 158–9
elites: in China 240–2, 243; as dominant coalitions 43–5, 47; evolution of capitalism and 34; landed elites, eighteenth-century Britain 90–2; in limited access orders 191; powers of 7, 44; in Tanzania 206, 207, 208; and the transition to open access orders 46
emerging market economies **27**, 264; *see also* Tanzania
equity markets: in America 176–8; in coordinated market economies (CMEs) 54; in France 131; in Germany 131; in liberal market economies 54
extractive institutions 22
extractive states (colonial) 18, 19, 162–3

financial systems: bank-based 59, 137–8; equity-based 59
fiscal capacity: in America 168–9, 195, 264–5; in Britain 78, 93, 95–6, 126–7, 264–5; in China 239; in France 126–7; in Germany 129–30; and legal capacity 93, 95–6, 126; and national growth 41–2; and state capacity 41–2, 78, 257–8
Fohlin, C. 133
football leagues 68–9
France: Banque de France 137; capital markets in 136; centralized state of 118–19, 127, 144, 167, 262–3; civil codes 118, 124–5, 262; company ownership data 54, **54**; corporate governance institutions 144–5; corporations in 63, 106, 131, 134–5, 173; equity markets in 131; étatisme 120; financial institutional forms 119; financing institutions 136–7; fiscal capacity 126–7; French High Speed Rail Network (TGV) 21; labour markets 141–2; legal systems 125; Napoleonic Code 125, 131; partible inheritance of land 83; peasant landowners 121; per capita GDP (1990) **5**; private limited liability companies 131, 132; property rights 120–2, 124–5, 143–4; proportional representation 142–3; publicly listed companies 131; stakeholder focus 145–6; state capacity and government debt 136–7; state-business-elite nexus 119; trade unions in 141–2; transition to an open access order 46
Franks et al. (2006) 133
Fukuyama, F. 47

Galbraith, J. 175
Germany: Berlin Philharmonic 68–69; centralized state of 118–19, 263; civil codes 118, 124–5; codetermination 119, 139–40; company ownership data 54, **54**; company ownership structures 132–4; corporate governance institutions 144–5; corporations in 63, 106, 120, 131, 132–4; creation of the nation state 128–9; education system 129–30; equity markets in 131; financing institutions 119, 137–8; fiscal capacity 129–30; Hausbank 137; industrialization 140–1; investor protections 138; labour markets 60, 138–41; management ideologies 60–1; national football team 69; peasant property rights 123; pension systems 143; per capita GDP (1990) **5**; private limited liability companies 131–2; property rights 122–3, 124–5, 143–4; proportional representation 142–3; publicly listed companies 131; stakeholder focus 142–3, 145–6; state capacity 127–9, 130, 136–7, 144; trade unions in 139; universities 70; works councils 140; *see also* Prussia
Green, E. 202–3
Greif, A. 29, 35, 36, 37, 41, 46, 67, 93
Guinnane et al. (2007) 132

Hall, P. and Soskice, D. 1, 53, 56, 57
Hannah, L. 102, 103, 104, 105
Harling, P. 98, 99
Harris, R. 102–3, 104
High Speed 2 rail link (HS2) 20–1
Hill, C. 84
Hoffman, P. T. 42
Horwitz, M. 165–6
Huang, Y. 223, 224, 231–2
Hughes, J. 163
Hughes, J. and Cain, L. 156

inclusive institutions 22
individualism 32, 79, 109
individualist societies 36, 37
individualized property rights 39, 40–1
individuals: and the formation of institutions 29–30; grid and group schema 32–3; individual liberties in China 229; and informal institutions 32; and socially constructed decision-making 30–1
informal institutions 31, 32, 257
infrastructure 20–1
institutional evolution 22
institutional theory 57, 58
institutions: academic literature on 18–20; colonization and the development of 19, 162; definitions of 28–9; and economic development 4–6, 17–18; evolution of 29–35; 'good institutions' 19; ideologies and 31; and individual decision-making 30–1; instrumental variables 19; primary institutions 28; as social contracts 21, 29–30

Japan: company ownership data **54**; labour markets in 59–60; management ideologies 60–1
Jefferson, Thomas 158–60

Kagan, R. 89, 163
Kennedy, David 226, 228
Kopsidis, M. and Bromley, D.W. 123
Kraus, Christian Jacob 128
Kuznets, S. 34

labour markets: in the Anglo-American system 59; capital-labour relations in America 178–9, 270–1; capital-labour-management relations in Britain 108–10; capital-labour-management relations in CMEs 67; capital-labour-management relations in LMEs 66–7; capital-labour-management relations in social democracies 61, 64, 65; in China 227, 249–50; in the continental European system 59–60; in coordinated market economies 67, 263–4; in France 141–2; in Germany 60, 138–41; insider/outsider employee distinctions 64–5; in Japan 59–60; methods of collective bargaining 53; representation rights 59, 60; skill formation 59–60; slavery in America 160–2, 261; union organization 59; United States of America (USA) 152; *see also* trade unions
land ownership: in Britain 83–4, 90–1; and the Civil War in Britain 84–6; and colonization in America 156–7; extra-legal squatter settling in America 157–9; land enclosures in Britain 83–4, 85, 91; land tenure regimes in Sub-Saharan Africa 200–1; partible inheritance in France 83; peasant

landowners in France 121; rural property rights in China 228, 230; state vs. customary/rural land rights in Tanzania 24, 195–6, 198–9, 201–4, 217
Landry, P.F. 243
Larson, J.L. 168, 169
Lee, H.Y. 243
legal systems: centralized 40–1; in China 234–6, 247–9; common law in America 160, 163–6; common law systems contrasted with civil codes 125–6, 261; common-law-based property rights in Britain 87–90, 112, 125; and contract enforcement 36; contractual law in America 165–6; decentralized 40–1; and economic development 225; evolution of 23; extra-legal squatter settling and property rights in America 157–9; and fiscal capacity 93, 95–6, 126; in France 125; and individual property rights, liberal states 23–4; and individualized property rights 39; judicial independence in China 236–8; judicial review in America 164–5; legal origin debate 124–5; in limited access orders 190, 191, 235; and market development 40; prerogative law in Britain 88; and property rights 40–1, 228, 257; and property rights in China 228–30; protection of capital property rights 58–9; role of the rule of law 193–4; statute law in Britain 88
Leonard, T. 170, 179
Lerner. A. 20
Levy, B. 205, 207–8
Levy, B. and Fukuyama, F. 193, 267
liberal market economies (LMEs): capital-labour-management relations 66–7; company ownership data 53–4; comparative corporate governance in 56; contrasted with coordinated market economies 53–4, 55, 68–71; equity markets in 54; methods of collective bargaining 53; overview of 1–2, **25**; protection of property rights 66, 259–62, **259**; state-business relationships 54–5; *see also* Great Britain; United States of America (USA)
liberal states: coevolution of property rights and the state 23–4; the individual and the legal system 23–4; nature of 6–7
limited access orders (LAOs): applied to China 187–8, 267–8; applied to Tanzania 188, 204–5, 267–8; basic LAOs 190; compared to open access orders 191–2; democracy in 192; and developing countries 189; elites and the rule of law 191; enforcement of property rights 46–7; fragile LAOs 190; leaders in 46; legal systems in 190, 191, 235; mature LAOs 190; rent allocations 189–90, 192; and state capacity 190; and violence 189, 190, 191, 192, 204–5, 216
Linklater, A. 83–4
List, Friedrich 129
Liu, Q. 247, 248
Locke, John 86

Macfarlane, A. 82
management ideologies 60–1
Mandler, P. 98, 111
Mann, M. 31, 42–43, 97, 107, 128, 159, 162, 164, 178, 179
markets: and contract enforcement 35–6, 37; development of and legal systems 40; *see also* capital markets; equity markets
McGaughey, E. 139, 140
Milhaupt, C.J. and Pistor, K. 23, 28–9, 40, 125, 134, 163, 225, 228, 236
Mokyr, J. 96–97

Naidu, S. and Yuchtman, N. 178
Napoleon (Bonaparte) 124, 125, 127, 128
Naughton, B. and Tsai, K. 251
North, D. 29, 31
North, D. and Weingast, B. 82
North et al. (2009) 23, 29, 43, 44, 45, 46, 47–8, 83, 86, 87–8, 90–1, 111, 189, 191, 192, 205, 226, 235, 267
North et al. (2013) 189, 191
Nyerere, Julius 195, 199, 205, 209–10, 211

O'Brien, P. 94–5
open access orders (OAOs): characteristics of 45–6; compared to limited access orders 191–2; impersonal relationships 45, 46; leaders in 46; and the rule of law 235; transition to 46–7
orchestras 68–70
organizations: as coercion-constraining institutions 47–8; corporate

organizations in Germany 130; definition of 29; in open access orders 45; perpetually lived organizations 45; as types of CEIs 37–8

Piketty, T. 81, 130, 161, 261
Pinkertons 152, 166, 178, 191
Pistor, K. and Xu, C. 227, 232
Porter, R. 90
primary institutions 22; *see also* coercion-constraining institutions (CCIs); contract-enforcement institutions (CEIs); fiscal capacity; legal systems; property rights
property rights: abuse of by the state 35, 37; and asset protection 228; in Britain 81–2; and changes in political power 39; in China 224, 225–6, 228–30, **259**; and civil codes 126; and coercion-constraining institutions (CCIs) 35, 67; and colonization in America 156–7; common-law-based property rights in Britain 87–90, 112; and constraints on the state 266; within continental economies 23–4; and contract-enforcement institutions (CEIs) 35, 67; in coordinated market economies 24, **259**, 262–4; customary (traditional) property rights 39; customary vs. formal property rights in Britain 91–2; definitions of 38; and economic development 198; in emerging market economies 264; eminent domain 39; and evolution of capitalism 38; and extra-legal squatter settling in America 157–9, 200; formal property rights vs. customary rights in Britain 91–2; in France 120–2, 124–5, 143–4; in Germany 122–3, 124–5, 143–4; the individual and the legal system 23–4; individual and the nature of the state 20–1; individualized property rights 39, 40–1; land ownership and the Civil War in Britain 84–6, 87–8; within the legal system in America 164–5; and the legal system in China 228–30; and legal systems 40–1, 228, 257; in liberal market economies 66, 259–62, **259**; maritime property rights 38, 81; and Parliamentary Acts, seventeenth century Britain 91; private individualist property rights in Britain 82–4, 86–7, 111–12, 260; protection of 66, 258–9, **259**; rural property rights in China 228, 230; and shareholders 58–9; slavery as property in America 152, 160–2, 261; and state capacity 41, 66; state vs. customary/rural land rights 24, 195–6, 198, 201–4, 217; statist property rights 39, 40, 200, 203; in Tanzania 159, 217–18, **259**; and township and village enterprises in China 231–2; of tradable assets 39, 256–7, 260; tradeable property rights in Britain 7, 90, 92, 110, 112; *see also* land ownership
Prosterman, R. 228
Prussia: absolutist sovereignty in 127; civil codes and eminent domain 118–19, 125; and creation of German nation state 128; education system in 129–30; land ownership 123; *see also* Germany

rents: rent allocations in limited access orders 189–90, 192; in Sub-Saharan African countries 191–2
Rodrik, D. 19–20
Rodrik et al. (2004) 18
Roe, M. 61, 64
Rueda, D. 64–5

Scott, Dread 161
Shamburgh, D. 241, 242
shareholders: in corporations 63; insider/outsider models 151, 154, 173, 174; property rights and 58–9; shareholder capitalism in America 173–5; shareholder capitalism in Britain 106–7, 112, 268–70; shareholder democracy in America 120; shareholder democracy in Britain 120; shareholder primacy (dispersed shareholdings) 151; shareholder primacy in America 151, 173, 174, 175–6; shareholder primacy vs. stakeholder considerations 61, 62, 63–4, 142–3; shareholder protection in China 247–9, 251; in social democracies 142
Shi, T. 236–8
slavery: and common law 160, 161, 261; and historical racial segregation 161, 163, 180, 262; and the plantation economy 160, 161, 261; slavery as property 152; slavery-based capitalism in America 8, 153; slaves as assets 160–2, 261; and the War of Independence 160–1

Smith, Adam 28, 36, 91–2, 128
social capital 47–8
social democracies: capital-labour-management relations 61, 64, 65; decision-making in 61; shareholding systems 142
social orders: concepts of social power 43; and the formation of institutions 29–30; Great Britain 91; grid and group schema 32–3
stakeholder capitalism 119, 120, 268–70
state capacity: and bureaucratic capabilities 96; and contract enforcement 35–6; and fiscal capacity 41–2, 78, 257–8; in France 136–7; in Germany 127–9, 130, 136–7, 144; and government borrowing 96–7; and government debt in Britain 96–7, 136–7, 265; and limited access orders 190; and Party control in China 226, 240–1; and property rights 41, 66; in Tanzania 216–18
state power: and abuse of property rights 35, 37; authorative/diffused powers 43; collective/distributive power 43; concepts of social power 43; constraints on 37, 78, 257–8, 265–6; extensive/intensive powers 43; sources of 31; and violence 28, 35
states: eminent domain rights 39; mutual relationship with dominant coalitions 44–5; relation to business in coordinated market economies 55; relation to business in liberal market economies 54–5
statist property rights 39, 40, 200, 203
Stevens, M. and Teggemann, S. 207
Sub-Saharan Africa: development and property rights 198; land tenure regimes 200–1; rents in 191–2; *see also* Tanzania
Sutton, J. and Olomi, D. 197

Tanner, D. and Green, E.H. 108
Tanzania: agricultural cooperatives 196, 208–9, 217; agricultural cooperatives, historical evolution 209–12, **210**; Arusha Declaration 199, 202, 210; as basic limited access order 188, 204–5, 267–8; bureaucratic capabilities 207–8; centralized state of 196, 204, 205–6, 216–17; coffee cooperatives 209–10, 211, 212–15, *213*; economic overview 197; elites 206, 207, 208; ethnic divisions 196; extra-legal property rights 159; industrial development policies 206–7; liberalization 202, 207, 211; per capita GDP **5**, 197, 223; post-colonial history 205–7; protection of property rights **259**; role of the rule of law 194; as single-party state 207; sisal production 206; state capacity 216–17; state capacity and property rights 217–18; state vs. customary/rural land rights 24, 195–6, 198–9, 201–4, 217; tea associations 196–7, 215–16, 217
taxes *see* fiscal capacity
Thane, P. 99–100
Tilly, C. 88
Tocqueville, Alexis de 9, 91, 121, 122–3, 126, 152, 155, 159, 160, 167
trade unions: in Britain 108, 109; in China 249; in coordinated market economies 53; employee representation rights 60; external control 60; in France 141–2; in Germany 139; internal participation 60; in liberal economies 53
traditional (customary) property rights *see* customary (traditional) property rights

Unger, J. and Chan, A. 245
United States of America (USA): capital-labour relations 178–9, 270–1; colonial legal system 157; colonization and formal property rights 156–7; common law system 160, 163–6; company ownership data 53–4, **54**; concentration vs. competition 170–2; contractual law 165–6; corporations 63, 172–6; debt mechanisms 169, 265; decentralized nature of the state 166–8, 262; democracy in 152; equity markets 176–8; evolution of capitalism in 194–5; extra-legal squatter settling and property rights 157–9, 200; fee simple 83; fiscal capacity 168–9, 195, 264–5; inheritance laws 159; judicial review 164–5; labour markets 152; labour representation rights 60; laissez-faire liberalism 169–70, 260–1; management ideologies 60–1; numbers of organizations 47–8; per capita GDP (1990) **5**; political rights 167–8; private capital markets 170; property rights 155; property rights and the legal

system 164–5; protectionism in 168–9; racial segregation 152; shareholder capitalism 173–5; shareholder democracy 120; shareholder primacy in 151, 173, 174, 175–6; slavery as property 152, 160–2, 261; transition to an open access order 46; the trust problem 170–2, 175
universities 69–70

Villaverde, J.F. 86, 163
violence: and contract enforcement 35; and limited access orders 189, 190, 191, 192, 204–5, 216; management of and classification of states 43–4; and state power 28, 35
Vitols, S. 137

Walder, A. 243, 244, 250
wars: and fiscal capacity 78, 94–5; land ownership and the Civil War in Britain 84–6, 87–8; and state formation 42, 94–5, 265
Weingast, B. 29, 35, 37

Xu, C. 231, 233, 238–9, 240

Zhang, Y. 229

For Product Safety Concerns and Information please contact our EU representative GPSR@taylorandfrancis.com
Taylor & Francis Verlag GmbH, Kaufingerstraße 24, 80331 München, Germany

www.ingramcontent.com/pod-product-compliance
Ingram Content Group UK Ltd.
Pitfield, Milton Keynes, MK11 3LW, UK
UKHW021012180425
457613UK00020B/912